To Mom, Nanny Louise, Lori, Linda, Denise,
Sarell, Sonia, Stacy, Angle, Jo and Mandy.
Thank you to each of you and the role you've
played, and in some ways still play, in my story.

rePeatedly reVised

Learning to start over again…and again

Introduction

It took me three years to get the courage to even think about sharing this story, but now it's done. There were several tears spilled on my keyboard as I returned to remember old pains and hurts in order to share them with you. However, through all my time spent writing, I was reminded of how great my Heavenly Father's love is for me, his daughter. It is only by His redemption and forgiveness that I have a voice and a platform to share this part of my life. All credit and glory goes to God my Father for how He loved me through some of the most difficult days of my life.

A few things you need to know about the words you are about to read:

- Some of the names have been changed to protect the lives that are now part of my own story.
- The details surrounding my court appearances and my case have been strategically left out – not to withhold information, but to keep from creating any legal ramifications that might arise.
- Although there were others who played a direct part in my case and sentencing, their story is just that – their story. I chose to focus on my personal part of the story and that is all.

- Excerpts from my personal journal kept while imprisoned are shared throughout this book. You'll see them in italicized font. It's personal and honest. I wanted to share my personal experiences, which are not meant to mirror or mimic the experiences of those still incarcerated. Our time spent locked up is uniquely ours – each of us dealing with it and getting through it in our own way.

It's my prayer that you will read my story and not just be shocked or startled by my mistakes and failures, but that you will be encouraged to make a change in your own life. Maybe you'll see God's forgiveness and redemption in a new light, in a new way and with a new trust that He can deliver you, renew you and revive you.

I titled this book, "rePeatedly reVised," because that is what I am – constantly having to relearn, revise and revamp myself. Even now, I am learning, growing, and working on becoming the best version of myself. I don't always get it right, and what helpful concepts you pick up here are offered from a humble heart that's faltered and failed more times than what's simply disclosed in this book.

However, there are some aspects of my life and of my

persona that are permanently revised and for that I give credit to a God whose forgiveness knows no end and His patience is everlasting.

So this is the book where I share some remarkable things God has done in my life, lessons I've learned and encounters that forever changed me. I hope it has the same impact on you.

---Christie Browning

February

"I've known since I was a young girl that my life was not going to be normal. I knew in my gut it wasn't going to be the same ol' life for me. Of course, even knowing my path would be different, and sometimes appear odd to others, I never dreamed I would be here."

"Guilty."

There is no way to sugar coat it. I sat in a courtroom where a jury found me guilty of fraud. The courtroom scene was not nearly as dramatic as what plays out on primetime television, but that didn't diminish the feeling that hit when I heard...

"Guilty."

It was as if someone kicked me in my gut, forcing all the air out of my lungs. I was guilty, according to the jury selected for my trial, of fraud and was now going to face jail time. What the judge said afterward met my ears coated in a heavy fog. Not much made sense and not much penetrated my mind. As I tried to stand up from my place at the defendant's table, my legs moved as if there were large weights attached at my ankles. I remember trying to be polite as I conversed with my attorney, trying to absorb her direction. Nothing soaked in. All I knew was that I would be coming back to that very seat, in that very courtroom in a month to be sentenced for the crime in which I was found guilty.

I'm not sure how you're supposed to function during that 30-day waiting period – from the time you're found guilty to the time you're sentenced. The judge said it was time for me to "get my affairs in order," but I didn't know what that meant exactly. I went about working, cleaning my house, going to church, preparing meals, grocery shopping – all the things that a "normal" life would include. However, everything I did and all the plans I made had an expiration date.

My trial came and went within the same day. Jury selection started the morning off and by mid-morning questions were being hurled at the witness stand. There wasn't anyone in the courtroom outside of the major players. No audience had come to watch the drama unfold.

By late afternoon the jury was back with their verdict and everyone was home having dinner like any other night – but not I. I sat at my dinner table knowing that in a month, I would find out what my punishment would be and how that might impact the rest of my life.

My charge was classified as a Class D Felony for Fraud. But that was a vague description of the crimes painted during trial. My character, my ethics, and even my faith were called into question. In the end, my case centered around mishandled funds that equaled less than $600.

I sat in the courtroom trying to focus on what was being said by the attorneys and the other witnesses. However, the process was so full of legal jargon and fast-paced action that most of the day flew by in a blur. What I can't forget were the comments and remarks that stung and cut me deep. The day was emotional, exhausting and overwhelming.

When all the questioning was over and both sides had come to a rest, it was time to wait for the jury to make their decision. Upon dismissal, the attorneys went their separate ways and I found myself sitting in a small room inside the legal library. The outdated furnishings and limited décor told me this room wasn't meant to inspire hope and justice, but only there to allow for some legal mind to do his homework on a case.

I prayed. I prayed using scripture. I prayed in faith. I prayed with the boldness that could move mountains. I *knew* God was going to work on my behalf. I trusted without doubt that I would walk away from that day as a free woman, the court having seen what a huge misunderstanding this all was. I leaned on all the promises found in the Word. I sought God as my refuge, my strength, my help in that very specific, real time of trouble. I was ready to watch Him work a miracle on my behalf.

When my attorney knocked on the door of that little room, I stood with my head held high, sure that my prayers were answered.

Disappointment doesn't begin to describe how I felt when the jury didn't get my prayer request. When the verdict was "guilty," I felt stunned and confused. Did I not come to the Throne with great faith? Did I not assure God that I would give Him all the glory when He set me free? I did everything I thought I was supposed to do. I followed the right formula. Didn't I do enough?

Once I returned home, the 30-day clock started ticking. I lay in bed that night, asking God "why?" I resolved that God was doing some miraculous work, and His deliverance would be seen at the sentencing in a month.

For the type of charge I was found guilty of, the judge could choose to simply give me some community service, assign some fines and fees and there would be no jail time to serve. On the other hand, the law allowed a sentence of up to five years to serve. Quite the large margin, but I wasn't worried. I knew God was going to work out the "no time to serve" option in my favor. I had already pictured that in my mind and could see me leaping to my feet in victory as the gavel came down. I would walk out of the courtroom prepared to tell everyone I met about the wonder-working power of my Heavenly Father.

I prayed and lived that month in complete faith. My church did the same, sending their strongest prayer warriors to pray circles around the courthouse on my behalf. We all believed God was at work.

You've probably put two and two together to realize that once again, that prayer request wasn't answered as I had hoped. If so, this would be the end of the book....not really your money's worth now is it? Lucky for you and your dollars, the story continues.

Chapter 1

In the beginning

I grew up in a home with parents who loved me deeply and an extended family that offered love abundantly. My parents were high school sweethearts who married young and became parents of their first born, yours truly, at age 21. In a few short years, they started going to church and soon decided to live devoted lives to following God's plan and accepted the fact that Jesus Christ died for them in order to offer all those who believe eternal life in Heaven.

Each Sunday we were in church. My parents were involved in children and youth ministries as teachers. Wednesday nights you would find us back at church for Bible study and prayer meetings. I remember tent revivals with all the stereotypical nuances, paper fans and fiery preachers.

My family, which eventually included a younger sister and a younger brother, would have dinner together most nights. Afterward, Dad would read the Bible and lead us in a short lesson. Early in the morning as I ate my breakfast, Dad would sit across the table reading his Bible before he was off to work. He finished with head bowed and hands folded, praying for his family I'm sure.

Free time would include music. Dad played the drums and all things percussion, but he could also strum a guitar. I have fond memories of him signing good ol' gospel songs sitting on the couch, guitar on one knee and myself happily planted on his other knee.

It was a good life. Dad worked hard to provide for us all, and Mom stayed at home to take care of us kids and our home. There were buckets of laughter and funny moments that still make us chuckle all these years later. We had a family dog and we spent family vacations camping and fishing. My grandparents were in the middle of it all, participating in holiday feasts, Sunday dinners and family birthdays.

This is not the upbringing you expect to attach to someone who now had to declare "felon" on every job application from now until retirement. However, somewhere things took a turn for the unexpected.

I loved being at church. I loved studying the Bible and learning about the stories and characters that exemplified a believer's how-to in following God. It was my grandmother who instilled my love for digging into the Word. She always had several Bibles she read and maps that depicted important journeys and cities relevant to Bible stories. When Easter rolled around and the quintessential Biblical movies would air on television, she would sprawl out on the floor, her maps in front of her and me by her side. She would show me where those iconic scenes took place and she would read the real facts from the Bible, void of Hollywood's embellishments.

My mother leaned on the Bible for answers to life's tough situations and circumstances. I remember when it was time for her to have "the talk" with me, she pulled out the Bible and walked me through the scriptures where God created Eve for Adam. She pointed me to scriptures that asked for purity and explained marriage. As society toed the line for morality and values, Mom would always point back to the scripture for truth and direction.

Childhood experiences such as these led me to become a faith-filled teenager, carrying my values and morals proudly into the halls of my high school. I stood around the flagpole for the annual See You at The Pole – a national movement for students to pray for their schools. I was president of our Bible Club and a leader in my church's youth group. I wasn't the top of my class academically, but I was strong enough to earn an academic scholarship to college. I didn't party, drink, smoke or have sex. I followed all the rules.

So what went wrong? How did a girl who had every

opportunity afforded her, was raised in a stable home, taught Biblical principles and lived by them, end up with a felony conviction? It started when I was a child… in the very home where Bible verses were memorized and songs of Jesus were sung.

Small insecurities started taking root when I was in elementary school and struggled in my math assignments. Dad would spend hours with me each night going over my homework, desperately trying to get me to understand long division and fractions.

It wasn't the math that put me in that courtroom, but it was the fear of disappointment that took me down a slippery slope. With each problem completed incorrectly, I watched the frustration flicker across my dad's face. Don't get me wrong, Dad did everything he could to help me and all his actions were built on the best intentions with a loving heart. But I hated seeing the disappointment in his face and I hated that feeling of letting him down. I hated that gnawing guilt and worry that swelled up in my gut every night when it was homework time. In my little girl heart, I decided to do whatever it would take to keep that disappointment at bay.

As a child, this meant acting in small ways – hiding a mistake, embellishing a few details, covering up some failures.

It never failed that Mom and Dad would eventually find out about my cover up. The punishment was always worse because I had lied or hidden the issue, but even though I knew the worse would come, I still followed the same plan of attack. The punishment for having lied wasn't near enough to move me to be upfront with my parents. I was willing to take the hit if it meant avoiding those disapproving, disappointed faces even for one more day.

Punishment in my home was delivered justly and with love. My parents didn't act in an abusive way. They wanted to teach me the right way to live, the better decisions to make, and the Godly way to act.

They loved me so much. That may have been the reason why it hurt to disappoint them so. I just wanted them to be happy with me, be proud of my choices and my actions, and to be the girl they wanted me to be.

One night I remember lying in bed on the bottom bunk while my sister camped out on the top bunk. It had been a long night of frustrating homework. I went to bed feeling like I had failed and was worried about class the next day. My sister leaned over the edge of her bunk and said, "I hate it when you have homework. Everyone in the house gets so mad and angry. Why can't you just do it right?"

In her young mind, the tension that was in our home came directly from me. I remember feeling like I was hurting my whole family. I know she was just speaking from her own perspective and didn't realize what her brutal honesty did to my heart in that moment, but I was crushed. That night I took a big leap in the wrong direction – the direction to do whatever it takes to make everyone happy and gain everyone's approval. I was done being the source of let-down and disappointment.

When my teen years hit, I learned how to keep that approval going. I wanted to do whatever my parents wanted me to do. I wanted to date whoever they wanted me to date. I wanted to take whatever classes they wanted me to take. I wanted to dress however they wanted me to dress.

Every decision I made went through the "parent filter." If they liked it, so did I. If they were against it, so was I. For the most part this didn't fail me on principle. My parents were and are great people with a high standard for living. But something was off when it came to making some real-life choices for myself. I didn't know how to discern what *I* wanted. I was unsure of myself, what direction I wanted to go and who I wanted to go along with me. More importantly, I didn't know how to listen to my own heart. The quiet whispering of the Holy Spirit was easily drowned out by the voices of those in my world.

When my parents suggested that a local college would be a good place for my education after high school, I agreed and eagerly looked for a major I might be interested in that was offered at that campus. I just didn't know any other way to function. Whatever Mom and Dad wanted; Christie tried to comply.

There's no blame to really place here. My parents didn't do anything wrong and I don't believe I was in the wrong. It was simply a series of circumstances that, when built on each other, developed this shell of a girl who was insecure and unsure of herself. However, as insecure and unsure of myself as I was, I was still outgoing, well liked and socially active. But then again, of course I would be... that's what was expected and that's what was seen as "good" and "together."

High school brought relationships that were mostly founded out of guys I knew and met through church. My parents had a philosophy when it came to dating – keep it casual, don't get too serious. They believed this philosophy would keep me from getting too hung up on just one guy, leaving everything else I loved and was interested in behind for him and him alone. When things would get a little too serious or if the relationship was getting a little sideways, my dad gave a word of warning – "You can break up with him or I can break up with him for you. You decide."

For years I took solace in knowing that my dad was always there to be my rescuer. He would swoop in and save me from a bad boyfriend and even from myself. I saw him as a protector and shield that would keep me safe. It was comforting, hard at times to come to terms with, but comforting all the same.

I leaned on my parents to make my choices and now, when it came to dating, they dictated my relationships. I really had no sense of how to make a decision on my own and when it came to dating... I really had no idea on how to spot a good relationship. Yes, I had my parents as an example of a Godly, loving marriage where soulmates are best friends totally devoted to each other. I just lacked the ability to know how to get there and who was the right person to travel with.

The very last semester of my high school year, I had just experienced a breakup. This time I was the one left with a broken heart instead of the other way around. It crushed me and I was devastated. One afternoon, right after school, I walked down the street of my housing addition to visit a male friend who had graduated the year before me. He had heard that our yearbooks were in and he was anxious to see it. So, he invited me over. There are three crucial warning signs I should have seen, that should have stopped me in my tracks that day. One, I was going down to a boy's house and I knew his parents were not going to be there. That was a deal breaker in our family. Two, on that particular day, I was grounded and was not supposed to be venturing off from home after school. What I was grounded for, I don't remember, but I knew my parents wouldn't be home for hours so no one would be the wiser. And third, *"let me see your yearbook???"* Isn't that a sorry excuse for a pick-up line?

When I got to his house, I was nervous. All the butterflies had taken flight in my stomach. This was a kid I had hung out with for hours and hours and under this pretense we were just going to hang out like we normally did, so why was I so nervous? Maybe it was knowing I wasn't supposed to be there. Maybe it was sensing that there was a little bit of an attraction on both sides. Whatever it was, all the bells and alarms were going off, but I didn't heed a single one of them and I crossed the threshold eager to do what I wanted.

A simple flip of a few yearbook pages quickly turned into kissing and then into a heavy make-out session. When things started traveling faster and farther than I wanted, I tried to say, "cool it," but he didn't listen. When I tried to move away, he just held me closer. When I tried to push harder, he pinned me against the ground. When I slammed my fists against his chest, he just smiled and squeezed my mouth to push my lips together and kiss me. He was strong. He had been a high-school standout in wrestling and had just come home from basic training before getting his orders to leave for the Army. I was overpowered with no hope of an escape.

But even then, in that moment when I was in the wrong place at the wrong time, God was not far. He was watching out for me and in a stroke of grace and protection, the low rumbling sound of the garage door lifting open startled us both. His mom was home. In that instance he dropped his guard and I kicked my way out from underneath him and bolted out of the front door. She never saw me there, and to this day, I assume she never found out what was about to happen in her home, in her living room while she was away.

I know this is not every victim's story. I know there are those who are abused and assaulted in the worst ways and wonder why. If this is you, I know you've wondered where God was in those moments. Why didn't He provide an out or a savior in that moment for you? Dear friend, I don't have the answer to that other than to say, we live in a crappy world with crappy people who do crappy things. But I know God sees your scars, hears your cries, feels your pain and His heart breaks with yours. One day I know we will understand why we experienced the bumps in the road or the very pits that consumed us at times, but for now I believe this – all the things that happen in our lives, whether it's our fault or whether it's not, all of them can be used for good and for His purpose if we trust Him enough to let go of the past and the pain. To lay it down every day and choose to not be held there anymore. When we make that choice, we can experience freedom from the weight of those memories – not that we will ever forget them – but we aren't defined by them or defiled because of them. In that choice also awaits healing, in small doses and in small steps, but healing that makes us whole again.

As I left that house, I ran up the street to my home crying and fumbling to try to put myself back together. When my mom got home that day, she knew I was upset and could see that I had been crying. She chalked it up to breakup blues, and I was not going to tell her anything different. I was so stunned by the whole encounter. I was ashamed that I had let myself fall into that trap. I feared the trouble I would be in if I told my parents I had broken the rules. And I think mostly I was scared of being told I got what I deserved because I was in a place I wasn't supposed to be in. That thought ripped through me, because it would sum up the afternoon as failure, as disappointment and as disgust. Those were labels I didn't think I could handle, so I just pushed the whole thing aside. Afterall, I wasn't supposed to be there. It wasn't rape or a sexual assault if there was no sex, so I dismissed it. I also knew that the likelihood of my ever seeing this kid again was minimal so he would go his way and I would go mine and no one would ever need to know. At the time, all I thought I was out was the cost of replacing the yearbook I had left at his house. That was a minimal cost to keep my secret. And I went on about my life, focusing on graduation and college.

My freshman year of college left me feeling restless and unsatisfied. I wanted more and felt as if there was something else for me out in the world. Looking back now I see that what I really wanted was to escape. As much as I had wanted to get on with my life, I was haunted by that incident, but I had no way of recognizing what I was feeling, let alone deal with it. My coping mechanism began to be busy. If I just stayed preoccupied with "stuff," I could escape what I was feeling inside. So, I began looking for other opportunities to get a fresh start, to get away, to run.

I was fortunate enough to land a spot in a ministry organization that encompassed music and drama to deliver a faith-based, anti-violence assembly program in high schools and middle schools across the United States.

The position required me to devote a year to the ministry as well as raise financial support to off-set my expenses. I would also have to relocate to Michigan where the training facility was centered and be willing to travel with eleven other members for the year. To my surprise, my parents were on board with the idea, once they had done some research and verified it as a legitimate program. So, in the middle of July we made the trip to Michigan. It was the first time I had been away from home and away from my family. I was eager to fit in and experience success in this new experience. I began training and prepared to start the tour once the school year began. My family and church were supporting me from home, and everyone believed I was fulfilling my God-given purpose. The voices at home whispered,

"I just knew she was going to do something big,"
"She is so talented, it was just a matter of time,"
"God is going to use her for something great."

But…I met a guy. I could stop right there because any wise woman knows how this story is going to end. Emotions in a young woman blind her easily to truth and reality, but the heart calls strongly.

Yes, as you probably expected, I followed my heart and began a relationship with a guy who was in my touring group. He was tall, dark and handsome. He played the bass and was incredibly intelligent, well read and well spoken. He was charming and knew how to win over anyone who was in his space. But, quickly, when we were alone, the relationship turned sour. He became overbearing and controlling, constantly picking at my weaknesses or short-comings. He would call me names or put me down in front of others. He was older than me by a few years and would tell me I was immature, and I just didn't know what it was like to be with "a real man." I tried to do all that I could to keep him happy and the be the girl he wanted, but it was never enough. I built a "love" on sacrificing everything to get just a crumb of his affection in return. This relationship was toxic, unhealthy and destroyed what little self-confidence I had. After six months, I tried to break off the relationship and was met with violent outbursts and on-going petty fights that made me and the rest of the group walk on eggshells.

The mess of our relationship was no longer a secret. Eventually our managing company sent me home to take some time off, while he got to stay on as if nothing happened. While

I was at home, I was so embarrassed. I had let everyone down. Anyone who knew me knew what I was doing and now I was home to say I ruined the chance I had. Eventually, the tour manager called and asked if I would be willing to come back and I was transferred to another team located in a different part of the country doing the same type of programming I was already trained to do. I took the chance to go back and finish what I had started. All the while, I was confiding in our group's road manager.

He was calm and listened to me. He paid attention to me and acted as my protector. He cheered on my talent and made me feel wanted, accepted and special. It didn't take much more for me to jump from the toxic, abusive relationship I was once into the waiting arms of a guy who would rescue me from the drama.

After six months of cultivating a relationship, we both left that tour, got engaged and moved to Indiana where he was from originally. It happened quickly. My parents were concerned that the speed of this relationship was startling, but given my age, they weren't in a position to stand in the way. Silently they watched me pack up and head to Indiana.

My first year in Indiana was spent getting used to a lot of firsts – my first fulltime job, my first car, my first time to live on my own, my first rented space. I was swept up in wedding details and this new, independent life. However, what I was doing was far from independent.

When my fiancé said "jump," I asked "how high?" It was the same technique that I had mastered while avoiding conflict with my parents. I would do anything to avoid disappointment, upset, failure or conflict. No matter if it was picking out flowers for the wedding or picking the right outfit to wear to an event, I didn't make a decision without first running it through the "what-would-my-fiancé-think" routine. I literally was incapable of making my own decisions or having my own opinions. I was so consumed with keeping the peace. I was overwhelmed with making sure those around me saw me as a success and saw a girl who had it together. I had failed in so many ways before, this was finally my chance to get it right. I had connected to a guy who looked to be a perfect fit on paper. I was mature and brave to have started a whole new life. But it was a lonely, empty life, and it was far from over.

Chapter 2

Married but not happily

In the summer of 1998 I walked down a cobblestone path in the middle of a beautiful rose garden to marry Tom. Looking back now, I can see that I made the decision to say "yes" based on a few things: Tom looked good on paper and my parents liked him. That was it. There was no romance there on my part, no love that was splendid. It just made logical sense. It didn't hurt that everyone else liked Tom, I liked him too. Looking back now, I realize what I really liked was that he could take me away and give me a fresh start. He knew about some of my screw ups and had witness my toxic relationship before. When I declared that "screw up" was all my fault, he loved me despite my mistakes. I thought it was the best I could hope for, and I liked the idea of us as a couple. He was into stage productions and sound. I was into performing and music. Seemed like a no brainer! So, when it came to the proposal, how could all of this be wrong? I had to agree to marry him.

After the wedding, Tom and I went off to our honeymoon. Of course, hindsight is 20/20, but I should have known something wasn't right in our relationship even then.

While other couples look for their honeymoon to spend time together, wrapped in each other's arms, creating memories and establishing the early stages of married intimacy, our time was nothing like that. In fact, Tom was inclined to sleep the day away and lie in the hotel room watching movies. There was no romance, no intimacy, no marital memories. Since I hadn't been sexually active before marriage, I assumed that my idea for sex in marriage was off-base and my expectations were set too high. When I pushed the issue, Tom reminded me that my run ins with bad boyfriends, and my encounter with an attempted sexual assault, had twisted my expectations of sex. Our limited physical relationship was normal.

I made the most of our vacation and figured life would magically get better as time went on. However, if you've been married, you know that relationships don't magically get better. They take work and intent.

Shortly after the wedding, Tom and I bought our first home. I immediately got caught up in decorating and making this house a home for the two of us. Tom, being a handyman, immediately launched into all the updates and repairs that would better our home. It wasn't until two years later that the dust settled, literally, and I woke up feeling something was wrong.

It was hard to put into words, but I felt empty, dull. I looked at what had been the past few years and thought, "If this is what it's going to be like, what's the point?"

Just like any good girl, I called my mom hoping she would have some great words of advice. When I tried to explain what was going on, she encouraged me to not be discouraged. She figured this melancholia was just life settling in after the whirlwind of the past few years. I took her perspective as gospel, she was indeed married longer than I had been. Certainly, Mother knows best, right? So I sucked up my whining and complaining and forged ahead. I threw myself into my career and into my church. I volunteered for everything and got involved in anything that I could squeeze into my schedule.

Remember, my defense mechanism is busyness when it comes to avoiding conflict or dealing with unfavorable situations. And I became a pro at being busy.

In the middle of all that I was doing, I launched a business and so did Tom. He was off in one direction doing his thing and I was off on my own adventure. We weren't even ships that passed in the night... we were ships that didn't sail the same waters. But I kept on keeping on, doing all the things I thought I should be doing, keeping the peace, putting on a smile and acting the part.

My days were quickly filled attending church, singing in the choir, volunteering with the youth program, going on women's retreats and daily spending time reading and studying the Word.

I was able to keep up appearances for a few more years. I made myself believe all was right and I was happy. Until one day something happened that threatened to throw reality in my face. I was pregnant.

When fear sets in

Tom and I had just returned home from being out of town for my sister's wedding. I had been feeling sick while we were there, but I chalked it up to all the anxiety and excitement of the wedding. But my curiosity got the best of me and I bought a pregnancy test. I remember being in our upstairs bathroom. I could hear Tom downstairs on the phone talking to a contractor in regards to his business. I unwrapped the test, read the directions and did the deed. It didn't take long for the test to confirm my suspicions – I was pregnant.

In that moment, fear slapped me in the face followed by a punch of panic in the gut. I started crying and muttering to myself, "NO! I can't be pregnant. Not when I am so screwed up and so unhappy. I can't be a mom when I feel like such a train wreck."

It was the first moment that I said out loud how unhappy and unsatisfied I was with my life. When other women would be crying tears of joy over this new little life, I prayed between sobs that this pregnancy test was wrong. The last thing I wanted was a baby. The last thing I needed was another aspect of my life in which I felt totally insecure but had to look like I had it all together. I knew our marriage wasn't right. And although I couldn't put my finger on it, I knew it wasn't the home I wanted to bring a baby into.

Minutes that felt like hours ticked by and I eventually talked myself into being happy. I coached my heart to get in line and to suck it up. I washed my face, took a deep breath and put on my happy face. As I told Tom about the pregnancy, he seemed pleased. I remember him joking that he must have "special swimmers" that could get the job done with just a once or twice encounter. I could never tell him how I really felt.

We didn't wait long to start telling family members about the baby. We also didn't wait long before we started buying cribs, furniture and baby items. My attention was kept busy in all the planning. I spent my free time picking out wallpaper for the nursery, looking at designs and ideas to transform our guest room into the perfect place for our little one to grow up.

Busy. Always busy. Never a dull moment. Never a quiet life. One whirlwind after another.

Then it happened. At a checkup with my OBGYN, it was confirmed that I was going through a miscarriage. Some cramping and bleeding led me to make the appointment. As the nurse held my hand to console me, the doctor tried to explain what the next steps would be. The helpful nursing staff took my tears for a sign of sorrow over the loss. But I knew they were tears of guilt. I didn't want the baby in the first place, and now I had gotten exactly what I had hoped for. The baby was gone.

The amount of guilt I felt made me sick. My thoughts were racing around one singular thought...I had prayed for, pleaded for, begged for this to not happen and now I was getting exactly what I had asked for.

The next thought that crept into my mind... and here's another point of failure. I would now have to tell all those approving family members and friends that I had screwed up and it wasn't alright. I had lost the baby.

A few weeks went by where doctor appointments and exams diverted my attention from the loss. I kept my eyes forward and focused on the future, never letting my heart grieve or heal from the condemnation I carried on my shoulders.

Again, my quest for perfection, for approval, for peace-keeping, for keeping up appearances took over and the fake way of living I had created as my standard became a way of life again.

The shell of what was my fake persona grew a little thicker, a little stronger. I was becoming an expert at swallowing my feelings, painting on a happy face and pretending I was okay. But in the end, I was only lying to myself.

Chapter 3

Change brings nothing but frustration

After losing the baby, I could only be still for so long. My heart began to feel unsettled. I knew something was wrong. I knew this wasn't how I was supposed to feel about my life. So I began to make changes. I changed my hair, my job, my eating habits, and my exercise routine. I closed my business and started another one. I changed where I volunteered, who I hung out with, and where I spent my free time. I took up painting, playing guitar, writing, photography and crafting. Nothing seemed to help.

I changed the furniture in my house, remodeled, repainted and reorganized. I even went as far as changing the mattress on my bed trying to figure out why I felt so bad. When none of those proved to be successful solutions, I changed churches, but nothing helped.

It was during this time, Tom and I fell into some serious financial issues. While he was busy running his business, I was left to monitor and handle our family finances. But without communication between what we needed for our personal budget, Tom went ahead with his business and I did what I could to keep the bank account positive. Financial stress began to weigh on me. Tom was daily under the pressure of keeping his business competitive in a saturated market. We went to bed each night with the weight of the world on our shoulders and no communication with one another to help ease the stress. To add to the situation, God was nowhere to be found in our marriage. Tom had stopped going to church a long time ago and my attendance, while regular, was for show and not much else.

My solution for keeping us afloat was to finance our debt into more debt. I took out second mortgages, refinanced our first mortgage to take advantage of the equity in our home, racked up credit cards and juggled money like a pro. Robbing Peter to pay Paul was my mantra and as long as no one knocked on our door to shut off our electricity, it was a good day.

I was working in the mortgage business and was able to get an appraiser to overstate the value on our house so we could squeeze more money out of our home. We were more than upside down on the property. When Tom's business had to close, we were faced with a mountain of debt. Bankruptcy was our only recourse and we were forced out of our home due to foreclosure. Our cars were repossessed, and our financial credibility ruined.

Talk about feeling the weight of failure. And so much of this failure was public. We lived in a small town and folks knew us. Naturally, they knew when a sheriff sale happened at our home and when things began to unfold. I'll never forget coming home to a message on our answering machine from a well-meaning friend.

"Saw the sheriff's sale in the paper and I am so sorry you are having financial difficulties."

I wanted to just run away.

We had to pick up and move, literally and figuratively, but nothing much changed. We simply moved to the next town. Although we didn't launch businesses, our marriage dynamic did not change at all. Our schedules were much the same and our lack of communication was now worse. Tom was frustrated and unhappy with his having to go back to work in a corporate environment. He viewed our financial problems as completely my fault and "punished" me by shutting me out. I was put on a short leash when it came to money. Instead of creating conversations that kept us both accountable and built unity in this area of our marriage, I felt like I was being monitored. Tom acted like he was my father, reprimanding me when I took a wrong step. He would remind me of my past mistakes and used that failure as justification for putting a financial control on me.

40

He did not allow me to have any say or ownership once we got back on our feet. I didn't have my name on the checking account, I didn't have my name on the utilities for our new place, I didn't have my name on the lease agreement. Soon the control turned into manipulation and our already weak relationship turned toxic and unhealthy very quickly.

Bad habits resurfaced and became worse. They resurfaced primarily because we tried to rebuild on a false foundation. Neither of *us* changed and therefore, *nothing* changed in the long run. Tom was off working a new job and throwing himself into a side project that kept him away most nights of the week. I was left home alone.

Tom didn't want me to work. He enjoyed knowing that I was at home where I couldn't "get into any trouble." We had just one vehicle so I didn't go anywhere without his permission. If I did take the car for an appointment or to go to church, I had to be home at a certain time or Tom would begin calling my cellphone without ceasing until I answered. On more than one occasion, I would come home late from Wednesday night Bible study to find that Tom had set out on foot to hunt me down and bring me back home. Don't mistake this as a husband's concern for his wife. This was manipulation at its best and the guilt trips were many. Money and anything that would give me any sense of freedom was forbidden and I was kept at home, removed from my family and friends.

Why did I put up with this behavior? Somehow in my approval addict mindset I believed I was being a good wife by adhering to these rules and expectations. I considered it as the way I was to be submissive to my husband. All the while I was submitting to a man that wasn't led by God, but by his fear and insecurity. At the same time, I had bought into the lie that our bankruptcy, and any other hardships or bad days in our marriage, were my fault. I solely carried the burden of that financial meltdown and therefore was the only one "punished," the only one that "needed to learn a lesson." I felt like I didn't deserve to have a life, to enjoy it or to be free to live it. After all, the reason we only had just one car was because of my poor financial management, so who was I to be trusted to drive it? Looking back at it now, it sickens me to see how twisted my reasoning had developed. Every time I let fear win and I let approval addiction take over, I let the mess get more twisted.

Needless to say, my marriage was not a happy one. We weren't filled with love, but with bitterness, resentment and mistrust.

Chapter 4

The door to deception swings wide

In a fluke incident, I somehow convinced Tom to let me join a direct sales company. I sold him on the work-from-home concept and that this opportunity would allow for me to make some extra money.

By this time, Tom was enthralled with his full-time job and a hobby that was almost like having a second full-time job. I believe he signed off on the idea of this direct sales business as a way to keep me busy and out of his hair. But I saw it as an opportunity to have something for *me*, something that would make me feel good about myself and something that would grant me a bit of success.

I started the business with great gusto. It didn't take long for me to fall in love with what this new opportunity offered. I had joined a company that centered around wonderful women who encouraged me, cheered me on and applauded my accomplishments. It was a breath of fresh air and the shot in the arm I needed.

In this business opportunity, I was applauded for success. Prizes were earned, the spotlight was bright, and the atta-girl came in heaps. Although the company meant for these things to be motivators, it was like an addictive drug for this approval junkie. I would do whatever it took to reach the next level of success, to earn the next prize or get the next round of recognition. I even bent the rules to make them play in my favor.... And that is what landed me in that courtroom.

A decision to finagle hostess credits and party purchases, all in the name of climbing the ladder of success, led me down a heartbreaking path that ended in a courtroom with a guilty verdict.

Looking back on those years where I was lost and worried more about what others thought than what was right, I can see that the fall wasn't sudden. It was little by little, but the more comfortable I became walking on the outskirts of what was true, the easier it was for those judgement calls to get blurry.

I realized I was in trouble when I got a phone call from a county detective wanting to ask me some questions. I retained an attorney who found out what the questioning was all about, and it wasn't long before I was told there was a warrant out for my arrest. Before I could turn myself in, a sheriff showed up at my home to serve the warrant and take me in.

It was a Friday afternoon in the middle of summer. I was in a T-shirt and a pair of gym shorts. The sheriff was very polite as he knocked on the door and asked for me by my full name. Tom was there to watch the scene unfold. The sheriff explained what was going to happen. I was going to be taken into custody and brought to the county jail where I would be booked, fingerprinted, have my mug shot taken and frisked. I would spend the weekend in jail until I could be seen by the judge on Monday. He would determine if bail would be set and at what amount. Either way, I was spending a few days in jail.

It was a lot to take in. I cooperated with the sheriff, letting him cuff me and lead me out my front door into the summer sun. I remember being placed in the back of the sheriff's car. The front seat was pushed back so far that there was little-to-no leg room and the cuffs were digging into my wrists that were forced behind me. As he shut the door and made his way to the driver's seat, I was left in the car alone for a few minutes while he jawed on his walkie-talkie. The heat in the car was oppressive and made it hard to breath. I felt claustrophobic as the emotion of it all started to make its way to the surface.

The twelve-mile trip from my home to the jail was long and fast all at the same time. I went through the routine of being booked, fingerprinted and photographed. I changed out of my clothes and into a set of orange scrubs that was to be my attire for the weekend. Carrying a plastic tote with some personal hygiene items, a bath towel and a sleeping mat, I was led to the cellblock for women.

The walls in the cellblock were gray and there was nothing but concrete, floor to ceiling. The lights were yellow and dull, casting a sickly glow on the dingy walls.

The women's block was loud. Women talking, shouting while playing cards, a small television was blasting music videos, and all the noise bounced off the concrete walls, metal doors and picnic table in the center room.

Off the center room were fourteen, two-person cells. They were dimly lit with a set of bunks, a sink and a toilet. My cellmate was an older woman who was serving time for solicitation. She could see that I was overwhelmed by the surroundings and began to help me settle in. I couldn't breathe. The air was stale, and my chest was heavy. I couldn't imagine waiting here a few days for my court appearance let alone spend any length of time there.

Lydia, my roommate for the weekend, was babbling on about what was what there in the block. I couldn't take in what she was saying. However, in a moment of desperation, I looked at her and said, "I don't know if you are a Christian or not, but I need to pray, and I need to pray out loud with someone. So, will you let me pray with you?"

I am sure my request stunned her a bit, but Lydia agreed, and we sat next to each other on her bottom bunk and I prayed. I just needed relief from the emotions that were suffocating me. I remember choking out the words to my desperate prayer, but earnestly pleading that God would somehow make Himself present in that moment. I pleaded for peace and that He would lift this oppressive pressure off my chest. As I prayed, I felt a physical wind blow through that cell. Lydia and I both looked up at each other because she had felt it as well. It was palpable, and peace washed over me in that moment. I knew that God was with me. I had felt His presence in the most powerful way. My mistakes were mine to account for, but God hadn't written me off. I had run from Him in so many ways, all while still looking the part, but He was waiting for me to return to Him. I wanted to give Him perfection. He only wanted a relationship with the real me, including all my imperfections.

Dear Friend, you may believe that your mistakes have disqualified you from the love of your Heavenly Father, but let me tell you this one solitary truth that rises above anything the world has to tell you:

You are _not_ disqualified. You can have the love and forgiveness and acceptance you crave, all you have to do is ask, accept it and believe it is yours. You have a Heavenly Father who loves you. In fact, nothing you do can make Him love you any less. And nothing you do can make Him love you more than He does right now. That's a powerful truth to grab ahold of, especially if you're a people pleaser like me!

The weekend came and went. On Monday, I went before the judge, pleaded not guilty and was allowed to post bail and return home until my next court date. My attorney went to work on my case and the days ticked by. The whole ordeal took about two years – from arrest to sentencing. It was not a fast process. But each day, I was determined to see God in the situation and I was confident that He was going to bring about an outcome that was in my favor. I would have bet my life on it. There was no shortage of faith on my side.

But my faith wasn't going to be tested in my victory. The real test would be in what seemed like a dead end.

Chapter 5

Felony becomes final

A week before my sentencing, my mother called to tell me she was coming up from Tennessee to be there in the courtroom. She was bringing my younger brother with her, so she didn't have to travel alone. My dad wasn't going to come – he didn't think he could handle watching the events unfold. I can only imagine what emotions my parents went through, watching their daughter being put through her paces and wondering what the future held for her.

I remember spending the day before my sentencing at home alone. My mother was traveling and would arrive that evening, and I took time to gear up for the day ahead by reading the Bible, praying, and journaling. As a natural-born writer, journaling is a form of therapy for me. It helps me cope and allows me a safe place to vent and sort out my emotions.

After meditating, praying and feeding my heart and spirit, Tom came home from work (yes, he had worked that day) ready to meet up with my mom and brother. However, he was not pleased with the way I had chosen to spend my time.

"I am about to be left alone to do everything myself, the least you could have done was made sure the laundry was finished and the house was cleaned. The whole reason we are here in this predicament is because of you in the first place!"

He raged at me for an hour over my decision. I was crushed that in those final moments, I had failed… again. The feeling that I could do nothing right was almost tangible. I had been called a "train wreck," "hopeless," a "burden," by the very man who was supposed to love me for better or for worse.

I met my mother and brother that night for dinner feeling so alone and so ashamed. Sure, I kept up conversation and tried to not focus on what the next day would hold, but inside I was crushed, already defeated and afraid.

The night before my sentencing, I remember lying in bed, while Tom stayed up to work on the computer. I prayed for God to somehow intervene and move the judge to have great mercy on me. After praying I fell asleep exhausted from the weight of it all.

The courtroom was empty minus my family and a few close girlfriends. Thirty days had gone by from the date that I stood in the same spot, hearing a jury declare me "guilty." Now I waited for a judge to determine my fate.

I stood in my tailored pant suit and heels, an outfit I wore to church many times. The judge read my charges and declared my sentence to be two years spent in the state's department of corrections - prison. I don't remember a thing that was said after that. All I knew was that I had believed that God would intervene, but He didn't. All I asked was that He show mercy, but He didn't. All I wanted was to know I was alone, but He had abandoned me. I was hurt and betrayed.

I was ushered out of the courtroom and into a side conference room to complete some paperwork. Part of my sentencing included a year of probation after serving two years in prison. Before I would be moved to the jail, certain forms needed my signature and I was to be instructed on my probation terms. It just so happened that the probation officer tasked with managing my case also was a friend. I had spent years standing beside Jamie in our church choir loft and on stage with our praise and worship team. She was a great alto and I was a strong soprano. We had participated in several Easter cantatas and Christmas pageants together. On that day in March, Jamie and I didn't harmonize our voices in worship, but we both cried tears of sorrow. Jamie was shocked at the day's outcome. Weeks later, in my journal I wrote:

"Even while at the courthouse, while sitting with Jamie reviewing my probation paperwork, she told me, 'You'll do great things in prison. I know you will. They need you there.'"

After the administration part of that meeting was over, I was brought out into the hallway with the chance to say goodbye to Tom, my family, and friends. There were tears and promises of prayers. But nothing stuck. I only felt the arms of those I love wrap around me. I only saw the worried look on my mother's face. My words were muffled underneath the emotions I tried to keep under control. The most scaring memory I have from that moment is of my brother, six years younger than me, standing tall and handsome next to my mom as her support in that moment. He may have hugged me and said goodbye, I don't remember. I do remember his piercing blue eyes full of emotion that said it all. He was confused. He was worried. He looked at me like he didn't really know who I was. He was disappointed. The very thing I had worked so hard to avoid was in fact all that I had to show for my wasted efforts.

Then, with my hands cuffed to a chain around my waist, a sheriff walked me from the courthouse, across the street and to the jail where I would wait until the state's department of corrections had a place for me. That time was undetermined.

The logistical part of my case was frustrating. I had jockeyed around some hostess credits and offered a payment plan to a group of ladies that came to bite me in the behind. Later, while serving my sentence, I realized that God didn't have me there for the silly mistake I made in that business transaction, He had me there to get my attention. I might not have deserved a two-year prison sentence for fraud in the amount of less than $600, but I did deserve the sentence for the way my life was displeasing to God and so far removed from the plans He had for me.

Chapter 5

March

"At first, my beginning was full of frustration and anger. I wanted to know why God put me here. Most importantly, I wanted to know why God seemed to be absent."

Coming back into that jail, into that women's block, I couldn't believe I was back. Although now I was back for a long time, or at least until the prison had room for me.

I was angry. I was bitter. I was hurt and mad that God would let me end up there. I was a ball of twisted emotions, left to sort it out in a desolate, hopeless place. Enter in a few well-meaning women who were from the area church visiting the block to minister to the women. I heard the familiar voice of a girlfriend I had once attended church with where we studied in a women's Bible study group together and spent many hours sitting around her kitchen table sipping coffee, talking and laughing about life.

She should have been a welcoming bright spot in that dark space of my life, but I was ashamed and quite frankly, the last thing I wanted to hear was how God loved me. So, I hid. I tucked inside my cell and waited until she left. But the conversation floated on the stale air and my heart couldn't help but absorb a bit of the truth she was there to share.

A few days later, while sitting in the dayroom, the block door opened and in walked the prison chaplain who I had known from previous church-related interactions. Pastor Alice was an elderly woman who had a big smile and an even bigger heart for the women serving time in our county jail. She brought a warmth and energy with her that somehow softened the cold, metal world we lived in. She spotted me, and I couldn't run. She swooped in with a big hug as if she had spotted her long-lost friend. She was so glad to see me. I was stunned by her excitement and disappointed that I couldn't run.

Pastor Alice grabbed me by the arm and sat me down at the picnic table where she eagerly shoved her Bible in front of me. The other ladies in the block had gone to retrieve their Bibles and were gathering around the table to participate in what was becoming clear to me ... a Bible study.

As everyone settled in, Pastor Alice began by telling the ladies how she knew me.

"Ladies, you need to get to know Christie and her story. It is powerful and she's a very special person. She has a gift for teaching

the scriptures and sharing divine, inspired application. And you should hear her sing! I've told her many times she needs to speak and preach."

My mouth hung open and I was shocked by her faith in me. Even in that depressing state she saw worth in me. That day she spoke power and purpose over my life, and I felt encouraged that this part of my story wasn't the ending, but just the beginning. In my journal I wrote...

I had prayed for God to give me some sort of solace and in return I heard Him say to me: "Here in this place I am going to build your character. This is the 'fire' in which I am going to refine you. I am preparing you to do my work. So, although you see this as a delay or even a roadblock, I see it as a necessary tool that will be invaluable to your calling and my relationship with you. Always remember that I make all things work together for My good, even in this."

Four weeks went by before I was told I would soon be transported from the county jail to the prison's intake facility in Southern Indiana. However, for security purposes, I would not be told the specific date this would take place. That meant my family wouldn't know either. Thankfully, a few girls in the county block had a few experiences with the department of corrections and gave me a tip: Write a letter to your family, addressed and ready to go so that when you are transported, someone you trust on the block can mail it for you to notify your family. And that's what I did. On the morning that I was transported, I left my letter with my cellmate and gathered what little belongings I had and was able to take with me, settled in to the sheriff's transport car, and was soon headed south.

The trip took a few hours and there were few words shared between the sheriff and I. When we arrived at the facility, we passed through a series of security checkpoints and then I was finally dropped off in a folding chair, sitting in front of the prison's "greeter."

A woman who fit the stereotypical description of a prison guard gruffly asked me a list of questions and then directed me to a concrete stall where I was told to strip down to my birthday suit. I was told to spread my legs and place my arms over my head. She quickly frisked me to ensure no contraband was being brought in between my butt cheeks, under my breasts or between my thighs.

After I was checked, she handed me a pair of white briefs, a white bra, a pair of white socks, a set of orange scrubs and a pair of white Velcro sneakers. My photo was taken, my corrections number was issued and was to be my ID for the remainder of my time in prison. I was then escorted by another inmate to the intake building.

This ominous building was concrete with few windows. Its two-story building held approximately 600 women – 300 on one side and 300 on the other. Large rooms were caged off with eight sets of bunks in each and a matching set of lockers for storage. The noise level was off the charts and guards seemed to be yelling nonstop. In the center of it all was a large open area outfitted with tables and chairs. Two small televisions hung on the wall with closed captioning words scrolling along the bottom. In the back corner was a small room where a nurse was stationed. I took a seat and she worked on collecting my blood pressure, temperature and weight. She looked at me with an expression of concern when my blood pressure came back higher than normal. "Your blood pressure is really high? I wonder why that is?" I wanted to scream at her "BECAUSE I JUST ARRIVED AT PRISON!" However, I just shrugged and complied with her requests as she took a blood sample, counted my teeth, and asked another long list of questions to gather my medical history.

At the time I didn't know what an odd thing it was to be

going through this process as the only offender. In prison, inmates are called "offenders," a term I had to get used to really quick. No one calls you by your name, just by your prison ID number or "offender."

Offenders are transported to the same intake facility from all over the state each business day. At the time I was serving my sentence, on average eight women were taken in each day and about same went out to whatever facility they are to be permanently placed. Do the math. That averages to be one thousand nine-hundred and twenty women a year. That was the conservative average at the time. I can only imagine what that number is today.

However, on my day, I was the only one. I believe this was God's way of making a rough day just a little more bearable. I quickly found out that if I was patient, polite, respectful and took my punishment like a big girl, the prison staff was almost kind. At the very least they went a little easier on me because they recognized my humility and my willingness to comply.

Never did I experience this more than on that first day. While I was being take through my medical checkup, the laundry department was supposed to be getting together my bedding, linens and extra state issued undergarments. They were to be delivered to the intake building with my name on them, but they never came. When we had all returned from dinner and there were still no drop offs from the laundry department, I knew I had to say something.

I meekly approached a large counter where two guards were stationed tasked to watch over the heap of us women. One lady was working who had a reputation for being nasty. I had already witnessed her bark as she interacted with some of the other offenders and I knew she was someone to approach with caution. She was downright scary, but I knew I had to do something.

Let me just stop for a moment and parallel this fear-driven humility with how we may act when we come to talk with our Heavenly Father. If we've been broken and bruised, or if we feel the weight of our failures, we may find that we tiptoe up to the throne to beg for our Heavenly Father's attention. We may seem Him as a fearful force, one that makes us afraid to even ask Him for anything. But unlike my prison guard encounter, Heavenly Father is not there to beat you down or make you feel less than. Dear Friend, please hear me when I say He loves you. He loves you so much and wants so badly for you to not just come up to Him, but to run to Him with complete trust and abandon, leaping into His arms for Him to hold you and carry you. That is who we are dealing with.... A persona my prison guard friend hadn't any connection with.

A yellow line was painted on the floor that followed the outline of the counter creating a three-foot gap between you as the offender and the guards. This apparently was a line you didn't cross without an invitation. I didn't need to be told that, it just seemed like common sense. So, I stood at the line waiting to be acknowledged. There's no motivating a prison guard if you are an offender. You simply move at their pace and in this case, it seemed to move like molasses. But finally, I got the nod to move up to the counter and I explained to the terrifying guard that I was without my laundry drop.

It must have been something in the way I spoke to her or it was God's favor in that moment, but her response was not yelled back at me in a demeaning tone. She softened her approach, took my name and ID number and said she would check on things.

That night I slept soundly. Probably from the exhaustion of the day, but I didn't sleep on any linens. The bed sheets, bath towels and second set of undergarments didn't come. No, I slept on plastic with no pillow, no blanket to curl up under and hide. I laid on the top bunk in the middle of that caged room exposed, vulnerable, lonely... but exhausted and therefore sleep came.

After returning from an early breakfast, the same guard pulled me off to the side to inform me that my laundry drop had arrived. I was never so excited to have something that I felt was mine and to have at least a little of something that resembled creature comforts.

The other ladies in my "room" were fine. We didn't have any fights or run-ins and I never felt unsafe or uncomfortable. Contrary to other prisons (I am happy to say I only have the one experience to compare), and despite what might be portrayed on television, prison was well managed. There were high cleanliness standards and such a care for the offenders' well being that you had to go looking for a fight or for a sexual encounter. I assume this "care" wasn't necessarily for the welfare of the prison population, but more to save the State from having to explain anything that might pop up in an investigation or lawsuit. Don't get me wrong... it's prison and we are talking about a population of troublemakers to some degree. Sure, there was the occasional theft among thieves, arguments over who's turn it was in the shower and so forth. But nothing like I had seen depicted. My biggest complaint was that it was loud all the time, except at night when the guards demanded quiet, and it was lonely. With the number of women coming in and coming out of the intake facility, no one was there long enough to invest in any sort of a friendship with me. I spent days without talking to a single person. There's no music, not even from television commercials because the television runs on mute with captions only. It wouldn't matter, there is so much noise you couldn't have heard a commercial jingle even it was on. Why was it so loud? Well, when you cram 300 women in one space with nothing really to do other than sit and talk, even 150 conversations going at a normal level would equal "loud."

It takes several weeks before an offender can have anything while going through intake. To buy any items on commissary such as pens, pencils, paper or envelopes, money has to be added to an offender's prison account. However, the State only allows those who are approved to apply money to the account. This process takes time.

In my first couple of days, a staff member sat all of us new offenders down and walked us through creating a list of individuals who we wanted to be on our approved list. This list would be the folks allowed to apply money on our account, but also would be the people we could call once we had enough money to buy a phone card to pay for the call. It was also the list of people we would want to visit us when we were allowed visits at our permanent facilities once we were placed.

All of that meant a few weeks of isolation. No phone calls or letters to and from anyone while the list was getting approved. I panicked. I knew my mom and dad were worried sick. Since no one had gone through this process before, they wouldn't know that they couldn't write to me or why I hadn't written to them. I was disappointed that I was going to go without a pencil and paper to jot down my own thoughts. I was going to go without something as simple as a ponytail holder until my list was approved. It was a long couple of weeks.

I remember finally getting the chance to make a call to Tom and my Mom and Dad. They were two very different conversations. My call to Tom was met with more shame and bitterness. There was little to no encouragement and I was given a lecture that informed me that I better learn my lesson.

My parents wanted to assurance that I was okay, and I was safe. My mom wanted to know if there was anything she could send. She had already figured out where I was, had called the prison to learn more about where I was, and had already learned the rules of what she could send and not send. Leave it to a mom to do whatever it takes to hunt down the facts about her kid. I am sure she didn't sleep until she knew it all. I asked her for a Bible.

In that space, the only thing I wanted to cling to was

God's truth. It took one day of being in prison for me to realize I couldn't go through this without leaning on God's help. However, there weren't many Bibles around. I found myself walking around each day repeating in my head scripture I had memorized. Never was I so thankful for scripture memory disciplines my parents instilled in me. It gave a whole new meaning to "thy word I have hid in my heart."

One reprieve I found was in a routine I established early in the morning. We would wake up at about 4:30 in the morning for breakfast. Everyone had to go whether you wanted to eat or not. We would all line up and file down to the mess hall to eat. I have to say, the food wasn't all that bad. You just had to eat on their time and at their pace, which was fast.

As we all came back from breakfast, most of the women would go back to bed for a few hours. I found this to be the perfect time for me to take a shower because I had the bathroom to myself. I also participated in the morning recreation time. That consisted of being allowed to go outside and walk the sidewalk around the prison grounds. I would stay awake through lunch and then in the afternoon take a nap while my room was empty and everyone else was in the large group room playing cards and watching television. I got up for dinner before retreating to my bunk to read. That was until I met Sarah.

Chapter 6

April

"The turmoil of being incarcerated, of going through the court drama, has torn me up. It's like a till going through soil. I've been overturned, ripped open and roughed up. But because of that, it is the perfect ground and the perfect time to plant seeds in the heart- seeds of redemption, change, transformation and restoration."

It was a cold day, but the sun was shining. A bit of money on my prison account had afforded me a radio with some earbuds so I could listen to some music. I could pickup a Christian radio station if I was lying in my bunk or if I was outside. During my morning walks, I would put on that station and walk circles around the yard. That time was spent praying with tears running down my face, but it was a time I looked forward to each day. This day was no different.

As I walked, I prayed a prayer that I had been offering to God for several weeks. Each time I got the same response:

"God, I desperately need for you to bring me a friend, at least for the short-term stay here. I am so lonely, and I need someone to

break that loneliness."

God always replied:

"I know. But I am closer than a brother and you are a friend of God. When I am all that you have and all that you need, I'll bring someone else."

That was a hard answer to swallow, but I knew if I was going to ever recover from my need to please, I had to be in a position where there was only God. However, on that brisk Spring day, I was given a friend in Sarah.

I made my way around the circle. In the middle of the sidewalk circle were picnic tables scattered throughout. If an offender chose to take the offered recreational time sitting down, it was allowed. Some women came out to sit in the sun, some came out to read. The first time I passed Sarah I could see she was reading. She was an older woman with a soft face, and she seemed quiet. The second time around I thought I saw *what* she was reading... a Bible! The third time around I knew for sure and I made a beeline straight for her.

I sat down across from her and introduced myself. I asked her for her name and then eagerly asked if she would like to read together. I was so excited to find someone who might want to talk about the same things as I did and someone who might be on the same page as me! She probably thought I was crazy. I am sure I came at her like a lunatic, but I was overjoyed that she was the one I had been praying for.

We started meeting each day to read. Soon we started sitting together a lunch and dinner and then before you know it, we weren't retreating in solitude to our bunks each night, we were sitting it the group room playing cards together. In the days that soon followed, a few other offenders from Sarah's county had arrived. They were much like Sarah and our group grew from two to four and then to five. We were all going on about four weeks of the seven-to-eight-week intake process. It sure was nice to have a group of gals to befriend.

"Today Sarah and I were studying the second chapter of Romans. Paul writes about rules, rituals and the law. He is working to encourage the reader to go a little deeper than just checking off a list. We then read in Proverbs 21 as a reference to this material.

Sarah and I came across the same theme three different times. I asked her what she thought the significance of this might mean since we've read it three times. We agreed that God wants us to realize there is more for our future than just not committing the same mistakes again. There is more to our life than just keeping the law. There is more than a simple list dos and don'ts. We need to grab ahold of the relationship. *We need to fully open out hearts to the idea that it's God's kindness that draws us to repent and change not just our own desires to follow the rules and get it right to avoid trouble."*

A note to instill hope

Somehow through the weeks, my church at home had captured my address so they could write to me. Being that it was from a church, the prison allowed it and I received many encouraging letters and cards throughout my entire prison term. But two ladies were real powerhouses at keeping me encouraged. They were both single women who had gone through a divorce and had learned firsthand what it was like to walk through tough times alone with only God at your side. One of these two gals wrote this prayer for me:

"I am asking God to speak to you in a very personal way. To replace panic with confidence. To speak to you in a way that you will never question if it was Him or not."

It meant a lot when I received her note, but I had no idea what that prayer would mean to me in the months ahead. Those two ladies will never know how much I needed their letters and cards. It was a simple act, but it filled me with hope when I had none. Their friendship would turn out to be a valuable piece to my story in the years to come.

A Good Friday to remember

It was the night before Good Friday. Sarah and our group were gathered around the table playing cards when I realized it was soon to be Easter weekend. The prison offered church services each Sunday, but due to the number of women who would attend, the services were offered on alternating weeks to each side of our intake building. That meant we could only attend church every other week, but our week happened to fall on Easter Sunday. We were looking forward to the service, but we agreed that Good Friday was just going to be a day like every other, unless we could figure out a way to make it special. How could we choose to focus our hearts and minds on what that day means and what the Easter weekend was all about?

Sarah and I agreed to fast on that Good Friday. If Christ could suffer through being beaten and humiliated and then hung on a cross to die for us, how could we complain about passing up on a few meals?

The pact was set and the next day we set out to commemorate Good Friday by fasting. While going through

70

intake, you can't purchase snacks or other food. You are stuck just eating the three meals prepared for you by the prison. That being said, if you are used to hoping up and grabbing a bag of chips from the pantry in your home, prison is a bit of an adjustment for that reason alone. Plus, you don't get to ask for seconds. So, if you've never been disciplined about your portion controls, prison will do it for you! Let's just say, a lot of gals lose a lot of weight while being incarcerated. In total, I lost about sixty pounds. Not really the plan I would recommend, but I did lose the weight.

Our choice to fast was made even more challenging because it was a "holiday meal" for the prison, which meant they made something extra tasty for the offenders. And remember, we all had to go to the meals even if we didn't want to eat. We all had to take a tray of food and sit there during the meal time even if we were choosing to not eat.

So, as lunch and dinner came, Sarah and I got in line, marched to the mess hall, took our trays of amazing food (at least amazing in sense that it was an upgrade from the traditional fare), sat down at the table and watched everyone around us dig in. We sat there. Soon people began to ask why we weren't eating. We explained. We got a lot of strange looks that day. Sarah and I kept in touch after we both were released from prison. We're friends today and not a single Good Friday goes by without us somehow reaching out to each other to remember that day. It was like none other, and by far the hardest fasting session I have ever done. But what an appropriate sacrifice to make in that place, on that day, for that reason.

"This whole experience has made me view the Easter story through new lenses. It's made me appreciate the exhausting saga Jesus went through even before he encountered the cross. The fact that He'd love me enough to do that... I cannot grasp it fully."

Easter reflection

"Easter Sunday service. It was quite an oxy-moron to sit in a chapel, listening to the account of how Jesus died to set us free, but from where I was sitting, I could see out the window to the barbed wire fences and guards.

For an hour and a half, the orange melts away and I am lost in the presence of God, lost in song and immersed in the powerful teaching of the Word."

The Easter story has such a deeper impact when you hear it as one in prison. We look to the Cross to see our redemption, but when that term is used in the scriptures, it a term borrowed from the same root as the word used to describe a slave market. It's someone who is in bondage, written off, worth just a few cents, but when Christ makes the purchase, we have new worth. We were worth His life! He stood in the place for me. And even though He wasn't standing in my orange scrubs wearing my prison number, He died so that I didn't have to be alone in that experience. He died so that my prison experience wasn't the end of the story. He died so I could have new worth, new purpose and new meaning. He did that for you, too!

The preacher spoke that Easter Sunday on Romans 3:24-26. He spoke of Christ's atonement for our sins. Atonement being a word borrowed from the Old Testament that describes the animal sacrifices the Israelites would make to be forgiven. The blood of that sacrifice turned away God's wrath, gave them forgiveness and created a way for them to have God's presence around them again. Isn't that what Jesus did for us? In that prison sanctuary, I felt the scripture reference, "where the spirit of the Lord is, there is freedom." Because even though I was locked up, God was beginning to set my heart free from the weight of my mistakes and failures and shortcomings. He was unveiling the true meaning of Christ on the Cross and what it meant for me right there in that situation. It wasn't just a ticket to Heaven. It was so much more than that. It was about a plan for me to have a life, a relationship, a personal connection to my Heavenly Father without barriers and without rituals. It means I can come as I am, and I can come freely.

Chapter 7

May

" God, when intake is done and I am placed in my permanent location, I know you are going to put me where I need to be. I know you are going to protect me. I just ask for your overwhelming favor in this process. God, go before me and prepare the place where I'll be. I ask for a smooth transition. I am scared of starting over again somewhere new when I am just getting used to being here. Ease my anxiety. Overwrite my fear with your courage. You have blessed me so much. Thank you for never leaving me."

As May rolled around, I had completed six weeks of the intake process. I knew my time was soon to come that my evaluation would be completed, and I would be transferred to the facility where I would finish my time.

Intake consists of physical and mental evaluations. In addition to having a complete checkup, each offender is given a dental exam, tested for all sorts of transmitted diseases, and is put through some psychiatric screenings. All of these were rather mild for me, except the psychiatric screening.

This screening started with an initial multiple-choice

survey of all sorts of life aspects. From assessing tolerance for authority to understanding rationale for decision making and even capturing an age range on a person's first sexual encounter, drug use and so on, this test ran the gauntlet. I completed the test much like those standardized tests in school, number-two pencil, and all. A page of circles was filled in and then returned to the test administrator for scoring. After a few days, I was called to meet one-on-one with the facility's psychiatrist, not because he felt I had a mental health concern, but because he thought I lied on my test.

The conversation started with him urging the importance of the test and that the evaluation would not incriminate me or get me into trouble. He kept pushing the critical need for honesty and transparency even though my tendencies may be to not "trust the system," he assured me he was here to help. I sat in his small office with outdated furniture while he reiterated himself without ever actually asking me a single question. When he was done, he asked me if I wanted to change any of my answers. I said no, my answers were honest. After much discussion back and forth, he finally believed me. He said, *"I just can't understand how someone who provides these answers ends up in a place like this?"* You and me both, Doc!

A hard healing process

I kept a pretty complete journal while I was incarcerated. Not knowing what I would be allowed to take home with me when I was released, I wanted to preserve my journal entries which were just written on pages of notebook paper. To do that, periodically, I'd mail home to Tom my pages and ask that he keep them safe somewhere. I had numbered the pages and dated them so that I could put it all back together when I got home.

That being said, it is easy to walk through each day of my sentence. Some days were more exciting than others, but one constant note in my journal was a prayer for my marriage.

The overwhelming scene of going to court and now being in prison didn't overtake the initial concern that something wasn't right in my marriage. Even sitting in a cell, I knew something wasn't working. I knew something was up. I knew if there was any hope of my returning home and having a marriage that lasted, I need God's intervention. I actually looked at the time away as a time for Tom and me both to assess our needs and work on ourselves so that when we were reunited, we were ready to reinvest in our relationship. At least that was my focus, and my journal entries are full of prayers on this matter.

"Maybe the hectic pace of life has damped the romance. Maybe the stress of the situation has wiped out all hope. Could it be that the scars are so fresh, so many hurts and past pain that we don't dare let ourselves be close? For some reason I have this deep-seated feeling that we'll be together at the end of this and we won't know each other. It won't be the same. Time has passed. We will have realized life is different on our own or he'll realize life is easier without me.

How do I be a wife when we are so far away from each other? We are distanced by miles, separated with limited conversation and reeling from hurt and frustration. God, give me wisdom to know what to do. Help me."

This was just one prayer. I prayed many. As much as God spoke to me, revealed things to me, answered prayers for me throughout my incarceration, on this topic I received no answers. God was silent. I think that concerned me even more.

My fear was only made greater by Tom's lack of communication. There was little to no mail received from him and our phone calls were very business-like. Most calls centered around what was going on in my world and anything I might need. He would share what was going on in his job, ask where something might be found around the house and end with a story about our dogs. There was hardly an "I love you," or an "I miss you," or "I can't wait until I can see you again." Prison calls are closely monitored but I can tell you one thing – the guy tasked to listening to our calls was bored stiff!

Being in prison made me stop and think about my relationship, not just with Tom but with others such as my parents. I decided to sit down and write letters to each of them asking for their forgiveness. For Tom, that meant asking for forgiveness for not being more upfront about things, for not being bold enough to communicate what I needed or what I was feeling and to say I was sorry for not working on our marriage. I know it's a two-way street, but my side of the street was certainly shut down, too.

The letter to my parents was a lot of the same. I needed to clear the air and say I was sorry for not including them in my life. A move ten hours away and a controlling spouse who didn't let me visit often made it easy to dismiss them. That left them feeling hurt, as if they had done something to drive myself away. I knew the letters wouldn't fix everything, but it was the starting point. I prayed about each one before I wrote it and as I mailed it. I am happy to report that God restored the relationship with my parents along with my sister and brother and brought us all closer together. Geographical distance still separates us at times, but thanks to technology we communicate more frequently and try to share openly and honestly about our lives…even the tough stuff.

Learning the lesson

"When I look back at how I felt, decisions I made or didn't make, or choices I'd make out of desperation, it really comes down to insecurity. People pleasing, approval addiction, all of it is insecurity driven. The root problem is where my security is placed. It's been placed in me, who I am and what I can do. It's been placed in the appearances I can create and the standard I can live up to, but never placed where it needed to be. It's time for me to look at placing my security in my Heavenly Father."

Up until a transformative point in prison, my adult life had been much like that foolish man we read about in the Bible. He chose to build his house on sand, and when it rained and the flood waters rose, his house washed away. It wasn't that he had no foundation, it was just that his foundation was built on the wrong thing… shifting, unstable sand. In comparison, a wise man built a house and he chose to build it on a rock foundation. When it rained and the flood waters rose, his house stood firm.

What I love most about this parable we read about in

Matthew 7:24 -26, is that both builders, the wise one and the foolish one, both experienced the rain. They both experienced flood waters and threats to their homes. The difference was the foundation they chose to build on.

We are never promised to have a care-free life if we choose to follow Christ, a reality we sometimes miss when the rain starts to fall. We are promised over and over in scripture that we will have strength, that God is for us so no one can be against us, that He is a firm foundation and a cornerstone for our lives.

The wise builder looked at his skills and the firmer foundation and concluded that while he might be able to build a mighty fine structure, he would be even more successful if he paired what he had to offer with a rock-solid foundation.

I like to think the foolish builder wasn't dumb. He had to be smart if he could build a house, but I think pride is what got him in trouble. He thought his abilities to construct a house would be good enough to hold no matter what the foundation was underneath. He didn't see the importance or the need for the foundation.

When I compare myself to the foolish builder, I see how, up to that point in my life, I was prideful. I thought I knew how to construct my life better than God. Now, certainly at the time,

I didn't think that was the case. I was all about Bible study and church attendance, even in prison. But my heart was headstrong on building on my foundation, with my materials and my know-how.

Once my "house" was built, I would get worried about its stability. As the storms of life would threaten to beat down my door and rattle my windows, I wouldn't lean on the Master Carpenter. No, I would slap on a coat of paint or hang a decorative piece of art. It was always about dressing up the space, but never dealing with the bones of the place. I just bought more time, but I never invested in the hard work necessary to shore up its footings and foundations.

My heart was deceived. I was so insecure in everything I did. It was why I worked so hard to keep up appearances and make everyone happy. I worked to gain value and worth from position and people, not for God. Naturally, those positions and those well-meaning people let me down. At one point in my search for something to "fix" me, prior to prison, I had seen a counselor. He succinctly summed up my issues in one picture. He said to me, "Christie, let's pretend that your parents and other people who are important to you are sitting on your left. On your right sits God. Both sides want you to do something great. Their ideas of what you should do are very different, but great. If you were getting direction from both the right side and the left side, I think you would choose your parents' side every time. I think you value the opinion of your family and others who matter to you far more than you trust and value the direction of God. That's a problem."

I knew he was right. Never had someone identified the problem so clearly. Just like a house that is doomed to fail when constructed on a weak foundation, it was only a matter of time before my life would unravel. Not because I was dumb or brought up in a bad situation. It was simply because I chose to live by the opinions of others, not God's plan.

When I journaled that revelation, I had no idea exactly how that transformation was really going to unfold. It wasn't the turning point for me...not yet. But it was the start of my heart opening to the fact that I might be responsible for some of my circumstances and that I needed to change.

A change in venue

May finally brought the end of my intake process. I had been classified and was waiting for my new facility to have an open bed. Within the week of finding out intake was coming to an end, I received notice that one of the ladies involved in my case lived in another county. Once the court process caught up with itself, another suit was filed against me in that county. Same charge, just different county. The news was devastating. What was even more debilitating was knowing since I already had a conviction on the current case, I would likely have the same outcome in the neighboring county. To add to the issue, I was incarcerated and couldn't as easily defend my case as I could if I was at home. A public defender would be assigned if I didn't want to hire an attorney and when the court was ready to address my case, the county would contact the department of corrections to have me transported to court for the hearing. I was scared of what this all would mean to my time to serve and I was not looking forward to the process at all.

As it currently stood, I was given a two-year sentence but in Indiana, offenders earn credit for time if they behave and follow the rules. That meant my two-year sentence would be one. But now that a new case was in the mix, this could mean lengthening that timeline or the court could rule that the time served would run at the same time as the current case, sort of killing two birds with one stone.

The news of this case just about blew out any flicker of hope I had worked so hard to coax. However, regardless of how I felt, the process was moving ahead, and I soon learned that I would be heading to Indianapolis without any of the friends I had made. They were all going to a more lax security prison, but my additional case classified me at a higher risk, and I was off to a medium security facility without them.

The same routine happens when offenders move into a new facility. There's a day of processing information and evaluations before offenders are taken to group housing while that facility assesses and decides where offenders will go within that prison. Part of this process is meant to determine if offenders were eligible for any educational programs, any substance abuse classes and what job they might be suited for. The entire prison was run by offenders. From maintenance to kitchen crews to lawn care to running errands and filing. Each function was completed by offenders with the supervision of a prison staff member or guard.

"I left for Indianapolis this morning. The transition wasn't as bad as I thought it would be. I only cried for a few hours. Walking into this new prison was a lot less scary because I went in with about five other offenders. Once we were settled into the group dorm, I realized that a lot of faces were familiar. Many of the offenders who left intake just a few weeks ahead of me were in this dorm. I also ran into Cathy, a gal I met while in the county jail. She isn't in my dorm, but I saw her as we were walking from one building to the next. We met up at

rec time to catch up a bit. The best news of the day... my radio picks up a great Christian radio station."

Even though I wasn't officially in my permanent spot, being out of initial intake process came with more freedoms. For instance, I could choose to go to meals or not. There were more options for things to do and sign up to be a part of. The rules were more relaxed. We didn't have to walk in a group or in a single file line every time we went somewhere. We could have more things in our rooms, and there was a bigger list of things to choose from the commissary. Speaking of rooms, most rooms were just two-person rooms, much like a dorm room. There were community showers on each hall and a large common room where offenders could watch television, play cards, hold meetings or converse. Offenders were free to move in and out of their rooms as they pleased and into the common room or outside to an activity for which they had signed up.

Activities ranged from recreational time, to going to the library, to visiting the computer lab, attending church services, participating in support groups and more. I couldn't believe all there was to do.

The population was a mix of women like me that had the lowest level felony and little time to serve to those who were "lifers," meaning they had a life-long sentence to serve.

The food at this facility was nowhere near as good, but the grounds were pretty. This prison also housed a few select programs. One was a special program that allowed offenders to work with and train service dogs. As the prison broke for recreational time, I could see the women with their dogs training them in the yard to do specific tasks. Most were young dogs or even puppies. It was a fun thing to witness. The other program was offered to mothers who were pregnant at the time of their incarceration. There was a special dorm that came with some added perks to help the expectant mothers be a bit more comfortable. It also housed a special wing for moms once their child was born. Women who qualified for the program could have their child there with them for up to two years. Everyone wanted to get in on the "baby dorm," because of the babies, but also because of the perks. The baby dorm had more comfortable furniture, a nicer common room, more lenient guards and was decorated a bit brighter.

Within the first few days of being there, I put my name on the list to be added to the prison's choir, to attend church and any Bible studies. I also put my name down to visit the library.

I arrived at this new location on a Wednesday, and by

Friday was already attending my first church service. I wasn't too sure how I felt going to this service. It was a weekend-long event billed as a "revival" and was to be held outside in the prison yard. An area church was coming in to host it alongside another community group that was providing a large cookout. Like any gal who likes a good burger, they had me at "cookout." I went to the Friday night session and it was okay. I more enjoyed sitting in the beautiful weather, soaking up a bit of the May sun. I remember enjoying sitting still for a few hours. The events leading up to the transition and the days that followed had been packed with a lot of meetings and appointments. It seemed I was being hustled all over the place to get settled in. Yes, I enjoyed getting to sit outside, hear some positive messages, soak up the sun, and catch my breath.

Saturday came with a morning session, the cookout, and an evening session. It was much of the same type of structure as it was the night before. The food was good and a bright spot in the weekend. They served us ice cream! It had been almost two months since I consumed any sugar. Prison food tends to be high carb, low salt and lots of sugar substitutes. To have real burgers and real ice cream was like being served a five-star meal.

Sunday morning service was full of praise music that we

could sing along with. It was powerful and moving. In my journal I wrote:

"There is no genuine worship like those in prison who have nothing to lose and only Him to live for. In this service no one is judging me or cataloging my mistakes. I don't have to measure up because we are all flawed. We all are wearing the same thing, are labeled the same and there is very little uniqueness. However, we all worship a God who knows us by name, not by prison ID numbers. He knows our name, sees past our felonies, and loves us like His own. That is cause to praise Him with total abandon."

Unlikely spot for a change of heart

The last night of our weekend-long service was moved indoors due to a threat of rain. The church volunteers had set up inside the prison gymnasium and a large group of offenders filed in for that night's service. The gym was a dull gray and smelled of old stale air and disinfectant. Dim lighting made the place seem even more dingier. The floor had been treated with a plastic coating to make it a bit softer than plain ol' concrete, but that substance mixed with layers of cleaning solution made the floor sticky. It wasn't a beautiful scene.

By my best guess, about 300 women offenders sat in folding chairs that night to listen to the music and the speakers.

I don't remember a single song sung or a single word spoken. I do remember at the end, the preacher instructing his entire team to line up at the front. He then invited us to come forward and partner up with one of the volunteers if we wanted prayer. It seemed that all the ladies got up at once.

I found myself sitting alone in the middle of the gym, in the middle of the row, among a sea of empty folding chairs. I had no intention of going forward. Sure, God and I were on speaking terms and I was starting to find solace in scripture and prayer, but I wasn't ready to make a show of it. So, I sat in my seat. I watched each of the women be embraced by the church volunteers as they were enfolded in prayer. Ten minutes went by if not more and I started to feel a stirring in my heart. A tear slipped from my eye down my cheek. Then another. Then another. I knew I needed to pray, but I knew I wouldn't make it through the masses that had accumulated up front.

I made my way through the rows of chairs to the side of the gym, away from the crowd. I wanted to be by myself. There, on that sticky gym floor I knelt. Next to the gray cinder-block walls, away from the group, I bowed my head and prayed. Three words didn't come out of my mouth before I was face down on the floor, sobbing uncontrollably, pouring my heart out to God.

"I can't do this. I need You to intervene. I need You to do the work. God, change me. God, transform me. Help me to be teachable, pliable so that I can reformed and renewed. Your promise is life more abundantly. God, I hold to that promise in place of the fear that I have held onto for so long. God, I give you my whole heart, my whole self. Take me and lead me. I am yours and I make you Lord of my life in all ways and in all areas."

I stayed face down for what seemed like hours. I just wanted to empty all of myself in that moment. For years, for decades, I kept God just on the outside of my life. I never truly surrendered to His plan, to His will, to Him being God of my life. I controlled things, manipulated things, let everyone else have a say, all the while keeping God at arm's length. This was the surrender He was looking for. This was the moment He had brought me here for.

God is so good and forgiving of all our mess. I have a real, personal testimony of that because of that night. While I was lying there, face down, a pool of my tears on the sticky ground beneath me, I felt a physical change in my gut. I felt a lightening of my heart. I felt a new countenance, a filling of God's love radiating from me. I went down on the floor as one person and came up off the floor changed.

The gym had mostly cleared out, offenders making their way back to their dorms. I was given a hug and some words of encouragement by the church volunteers as I stood up and headed out of the gym.

It was a nice night as I walked out of the building, my lungs trading the stale gym air for the fresh summer breeze. I walked alone across the yard to my dorm feeling like I was on cloud nine. I felt free, even though the barbed-wire fencing loomed off in the distance. I remember saying out loud:

"Okay, God. You've got about nine months left of my time to serve, so let's get to work. Whatever needs to change in me or purged out of me, let's do it. Don't let me leave here the same as I was when I arrived."

Chapter 8

June

"Since the weekend-long church service I have been asked by a couple of gals to lead a Bible study during our morning rec time. I was able to join the church choir and I found a large selection of faith-based books at the prison library."

A few days after I stood up from that gym floor, I was given my permanent placement at the prison. I moved from the intake dorm to the coveted "baby dorm" where I would be an in-house porter. My job would be to clean the dorm each day. Of all the jobs that could have been mine, that seemed like the best one. I rather enjoyed cleaning and I felt like the luckiest gal in the world to be living in what was deemed the nicest, most laid-back dorm at the prison.

My cellmate was a woman about seven months into her pregnancy and about four months left on her sentence. Her name was Charlotte. The dorm was set up like the rest, large common room with tables, chairs and televisions with hallways that led off to two-person cells. Once again, we were free to come and go from the cells into the common room and most of us kept busy with different prison activities.

Each dorm had a guard who kept an eye on everyone and everything. There was also a counselor on each dorm. Her role was to facilitate communication between each offender and the prison staff, coordinate an offender's participation in programs and classes, and help an offender prepare to leave the facility when their out date came up.

Upon moving into the dorm, I was called to the counselor's office. She was a petite lady with curly red hair and a big personality. She was kind and welcoming. In the facility each of the prison staff went by Ms. or Mrs. Her name was Mrs. Bennett. I sat in her office as she plugged in some details on her computer. She was chatting away about the dos and don'ts of the dorm and explaining my job responsibilities.

As I took in the pictures of her family, some doodled artwork given to her by her kids and other personal mementos, I noticed a bumper sticker from the Memphis Zoo tacked up on her corkboard. Having been born and raised in Memphis, this caught my eye and I asked her if she had traveled there. She laughed and said, "No. I am originally from Memphis...well, from a suburb of Memphis."

I about fell out of the chair when she told me that and I

shared with her where I was from. We started swapping notes and discovered that we were from the same suburb and lived just a few streets apart from each other at one time.

That day started a special connection between Mrs. Bennett and I. She looked out for me and made time for me while I was there. She was kind and compassionate. I am so grateful for her.

Even in the worst situation, God was there and was making the best of it all. I could see little ways He was working. He hadn't abandoned me. In fact, He was walking just ahead of me, preparing the way.

Although I had experienced a spiritual awakening that night in the gym, I still had to finish my prison sentence. That's how life works. We can experience God's forgiveness and His grace as He accepts us and loves us even though we have failed, but we still have the consequences to live out. Sure, I had a change of heart, but the prison gates didn't fling open. I had to finish the term. And, to add to the mix I was about to learn how this additional case in another county was going to impact my time.

The jailbird can sing

Each week I enjoyed singing with our prison choir. We'd

have practice during the week and then sing a song at our weekly church service. It wasn't anything special or fancy. Most times we sang without any music. But there was still something very satisfying about being in that choir. Maybe it was because of a gal I met there named Jolene.

Jolene sat on the back row of the choir loft and being new to the group, that's where I landed, sitting right next to her. Jolene had a smile that lit up the room. She was so kind and had a very genuine love for God that was contagious. Each week we got to know each other more and more. I think I enjoyed our conversations more than the music. We'd swap Bible verses we had read that week and share ways we saw God show up in our lives. She was encouraging and I enjoyed every encounter with her.

One day we sat on the back row having our normal discussion when I turned to her and said, "Jolene, how is it that someone like you is in a place like this? What on earth did you do?"

She smiled, grabbed my hand and looked me straight in the eye and said, "I killed my three kids in an angry fury to get back at their dad. I killed them, then cut them up and left them for him to find."

I don't even know what my expression was – probably

one of shock. Jolene's eyes never left mine. She patted my hand and said, "Sweetheart, if you are gonna make it here, you have to not ask questions you aren't ready to hear the answers to. It don't matter why someone is here. We're here. You're here. We all just do our time."

Jolene quietly picked up her sheet music and jumped back into the rehearsal. I will never forget that encounter. I can still feel all the emotions that accompanied the details of her story. I had a hard time seeing her as I did before, but I often reminded myself of what she said… I'm here, she's here. We are all felons. For what it didn't matter.

Revelation comes slowly

When I wasn't cleaning the dorm, I filled my time reading. I visited the prison library regularly and eventually read every faith-based book the facility had to offer. When I wasn't on my way to church or at rec, I was tucked away on my top bunk reading, studying and journaling.

My journal pages were like letters to God. I would write out my prayers and my thoughts, trying to capture the lessons I felt God was teaching me. I also spent a lot of time trying to understand where it all went wrong. I figured if I knew what got me to where I was, I could avoid ever ending up there again.

"God, if I could have just been content with your approval, then my actions would have reflected my faith. For my love of approval is the result of, the root of, all kinds of evil for me. I see so clearly that what I chose was wrong. But it was so much more than just getting the answer wrong. I was in such a destructive cycle. The consequences of my choices went beyond just the surface to some deeper. It choked my spirit, my vision to see God and hear His voice. God, please never let me be this blind again."

My time spent in that top bunk was healing. I didn't socialize a lot or get to know any of the other girls in my dorm. I just wanted to be alone. Looking back now I realize the power of that solitude. There's a difference between isolation and solitude. We see Jesus seeking solitude in the scriptures. He needed a still, quiet place to reflect, pray and be closer to Heavenly Father. Isolation shuts the world and everyone in it out. It's a defense mechanism where solitude is a healing space.

In those times where my heart was heavy and burdened, I would want to turn to someone to talk with. When no one was there, I knew God was. He was my one true friend. My prayer requests shifted from a long list of requests I wanted God to answer to simply just talking with God to know Him more.

I became less consumed with what God could do for me and more focused on how important God could become to me. I wanted to be closer to Him, to know Him better. I began turning my journal pages into pages praising God instead of petitioning God. I believed that if I just put my focus on Him, the rest of it would fall into place.

This dependency was going to prove valuable in the months to come. While my relationship with God was growing deeper and stronger, the relationship with Tom and members of my family were on shaky ground. I knew my family loved me and that they were praying for me, but there were long-term hurts there that needed time to heal. With Tom, the experience seemed to be pulling us apart. Our conversations were less than loving. Tom was consumed with things he was involved in and was far removed from my needs or my reality. At the time I chalked this up to his way of dealing with the separation, but I would later learn it was more than that.

In a June journal entry, I wrote:

"There was a comment Tom made in his letter that said he was learning some things about himself. Something about it didn't sit well with me and made me a bit scared. I don't know why, but I have an uneasy feeling about things between us. God, I don't know why I feel sick in my stomach – this uneasiness about him, about us. I feel like

the bottom is about to fall out. Maybe it's just the severity of our situation. I feel a sense of desperation to hold onto this marriage, but I feel it slipping. God, I know this… my faith and trust are in you, not Tom. I know that if he's not there, you will continue to be."

Dark nights ahead

"This week I have been exceptionally down. My emotions are getting the better of me and I really miss my family."

As the middle of June came around, the days grew hotter and the pressure mounted as everyone was a bit on edge. The air conditioning in our dorm couldn't keep up and the nights were suffocating. The heat and humidity made it near impossible to sleep, which made the days long and miserable for most.

I learned that my second case was going to move ahead with a combined court date that would roll the plea hearing and sentencing into one. That meant I would only need to be transported to that county one time. Finally, I would have some closure on that case. In the meantime, Mrs. Bennett had been trying to get me into a few programs that could cut some of my time to serve. But most of the programs are only for those offenders who have a minimum time of one year to serve from the date they came into the facility. I came in at nine months, so I don't qualify.

Each week I would have a scheduled call with Tom. The call typically centered around what things Tom was doing to fill his time. I hardly ever got a card or a letter from Tom. It was just usually the weekly phone call. Each week I would ask for him to let my parents know how I was doing. Although I would write to my mom and dad regularly and they would return the correspondence, I felt Tom could deliver some assurance that all was okay. I got my wish one week… a wish I might not have wanted to be granted.

"I feel like I have been punched in the gut. I am hurt and angry and feeling hopeless. I feel as if the past few months have been for nothing. All the work and progress and soul searching has resulted in nothing more than still being a 'train wreck.'"

My call that week to Tom consisted of his report from a recent conversation held with my parents. He proceeded to tell me that my mom felt as if I wasn't doing enough to make the most of my time in prison. She told Tom it seemed I was attending some "big church camp." And I was "delusional" about the reality of my circumstances.

Tom said he agreed with her. They both suggested that I get together with a counselor or therapist there at the prison to get some "professional help." I was stunned by the accusations and hurt that although I could see the change in me, the people I wanted to notice the most were blind to it all. No one had come to visit me. It was a few letters that were all they could go on and a couple of weekly calls. I hung up the phone feeling the weight of the world and a thousand different emotions.

The timed call had come to an end before I could respond to Tom. It was probably a good thing. I needed time to really think about all that was said. I went back to my top bunk with a heavy chest. I took to my journal to empty my heart on paper. I wrote all night long. I never went to sleep, but poured my soul out on paper, looking for some perspective and praying for some clarity.

"I am mad because I feel like I won't be anything more than my failure and mistakes. Heavenly Father, I don't know how to begin to sort through this wall of emotions. In one conversation I feel like I'm drowning in a sea of hopelessness. My knee jerk reaction is to give up. How can you ever work to be different if all you are to them is your past?"

I don't know if you relate to what I was feeling that night. My guess is if you have ever felt defined by your mistakes, you get it. There's that gnawing feeling in your gut that you will never be more than the last mistake you made. You feel labeled as a failure and that nothing can ever be different. It's not a pity party. It's not even playing the victim. It's a harsh reality that you come to grips with... you are a screw up. A hopeless failure that will never change.

Friend, that is a lie. I know it is a lie because on that night, sitting in that top bunk with my tears drenching my notebook paper, I realized these truths:

- I am a recipient of God's grace and I belong to Jesus
- Yes, I have sinned, but I am justified, meaning no charges are brought against me because of Jesus' blood shed for me on the cross.
- I have been freed from sin and become a slave to righteousness
- There is no condemnation for me because Jesus has died to set me free
- If God is for me, which He always is, who can be against me? Who will bring any charge against me who God has chosen?

The morning after

"God, I love you and I love that you see me in my pain and frustrations and my low points. I love that you love me enough to work on me and in me. You would be worthy of my worship if it was for nothing but the cross, but you went further – you want an ever-evolving relationship with me.

God, clear my mind and heart so that I can hear you, so I can see what you've done in my life these past few months. I have given you my heart to do with it what you will. I have let go of fear and anxiety so you can mold me. You have an all-access pass to the dark spots and deep crevices of my heart. God don't let this time go by without radically changing me. If what Tom and my parents have said are true, then show me. Don't let my pride stop your work. If I am not taking every opportunity to heal and work on myself then show me. But God, if I am right where you want me to be, if I am absorbing all that you have for me, then give me that confidence. "

I spent that day fasting, preparing for a follow up phone call with Tom that night. Luckily, the call was a bit more positive than the night before. I know it was because there was time for me to cool down. I took time that night to write down the things I missed most, and the ways prison is NOT like a Bible camp. I then shared that with my parents in a letter.

I missed having a pillow to sleep on. In prison, the beds were made with a built-in pillow, but it wasn't the same. I also missed having milk to drink. The mess hall served powdered milk and believe me... it is definitely not the same.

In the weeks that followed, I did get a chance to meet with a counselor at the prison. When I sat down with her to discuss my situation, she spoke honestly and said she had no time for me. She was consumed with helping women who had serious mental health issues or who were suicidal. Her best advice was to read some good books at the library. Even thought it wasn't the advice I was looking for, I can say I tried.

While we think prison is a place of rehabilitation, my experience is that it is anything but. An overcrowded population strains the resources of the staff that are there to help. Soon the job is more about keeping the peace, not healing the sick. Hence, when offenders are released, it's no wonder we see so many repeat felons. Nothing has changed for them. They just marked time until time was up. That's why prison and jail ministries are vital. Those who volunteer to do such work are amazing folks and should be supported and prayed for.

My day in court... again

Early in the morning, the dorm guard came to wake me

to have me prepare to leave for my hearing at the county courthouse. I was transported by the prison to that county's jail to see the judge.

Later that day, conferenced in by closed-circuit video, the judge announced his sentence to be three months added to my sentence. It was a relief as it could have been a lot worse. I was taken back to my cell to wait until the following day when I would be transported back to the prison.

Shortly after dinner was served, the jail guard asked if I wanted to go outside. It was a nice June evening and he said he had one other female who wanted to go out. He led me down a hall and out to a caged off yard where another woman was sitting at the picnic table. I recognized her immediately. She had been in the county jail while I was waiting for a bed to open up at the state's intake facility. Here we were, almost six months later, in a different county, seeing each other again. It was a bright spot in the whole ordeal. We chatted about what was going on in our lives at the time. Ashley was back in county about to be released for her time served. She had no one to go home to and no one to even pick her up from the county jail. Of course, I didn't have any quick solutions for her, but we prayed together in that courtyard and I promised to keep her in my prayers. Even today I think about her and hope she is okay.

It may seem odd that these little occurrences were so monumental to me, but it was in times like these that I knew God had not forgotten about me. It was proof positive that my Heavenly Father was finding small ways to bless me, and if I was paying attention, I would notice them and thank Him for it. He delights in blessing His children and we should find joy in thanking Him.

Returning to the prison, my cell was just as I had left it, but a found that just one thing was missing... my wedding ring. Each county has their own set of rules. Some allow women to have a ponytail holder, while others do not. Some are okay with you wearing jewelry and some are not. If you are caught with something they didn't allow, it would be confiscated. Not knowing for certain if my wedding ring would be allowed or not, I secretly tucked it away under my bed in my cell. I thought I had done a good job hiding it, but clearly, someone had found it.

Women who had life-long sentences were always on the hunt for things such as rings and earrings. People would trade these items for food, hygiene items, radios, hairdryers and other things. No doubt someone got a hold of my ring and raked in a hefty load of goodies. But in prison, you have to let that stuff go. You can't go on the hunt or point fingers. You just let it go.

The good news from my return was that the three additional months now meant that I would officially have twelve months at the prison, now qualifying me for a program or class. When the news reached Mrs. Bennett, she was elated and immediately began working on a class I could get in on. As it turned out, a few weeks later I was enrolled in a horticulture class provided by a local college. The class would cut three months of my time off my sentence. If you're doing the math, that meant I wouldn't have to spend any additional time in prison. My release date would be the same as it was before the additional case. It just took the additional case to get me there!

Chapter 9

July

"Yesterday was one for the record books..."

Every other week it was our dorm's turn to receive commissary. Commissary is prison's version of clicklist. You take a paper menu, select the items you want, turn it in and if you have the money in your prison account to make the purchase, your order arrives in the next week or so. Each dorm had an assigned week and when it was your turn, you had to walk across the yard to the administration building to pick up your order.

Commissary offered a variety of items from snacks and microwave fixes to hygiene items and some small articles of clothing. It was always a good day when it was commissary day. Just like everything else in the prison, commissary orders were handled by other inmates. In fact, commissary orders were first filled at one of the male prisons and then shipped to our prison to be distributed. That being so, occasionally a male offender might try to slip a note in an order in hopes of creating a prison pen pal connection. Or, in other situations, when a connection was made, a commissary order might get a few extra items in it that the offender didn't order. If you were caught participating in such activity, it was bad news. Although, most of the women found it to be a bonus if some extra items were found in their order.

On this particular July day, I went over to the administration building to get my order with the rest of my dorm. I was anxiously awaiting some snacks and instant coffee. When I got back to my room, I started unboxing my items only to find that I had several things in my box I didn't order. I quickly referred to my order list tucked into the box to see if I was charged for these items. When they didn't appear on the list, I knew exactly what had happened. I did not want to be caught with something I didn't order, but there was a part of me that was excited to have the freebies. Who would know anyway? I kept a low profile and I wasn't going to somehow return the favor so no one would be the wiser. Then it hit me… regardless of who at the prison would know, God would know. I couldn't keep what wasn't mine.

"I got four pens, a highlighter and three pencils, just to name a few of the things I didn't order. It was probably less than five buck's worth of stuff. And let's face it… I could always use more writing

utensils. But I felt the Hoy Spirit say to me, 'You didn't pay for it. You are here because you weren't always honest. Honesty is a trait I am working on building in you. If you can't be honest here, in this little way, you'll never be honest outside of here.'"

I took my receipt and my additional items to the dorm guard and explained the scenario. When I asked her what to do, she chuckled and said, "I guess it's your lucky day." I urged her to understand why I couldn't keep the items and I asked if there was any way I could take them back to the commissary department in the administration building. She looked at me like I had four heads, but she put a call in to the commissary guard to let her know I was on my way.

When I got to the administration building, another dorm was there getting their orders. When the guard spotted me, she called me to the front of the line where I had to explain the whole thing again. The other offenders heard my story and began whispering it down the line. The gal right behind me said, "Whatcha bringing it back for? Their loss is your gain."

The guard reviewed my receipt and agreed that I wasn't charged for the items. She too looked at me like I was crazy and said, "I've had a lot of things happen in my years here, but I don't think I have ever had anyone bring back items they didn't pay for." She laughed and shook her head in disbelief. My response was, "Well, I'm here for a theft charge, so consider this evidence that I have changed." To that she replied, "Well, God bless you." I laughed and turned to leave saying, "Oh I know He will."

For a few days after that, the prison was a buzz about the crazy offender who returned her extra commissary items. I just chuckled to myself knowing what my real motivation was all along.

A star-spangled shocker

To help celebrate the fourth of July, the prison was organizing a variety show that would feature a variety of talent from the offenders. Those who had a talent they wanted to share were encouraged to sign up to participate. I happened to be walking past the sign-up table when a woman asked if I wanted to participate. I told her I could sing, and she offered me a list of song titles that would be available to me. As I skimmed the list there was only one song I saw I knew I could sing without much preparation. It happened to be *"Hero"* originally recorded by Mariah Carey. Now, I am no Mariah, but I have sung this song several times. It was a standard audition song and then used as a sound check for myself back in the days when I toured as a vocalist. I was confident I could resurrect it again for this occasion. I didn't tell a single person I was going to do it. It was my secret.

A few days prior to the show, a dress rehearsal was held in the gym. As I was leaving the dorm to go over to rehearse, a few ladies inquired about what I might be doing for the show. I just smiled and said, "you'll have to come see."

The prison had its group of gals that sort of ruled the yard. These were women who had considerable amount of time to serve and had made themselves known as the group to watch out for. There at the rehearsal was this group's ring leader, affectionately known as "Crusher." We all were lined up along the gym wall as the coordinator called out each act. When she called out, "*Hero*" Crusher busted out a loud scoff and said, who's gonna be stupid enough to get up and sing that? I happened to be standing right next Crusher so when I moved out of line and over to the mic, I heard her say, "Ain't no way that white @#$%# is gonna pull this off."

I grabbed the mic, closed my eyes and sang my heart out. When I was done you could hear a pin drop. Then, breaking the silence was Crusher whooping and hollering her support, which then the rest of the crowd followed.

When the day of the variety show came, I sat in the

audience and waited for my turn. I was sandwiched in between a questionable dance act and a drum solo. As I made the way to the stage, the coordinator wished me luck and said, "someone needs to hear the message of this song... make it good."

I got up and gave it my all. A hardened crowd of women felons were moved to tears and I got a standing ovation. For days after that I was met in the halls and in the yard with congratulations from many. I soon became known as the "little white girl singer" and was asked to sing at a few other events.

On my dorm, it sort of became an ongoing thing that I would sing for everyone's birthday or on the last night they had before going home. It became my identifying thing, which I was happy to share with the prison.

Choir comparison

Prior to prison, I had traveled the country singing in all sorts of venues and on all kinds of stages. More recently, I had spent two seasons with our city's philharmonic orchestra and chorus singing some of the world's most melodic numbers. It made for a unique comparison, which I logged in my journal, on the first night I sang in a performance with the prison choir.

"Last night was my first performance with the prison choir.

Being in this choir is different than anything I have ever done before. From ballgowns to prison khakis. From elegant stringed instruments, finely tuned and expertly played to a very worn our piano in need of tuning and an outdated sound system. From ornate theaters and concert halls to a small stage squeezed into a small classroom. From classical pieces written by legendary composers to gospel spirituals written from the soul. From where I was to where I am now.... night and day."

The parallel should have been devastating, but the reality was that I felt more freedom in that prison choir than I ever felt in a ballgown in a historical theater. I was more in prison then than I was standing there in khakis and a prison badge. My fears and insecurities had driven me to a very dark, lonely prison of the heart. Things looked great on the outside but brick by brick I walled myself off from the genuine me. The times when the wall would crumble a bit, I was quick to repair it and clean up the rubble so that no one would notice. Each time a brick went into the wall, I became more and more imprisoned. I never let anyone in, not even God. He was there, but He was always on the other side of the wall.

Standing there with the choir that night, it hit me – where I was, what I was doing. It humbled me. My journey could be sad if I focused on mistakes that got me there. However, if I focused on the change within and the new journey I was on, it was all worth it to live freely.

Looking to the future

It was a night in July that my prayers started changing. No longer was I focused on the day-to-day survival of my prison journey. My prayers started to center around my future and what it might look like once I was out. My release date was still months away, but I felt prompted to begin praying for the future and how I could begin to prepare even while being in prison.

One particular night I was up late praying and journaling. I had been restless and couldn't get any sleep. While journaling I had a vivid vision of my future. I was on a stage in a large arena with a crowd of faces sitting in front of me. The audience was engaged in whatever it was I sharing. I don't know what I was saying but I could see that I was holding a Bible and speaking out of the scriptures. The vision was so real, so vivid that if I could paint or draw you a picture I could do it with exact detail. Even all these years later that vision is still burned in my mind.

I began journaling the vision as graphically as I could. I

had a confirmation in my heart that speaking and sharing God's truth and His Word was what my future would hold. For several nights I relived this vision. It was always the same. Each time it was over I felt the Holy Spirit whisper to me, "This is it." It took a couple of times to realize that my vision never included Tom. In fact, as I replayed the vision in my mind there was a very sad feeling that Tom wasn't there or wasn't involved. I remember praying and asking God to explain why Tom wasn't there. I didn't get an answer right away, but I did about a year later.

Unlikely audience of readers

I had checked out several books and Bible studies from the library and was running out of things to read. Soon my Bible study time became singular as I simply read the scriptures and tried to write any revelation, insights or lessons I felt as I read. This started a stream of mini devotionals in my journal. One afternoon I was sitting on my bunk writing furiously when the dorm guard happen to stroll past my room. She was a friendly guard who loved to get to know her offenders. So, it was no surprise that she poked her head in my room to ask me what I was working on. When I explained to her it was a devotional I was writing, she asked if I would let her read it when I was done.

I was taken aback but agreed to bring it to her before dinner to read. While I was at the mess hall, the guard was left to read my writing.

When I returned to the dorm, she pulled me aside and asked if I had anything else to share with her. I said no but I could probably come up with something. She urged me to come up with more and then asked if she could take the one, I had shared with her so that she could share it with her women's group at church.

I was hesitant to let it go. It was my only copy. I asked her if I might have a few minutes to rewrite it so that I could keep a copy. She obliged and I went to my bunk to rewrite the words. For weeks we did this – I wrote a devotional, she would read it and want a copy of it, I would have to rewrite it as to keep a copy, and she would go off with a copy to share with her ladies at church.

Somehow word got out about the devotionals and I soon had other guards and offenders both coming up and asking for copies of my work. At one point I was having to write my devotionals ten times in order to get copies to everyone. Keep in mind this was by hand! There were no copy machines and I wasn't typing it on a laptop where I could simply print another one off. No, this was my hand holding a pen and writing it all out on notebook paper.... ten times!

That began the first time I focused my writing skills to teach God's Word to others. It began in an unlikely place, from an unlikely space to a very unlikely audience, but God can do anything! He can use anyone, anywhere if we are willing. It would have been easy to think, "Oh, I'll get to writing once I get home and have a computer and lots of resources for research and such." However, God doesn't expect us to come with all the answers and all the resources. He only asks for our willing hearts and whatever talent He has placed inside us. It makes me think about the Little Drummer Boy. He didn't have but his humble talent to offer Jesus. So that's what he brought. What do you have to offer? It doesn't have to be much, but you do have to be willing to offer it up completely. I assure you the rewards and blessings are priceless in return.

Chapter 10
August

"Jolene gave me a Bible verse today to ponder. Ruth 2:12. She said the "2" and the "12" were from my prison ID number and that it meant something special. Most IDs start with a "1." She said she thought this was my life verse."

It took almost six years to get the impact of Ruth 2:12 in my life. To be honest, when I went back to my room that day and looked up the verse, I thought Jolene was crazy and off her rocker.

"May the Lord repay you for what you have done. May you be richly rewarded by the Lord, the God of Israel, under whose wings you have come to take refuge." – Ruth 2:12

If you look at the previous verses you get the context of this verse. Ruth has quietly and obediently followed her mother-in-law into a new land. She has helped take care of her as her sons have died and Ruth is now a widow. Their future wasn't going to be bright and glamorous. Widows weren't well received and usually didn't have a lot of means. Ruth's choice to follow her mother-in-law was without fanfare. She simply followed.

It was because of her faithfulness that she met Boaz, a wealthy land owner respected in the town. He recognizes her devotion and faithfulness and speaks chapter 2 verse 12 over Ruth's life.

As I take stock in my life and where I've come, I realize that God notices the little things we do in the day-to-day spaces of our lives. He blesses our faithfulness and obedience even when we feel as if they don't add up to much. Sitting in that prison for days and months choosing to invest in my relationship with God meant blessings. When I could have had an extra year added to my time, I got three months…just enough to get me into a class that allowed for a time cut. When I was scared and alone, God delivered several ladies to support me and encourage me…. even one who was from my hometown. Repeatedly, I can see God's hand in this situation, and it was simply because of a humble heart that desired more of Him.

In the New Testament Paul encourages new believers to be ready with their testimonies in case they have the chance to share it. I spent time journaling my testimony in August so that

I would be prepared one day to share it. Now, all these years later, I am afforded the opportunity to share it regularly. It may not be from a large stage or to thousands of people, but each day someone benefits. I think that's the way we can all share our stories of how God has worked in our lives…just a little every day to someone who needs it. I believe this is how we best change the world around us, by investing in the hearts of those we come in contact with each day.

A surprising birthday

I was outside helping to plant new flowers along a pathway in the prison yard as part of my horticulture class when a runner came to get me. I had someone here to visit me. I couldn't drop those flowers fast enough to race to the visitation center.

Visitation came with quite the hassle. First the visitors had to be cleared through the proper channels which included a background check. Once approved they were put on a list and allowed to come for a visit. However, once on the premises, visitors had to have their bags checked, had to leave their cellphones and car keys with the guard and then be frisked before entering the visitation room.

For us offenders, we had to be completely strip searched,

but on that day I didn't care. I couldn't wait to see who was on the other side of that processing room. As I entered the visitation room, I saw my mom and dad. It was all I could do to walk across the room calmly without collapsing in heap of joyful tears. Their warm smiles and big hugs meant the world to me. All the hurt and pain I felt I had caused was washed away in that moment. That visit was very sweet. It did my parents good to see that I was alive and okay. It did my heart good to see that they loved me and was concerned for me. The time went by too quickly and we had to part, but I was floating on air that day. No amount of words can describe how I felt.

As my birthday got closer and closer, family and friends sent me birthday cards, notes, pictures and well wishes that meant so much to me. I tacked most of them up in my room to be reminded of how special they made me feel. Even though I was removed, I felt their love and support. All except Tom...

"Yesterday was my birthday and all week I thought surely Tom would come and visit me. Surely, he'll be here. I know he can't come every week or every month, but at least he'll make an effort to be here this week of all weeks. But, yesterday came and went with no visit. I also thought that through the week I would hear from Tom in the way of a letter or a card. I could understand if he couldn't get away to

come for a visit but gosh, surely, he could drop a card or a letter in the mail. It's like I am out of sight, out of mind. That is what hurts the most. I feel very forgotten."

A week after my birthday Tom came to visit. He told me he hadn't planned to visit but he was in town to fly out to Colorado to visit his sick grandfather, a grandfather he hasn't seen in twenty years. He said he felt like it was his last chance to see him and he was flying out that evening. While he was in town and had some time to kill, he thought he would stop for a visit.

Class is in session

My horticulture class kept me busy. I was in class most of the day with about ten other offenders. The teacher was a tough gal who was passionate about the subject but didn't put up with any nonsense. In addition to our bookwork, we also got to work in the prison's greenhouse and maintain a few of the flower beds on the grounds. I loved the class. It got me out and about and kept my days busy. I especially loved getting to get my hands in the dirt. It was rather therapeutic.

The tests were rather difficult, and the class required a passing grade in order to qualify for the time cut. I studied hard

124

and late into the night. Class projects were particularly challenging because there were no computers to do research or even prepare a paper. All was done the old-fashioned way – pen and paper and a good ol' encyclopedia.

One particular project required us to create a complete landscape design to scale. All we had to work with were some rulers, colored pencils, a few stencils and some graph paper. It was challenging, but I loved the challenged. I put everything I had into that class. In the end, when I took my final exam, I scored the highest the class has ever seen since the start of that course offering. I was pretty proud of myself.

I remember sending home my landscape drawings just like a kid who can't wait to show mom and dad their latest art project. I know Tom didn't really appreciate the importance of it, but it was a feather in my cap all the same.

Chapter 11

September, November, December

"It's getting to feel like fall. The temperature dips a little lower each day. This will be the third season I've experienced in this state. I am ready to go home, but anxious for what the future holds. How will I ever find a job? What will my relationship with Tom be like? What is waiting for me at home? Will I be accepted by those that I know? I'm getting a little nervous."

As I finished my horticulture class, I was officially given my release date of January 8th. I was just months from being released, and although I had started counting down the days, I was starting to feel the anxiety of having to live life on "the outside."

It's easy to be a felon when you are in prison with a bunch of other felons. You are among the many and no one judges you there behind the fenced barrier. But in the real world, being a felon meant a label that I could not dodge. I knew my probation would require that I get a job, but I had no idea on how that would work out. For the meantime, I had a few months left to serve out on my sentence, and I just needed to focus on that for now.

Since I was attending class, I was to be assigned to a new job. I had long given up my cleaning post to attend my horticulture class, but now it was time for something new. As it turned out, Mrs. Bennett needed a new assistant, and she chose me for the job. I loved this new role. It required me to run errands all over the prison for her, for me to manage her schedule and to act as a liaison between her and the other dorm residents. I felt truly blessed to get to work with her.

As the fall turned to winter my release date crept closer and closer. The dorm was preoccupied with the holiday season and we all did the best we could to make the most of Christmas. A small amount of decorations went up around the common room and on the night before Christmas, one of the guards read the Christmas story to us all. We then all sang Christmas carols and watched Christmas movies.

Spending Christmas in that setting made me recognize the beauty of Jesus' birth. I am sure Mary would have preferred being at home and not in a barn. I am sure Joseph would have preferred a more comfortable bed for the baby Jesus instead of a feeding trough, but they all made the most of what they had, where they were. That's sort of what we did on that night... made the most of it, trying to remember the importance of it

127

and celebrating it for the real reason for the season.

Preparing to go home

When an offender's release date comes close, the prison does a few things to get everything in order. First, there is a confirmation that the offender has some place to go that is safe. Whether it's a family member's home, returning to the home from where they came or getting set up in a group home, the state wants to give an offender the best start it can.

There's also confirmation that some sort of transportation will be available to take you where you need to go. If not, the state will supply the offender with a bus pass.

If the offender needs clothes to wear home, there's a clothing bank where you can select clothing items to wear. Additionally, the prison's beauty shop will give you a new cut so you can look your best as you leave.

There's even a one-day reentry course aimed at helping offenders obtain state IDs, build a resume and make a few connections for job placement. All in all, the state seemed to work hard to help offenders to get off on the right foot.

All these steps didn't diminish my fears. I was terrified of what was waiting for me at home. I didn't know where I stood with Tom, I was scared to go through probation, and I

128

was worried about getting a job. When the day came to actually leave, I cried like a baby. The emotions were all over the place. As strange as it sounds, the place I couldn't wait to leave now seemed more comforting than the home I had left before. At least in prison I knew what to expect. In prison I couldn't make many mistakes. In prison, the expectations were low, but on the outside… it was a whole new ballgame.

Going home

I was transported from the prison to the county jail where I was from right before my release date. On January 8th, I left the county jail and was finally free. Tom had been told what date and time I would be released. However, he was late picking me up. While I waited, the jail commander told me I could go downstairs to the probation department and get things in order with my officer.

Down the stairs I went to meet a young officer. I think I was old enough to be his mother. But he was nice and treated me with respect. He asked some basic questions to ensure he had all his ducks in a row and then he talked with me about the probation requirements. My probation term was a year and we would meet once a month during that time. Over the course of those twelve months, my probation officer learned much about me and recognized that I wasn't his typical felon. Because we established a good relationship, he would ask me questions about my experiences. He wanted to see things from my perspective. He had told me it would help him be better at his job, and I liked the honest conversation with him.

On that first day when we met, I told him my fear of getting a job. We lived in a small town where jobs were hard to come by and I didn't think Tom would allow me to work outside of our town. Afterall, we had just one car, so we'd have to work together to get us both to work. My probation officer assured me there was no pressure on the job front. He was mostly concerned that I didn't sit idle and get into trouble. As long as I was filling my time with good things, and paying my court fines and costs, he was okay with my not working. That took a huge weight off my shoulders.

Chapter 12

January

"It was strange. Something was off. We were strangers. There wasn't a happy reunion. I mean, sure he was glad to see me, but there was no passion or sparks. It was like we were meeting for the first time and we didn't know how to react."

Coming home that day in January, I was greeted by two German Shepherds who had desperately missed their mom. I was covered with slobbering kisses and wagging tails. It was so good to see my dogs. I couldn't wait to take a shower in my own bathroom and change into my own clothes.

I remember going into my bedroom and lying on my bed. The texture of the comforter was so soft, and the bed was so warm and cradling. Nothing like the metal bunks I had slept on for the past ten months. My small bathroom felt like a five-star resort spa compared to the prison showers I was used to. I got to put on makeup and actually fix my hair in a mirror that could reflect my entire face instead of the tiny five-by-seven mirrors we had in prison.

It was the little things I noticed most. The house was

quiet. There was peace sitting on the front porch of my country home. I was home. It felt nice to say, although there was a real awkward feeling between Tom and me. I chalked it up to the time spent away from each other and assumed that with a few weeks of living normal life again, we'd be okay. Whatever it was, I knew I didn't want to go back to the way things were, a life we didn't really share, a marriage that didn't have any communication, the way we kept score and measured my faults against his successes. I wanted more. I wanted a real marriage. I was willing to work to get it and I wasn't going to be easily dismissed.

I didn't realize how much prison had changed me. I was focused, determined and somewhere along the way I had rediscovered my voice. I wanted to give my opinions and be involved in the life I was leading. No longer was I okay with sitting on the sidelines while I let others dictate my life. Suddenly, I had perspective, I knew what I wanted, and I was going to take the steps to put things in place.

I couldn't wait to share this with Tom. I thought he would be so proud of me and how strong I had become. I remember sitting him down one night and explaining my vision for speaking and writing. He came back with heavy reservations reminding me that my felony would hold me back

132

and people probably wouldn't want me in front of their congregations or groups. I was disappointed that he wasn't on board. He was focused on the here and now – paying my court fees and fines.

Even though I was met with some hesitation, I wasn't going to give up. I knew this vision laid before me was real and it was God-sent. I knew it wouldn't happen overnight, but I was going to chase it down no matter what.

Shortly after settling in at home, the elderly gentleman Tom and I rented our home from announced that he was selling the place and we would need to move. It sent us into a bit of a tailspin because we weren't in any shape to buy a home and finding a place to rent that accepted two large dogs was hard to come by in our small town. Tom went into planning mode. I began praying for God to provide something. While I waited for the perfect place to come available, I started packing and preparing to move.

In just a few short weeks, by way of social media connections, Tom and I found a perfect place that was all too accepting of our large dogs. In addition, the place was furnished, and the woman was completely willing to accommodate our moving time frame and anything else we needed. She was an angel. I was so excited for this new beginning. The timing couldn't have been better. I just knew this was the fresh start Tom and I needed.

We began packing and moving as soon as we could, anxious to get in and get settled. I told everyone that came within three feet of me about this amazing blessing God had provided. It was too good to be true and I was elated. He was really working all things out for us.

Since I had been home, I started attending church again, the same church that had prayed for me during that court hearing. They celebrated me home and welcomed me back into their family. It was just what I needed to feel grounded. My church family was the support I needed to begin this new life. It was all starting to come together.

Chapter 13

New identities, true identities

"It is amazing how God can move mountains for us. I have learned to take my hands off of so much. When I do, things are always better. He is much better at running my life than I am."

I never dreamed that anything would come of this little article I wrote. Tom and his friend had made some connections with the company and staff tasked with managing the Superbowl halftime show that year. That meant the week before the big game, they were both off to rehearse and prepare for the iconic performance. It was a fascinating process.

Tom would be part of the crew that would set up the stage, lights and sound for the halftime performance. In just a few minutes he and other crew members would run out on the field in an orchestrated, choreographed manner and put an entire concert together. It's rather miraculous how it all works.

Because not much like this happens in our little town, I wrote a little article about their involvement and sent it to our county's newspaper. I had shared the article with the note that said, "If you want to use it great, if not that's okay. I just thought it was interesting and that your readers might like it." I also thought it newsworthy because many people in our town knew Tom.

Not only did the article run in the paper, I got a call from the paper's editor asking me if I'd like to write for them as a freelance reporter when needed. I quickly agreed without even thinking about it. I was so excited! It was something I never expected. It had been years since I worked on a newspaper or had written in this capacity. But if they were willing to work with me, I was willing to give it my all.

No writing assignments ever came. In fact, I was about to give up on the whole idea. Almost three weeks had passed, and I had heard nothing from the paper. Then the phone rang. It was the editor. He wanted to know if I was willing to come in and meet with him and the publisher about a part-time reporter job. I couldn't say yes fast enough. I met with them the same day!

As I sat in the conference room listening to the two of them explain the job and the writing assignments I would be working on, all I could think of was how perfect this job was for me. Just as I was getting ready to shake their hands and accept the position, I remembered my felony. In a small town like mine, it wouldn't take long for the word to get out. So even though they had not asked for a background check, I had to be upfront with them, even if it meant losing this opportunity. Heck, just a few short years ago I was on the front page of that very same paper. I couldn't ever expect to hide this fact.

I shared with the pair of newspaper men where I had just spent my last year and why. I was ready for them to say "thanks, but no thanks," when the publisher piped up and said, "You aren't the first felon we've hired, and I am sure you won't be the last. Do a good job and we won't care."

I could have run home I was so amped about this chance. I would be writing! Something I loved to do and getting paid to do it! I couldn't wait to tell my probation officer I had been offered a job and I couldn't wait to tell Tom I could pay my own fines and court costs.

Let's just say my probation officer was more excited than Tom. When Tom came home and I shared the news with him, he was worried about how our one-car situation was going to work out. He couldn't believe they accepted me with my felony. He accused me of not being completely honest with them. He was upset that I had taken the job without talking to him first. I was floored. I couldn't believe his reaction. But I was excited for the job anyway.

I started that part-time job as a reporter and within the

first few months I had been promoted to a full-time section editor. It required more time and I was out at night and on the weekends to cover meetings, events and other community news. The car situation was getting to be more of an issue, but I tried hard to work things around Tom's schedule. Nothing was good enough.

While I was thriving in a job I loved, feeling back at home with my church family, I was finding more and more aggravation with Tom. I remember us fighting one night about my job when I said, "I feel like I finally have everything I want – a good job I love, a church I love, a home I love – but I am missing the marriage I want. What can we do to fix this?"

For months Tom and I went back and forth with this conflict between us – I was focused on making things better and building a new life while Tom was trying to figure out how to get used to this "new" version of myself. There was a lot of tension between us, but for me, I could not do enough to ease it, fix it or resolve it.

I was covering a community event for a faith-based nonprofit one night when I ran into a pastor friend and his wife. We were catching up when I sort of had an emotional breakdown right there in the banquet hall. I began spilling my heart over my marriage and the pressure I was feeling from the

138

strain of it all. For what ever reason I left nothing out and held nothing back. I shared it all. The fights, the lack of communication, the lack of romance and intimacy – I laid it all out on the line.

When I was done emptying my heart, my friends carefully encouraged me and told me to go home and become determined to get to the bottom of the issue. Without being demanding or abrasive, they urged me to ask questions and pray for the right words to say.

I left the event, red nose and puffy eyes, and returned to my office at the newspaper. I shut my office door and put my head in my hands and prayed. I prayed hard searching for direction and guidance. I knew I had to go home and face reality. Hiding out in the newsroom wasn't an option.

At home, Tom was in the back bedroom on the computer. When I walked in, he could see that I had been crying. I didn't wait for him to ask what was wrong. I asked if we can talk and began pouring my heart out. I shared my concerns, my fears and what I had been feeling the last few months. Tom didn't say a word. When I was done, I took a deep breath and prepared myself for his response. Without expression, Tom said, "Before you commit to doing what it takes for this marriage, I need to show you something. Can you wait in the living room?"

I walked out to the living room panicked. What could he possibly have to show me? Was he sick? Had he had an affair? What could I possibly need to see that might impact my decision to fight for my marriage?

Tom came into the living room with about ten computer pages printed out for me to read. He admitted that he had prepared the letter weeks ago but was waiting for the "right time" to give it to me. Of the ten pages, four pages made up a letter Tom had written. In the letter he explained his long-time battle with his desire with his sexuality. While he didn't particularly feel he qualified as "gay," he did identify better as a woman. I was shocked and struck speechless. He closed the letter by stating that he knew this would be a lifestyle I was uncomfortable with, but he hoped I would grow to accept it.

The remaining six pages were articles he had printed off the internet to support his choices and to help me understand his perspective. He had even found a top-ten list of reasons why his choice to live as both a man and a woman would be beneficial to me and our marriage.

One thing was certain. This was a shock to my system. I had not seen this coming at all. When I finished reading the letter, I asked Tom to leave for the night. I needed time alone to grasp all that had just been unloaded on me.

I spent that night wrestling with this new information, getting counsel from my parents and trying to decide where to go from here. The next morning, I called Tom to let him know that I was okay with him coming home, but I had not made any decisions on the subject. In fact, I had more questions I needed answers to.

As we met back at the house, I found out more to the story. This was a sexual desire Tom had been hiding since before we met almost thirteen years ago. At one time he was caught dressing in women's undergarments by his father who called him ugly names and threatened to disown him if he was caught doing it again. This made Tom repress he feelings for a while. However, in his early adult years he had toyed with the notion again and again. While we were married, he hid his lifestyle and only "acted it out" when I wasn't around. He admitted that my being in prison had given him a lot of freedom to explore his desires and he lived out some of his fantasies even going as far as dressing up completely as a woman and going out to a club. He had invested in a complete wardrobe with wigs and makeup to go with it all. He had secretly stashed this away in a storage unit I had not known about.

I told Tom I needed time to sort through all of this. He told me he felt free now that his secret was out. He even expressed his excitement to take part in shopping dates and spa days together now that we could be both married and best girlfriends. To this I had no response. I was stunned.

The revelation did answer a lot of questions as to why there was so much anger in Tom towards me. Why our relationship had always been rocky and deceitful. It explained why we never had sex or had any sort of physical connection. When I asked Tom if this is what kept him from being intimate with me, he said it was. But he quickly added that if I would let him wear women's garments to bed, he would feel more "in the mood."

Within the next week, Tom was asking to move his wardrobe into the house. He began shaving his body hair, he purchased skin products and started painting his toe nails. It all spun out of control very quickly. When Tom realized I was not getting on board with this new lifestyle, he suggested we go to marriage counseling.

We did attend marriage counseling, but it was apparent in just a handful of sessions that Tom wanted me to accept what he was, and I wanted him to change. We were not going to move to any common ground anytime soon.

There is something to be said for tolerance and for even choosing to stand by a spouse or loved one while they deal with an addiction or unhealthy way of life. I believe we all deserve that sort of grace and space to sort through our "stuff." However, Tom and I were coming at this from two very different angles. Our entire marriage had been built on lies, deceit and secrets. There was nothing to reach back and build on because it was doomed from the start.

In my heart I believed the Bible spoke clearly on this subject. God created man to be man and woman to be woman. There are no blurred lines here. Although I wanted Tom to be happy, I also didn't want another girlfriend. I wanted a man, a partner, a husband who could be all the things God created a man and husband to be. At the same time, I wanted to be free to be a wife and a woman without competing over who wore it best.

In the weeks and months to come I felt like a stranger in my own home. I felt as if I couldn't be comfortable or relax. All the while Tom was getting more and more comfortable with his freedom. I knew the only way I was going to get any perspective on the subject was to get out and away from it all being flung in my face.

A single woman at church, who had become a great pen

pal for me when I was in prison, approached me at church one Sunday and said, "I don't know why I feel the need to tell you this, but if you ever need a place to stay... I have a room for you."

I collapsed in a relieved heap of tears as she gave me a hug and worked out the logistics. She never pushed to know more of what was going on, she was simply there for me.

In the weeks while I stayed with this single woman, things unraveled fast. Tom was angrier than ever that I would be so bold as to move out. He became irate, showing up at my work place to threaten me, following me to different events I was covering for the paper. He left me mean, manipulative notes in my car. Shoved old anniversary cards in my face to remind me that I either loved him at one time or lied about it. The whole scene was my fault.

At a counseling meeting, Tom finally admitted that he was jealous of me. He resented the fact that I had "screwed up our lives," and then got lucky enough to land my dream job. Instead of supporting me and cheering me on, he tried to rob me of any sense of self or success. All his actions were rooted in his own fears and insecurities.

Surprisingly, I wasn't mad at him for his secrets. What I was upset about was the fact that he knew how I threw my self on the sword for every bad thing that ever happened to us. I quickly took the blame for every mistake, for every shortcoming, for every shortfall we experienced and beat myself up for it – he right along with me. For almost thirteen years I was the screw up, the disappointment and he gladly let me take that label, and sometimes he applied it in spades. Yet, he never was honest for what he was struggling with. He waited all those years to come clean. I devastated and hurt that someone who supposedly loved me would let me take the fall like that. In the end, I wasn't someone he loved. I was someone that he could control and persuade to comply with his story.

By the fall we had filed for divorce and in October it was finalized. It wasn't what I wanted when I got married at the age of twenty. I surely didn't start the relationship looking for a way out, but it had happened. There were many who didn't agree with the decision, but prison had prepared me to stand on my own even if no one else stood with me.

As the divorce became final, I found myself living alone, in a two-bedroom apartment with nothing in it. I took no furniture, no decorations- not even a single dinner plate from the house. But it wasn't about what I could get or what was mine or what was even fair. It was about a new beginning.

I lived in a small town that knew Tom and me well but

had no idea the real reason for our marriage ending. The friends that still chose to hang around after I came home from prison quickly departed, minus a very select few. The pastor at my church that lovingly accepted me after my prison stay soon became uncomfortable with the divorce. When Tom decided he wanted to attend the same church, I was asked to leave. He had a creative spin on the failed marriage that didn't include his choices, just my mistakes. I was painted as the felon that was a fake. It hurt to move away from the church family I grew to love, but that didn't mean I was cut off from God. Man may have failed me in that moment, but God didn't. I knew the truth. I knew what was happening behind closed doors. In my own nature, I wanted to prove my case, but it wasn't my battle to fight nor my secret to tell.

In the beginning of it all I had prayed that God would show me what to say and do to honor Him as I walked through this divorce. It may not have been God's plan for this marriage to end, but it sure wasn't His plan for me to be snotty or vengeful in the process. So, in many situations I kept my mouth shut, letting people come to their own conclusions which were never accurate.

At one point, my mom had called and invited me to move back home. The offer was tempting, but I knew I needed to stay put and walk through this thing on my own two legs – just God and me. Prison has hard, but the divorce was harder. Had it not been for prison, I wouldn't have had the emotional and spiritual stamina to stand the test and weather the storm.

That year I accepted a promotion at the newspaper to be the editor-in-chief and won five press awards for articles I had written. Yes, I was staying put and I was going to fight to have the life laid out before me in a vision that night in my prison cell.

When it came to my felony, I knew I was to blame, but the hard lessons had been learned. I had been put through the fire and come out more refined, stronger and ready for the next challenge.

When it came to my marriage, there was blame on both sides. Tom had his issues and I had mine. I don't harbor any anger or ill will for Tom. There are aspects of him that still haunt me and some of his damage is still evident down deep inside me. I suppose dealing with it will be a life-long practice. But in the end, I hope Tom comes to recognize who he truly is in the eyes of his Heavenly Father and accepts the love that is waiting for him there.

People often ask why bad things happen to good people? To that I say we are asking the wrong question. The real question is how are good people made stronger and better in the middle of bad situations? In my case, it was a test that would craft this testimony that would impact the lives of many. I am far from perfect, but in prison, God changed me. I am far from being finished, but through my divorce God shaped me for better. Our bad situations, whether dealt to us by chance or because of our own consequences, don't have to define us. If we let them, those situations can shade us in deep, rich colors. Those situations can shape us to be more compassionate, more forgiving, more understanding... more like Christ.

The word "revise" means to re-examine and make alternations to; to reconsider and amend something especially in the light of further evidence or to reflect a changed situation. Prison became the field where I made a lot of revisions to my life. The beautiful lesson in that is that the revisions didn't stop. There were alternations made to my relationship with my Heavenly Father, my career, my mission in life and my marriage. It wasn't all perfect and I can assure you today it still isn't perfect. I've learned how to be repeatedly revised – to be okay with the constant improvements made in my life. I've found joy in working a little each day to be better and I've come to grips with the fact that I am not perfect and that's okay too.

I promise you that in the middle of life there is grace

afforded you from the Heavenly Father who loves you so deeply. He doesn't expect perfection. He requests devotion. In the day-to-day walk of life, He knows we will fall. He knows we will stumble, but He is always right there beside us with a heavy portion of forgiveness and patience. How do I know this? The pages of this book are filled with examples of how God showed up for me. I am nothing special. I have nothing extraordinary that would demand God's attention over any of His other children, yet He saw me, He loved me, He walked beside me patiently as I tried to get it right. He applauded when I did, and He lovingly picked me up when I didn't.

As you read the words on this page, I am praying for you. I don't know who you are or where you came from, but I am praying that in this moment you feel God's presence. I pray for you to experience Him in new ways that can mean freedom from your past, redemption for your mistakes, and hope for your future. There is more to your story, so don't give up. You can have a repeatedly revised existence.... it's okay. Be okay with small progress, not perfection. Be okay with not always being okay. Seek out those who can help you along the way. God sent many women and men into my life to encourage me and lift me up, for that I am eternally grateful. He will do the same for you.

For the woman who knows the label "felon," my heart especially goes out to you. I know first hand the struggle of that label and the disappointment and shame you feel. It is like a scarlet letter you can't get away from. Know this – even you are loved by God. He doesn't see you as a disappointment or a mistake or a felon. He sees you as His daughter, an heir to His kingdom with all the blessings He can bestow on you. I know it may not feel like it at times, and you may not even believe there is a God who could love you. Let me challenge you to let a little belief creep into your heart. Just a little twinge of belief can get you going. When you start there and keep looking for answers, I promise you He will deliver. He is calling to you, sometimes we just have to quiet our hearts to hear Him. But don't just hear, act. Slow down long enough to respond and trust Him even just the slightest to come nearer to you. You won't regret it.

I am so grateful for these lessons learned...and sometimes still learning. It has taken an odd mix of surrender and submission with a dose of strength and persistence. But the recipe was the right concoction for what was yet to come....

Enter my new future and love of my life, Mat. That's another story for another time, but let me just say, Yes! God does give second chances.

About Christie

Christie Browning is on a mission to encourage, empower and inspire others to uncover their purpose and live it with passion. She is a TEDx speaker, an award-winning writer and the author of 7 books. Christie publishes "Revision Magazine" a quarterly motivational publication for women and hosts the "Live Revised" podcast each week. She speaks at motivational events across the US and is the Owner and Founder of Revision Motivational Company. Christie's "live revised" mantra has compelled followers to uncover their purpose, live life with passion, and embrace new opportunities while fighting to be free from past mistakes, failures and disappointments. Be warned... Christie will shake you up and leave you motivated to live a bigger, bolder, brighter life. Originally from Memphis, Tennessee, Christie now lives in Indiana with her husband, her stepson, and their two dogs

Follow Christie on these
social media channels:

Facebook @ ChristieBrowningOfficial

Instagram @ christicbrowningofficial

LinkedIn @ christiebrowning

YouTube @ christiebrowning

For more encouraging books, empowering studies and inspiring videos or to inquire about booking Christie to speak at your event, visit www.christiebrowning.com

First
Leaders

LEADERSHIP PRINCIPLES
OF FIRST NATION SOCIETIES
FOR THE MODERN LEADER

Andrew O'Keeffe

First published 2023

Published by Roundtable Press
PO Box 415
Bellingen NSW 2454
Australia
Phone: +61 (0)412 616 047
Email: wisdom@firstleadersbook.com
Web: www.firstleadersbook.com

We acknowledge the traditional owners of the country on which we live and work,
the Gumbaynggirr nation. We pay our respects to Gumbaynggirr elders, past, present
and emerging.

Cover design and interior composition by Sheila Parr (sheilaparr.com)
Edited by David Brewster (davidbrewsterwriter.com)
Graphics and map by Merrilee Fleeting
Cover images used under license from © The Noun Project: kareemov (acacia tree);
Jhonatan (grass); Hopkins (leaf); Josh (fern).
Author photo by David Michael Thorn Photography
Interior photography mostly by Jude Tasker and Andrew O'Keeffe

A catalogue record for this book is available from the National Library of Australia.

978-0-6456279-0-9

This book is for the next seven generations of leaders.

Also by Andrew O'Keeffe

The Boss — Based on True Stories About Bosses at Work (a novel)

Hardwired Humans — Successful Leadership Using Human Instincts

Contents

Introduction

I SET OFF ON my adventure to write this book soon after talking with several Maasai elders. Seven years ago, my wife Jude and I holidayed in Africa. When we reached Kenya, I'd arranged to learn about leadership in Maasai society. My career has been in leadership, in workplaces, and I was curious to hear this different perspective on the subject. The conversations on this trip inspired me to investigate leadership in twelve First Nation societies. Their wisdom, I found, helps workplace leaders fix their major leadership challenges.

The first Maasai I met was Ngila Loitamany Johnson. He became a key contact and our dear friend. After talking with Ngila I had a series of individual meetings, usually sitting under an acacia tree, with several other people. Each person happened to 'report' to a different chief. About half-way through the conversations, I changed the focus. I'd been asking about leadership processes in their society, such as how an individual is chosen to be the chief. Now I made the conversation more personal. 'How about *your* chief?' I asked. 'Are they a good leader?' Their reaction stunned me. Each person instantly teared-up with loving thoughts of their leader. This misty-eyed response by followers, I discovered on this and a later visit, applies to both men and women. I made a beeline back to Ngila.

'Ngila!' I said excitedly. 'When I ask people, "Is *your* chief a good leader?" their eyes instantly glisten with tears just thinking about their leader. I don't know many workplace leaders who trigger this reaction! How do you get leadership so right?'

He told me more about the process of leadership selection, of the time-frame taken to appoint a chief and the attributes required of a leader. He told me about the role of followers in the selection of their leader. Some of what Ngila and other Maasai told me resonated with conventional workplace practices, which points to the fundamentals of good leadership practice. Yet much of what I heard caused me to question orthodox approaches and I saw the wisdom of the Maasai way.

Back home in Sydney soon after that holiday, I was enjoying an afternoon stroll around our local bay. As I walked, recalling the Maasai visit, a sense of euphoria swept through me. I felt invigorated by the insight I'd gained and from the stimulation of meeting people with a different perspective. Yet I was also disturbed that I'd reached a mature stage of my career in human resources and leadership development without touching on ancient wisdom. Where had this information been all my life? And I'd only scratched the surface. Excited by how much there must be to learn, my pace quickened. In 10 more strides the idea struck me: I will visit traditional societies in different parts of the world, if they will have me, to learn about their approaches to leadership. With that, I ignited a personal passion and set out on a quest to learn and share First Nations wisdom.

Since resolving to embark on my mission, I've had the privilege of visiting **Ju/'hoansi Bushmen** in the Kalahari of Africa, **Arrernte** and **Pintupi** in the arid centre of Australia, **Waorani** and **Kichwa** in the Amazonian rainforest of Ecuador, **Himba** in the dry sparsely-wooded hills of Namibia, **Maasai** (again) and **Samburu** on the Kenyan savannah, **Haida** on the Haida Gwaii archipelago in the far northern Pacific Ocean of Canada, **Māori** in New Zealand and, near Montreal, the **Mohawk** nation whose traditional lands include much of today's upstate New York. My visits occurred between January 2016 and January 2020. My research was to conclude in May 2020 with a visit to **Piegan Blackfeet** at the base of the Rocky Mountains in Montana, USA. Unfortunately, the COVID-19 pandemic caused that trip to be cancelled. However, in preparation for the visit I'd read extensively about this Great Plains nation, including books recommended by my would-be host, so I have included Blackfeet in this book. See the world map on pages 4–5 for the locations of the societies.

The 12 societies cover the spectrum of organisational complexity of First Nations, from small hunter-gatherer bands to those organised into divisions up to those organised as nations of 25,000 citizens. In comparison to workplaces, they cover the equivalent of small family firms up to large, complex corporations. The choice of societies was from a mix of design and good luck. For example, at the outset I was keen to visit Himba people in Namibia because I knew from a visit years before that Himba overwhelmingly continue to live their traditional lifestyle. Given I'm Australian, I was eager to visit one or more Aboriginal or Torres Strait Islander nations and Central Australia became possible when a friend took an interest in my project. At the outset I was keen to visit our neighbours in New Zealand. Visiting Waorani in the Amazon came from a lucky break, when a friend introduced me to a guide who had guided him into the jungle on several birding conservation trips.

In addition to personal conversations, I've read extensively the anthropological literature on the people I've visited, as well as the literature on many other ancestral societies. I've read the observations of early missionaries who were often the individuals making first contact with people and who frequently included anthropological information in their memoirs (before anthropology emerged as a discipline).

Given I'm interested in life prior to the influence of Europeans, a remarkable part of my adventure has been meeting people who grew up living the life of their ancestors. In the Kalahari Desert, in the Amazon and in the Western Desert of Australia, I met people who told me about their first contact with Europeans. When I started on my journey, I could only dream of having the good fortune and privilege of meeting the people I have met. I remain in contact with many of them. As well as enjoying their friendship, being in contact has allowed me to check with them that what I have written is an accurate record of our conversations and my understanding of their society. I have been able to check back with members of most of the societies I visited.

Continuously, I was struck by the warmth with which people welcomed me. To give just three examples. When I visited the Kahnawà:ke Mohawk community near Montreal and was able to thank Kimberly Kaniehténhawe Cross for hosting me and organising interviews with 10 senior people, she responded that when I first contacted her, she instantly felt honoured that I was including Mohawk in my research. Or Pintupi Marlene Nampitjinpa Ross who, after we talked in Central Australia, offered to contact me

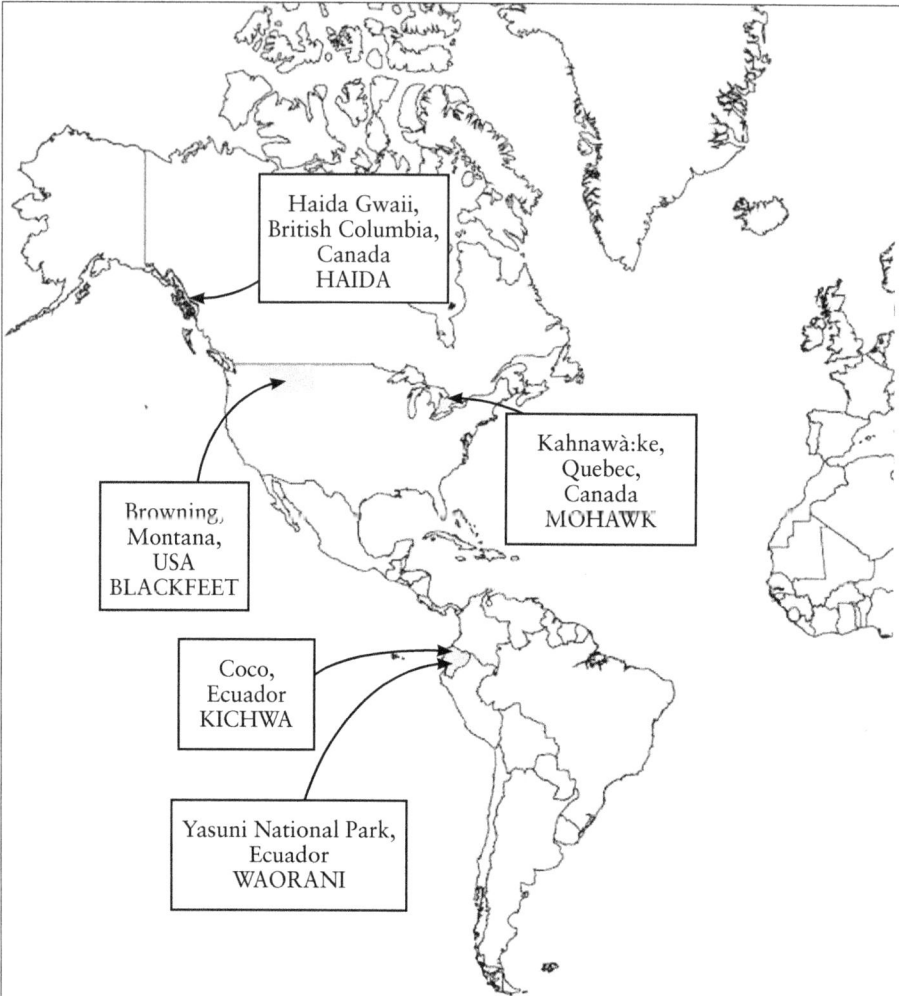

World map: The location of the 11 societies visited on the travels to write this book. Plus the location of Blackfeet society which unfortunately was not able to be visited due to the COVID-19 pandemic.

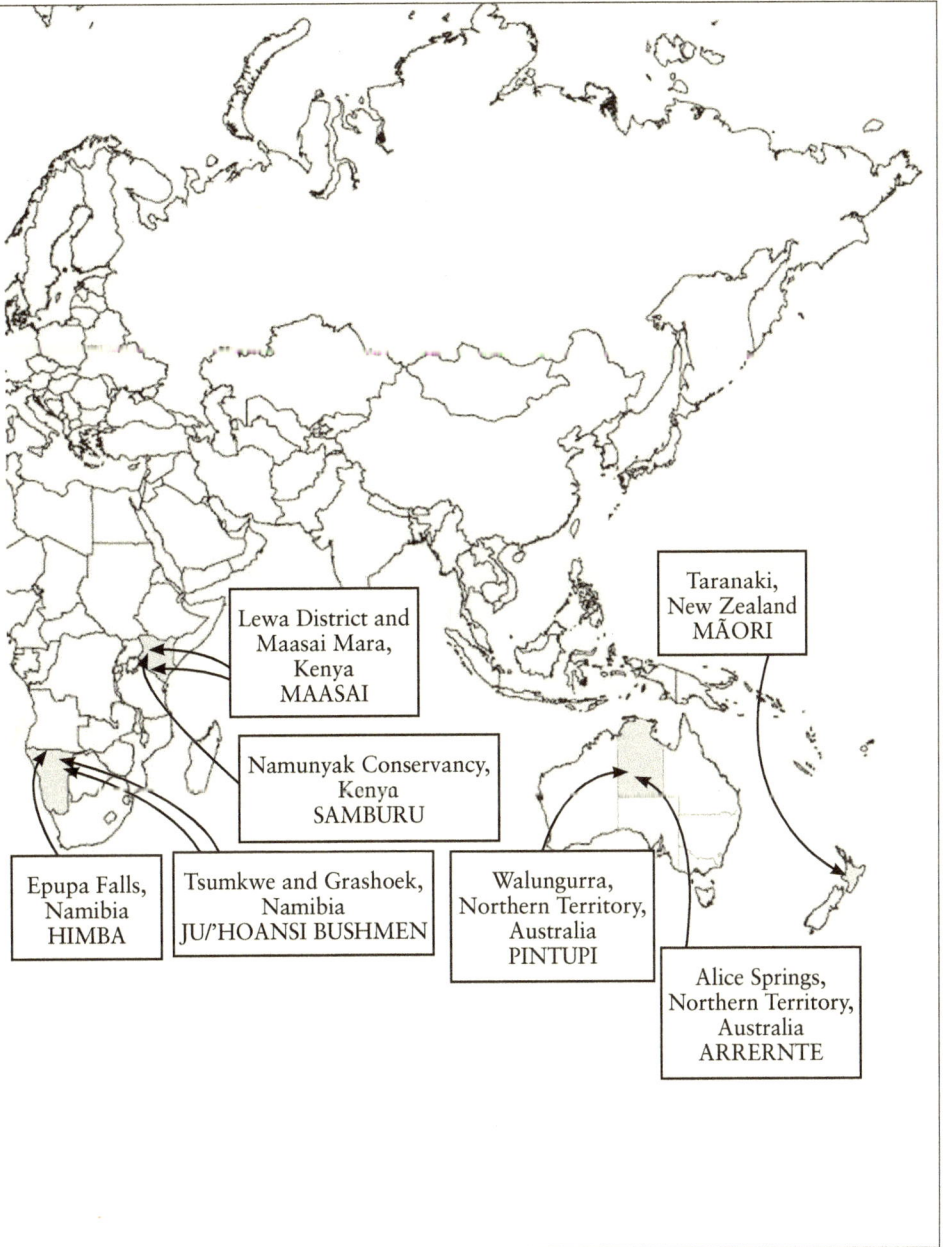

Lewa District and
Maasai Mara,
Kenya
MAASAI

Taranaki,
New Zealand
MĀORI

Namunyak Conservancy,
Kenya
SAMBURU

Epupa Falls,
Namibia
HIMBA

Tsumkwe and Grashoek,
Namibia
JU/'HOANSI BUSHMEN

Walungurra,
Northern Territory,
Australia
PINTUPI

Alice Springs,
Northern Territory,
Australia
ARRERNTE

when she would soon be in Sydney, which she did, so we could continue our conversation. Or Keri Opai in New Zealand who took three days off work to host me at his community. He and one of his community's senior women, Peeti Wātene, honoured me with a pōwhiri, a ritual welcome, at their marae (ceremonial centre).

Apart from their generous natures, the people I met were keen to share their knowledge as they saw this book as a vehicle for sharing their culture and giving voice to their ideas on life and leadership. They were attracted to the idea that workplace leaders might learn from their people's wisdom.

———

In the span of human history, we've been operating in workplaces for only a short time. Clearly, leadership in this environment is a relatively recent challenge. Workplace leadership only emerged as a discipline in 1911, according to the great organisational scholar Peter Drucker, when J. P. Morgan appointed the first professional managers. And only a few years before, in 1908, Harvard University started its business school. Those must have been heady days for industry leaders and scholars turning their minds to what constitutes good leadership in this new environment. Regrettably, in developing the theory and practice of good leadership, they ignored all that had gone before in the leadership of First Nations that was an available source of leadership wisdom and decided instead that they were beginning with a clean slate.

And what was the first workplace leadership model that appeared on that clean slate? The aloof and autocratic concepts of Frederick Taylor's *The Principles of Scientific Management*, published in 1911. What an alarming model as the starting point — as the foundation upon which we have built workplace leadership. Taylor's philosophy was that a worker engaged in manual labour 'shall be so stupid … that he more nearly resembles in his mental make-up the ox than any other type'. Taylor claimed he could 'train an intelligent gorilla to be more efficient' at manual work than a person. This bleak outlook led him to define the role of management: 'It is clear that in most cases one type of person is needed to plan ahead (management) and an entirely different type (of person) to execute the work.' In Taylor's view, the key function of management was 'at least one day in advance (give to each worker) complete written instructions, describing in detail the task to be accomplished as well as the means to be used in doing the work.'[1]

Significantly, the concepts and practice of workplace leadership we use today are built on the foundation of Taylor and the research, theories and models that followed. When the modern leader looks for ideas on leadership, they will likely be guided to the thinking and frameworks that have emerged in the last 100 years — built slowly and methodically but only from that starting point.

We could have built on a better foundation by tapping into all that had gone before our relatively recent move into industrial organisations. Traditional societies had the same fundamental challenge as modern workplaces — people existing together harmoniously and working cooperatively. Traditional societies that have endured for so long must have done a lot right in the area of leadership. First, they had a long time to work it out. Second, as a matter of survival they *had* to get it right. And third, given that I've found the patterns of leadership are mirrored across continents, my proposition is that the solutions that emerged align with human nature.

Why didn't early thinkers on the subject of workplace leadership tap into traditional wisdom? The social setting in the early 1900s blinkered people horribly. Given the social setting of the time — just when the discipline of workplace management was emerging — Western societies were still inflicting bigotry and brutality on First Peoples. In that era of colonial suppression, when First Nations' languages and cultural practices were widely repressed and ridiculed, and in many cases outlawed, it would have been astonishing if captains of industry had asked indigenous people for guidance in leading their organisations. Surely, today, we're awake to First Peoples' wisdom.

Ignoring traditional thinking on leadership has been to our great detriment. Through my lengthy career, I know we're struggling to find leadership solutions to build thriving workplaces where people love to work. Leading employee survey company, Gallup, finds that across the world only 15% of staff are 'engaged'; for many people their work lives are barely tolerable. The single biggest factor driving employee discontent is poor leadership — people generally don't like their boss. From the managers' perspective, most leaders find the people dimension of their role the most challenging. Managers wanting to improve look around and often struggle to find good role models. And at the organisational level, whereas ancestral cultures endured, organisations generally don't. Many organisations that were among the most admired say 10 or 20 years ago are today shadows of their former selves, if they still exist. The principles of leadership that I've discovered from my time with First Nations people, which I'll share in this book, provide practical initiatives to improve modern leadership.

My objective in writing this book is to help both individual leaders and organisations. For individual leaders, the principles followed by first leaders provide practical guidance to enhance their people-leadership ability. By following these timeless principles, leaders can lift their team's cooperative spirit and performance. Also, by having clarity of what's required of them in their roles, leaders will enjoy their leadership role more than they possibly do right now. For organisations, the principles show how to align leadership systems to what traditional societies found works and to avoid what was found not to work. From the ancestral wisdom shared in this book, organisations will know where to focus their investment in leadership systems and capability. Ultimately, by individual leaders and wider organisations adopting ancestral wisdom, workplaces will be more inspiring places for staff.

The focus of my research was to identify the *practical implications* for how workplace leaders can apply the leadership principles of traditional societies. My career has been as a practitioner, first in industrial relations in mining and manufacturing industries, then in senior human resource roles in information technology and professional services. More recently, I have taught leadership and consulted in change management. My interest in tapping into ancestral wisdom is an extension of my work over the latter half of my career applying, teaching and writing about the leadership implications of our basic human nature.

As my mission unfolded, the patterns of wisdom shared with me crystallised into what I call the 11 'Principles of First Leadership' that form the structure of this book (listed below). Nine of these principles describe the positives of what I learned from this study of ancestral wisdom. Two of the principles — Principles 9 and 10 — focus on avoiding two significant negative features of ancestral life. At the end of each chapter are recommended practical actions leaders can take to implement traditional wisdom in their own leadership and in their workplace.

While the Principles of First Leadership provide a complete blueprint for leadership, implementation is extremely flexible. The principles can be implemented in any order that works best for you and your organisation. As you read this book, I suggest that you look for ideas that fire your imagination with immediate application — as an individual leader or to improve a practice in your organisation. Start by implementing that practice and build from there.

Here is a summary of the 11 Principles of First Leadership that form the structure of this book.

1. **Organising Structure**: Ancestral people had a consistent approach in organising their population. The core design characteristics are present irrespective of whether the society is a hunter-gatherer society or a league of nations. The approach helps workplace leaders structure their workforce to make work easy — and avoid the dysfunction arising from poor structure.

2. **Nature of Leadership**: The role of the leader in ancestral societies developed as the population grew and the society became more organised. If the nature of leadership didn't develop, the society couldn't expand. The pattern reassures leaders of their critical role for a group to function and provides a model for matching the levels of leadership to the organisational structure of a workplace.

3. **Attributes of Leadership**: Across cultures and across continents, there is stunning uniformity of the attributes that qualify a person for leadership. The required attributes are so clear that generally even in a hereditary system, the person next in line will be banned from leadership if they don't have the required attributes for the role. This consistency strips good leadership behaviour to its core.

4. **Selecting Leaders**: As societies become more organisationally complex, great care is taken in selecting the leader. The success rate of traditional societies in choosing leaders sets the benchmark of what's possible for workplaces.

5. **Appointments and Status of Leaders:** When a person is appointed to a leadership role, traditional societies mark the moment with ritual. The ritual signals the obligations of leadership. Ancestral communities don't merely do the equivalent of sending out an email announcing the appointment.

6. **Checks on Leadership Power:** Given the problems arising from ineffective leadership or from leaders abusing their power, ancestral societies generally have options to fix poor leadership. The society could not ignore the negative impact of poor leadership on group harmony and the group's survival.

7. **Cultural Clarity:** Traditional societies are clear on the meaning of membership of their society. There is clarity on the extent to which individual desires are to be conceded in favour of group interests.

8. **Individual Identity Through Learning:** Ancestral societies are learning organisations. A key role of the leader — and the elders — is to teach. Teaching helps achieve individual identity within the group. For workplaces, individual learning is the remedy to the anonymity that many people experience in modern organisations.

9. **Gender Equity — To Avoid a Feature of Ancestral Life:** A finding from my research that disturbs me is that in ancestral societies there is widespread gender inequity in favour of men. One aspect of gender inequity in traditional societies is that leadership is almost exclusively a male occupation. My discomfort about this finding is somewhat offset by the fact that at least if we know the deep-seated source of gender inequity, we can choose to take the tangible actions necessary to fix the problem.

10. **Inter-Group Harmony — To Avoid a Feature of Ancestral Life:** Almost all ancestral societies had hostile relationships with their neighbours, which were often people of their own language group. This finding explains why workplaces can quickly tribalise, and helps leaders watch for the first signs of rivalry so they can take swift remedial action before organisation performance is sabotaged.

11. **Initiatives for Group Cohesion:** Ancestral communities generate a strong sense of belonging amongst group members. They devote significant time and resources to bind their community and — given the negative feature of life in the previous principle — to reduce tension with their neighbours.

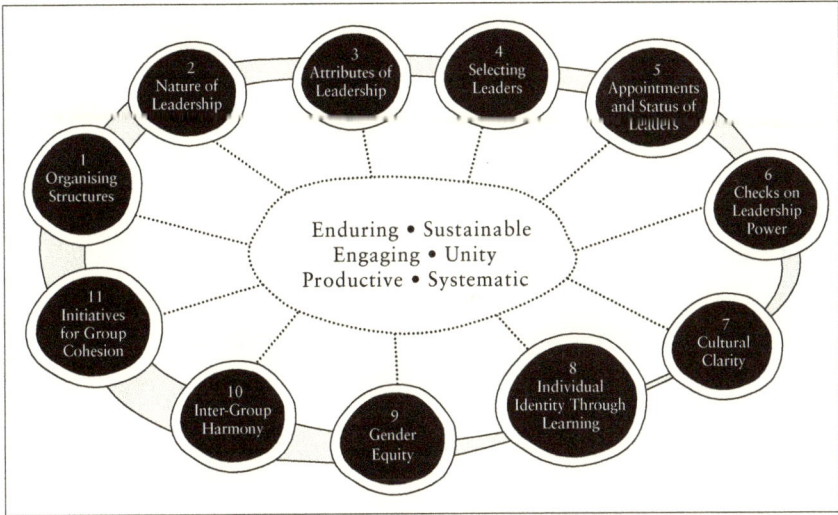

The 11 Principles of First Leadership are all connected, but are fluid and can be adopted in any order that makes sense to a leader or an organisation.

The outcomes that the leadership approach delivers to First Nation societies are admirable and equally relevant to organisations. From my investigation, as shown in the above graphic, there are key outcomes that in workplace parlance we call key deliverables. First Nation societies have **endured** through the millennia — a phenomenal achievement. Compare that durability to many other societies that have risen and fallen and, over the last century, organisations that have come and gone. First Nation societies manage their resources in a **sustainable** way. Their mindset is that they are part of the environment, not separate from it, and they manage their resources accordingly. They achieve high **engagement** of their citizens — individuals identify with the culture and everyone has their part. While moments of tensions occur, overall, each society and its component groups are **unified**. As I've just mentioned in Principle 11 above, we'll see in this book the extensive investment of time and effort that goes into achieving unity. The societies are **productive** human enterprises — food is produced, materials procured and tools manufactured. In the old days, even in the arid regions, except in bad drought years, there was enough food to eat and water to drink. The final outcome that stands out for me is that the societies are functional and orderly. I've called this outcome '**systematic**'. There is no sign of the bureaucracy that often surfaces in organisations; there are rules, but there are just enough of them and each serves a sensible purpose.

Workplace leaders share similar challenges to those faced by first leaders, and the eleven leadership principles assist in solving those challenges: how to grow your community, maintain unity, be productive and endure.

From my conversations with First Nations people, I have deep respect for their clarity of thinking, enlightened mindset and comprehensive approach to leadership. I hope you, too, are inspired by what they told me.

CHAPTER 1

Organising Structure

'My family lived in a pretty big village of about 150 people.'

SITTING IN THE SAND of the Kalahari in southern Africa, 70-year-old Komtsa told me of his early life as a nomadic Ju/'hoansi Bushman. He lived the life of his ancestors, hunting and gathering in his grandparents' band.

Bushmen are some of the earliest inhabitants still living in southern Africa. Their hunter-gatherer life endured for centuries but, beginning in the late 1950s, the governments of the day forced Bushmen to give up their traditional life and move into settlements. That's not long ago and in planning my visit for August 2017, I hoped to meet individuals aged in their 60s and older who still remembered the old ways. My hope was realised. What a privilege to meet and talk with Komtsa and two others who remembered, as teenagers and young adults, living the old way. I was acutely aware that the window to meet people who experienced the nomadic life is rapidly closing because of their age. There are several Bushmen peoples and my focus is on Ju/'hoansi (or !Kung) society, the most studied and the best known of the Bushmen. In this book, unless otherwise stated, when I refer to Bushmen I am referring to Ju/'hoansi.[1]

Komtsa lives on the outskirts of the town of Tsumkwe, just on the Namibian side of the border with Botswana. We were expected early and arrived at his hut around 8 o'clock on a bright sunny morning. He welcomed us with a broad smile and we soon settled in the sand. One of his neighbours served as translator. Komtsa shared his knowledge enthusiastically, happily reminiscing about the old days. He clearly misses the life of his youth.

In talking with Komtsa, I was transported back in time, back to when all humans lived the way he did. He's in direct contact with the fundamentals of the human organisation. He touched on the basics of organisation structure. He told me how work was assigned each day, such as deciding who would make up the group tasked with gathering nuts or a small work team to retrieve meat from a successful hunt. He told me about group dynamics, and the role of the camp leader in enabling the group to function peacefully. From his explanation, I saw the problems a group faces as it grows if the nature of leadership doesn't grow to match the increasing complexity of the organisation. He described the reality of occasional tension between group members — which I could readily picture from my career in workplaces. He told me that there was a need, occasionally, for the camp leader, his grandfather, to dismiss someone from the community because they were undermining the group's interests. I smile even now at the expression Komtsa said his grandfather used if he was evicting a camp member. This dramatic decision was much more elegantly expressed than what we tend to say in terminating the employment of a difficult staff member. 'One of the reasons for being asked to leave camp,' Komtsa told me, 'is if you were causing a pain in someone else's heart.'

The first topic we talked about related to the size of the group in which he lived. The principle of how societies organise their population is a first-order issue for understanding life, leadership and the social complexity of groups. In researching traditional societies, one of the topics I was investigating was whether a pattern existed for organising their population. For workplace leaders, identifying and applying such a pattern would mean we could use this wisdom, developed over the long journey of the human experience, to design our organisations to *enable* group identity, harmony and efficient work; we can avoid dysfunctional design.

If you were to study the organisational structure of 12 randomly selected workplaces, you would find, almost guaranteed, no similarity of design. Sadly, there's a good chance, too, that many of the 12 organisations in your study wouldn't even have design principles guiding the way they structure their workforce. But study 12 ancestral societies, as I have done, and a clear organising principle emerges, shared by them all. Traditional societies follow the same blueprint, and the blueprint handles scale. The principle applies irrespective of the way in which the society is organised: whether organised as independent nomadic bands, as independent villages, as independent divisions (clans) or even as nations comprising as many as 25,000 people. Likewise, the principle provides a blueprint for organising small, medium and large workplaces, so that by design we help people get along well and easily produce work.

Family and Band/Village as the Organising Pattern

The early morning sunlight highlighted Komtsa's closely cropped grey hair. I asked him about the size of the group in which he lived in his early years when he lived the traditional life of his ancestors. He told me that he and his immediate family lived in his grandparents' camp. He said the camp numbered at various times between 20 and 30 people. The size of his camp, or 'band' as I will refer to this group, was right on the norm for Bushmen. At the time when Komtsa was a youngster, anthropologists in the 1950s and 1960s, often making first Western contact with Bushmen, found that the most common number of people living in a band was around 25 people. Bands were comprised of families usually related by birth or marriage.

In his brief description, Komtsa revealed the pattern of human societies for organising a population: his *small immediate family* aggregating with other families to form *a band* or *village*. The two components of first, family and second, a band or village to aggregate the families, are the building blocks of human societies. (As an organising concept, 'bands' and 'villages' are essentially the same — the key difference for the purposes of this book is that bands are nomadic, and villages are settled or perhaps semi-nomadic.) In my travels for researching this book, I found that this organising principle of families aggregating into a band or village applies universally — across the range of societies on different continents (we'll look at the 12 societies in a moment). Even in societies structured to organise thousands of citizens — 25,000 in the case of Mohawk society before colonisation — the two building blocks of family and band (or, in Mohawk society, the longhouse) provide the foundation principle for organising their population. Based on this universal design arising from the long timeframe of First Nations' experience, I'm proposing that to be functional and productive, workplaces should adopt the blueprint to organise their people. To be *naturally* functional, staff need to be organised into small teams (equivalent to the human universal of family) within a department of a certain size (equivalent to the human universal of band or village). Large and small organisations should be built on this blueprint, just like the range of societies we will discuss. Workplaces that deviate from the blueprint that works for humans make it harder for staff to connect and do their best work.

The first level of structure, the family, represents the small intimate group in which we gain our strongest sense of connection. In traditional times, structuring around the family unit wasn't just about biology and the genetic and emotional connection of immediate family. Throughout the long haul of human history, the family was the primary economic unit of production of the 'organisation'. A husband–wife combination with their older children had the complementary knowledge, skills and muscle to produce and maintain the materials necessary for survival and the supply of food and other essentials of life. While materials varied according to the environment, there were tools for hunting and gathering such as bows, arrows, spears, spear-throwers, blowpipes, darts, poisons, boomerangs, fish nets, fish traps and digging sticks. There were cooking utensils and pots made from wood or clay. There were bags or containers for carrying food and water, and slings for carrying children. For many cultures there was the cleaning and tanning of hides for clothes. And there was the building of shelters, as varied as grass shelters by Bushmen, semi-permanent houses in the Amazon, transportable buffalo-hide tipis of the Plains nations of North America and palisade fortresses of Māori and Mohawk societies. Parents passed their extensive knowledge to the next generation, and while some societies such as Bushmen gave children an extended childhood, certainly by their teenage years children were valuable contributors to their family's wellbeing.

The second level of organisational structure, the band or village, provides the vehicle for aggregating family units and are large enough to provide support to individuals and families yet not so large that a person loses their identity. In traditional societies, the band or village served as the secondary economic unit for the sharing of food and the distribution of tasks, including water collection and caring for older and younger members of the group who could not hunt or gather. The band or village was the primary focus of territorial ownership and for the protection of group members.

The Size of Families and Bands/Villages

Part of the clear principle of organisation design around family and the band or village is the number of people in these two groups.

For the family unit, the group numbers about seven individuals (plus or minus two). In traditional times, the group included a grandparent or two, mum and dad and a few children. A group of about seven people is the size with which we gain our closest sense of connection with a shared obligation to deliver work. In a work environment, it's the size group where we have the best chance or being closely connected and where a manager can support and serve all team members. A team of seven plus or minus two in the workplace means that people should be organised into teams in which a manager has at least four, and not more than eight, direct reports.

The nature of the second unit of design, the band or village, is a consequence of the size of the human brain. Humans associate with groups of up to about 150 people, with a sweet spot at about 80 to 100 people. Early anthropologists didn't know why they consistently observed villages up to this size, but we know now, courtesy of Robin Dunbar of Oxford University. Dunbar found a link between the ratio of brain to body size (or, more accurately, the ratio of the neocortex to body size) and the group size of social animals. Humans have the biggest brain to body size ratio of any social animal. This large brain allowed us to live in relatively large groups, but the size of the group is capped by the level of social complexity we can handle. On Dunbar's analysis, the brain to body ratio of humans correlates to a community size of *up to about* 150, which is indeed the maximum size of ancestral bands and villages.[2] Applying this principle to the workplace means that the family-sized teams of about seven staff should be aggregated into departments of up to about 150 people. Small departments might number about 25 people similar to a Bushman band, some departments might number around 80 to 100 people and large departments would number around 150 people or a little more. As it does in ancestral societies, the village design concept handles scale in workplaces; it can handle a population of many thousands of staff through the creation of many villages.

Structuring a workplace around departments of up to about 150 people means the force of human nature is being harnessed. Challenges emerge — for workplaces and traditional societies — if people are in departments or villages much larger than about 150 people. In studying Yanomamo society in Venezuela from the 1960s, renowned anthropologist Napoleon Chagnon was curious about the pattern he observed in the size of villages. In his early career years, Chagnon was often making first Western contact with people. At that time, the Yanomamo population of about 20,000–25,000 people lived in 250 independent villages at an average of 80–100 people in each village.[3] Well before Dunbar's discovery of brain size, Chagnon was intrigued that he never found a village larger than 150 people. He was told of a village numbering 250 people, so he went up-river to investigate this abnormally large village. But on arrival he found that the village had split in two. It had grown beyond the 'tipping point' for humans and the social strains resulted in a fracture. Chagnon's conclusion was that as a village grows, the growing pains are too great and the internal political struggles overwhelm a single leader trying to keep the group united.[4]

In workplaces, we can of course create departments of 250-plus people. But the point from the long experience of First Nations is that departments much beyond 150 people are too large for people to feel a sense of connection and too large for a department leader to keep the group unified. Human nature wins the day, and a large department splits into separate units. Sure, on paper the department can be shown as a single group of 250 people and a senior executive might think the department operates as a united unit, but in practice the department will have split. People feel a greater affinity to a subset of the group. Because the fracture has happened informally, the line of the fracture might not suit the best operational efficiencies of the organisation.

Let's look at the 12 societies I've studied to examine the pattern and to show what I see as the overwhelming evidence that there is a design that works for humans. I'll then give examples of how the ancestral design pattern has been successfully applied in workplaces.

The Organisation of Traditional Societies: From Families to Nations

In covering the 12 societies, I'll do so in order of the level in which the society is, or was, organised — from nomadic bands, to settled independent villages, to being organised above the village at the divisional or clan level and finally to those organised at the level of the whole nation. I'll show that, without exception, each society applied the family/village design principle for organising its population. The only variable was the extent to which the environment supported smaller or larger numbers of people being coordinated and thus the level in which the society was organised — whether villages, for example, were organised into divisions to help people live together harmoniously. In abundant environments, such as the Great Plains of North America or the rich marine environment of the North Pacific Ocean, large concentrations of people could be supported which resulted in people being organised as divisions or as a nation. In arid environments, such as the Kalahari or the inland deserts of Australia, the concentration was capped at the band or village level.

Society	Level of Organisation Structure of the Society			
	Family	Band/Village	Division/Clan	Nation/Confederacy
Bushmen	√	√		
Pintupi	√	√		
Arrernte	√	√		
Waorani	√	√		
Kichwa	√	√		
Māori	√	√	√	
Maasai	√	√	√	
Samburu	√	√	√	
Haida	√	√	√	
Blackfeet	√	√	√	
Mohawk	√	√	√	√

Table: Organisation structure of the twelve societies investigated, showing the highest level in which the society is/was organised.

1. Societies Organised at the Level of Band or Village

In this sub-section we are looking at societies organised as family units aggregating into bands or villages. In the societies at this level of social organisation, bands and villages are independent and there is no level of organisation above the village. These societies are like small to medium sized workplaces.

Society #1 we have covered: Bushmen organised in independent bands of up to about 25 people comprising a small number of family units. In Bushmen society there was no organisation above the bands.

For Society #2 we travel to the semi-desert of Central Australia to visit Pintupi society. Pintupi country is in a remote part of the continent — 640 kilometres (400 miles) west of Alice Springs around the Northern Territory/ Western Australia border. In October 2019 I visited the Pintupi community of Walungurru, also known as Kintore. Part of the great privilege of visiting Pintupi is that they are amongst the last Australian indigenous people to interact with Europeans — the last Pintupi left their traditional life and made contact with outsiders as recently as 1984. Their arid country, driven mainly by low rainfall, shaped their social organisation. Pintupi lived in small family units and, depending on seasonal conditions, in bands of rarely more than 20 to 30 people.[5] One Pintupi elder I met, Marlene Nampitjinpa Ross, grew up living the life of her ancestors and was 11 years of age before she saw a 'whitefella'. (I'll tell that part of her remarkable story later.) Marlene is about my age. No, on second thoughts, given her youthful appearance, she must be under 60 years of age. What joy to meet, sit and talk with Marlene, to hear her stories and gain a glimpse of the life she has lived. The dry conditions of her country meant that she spent much of her childhood with her family unit of just six people: her father, her mother, her mother's sister who was her father's second wife and hence Marlene's 'other mother', two children of her other mother plus Marlene. Low rainfall with long dry spells and few permanent water sources meant the country could not generally support larger groups. During one of our several conversations, I asked Marlene how she and her family managed to find water in her arid country.

'We listened to that bird,' she said, cupping her ear with her hand and pointing to an imaginary bird over my left shoulder. 'It might be that small bird that would point us to water, or maybe a larger bird of prey.'

'And then how would you make it from one water source to another as you searched for food?'

'We carried a little water in a coolamon.' A little water in a shallow wooden dish would see Marlene and her family from one waterhole to another, of perhaps to a soak of water in the sandy soil if you knew where to look and how to obtain the precious resource. No wonder the group size was generally limited.

When rainfall and seasonal conditions permitted, Pintupi gathered in larger groups beyond the family. Just before the time of Marlene's birth, respected anthropologist Donald Thomson visited Pintupi country in the 1950s. This was a time when almost all Pintupi lived their traditional life. In reference to one group, and reflecting the usual organisation model, he wrote that 'the group comprised three families, each occupied a separate camp where the family lived as an independent self-contained unit'.[6]

Society #3 is nearby, the Arrernte society around today's Alice Springs. In the slightly more abundant environment than Pintupi country, Arrernte families organised as bands of up to about 40 people.[7] By way of comparison with the small bands of the peoples of the arid inland, such as Pintupi and Arrernte, in pre-colonial times in the south-east of Australia the abundant food and water resources supported people living in communities numbering up to about 120 people.[8] James Dawson and his family were amongst the first settlers in the Western District of Victoria. He and his family, despite dispossessing Aboriginal people of their land, were respectful of the traditional owners and curious about their society. Dawson's daughter learned the local language and listened to the stories about life before Europeans arrived through Port Phillip. The elders described life in substantial dwellings constructed of tree branches with roofs of bark sheets. Family units of parents and their dependent children lived in partitioned sections of the house, with separate sections for the young unmarried women and widows and one for bachelors and widowers. Up to 50 people lived in each house, in communities of up to about 120 people.[9]

For Society #4 we travel by canoe into the Amazon jungle of Ecuador to visit the Waorani people, which I did in May 2019. Peaceful contact between Waorani and outsiders only commenced in 1958. Their society was organised around six or so nuclear families living in a village or *nanicabo*. Settlements usually numbered up to about 35 individuals.[10] Two to three allied settlements positioned within about a 20-minute walk from each other formed a neighbourhood. A neighbourhood numbered about 90 to 120 people.[11] There was no unification of neighbourhoods. Some Waorani still live their traditional life.

Even in mentioning just these four societies, the pattern is emerging — there's an organisation structure that works for humans. Across these societies in Africa, Australia and South America, the pattern of families aggregating into bands or villages is the organising principle. There is nothing random in design. The only difference so far is the size of the band or village the environment could support, capped at about 150 people.

For Society #5 we stay in Ecuador to visit another Amazonian society, Kichwa, located along the headwaters of the Napo River. My guide into the Amazon, José Raul Aguinda Grefa, grew up in a traditional village. I asked José about the village of his youth.

'Our villages were organised as independent communities. Each community consisted of 10 to 12 families living in a single oval-shaped house. Within the house, each family had its own space, comprising a stove (*tulpa*) and bunk beds (*gaitu*).'

'What was the total population of a Kichwa village?' I asked.

'The community numbered about 50 to 70 people. The nearest neighbouring village,' he added, 'was about an hour-and-a-half's walk along jungle trails.'

Society #6 is back in Africa and another example of a society organised as families aggregating into independent villages. After visiting the Bushmen on one side of Namibia in August 2017, we drove to the other side of the country to visit the Himba people. Most Himba citizens continue to live their traditional life as herders of cattle and goats. Himba villages are marked by rough corrals constructed from dry branches. Villages consist of about eight to ten huts with a hut for each adult woman and her dependent children. In the dry northern district we visited, villages mostly number about 40 to 50 people. Villages are autonomous entities — there is no organisation of villages even within a district.

The grassless brown hills of the Himba homeland could not be in starker contrast to the lush green hills of New Zealand, and Society #7.

Māori migrated to Aotearoa (New Zealand) between about 950AD and 1350AD. Ancestry is vital in Māori society, and many individuals trace their ancestry by generation back to those migrations. I visited New Zealand to learn about Māori society in January 2020. The main feature of traditional Māori social organisation was the *hapū* comprising a number of extended family groups (*whanau*). In an 1870 census in one district in the Bay of Plenty on the North Island, five hapū ranged in size from 51 to 165 people. In the terminology I am using in this book, hapū was a village but not necessarily within the same physical space. Hapū membership was dynamic. Just like anthropologist Napoleon Chagnon observed for Yanomamo villages in South America, as a hapū grew in size, various pressures arose that might result in a hapū splitting to form separate new hapū. There were a number of possible reasons for such a split: family quarrels, breaches of customs, loss of authority of the leader, a division of land or defeat in war. The breakaway group would take a new name to mark their new identity.[12] A number of hapū were connected through a common ancestor to form an *iwi*, the higher level of structure. But for most of Māori history, iwi had no formal power or authority — hapū was the main organising unit.[13] It was not until the late 1700s that iwi began to feature more prominently in the political life of Māori citizens.[14] And slightly later still, in response to the occupation of their land by British colonists, many Māori took a further organising step and unified under a king in 1858.

2. Societies Organised at the Division Level

So far, we have looked at societies organised as independent bands or villages or, in the case of Māori society, the emergence of an organising layer above the unit of about 150 people. The next societies we visit are organised at a level higher than the village. Anthropologists variously refer to this level of social organisation as clans or sub-tribes. Because my focus is workplaces, I am going to use the workplace term 'division' (which is also the term used by the Blackfeet nation in North America). At this level of organisation, each division is autonomous, with no unification of the divisions at the nation level. Importantly, while at this level the population is organised into divisions, the design blueprint of family and village is still the building block of the society: families aggregating into a unit that, given the size of our brain, people can handle. There is still none of the haphazard design that we find in any randomly selected medium-to-large workplaces. The design feature at this level is that villages are organised into divisions.

For Societies #8 and #9 we are in Africa, this time on the savannah of Kenya to visit Maasai society and Samburu society. Most Maasai and Samburu still live their traditional village life as herders of cattle and goats. Samburu split from Maasai to form their own society, I was told, just a few centuries ago. Given that the split was relatively recent, the two societies are very similar. I visited Maasai in January 2016 and August 2017, and on the second trip I also visited Samburu society. Maasai and Samburu are examples of societies organised above the village into divisions. The contemporary Maasai and Samburu structure is like a large organisation structured as a conglomerate of independent divisions, without an executive team uniting all divisions. In fact, before 1963 Maasai society was organised as a nation. But after Kenya declared independence from Britain, the role of the paramount Maasai chief adapted into a role as the Maasai representative within the new republic. It was from that point that the Maasai divisions became the highest level of their organising structure.[15]

In Maasai society there are four layers of the organisation structure: Level 1 is the family; Level 2 is the village; Level 3 is an 'age set' (which I'll explain); and Level 4 is what I'm calling the 'division'.

While age set and division play a significant role in Maasai life, the building block of the society is still the family and village. A Maasai village, or *manyatta*, mostly numbers about 50 people, with some large villages numbering 100 to 150 people. During our 2016 visit to Kenya, my wife Jude and I met William Kinanta Sadera. William was our safari guide in the Maasai Mara region in southern Kenya. Between his brother and him helping Jude and me search for amazing animals such as a mother leopard and her two cubs, we had plenty of time to talk. While William works in the Western economy, he lives according to his traditions and when he's on a break between guiding shifts he heads home to his village.

'When I get home,' he told us, 'I always look forward to *real* food.'

'What's real food?' I asked, laughing.

'Milk mixed with cattle blood — *osaroi*,' he said, involuntarily licking his lips ever so slightly.

Some of my Maasai conversations were translated from Swahili, the common language of Kenya. In William's case, he has superb English skills. He told us he'd started school at age five. I asked him about his early memories.

'When school term ended and I headed home for holidays,' he began, 'I first had to find my village! A village moves following the rain and fresh grass for the cattle, so the first week of my school holidays was always spent wandering the savannah finding my family.'

'What did you do at night when you were searching for your family?' I asked, contemplating the wellbeing of a five-year-old on the African savannah.

'In our culture, we have a saying that "a child belongs to no one", meaning a child belongs to everyone. Back in those days, come sunset, whatever village I was near took me in and looked after me for the night. The next morning I'd set off again in search of my family.'

William's reference to his village prompted me to enquire about the population of his village as a key organising element. We were driving back to our safari camp having visited the monthly cattle market in the nearby town of Aitong. 'William,' I asked, cupping my hands as though holding the village population in a container, 'when your village packed up and moved site for the cattle, how many people are we talking about?'

He hesitated, obviously doing a rough count. 'My family lived in a pretty big village,' he said. He finished his count. 'About 150 people,' he said.

I laughed and told him that when he said a 'big village' I was anticipating his answer of 150. I told him about Dunbar's Number and the size of the human brain. He smiled, nodding at the explanation of the pattern he recognised in how his people are organised.

Later, William told me about the organisation levels above the family (Level 1) and the village (Level 2). Level 3 of the organisation is the age set, and Level 4 is the sequence of age sets that in effect form a division for organising the population. As I wrote this book, William generously clarified my understanding about Maasai society and confirmed or corrected my text.

An age set, Level 3 of the organisation structure, runs across a number of villages. An age set is formed when a generation of boys within a geographical district is organised for initiation as warriors (*moran*). Once established, the age set remains together for life. Each age set has a chief and a leadership group. Upon graduation from warriorhood, members of an age set are permitted to marry. Their wives become members of their husband's age set. The size of the age set varies, depending on the size of the district and the number of boys ready for circumcision. An age set might number between several hundred and several thousand young men. In William's age set, at the time it was formed in 1996, there were 500 boys.

The 'division', Level 4, is created by the series of age sets. When warriors graduate from warriorhood, they become junior elders. At this time a new age set will be formed below them. Above the junior elders are the older age sets, the number of these depending on surviving members of the oldest age sets. As an example, in William's line, the age sets that form the division, in order of seniority, are Inyanguzi, Iseuri, Ikitoip, Ikishili, Ilmejooli, Ilmeshuki le tatene, Ilmeshuki le kejienye and the recently formed Ilmirisho. Through the series of age sets, thousands of people are organised into an effective, harmonious organisation. We will see in Chapter 2 that the nature of leadership and orderly decision making in Maasai society matches the series of age sets.

From the savannah of eastern Africa, we travel to the abundant North Pacific Ocean and Haida society — Society #10 of the 12. The rich marine resources along the northwest coast of America and Canada supported large permanent settlements. Haida territory is the archipelago of Haida Gwaii in northern Canada and the nearby coast of Alaska. I visited Haida Gwaii in June 2018. Haida society is organised at the division level. But the two building blocks still exist — individuals being part of a family and families aggregating into a group, the size of which suits our brain. In traditional times, Haida families lived in longhouses, or lodges, accommodating several families up to a total of about 50 people.[16] A grouping of longhouses formed a town, with a large town potentially comprising several hundred people, though the main unit for belonging remained the longhouse. My host, Elsie Gale, told me that in the summer months, including in her childhood, the population of a large town would scatter in smaller family groups of around 25 to 30 people to fish and collect berries in preparation for the long northern winter. Haida society is organised above the layer of the longhouse and the town. The main organisation level coordinating the longhouses was the sub-division of the relevant clan to which the people belonged (a sub-division of the Eagle or the Raven moieties). The sub-division, or sub-clan, was the highest level of social organisation.[17] In traditional times, the estimated population of 9000 people was organised into 40 sub-divisions (or sub-clans).[18]

The Great Plains of North America also supported large concentrations of people, thanks mainly to immense herds of buffalo (nowadays called bison). Society #11 is the Blackfeet nation (Blackfoot in Canada). I mentioned in the Introduction that the COVID-19 pandemic caused me to cancel my visit to Montana planned for May 2020. In preparation for the trip I read extensively about Blackfeet society, including books recommended by my would-be host, so I am including the society in this book. There is plenty of anthropological information about traditional Blackfeet society. Unlike First Peoples in the American eastern states, Blackfeet and their neighbours only experienced wagon waves of settlers and gold enthusiasts from the 1860s, and Blackfeet was the last nation to reach a treaty with the American government. Not only is this period relatively recent, but by that stage anthropology was emerging as a discipline so the social life of traditional Blackfeet society is well documented, including from the stories of people who remembered the old life.

The organisation design challenge for Blackfeet was of the same magnitude as a substantial workplace: how to organise a population of 20,000 people.[19] The solution involved the fundamentals of family and band. The primary organising feature was hunting bands of 10 to 30 families numbering 50 to 200 people.[20] People lived most of the year in their band and then in summer for a few weeks the bands gathered in their higher-level division for celebrations, rituals and marriage partnering.[21] This higher level of organisation was one of three divisions: the Piegan Blackfeet (or Pikuni), the Kainah (or Blood) and the Siksika (or Blackfoot or Northern Blackfoot). The three divisions were independent and the extent of their affiliation was, generally, to support each other in times of war against common enemies. The jump from the band of about 150 people to the division of thousands is a big jump for the purposes of organising a population. So, like the Maasai system of age sets, Blackfeet sub-divided their massive divisions into fraternities. The Piegan division had 24 fraternities, with names such as Black Patched Moccasins, Blackfat Roasters and Small Robes.[22] As with the other societies, the family/band/division provided an effective structure enabling peaceful and productive relationships of a large population.

For large workplaces, the blueprint emerging from Maasai, Haida and Blackfeet societies is to organise people into small family-sized teams of about seven people, which then aggregate into departments of up to about 150 people which then combine to form divisions of between about 500 and 1,500 people in the division (roughly seven departments forming the division). That same blueprint continues as we look at a society of 25,000 people organised as a confederacy of nations.

3. Societies Organised at the Level of Nation

The highest level of organisation structure in traditional societies is the organisation of the whole nation. Yet even here the building blocks are small family units aggregating into units that the human brain can handle.

From the Great Plains we travel to the eastern side of North America to visit the Mohawk nation — Society #12, our final society. The Mohawk nation was the only society I visited that was organised to the level of the nation, and, in fact, in their case, as part of a confederation with other common-language nations to form the Haudenosaunee, or Iroquois, confederacy. Traditional Mohawk Territory is primarily in eastern New York state. The southern boundary was the Catskill Mountains in New York, the northern boundary was the St. Lawrence River Valley in southern Quebec and Ontario, Canada. The eastern boundary was the Green Mountains in Vermont and the western boundary was around present-day Utica in New York state.[23] Historically, the Mohawk nation and their neighbours were at war but about 1000 years ago a wise man of the Onondaga nation, another of the Haudenosaunee nations, persuaded his nation and the neighbouring nations that they should end the bloodshed and live in peace. This wise man was a great law maker and gave the nations 'The Great Law of Peace', the constitution of the Haudenosaunee League of Nations. Initially the confederacy comprised five nations and subsequently, in 1715, expanded to include a sixth nation.

In the early days of the colonial era, the Mohawk nation with the wider Haudenosaunee confederacy numbered about 25,000 people. Of that number, Mohawk numbered about 5000 citizens and, perhaps prior to the devastating impact of smallpox, the Mohawk population could have been about 11,000 people.[24] That's a major organisational challenge. Like the other societies we have considered, the design blueprint of families aggregating into groups of up to about 150 people provided the solution for the large population to function peacefully and productively.

The Kahnawà:ke Mohawk community near Montreal warmly welcomed me to their territory when I visited in June 2018. In making my inquiries to visit, I had the good fortune of being introduced to Kimberly Kaniehténhawe Cross, the manager of the appropriately named Welcome Center of the Kahnawà:ke Tourism Office. Kahnawà:ke (pronounced Garn-a-wah-gay) is home to about 8000 people. Kimberly and I had been in touch through email and telephone for months leading up to my visit, and how delightful it was, felt mutually, I think, to finally meet. I mentioned in the Introduction of this book that when I thanked her for warmly responding to my request to visit, she replied that she felt honoured that I was including Mohawk society in my research. Such is her grace and generosity. She organised a busy itinerary for me to meet 10 senior people, who generously gave their time and shared their knowledge.

Kimberly and my main conversation took place over lunch at a café near the banks of the St. Lawrence River. She was soon describing 'family' as the building block in Mohawk society. The theme of family as the key economic unit in Mohawk society is celebrated when a couple marry. In traditional times, the bride visited the home of her intended husband and presented to her future mother-in-law a few cakes of corn bread. The groom's mother reciprocated by giving to the bride's mother venison (deer) or other game hunted by the groom.[25] The sharing of gifts — corn associated with the primary female contribution from the fields and meat associated with the primary male contribution from the forest — represents the ability of the couple to provide for their household and to form a successful economic unit. In the modern version of this tradition, Kimberly told me, the bride and groom feed the longhouse, the ceremonial centre of the community. The bride provides corn bread and corn mush. The groom provides the meat.

'The gifts to the longhouse,' Kimberly said, 'show that the bride and groom can take care of each other and can take care of guests.'

While Mohawk society is organised as a nation as part of a confederation, the building block of family aggregating in a unit of about 80 people — the longhouse — was the key feature in traditional times. The longhouse is the equivalent of the band or village found in other societies. I was keen to find out what life was like in Mohawk society before the impact of Europeans. European impact goes back a long time. The Mohawk and other Haudenosaunee nations, placed as they are near the Atlantic coast, were among the first native North America peoples to experience European contact. The French arrived in Canada in 1534 followed by the Dutch through New Amsterdam (New York) in 1609. Because colonisation is so long ago, one of my challenges was to find material that documented life prior to European influence, or at least before significant influence. One gem I found is the diary of a visit to Mohawk Country in 1634. The book gives insight into both the abundant food resources that supported large aggregations of people and also the way the population was organised.

The early attraction for Europeans in North America was fur trading, mainly beaver furs. The local people trapped the beavers and traded with the Europeans. In the early 1630s, the Dutch were concerned that attempts by the French to the north to establish a truce with the Mohawk nation might destroy the fur trade between the Mohawks and the Dutch. In 1634, the commander of the Fort Orange Dutch settlement sent a young surgeon-barber, Harmen Meyndertsz van den Bogaert, and two colleagues to investigate the issue and to reassure the local people of the interest of the Dutch to trade beaver furs on attractive terms. The commercial value of the fur trade was stunning. Even by 1650, after years of hunting beavers, the number of pelts from just the Mohawk Valley in New York numbered 80,000 in just that one year.[26] The furs mainly ended up in Europe as hats worn by wealthy people. To protect the fur trade, van den Bogaert led his small expedition into Mohawk and Oneida country in the winter of 1634–35. Fortunately, he kept a diary which, through an amazing set of circumstances, has survived.

Van den Bogaert described the Mohawk's large settlements, or 'castles' as he called them. What impressive structures they must have been. Castles were fortified with palisades of long sharp posts. Archaeological evidence indicates that castles endured for up to about 100 years before people relocated.[27] Van den Bogaert visited one large castle comprising 66 longhouses protected by a double row of palisades measuring 767 steps — a substantial settlement.[28] Longhouses were generally '100 steps long' and 22 feet (7 metres) wide constructed of cedar poles and massive sheets of elm bark.[29] Here we spot the organising unit matching the size of our brain. Each longhouse housed about 50 to 80 people. Longhouses contained a series of compartments down both sides of a central aisle, with each compartment housing a nuclear family.[30] Nuclear families numbered about four to eight members.[31] Each family had their own cooking hearth and shared, with the family opposite, a larger hearth for heating. Van den Bogaert and his two companions were made welcome at most towns, enjoying foods such as 'bread with chestnuts, dried blueberries and sunflower seeds baked in it'.[32] The abundance of food was astonishing. One day he witnessed people catch 'six, seven or eight hundred salmon'.[33] No wonder large populations could be supported.

The Mohawk nation and the wider Haudenosaunee confederation was a complex society in terms of the size of the population and the level to which it was organised. As we would imagine with a large workplace, the Mohawk organising structure didn't jump from a longhouse to 5000 Mohawk and 25,000 Haudenosaunee citizens. There are mid-level organising layers allowing the population to be coordinated and to build up a sense of belonging. Beyond the longhouses and towns, Mohawk citizens are members of a clan (equivalent to what I am calling a division in this book). The three Mohawk clans are the turtle, the bear and the wolf clans, and each clan has a further three sub-clans. Children belong to their mother's sub-clan. Hence, the society was, in traditional times, built up from family to longhouse to sub-clan to clan to nation to confederacy. The sub-clan to confederacy levels still apply. And as we will find in the next chapter, the nature of leadership follows that level of organisation.

'Families' and 'Villages' in Workplaces

It's highly improbable that traditional societies across every continent shared their solution for organising their population. It's almost guaranteed that the pattern developed independently because it was found to work over the long timeframe of experience. My proposition is that the design works for humans. A consequence of this wisdom of traditional societies is that, rather than reinventing a very, very old wheel, workplace leaders can choose to use the design for organising their own population. Let's look at four examples where organising the workplace on family and village units is the key design concept. And the examples show that the design is scalable to large workplaces.

Flight Centre operates in the global travel industry. The company employs 20,000 staff (pre COVID-19) and credits as fundamental to its success the structuring of its organisation on the principle of families and villages. In its retail stores, call centres and central functions, Flight Centre has teams of no more than seven people. Graham Turner, the founding (and still) managing director, told me that in the early days of their operation, growing from a few stores in Australia, he and his leaders noticed that productivity dropped if a busy retail store grew beyond six or seven staff. And Flight Centre has a clear productivity measure: sales per sales representative. Turner said that in those early days, seeing the negative productivity impact, he and his senior team decided stores would have no more than seven staff. Flight Centre became famous for preferring to open a second store in a busy neighbourhood rather than adding more staff to a store that already numbered seven people. The company prefers to pay the extra infrastructure costs of a second store rather than suffer the predictable decline in productivity that accompanies a team larger than seven.

When he was Flight Centre's Human Resources Director, Michael Murphy told me, 'Any time we compromised the rule of seven and even had eight staff in a store, productivity dropped. From painful experience, we will not compromise team size — our family team — of seven in number. This family unit is a foundation of our business, in terms of both the connection of people and the accountability for performance. The same applies to contact centres and corporate functions. In the early days of our call centres, we wondered why engagement and productivity were low.

When we reminded ourselves about family-sized teams and restructured into teams of seven, things quickly improved.'

Flight Centre aggregates family-sized teams into villages of around 80 staff. These 'villages' are geographically based, usually a district of a large city. Flight Centre wisely knows that it's beyond human comprehension for people to connect to a group of 20,000 people. However, they also know that an organisation *can* have highly engaged staff if there is a strong sense of belonging at the family and village level.

Gore Associates uses the building block of 150 people to organise their workforce. Gore, the maker of Gore-Tex among other things, is a highly regarded employer. When Gore builds a new facility, it tends to build facilities that will be staffed by about 150 people. A facility's car park will have enough spaces for only 150 cars. When the car park starts to reach capacity, it's time to build a new facility. A manager of the company told me that this design principle means that even on the few larger campuses, buildings are spread out so people are in units of no more than about 150 people.

When I was HR Director of a global professional services firm, I experienced the dysfunction that arises from an organisation design that deviated from the natural principle I have outlined here. We fixed the problem by implementing family units. At the time, one part of the structure complied with the ancestral wisdom of family and village, but one part violated it. The 'village' part worked well, with staff organised into operating units of around 80 people. A 'village' consisted of people in the same professional discipline within a location, such as rail and road transport engineers in Sydney. The problem was, with the growth of the business, these operating units had grown over the years from small units closer to the size of a big family to now being the size of a village. As the operating units grew in size, so too did the job of the operations managers. As this happened, there was no organising unit inserted below the village — there was no family unit. As happens when organisations deviate from nature, a role of 'section manager' informally emerged as a workaround. The section manager was an informal leader of a unit of seven or eight specialists, assigned to look after the small team to make things work given the now unrealistic job of the 'village' operations manager. But the section managers had no formal responsibility, no delegated accountability, no training in people leadership and no time allocated to attend to the increasing demands of supporting and coordinating people. Further, the staff were confused about when to go to the section manager and when to go to the operations manager. The confusion showed in the form of high attrition among young, highly billable professionals and thus as declining revenue. When we formalised the structure into family units led by a section manager who in turn reported to the 'village' operations manager, it was as though we'd flicked a switch and people were freed from their frustration. The dysfunction disappeared, staff retention improved and revenue increased.

The experience of one client organisation that implemented families and villages shows that the structure does not have to be implemented as a one-off massive restructure project. In this case, families and villages were implemented at different times in different divisions. This approach was possible because almost all of the senior managers were educated in the ancestral design as part of a wider leadership development program. As the opportunity arose, and on their own volition because the approach made sense, the senior managers implemented the design in their part of the business. After a few years, through this smooth and seamless approach, most of the organisation was designed on the family/village model.

The organisation operates in urban transport. Key performance metrics are safety, on-time running of services, revenue, profit and customer satisfaction. All metrics improved, in each department, as the family/village structure was implemented. Take for example the department of train drivers. As part of the implementation of 'families', train drivers were organised into units of five to seven drivers compared to the previous structure of much larger departments. With a greater sense of belonging, clearer management accountability and managers now having the time to support train drivers, engagement lifted and absenteeism of drivers declined significantly meaning more drivers attended for work each shift. More train drivers meant fewer cancelled trains, a win for the business and for commuters. Safety improved with the lost-time injuries falling by half over 12 months. Other departments showed similar improvements following the implementation of families and villages. As one senior manager observed in becoming aware of the ancestral design, 'This is a no-brainer. Our structure is all wrong. The poor design means people are "chasing their tails". There's a lack of planning, higher management is dragged down to operational issues and there's a lack of accountability to see things through.'

Readers of my *Hardwired Humans* book will not be surprised that the principles behind the building blocks of ancestral societies — families and villages — apply equally to the modern workplace. The power of the principle derives from its universal application across ancestral societies — there is no exception that I'm aware of. Clients in different industries ranging from heavy industry to the not-for-profit sector have applied this ancestral organising principle. All have experienced improvements in engagement and productivity from the better organisation design.

Actions for Workplace Leaders

What are the implications of this analysis for workplace leaders? The experience of First Nation societies points to concrete actions for workplace leaders to structure their workforce that will best assist the creation of a strong sense of belonging and to help people do their best work.

1. **Keep organisational structure on your radar:** Within the scope of senior leadership roles, the subject of organisation design should feature prominently on your radar. From my experience, there are many senior executives who don't consider organisation structure as a key systems decision and they lack a set of guiding principles for organising their workforce. Roles that carry the responsibility to design the system of work include business owners, chief executives, divisional executives and human resources and organisation design executives. People in these roles should have a point of view — a mental model or conceptual framework — about effective design principles. The conceptual framework goes to your view of the primary economic unit of your organisation (the family unit), your view about the best way to aggregate those units to give people a sense of belonging and accountability and, conversely, your view about the maximum group size beyond which belonging and performance erode. Designing around the principles used by

ancestral societies, I propose, is compelling because they point to what's natural for humans. As one client CEO said as she opened a workshop where her executive team was about to consider organisation design, 'If not based on human nature, what then?'

2. **Design your organisation around 'family units' of about seven people:** The first unit of design is the family unit as the primary economic unit of society or a workplace. The principle from traditional societies, proven in the long timeframe of their experience, is that people should be part of a team of about seven people, plus or minus two. This means a manager has no fewer than four direct reports and no more than eight. It's no coincidence that survey company Gallup, in its global research of staff engagement, finds that engagement levels drop significantly in teams larger than 10 people, compared with teams smaller than ten.

3. **Organise leadership teams with about seven members:** At each level of the hierarchy including the top level, leadership teams should number about seven members. The more we deviate from this principle the more difficult it is to maintain cohesion, clarity of accountability and efficient decision making. A major element of a team of about seven means that the divisional or executive team leader has a direct line-of-sight over the subjects that represents their responsibilities. An executive team larger than about nine members means the leader is skating across too many subjects and also that accountability for outputs among team members will be duplicated and confused. A leadership team that's too small, with fewer than five direct reports, almost guarantees the leader will not have a direct line-of-sight to the subjects they should be directly across in order to be in touch with key aspects of their responsibility, to ensure risk is managed and to ensure balanced decision making. I've seen examples of both forms of dysfunction in top teams — executive teams too large or too small. I once walked into a meeting room for a first meeting with an executive team of a prospective client. I was surprised to find 12 leaders sitting around the table, and wondered about both the reason for that large number and the likely dysfunction arising from the structure. The reason

later became clear: following a restructure a year or so before, the state managers no longer reported to the CEO, but the CEO hadn't wanted to disappoint the state managers by excluding them from the executive team meetings. They continued to attend along with their own manager. The dysfunction meant that there was confusion as to the responsibilities of the state managers and their leader, and confusion as to the state managers' relationship with the CEO. The confusion was corrected when the state managers were told, sensitively, that they were no longer part of the top team, which they readily accepted as the current situation made no sense to them. At the other end of the spectrum of too few leaders reporting to the CEO, the standout example was an aged care organisation. The CEO had only three direct reports, and the practical effect of the design meant that the CEO had delegated too much responsibility into the hands of a Chief Operations Officer. This meant, among other undesirable things, that the CEO had distanced himself from the key functions of the organisation. The dysfunction was removed with a restructure and the removal of the COO role.

4. **Design 'villages' of *up to about* 150 people:** Above the small family team as the primary economic unit, the second unit of design should be departments or operating units the size of villages numbering *up to about* 150 people, with a sweet-spot of around 80 people. A group of this size is driven by the capacity of our brains and the size of a group in which people, with effective leadership, gain a strong sense of belonging and mutual accountability to deliver. Large organisations should be structured in blocks of about this number. There is no limit to the number of villages.

5. **Structure village membership according to a compelling purpose:** In deciding the basis on which the village-sized group will be organised, priority should be given to a compelling purpose for people being organised together. Ideally, people should be grouped together on the basis that they are delivering a service or product to clients — this keeps people grounded in reality. For example, it's more powerful to organise people according to a project outcome rather than as members of a professional discipline. Or for

example, being together for the purpose of operating an aged care facility is more compelling than according to people's functional discipline. Being grouped together for a compelling — real — reason gives people greater unity of purpose and pride in delivery.

6. **Organise villages into divisions:** For large organisations, as we saw in such diverse societies as Maasai and Haida nations, 'villages' should be organised into divisions. Divisions will number between about 500 and 1,500 people (seven departments of about 80 people up to nine departments of 150 people or a little more). As we covered with the unlimited number of 'villages' in large organisations, there is no limit to the number of divisions.

7. **Monitor spans and layers:** Monitoring the 'spans' and 'layers' of your organisation is an effective way to check that the principle of families and villages is being effectively implemented. The 'span' (the number of people reporting to a manager) will be driven by managers having about seven direct reports. This in turn drives the number of 'layers' (the number of hierarchical levels from the top to the bottom of the organisation). Calculating the desired spans and layers means the organisation will avoid too few or too many managers. It's important to include both spans and layers in your design. Specifying layers without spans leads to dysfunctional design. For example, some organisations, driven only by layers, might say, 'From the CEO to the bottom of the organisation there will be no more than five layers of management'. But in organisations numbering thousands of people, that objective can only be achieved if managers have huge teams reporting to them; teams perhaps numbering fifty people. Teams anywhere near that size cannot be functional and a manager cannot hope to support or hold accountable that number of direct reports. Enforcing the design principle of just enough layers and spans means that the organisation avoids managers with huge teams or, at the other end of the spectrum, managers with just one, two or three direct reports which leads to people being over-managed and controlled. We will return to this topic in the next chapter when we look at traditional societies having just enough leaders according to the

level at which their society is organised — they have clear layers of leadership.

8. **Avoid matrix reporting — ensure everyone is a member of a single family and village:** At any point in time, an individual employee should be part of only one family unit and one village. That is, an individual, at any moment in time, should have only one manager to whom they report. This means that matrix reporting is futile. Matrix reporting, where people report to two or more managers and are part of two or more teams, is unnatural. The frustration most people experience with matrix reporting is indicative of its dysfunction. In ancestral societies, people are part of one village. Being expected to be part of two operating units in a workplace erodes group identity and performance accountability. People can get lost, or receive duplicate directions from two managers with competing priorities. People calculate their primary unit, which most often is the one that controls resources, and they treat that unit as their place of membership. They pay lip-service to the other unit forced upon them. This doesn't mean that a person can't have a dotted-line customer relationship with an internal client. That works fine. The problem arises if we kid ourselves that it's going to work for staff to have two bosses with equal influence. Matrix reporting became fashionable about 20 years ago. Having observed the introduction of matrix reporting, my observation is that the idea was motivated around trying to simplify large complex organisations. But it didn't achieve that, and is an over-engineered attempt that dilutes and confuses accountability. Life in mega, global organisations is complex enough without complex design. The better approach is to keep it as simple as possible.

9. **Enable family and village members to work closely together:** There are other systems or design decisions that support — or alternatively, undermine — membership of a team and a village. One example is the physical connection between members of a team. Leaders who are persuaded by the design principle of family and village will have a *preference* to organise people into operating units that are physically connected — in the same office. Of course,

in today's global economy, it's often not feasible to have team members and team leaders in the same location. But given human nature, it's easier and more conducive to team identity if team and village members are in face-to-face contact with each other. Where teams are dispersed, team members and their leader have to work harder at social cohesion. A second design decision relates to office layout — where people sit. 'Family' identity is enhanced if team members sit together, as against the trend to activity-based (or hot) desking (where on any day a work station is allocated randomly to any spot in the building). While activity-based desking uses real estate in a more cost-effective way than allocated desks, it comes at a cost. The cost is reduced connection between team members. If you are persuaded to implement hot-desks, then the best approach is to at least have neighbourhoods where 'family' and 'village' members sit close together.

We will see in the next chapter how the structuring of leadership roles matches the organising model of the society. And we'll see the dysfunction that occurs through the annual experience of the Bushmen if the nature of leadership does not match the level of social organisation.

CHAPTER 2

Nature of Leadership

'Every camp had a leader. Leaders would settle quarrels and keep the peace.'

LEADERSHIP WAS **THE** GREAT social invention of ancestral humans. Without leadership, groups could not function harmoniously. And without layers of leadership, societies could not grow from bands and villages to divisions and nations. Without leadership we wouldn't have cities and countries. And without leadership we wouldn't have workplaces.

The development of leadership allowed early humans to do something no other primate species could do. While a form of leadership is present in every primate species, it's limited to small groups. The organising ability of chimpanzees, for example, is limited to communities of about 50 individuals (I know something about chimps from my time with chimp researcher Dr Jane Goodall and with zoo keepers). The limit to the size of a chimp community corresponds to the brain size of chimps per Dunbar's analysis mentioned in Chapter 1. Chimps can't organise at the level of the forest. But the nature of leadership that emerged for humans meant that we could organise much larger groups than our band or village. We broke out of the band constraint and could organise into clans and divisions and nations. We can organise massive organisations. This is a remarkable achievement that we could only accomplish because of leadership. The presence of leadership in human societies is universal, all societies having a leadership or executive function that serves to facilitate orderly social interactions. Leadership is present in every First Nations society I investigated, although there is variability in the nature of leadership in the different societies. Importantly, the nature of leadership varies to match the level at which each society is organised. The 12 societies I investigated have a style of leadership that we readily recognise, with the exception of Pintupi Aboriginal society where leadership takes a different form. As we will see in Chapter 7, in Pintupi society leadership arises from the spiritual Dreaming period and is irrevocably linked to the privileged acquisition of knowledge and not human intervention. But even here, although the nature of leadership is different to the Western sense, there is still the existence of respected elders with social influence supporting a well-functioning society.

This chapter looks at the nature, or design, of leadership roles. In the next chapter we will look at the attributes required for leadership roles in First Nation societies, universally. As we begin this discussion of my findings on the nature of leadership in First Nation societies, there are three key implications that underpin the discussion. The first is that, given leadership is universal, leaders at each level of the organisation should be reassured that their role as leader is vital for the functioning of the group. The second implication is that there are obligations that come with taking a leadership role; in workplaces we are not conscripted to leadership, so seeking or accepting a leadership role should be done alive to the social obligations of the role. The third implication is that workplace leadership roles should be at distinct layers to avoid overloading the organisation with too many leaders or indeed not enough leaders. We need leaders at the level of the family, the village, the division and the nation. But we don't need extra leaders squeezed in distorting the layers.

Bushmen society provides a case study on the nature of leadership and helps explain why leadership is universal. After considering Bushmen society, we'll then step through the levels of leadership in other societies that expanded from bands and villages to divisions and nations — a valuable template for the levels of leadership in workplaces.

Bushmen Society and the Nature of Leadership

As a hunter-gatherer society, Bushmen society represents the original human organisation. Bushmen society reveals three fundamental aspects of leadership that we will walk through. First, the key functions of leadership that explain why leadership is universal. Second, the problems that arise if the levels of leadership don't match the level of organisation structure (the workplace equivalent of not having department or divisional leaders doing their job). And third, the perpetual responsibility of the leader having to decide who joins the group and occasionally who needs to be expelled from the group.

1. Every Camp Had a Leader

Each of the three older Bushmen I met told me about the leader of their camp back in the old days. In my conversation with 70-year-old Komtsa, sitting in the Kalahari sand as the day warmed up, I wanted to ask him about the nature of leadership in his society. But I needed to raise the subject in a way that didn't guide him to use terms that he would not otherwise use. I didn't ask, for example, 'Did you have a leader in your camp?' If I'd asked that question, first, he might have felt inclined to please me by simply giving a 'yes' answer and second, I would have been uncertain about the validity of his answer. As my first boss, Norm Amos, taught me about presenting evidence in an industrial tribunal, I had to avoid leading the witness. Instead, I asked Komtsa an open question about how the camp functioned. In his answer, he introduced the term *camp leader*. That allowed me to ask about the role. In the camp of his teenage years, he told me that his paternal grandfather, Bo, 'was the camp leader. Bo chose the place to live. He started the camp and asked others to join him.' Komtsa told me that part of Bo's role as leader was to try to resolve quarrels that inevitably occurred. 'The leader would stand up and try their best to solve the problems. People could start fighting and using bows and arrows. Bo would talk to people to try to resolve the problem.'

Leaders intervening to reduce tension resonated with my experience in workplaces, including, periodically, of my own team.

Several other functions of a camp leader were added by another Bushman who grew up living the old life. About a half-day's drive north from Komtsa's community, near the town of Grashoek, I met 60-year-old !Gao !Naioi. He and I had two meetings on consecutive days. A young Bushman, Ghau, translated Ju/'hoan to English.

The Ju/'hoan language is one of the Khoisan 'click' languages and listening to !Gao and Ghau converse, waiting for the English translation, was like listening to music. While there are sounds that we recognise, their conversation was richly sprinkled with a variety of clicks. Linguistic anthropologists invented symbols to indicate the clicks in the various Bushmen languages. In the case of the '!' symbol in !Gao's name, the symbol indicates a 'pop' click.

In conducting my research, my preference was to talk with people one-on-one, and not as a group if I could avoid it. By talking with individuals, my aim was to avoid any groupthink or one person influencing another, which would cause me to doubt the validity of the information. The approach also allowed me to be flexible and allow the discussion to go in the direction the person wanted to take it. And of course, meeting one-on-one helped build rapport with the individual.

Building rapport with !Gao was easy. He came to our first meeting with a bow and a quiver of arrows (I later learned his bow and arrows were for demonstration purposes, not the real thing). I'd read a lot about the traditional method of hunting, and the poison arrows used by Bushmen. I asked !Gao about his first kill of a large antelope. I knew that would have been a coming-of-age moment for !Gao as a young man, showing that he was ready to provide for a family — to start a new economic unit. He beamed and told me his first kill was an eland (the largest antelope and the most prized animal because of the high fat content of the meat). He told me how he stalked the eland until he was close enough — about 20 paces — to fire an arrow. The arrow struck, and the poison slowly did its work. !Gao tracked the animal for three days before it died. !Gao couldn't carry all the meat on his own, so he signalled his family to move camp to join him.

'To signal my family to come to me, I lit a grass fire. They signalled back by lighting their own fire. They were telling me that they are on their way and for me to stay with the meat.' The Bushmen's tracking skills were so good that his family knew they were following !Gao's footprints, heading in the right direction, and not falsely following someone else's footprints.

In his early years, !Gao lived in a band of around 10 to 15 people which included his grandparents, mother and father and siblings. !Gao was the eldest of five children. As we talked about his early experiences, he also used the term *camp leader*. In his childhood camp his grandfather was the camp leader.

'Every camp had a leader,' he said. 'The leader might be male or female. The leader was the teacher who knows the whole of nature and passes on all that information. A key decision was about hunting and where to go hunting. The decision of the leader on where to hunt was always obeyed. Another decision was about marriage — my grandfather decided the marriage partner of all family members. Leaders would settle quarrels and keep the peace. The leader wouldn't quarrel.'

'What did people quarrel about?' I asked.

'If people picked food too early, there would be arguments. Or if people from another band came and harvested your food, there would be problems. You had to ask permission to pick food,' he said.

As !Gao explained the number of decisions the leader made or influenced, I imagined an important decision *someone* had to make was what to do if other people wanted to join the camp — the equivalent of hiring new people to an organisation. 'What would happen,' I asked, 'if other people arrived and wanted to live in your camp?'

'My grandfather decided whether other people were welcome to join the camp,' he said.

That sounded like a delicate moment if a family was denied their request to settle in the camp, like giving bad news to an unsuccessful job candidate. 'What did your grandfather say to the visitors if he did not permit them to join the camp?' I asked. I was impressed with the delicate way rejection was expressed.

'My grandfather would say, "Go past to the place you are going."'

Not surprisingly, Komtsa and !Gao's explanation about leadership from their early years matched what anthropologists living with Bushmen found in the 1950s and 1960s. While anthropologists found that there was not a leader with the authority of a village headman that we will see in a moment, there were patterns of leadership. Anthropologist Richard Lee, the leading researcher of Bushmen, observed that in group discussions the people with the leadership mantle spoke out more than others, were often deferred to by others and 'one gets the feeling that their opinions hold a bit more weight than the opinions of other (people)'.[1] One of the daily group discussions involved allocating tasks for the next day. In an average size camp of 25 people, two groups of five to six people might be assigned to gather plant food, probably with the two groups going in different directions. The hunters decided whether they would go alone or perhaps in pairs. Several adults, perhaps those who gathered food the day before, would stay in camp to look after the older people and the weaned infants who could play in camp rather than be out with their mothers gathering food. Some of the people who stayed in camp would likely collect water in the cool of the late afternoon.

One of the aspects of Bushmen leadership observed by anthropologists resonated with an example of good leadership that I've experienced through my career. Marjorie Shostak found that key individuals 'function very much as group leaders ... These people tend to be more prominent in group discussions, to make their opinions known and their suggestions clear, and to articulate the consensus once it is determined.'[2] This last element of articulating the consensus of a discussion reminded me of a good leader I observed at IBM early in my career. This leader, who later progressed high in the IBM global hierarchy, had a wonderful way of facilitating team meetings. When making important decisions, he was keen for each person to share their opinion, keen to have a free-wheeling discussion and to see if a consensus emerged. If a consensus emerged, like a good Bushmen leader, he summarised the decision. If a consensus didn't emerge, he willingly made the decision (sometimes different to his view at the start of the meeting). Team members felt engaged in the process and were supportive of the outcome.

A key element of leadership of a nomadic band is that the leader's position by itself provided relatively little power over the group. The leader mainly operated through influence and persuasion. If Bo or any other leader in a nomadic society tried to operate as an autocratic figure, camp members would generally resent such leadership. The easy response from a disgruntled camp member was to pack up and move out. Bushmen had only about 12 kgs (26 lbs) of possessions — try that next time you go on vacation — so packing up and moving on wouldn't have taken great resolve and wouldn't have taken long. If enough people moved on, the band collapsed.

The tactful style of leadership in Bushmen society was a fit for the nature of the relationships between members of a nomadic camp. The camp generally comprised extended relatives, mainly parents and their older daughters with sons-in-law who were performing 'bride service' (young men were obliged to hunt meat for their bride's family). Sons-in-law were motivated to keep on good terms with their bride's parents — to be considered as good 'team members' in order to retain membership of the group and remain betrothed to their bride. The remaining band members were friends: people who chose to be in each other's company and who the leader was happy to have in their camp. In this social dynamic of relatives and friends living together, authoritative leadership was not required and would have been a mismatch to the nature of the society.

The first lesson, then, from Bushmen society is that the leadership role is present in order to provide key functions to the group. Leaders like Komtsa's grandfather, Bo, decided where to live and who could join the group; they led the discussion of task allocation; and they led the attempted resolution of quarrels to restore peace and harmony. We'll look in a moment at the occasional need to expel a member of the camp.

2. The Problems if the Leadership Structure Doesn't Match the Organisation Structure

The second lesson from Bushmen society as a case study is the fatal short-coming if the nature of leadership doesn't grow to match the level at which the society is organised — even going from a band of around 25 people to a group of up to about 150 people creates problems if there is no leader of that larger group.

In the annual dry period in the Kalahari, water is scarce and is limited to a few permanent waterholes. In that dry period in traditional times, bands gathered in concentrated numbers at those few permanent waterholes and now rather than groups numbering up to about 30 people, they numbered up to 150 people. In his 1960s' studies, well before Dunbar's analysis of group size driven by brain size, anthropologist Richard Lee found that 'two to six groups camped together at a permanent waterhole generally numbered 80 to 120 people and we never found the concentrations to be larger than 150 individuals'.[3] Apart from the pressing need for water, the gatherings were times of social celebrations including trance dancing, gift trading and arranging marriage partners.

The big problem, though, was that none of the leaders of the bands of about 25 people functioned as the leader of the 150 people now gathered. A role didn't exist at that level, and no one had the authority, nor probably the desire, to take it on. What happened with this leadership gap is exactly what we would imagine in a workplace where there are team leaders but no department or division leaders (or where people appointed as department and division leaders do not act as leaders). Without a leader of this temporarily larger Bushmen organisation, the larger gatherings were dysfunctional. People had no way to peacefully resolve the disagreements that invariably arose; no one filled the role of adjudicator to listen to grievances and to relieve the tension by proposing a solution. People were soon at each other's throats. When I asked !Gao about tensions and arguments, he told me, 'Remember, we had poison arrows.' And there was no antidote for the poison. While Bushmen had no weapons of war, arrows often started flying during these heated arguments. Bystanders ran as much risk of being killed as the adversaries. One 1960s' study, analysing data over a number of years, found that Bushmen had a homicide rate close to the level of notorious crime centres of that era, such as Detroit and Cleveland in America. Most homicides occurred during the time when large groups gathered.[4] People could not live in these larger groups for very long. As soon as fresh rains fell, the large groups dispersed — back to the band level where people could live harmoniously. Back to the level of their leadership.

Interestingly, during the time he lived with them, Lee found that there was one large concentration of about 150 Bushmen which, as an exception, stayed together for nine months. How could such a large group stay together for so long without a leader? The answer is that they were in the vicinity of a camp of Herero people. When a dispute erupted amongst the Bushmen and people were trading blows, and hopefully before poison arrows started flying, someone ran to the Herero headman who would 'intervene, separate the combatants and mediate the dispute'.[5] The Bushmen couldn't resolve the dispute themselves — they had no leadership in the camp of 150 people — so the Herero headman took on that level of leadership by default.

3. Three Warnings and You're Out

We have covered two of the three elements of Bushmen as an example of leadership in hunter-gatherer societies: first, the functions of leadership that point to why leadership is universal; and second, the problems if the levels of leadership don't match the level at which the group is organised. The third element shows that even leaders in a small band had the unrelenting responsibility of leaders of all human groups: periodically, the Bushmen leader might need to expel a member from the group. As workplace leaders know, me included, dealing with individuals who are disrupting team harmony is a challenge, but one that sometimes needs to be occasionally exercised. As a leadership educator, I know that 'managing poor performers' is always towards the top of the list of the development needs of leaders. From Komtsa and !Gao, I learned that this leadership challenge is as old as human society. They also told me about their grandfathers' approach to this constant leadership challenge.

In my conversation with 70-year-old Komtsa, I took him back to what he was telling me about tension within the band, and his grandfather Bo's efforts to resolve the tension and restore peaceful relationships. I was keen to find out what happened if an individual continued causing trouble.

'I imagine,' I said to Komtsa, the sun now hot even in winter, 'that in a camp of 25 people there were times when a person was being difficult or acting against the interests of the group.'

He agreed there were such occasions.

'What did Bo do?' I asked.

'He had an approach of three warnings.'

If I wasn't sitting down, I would have fallen over in shock at his answer. During his long life, Komtsa has been nowhere near a workplace. His answer was straight from observing leadership in a nomadic band. The three-strikes-and-you're-out approach of decent workplaces goes back a long way in the human experience.

'What happened,' I asked, 'if the offending individual didn't change their behaviour after three warnings?'

'They were kicked out of the camp,' he replied.

Wow, I thought, that's severe punishment to be sent to live on your own in the Kalahari Desert.

'What might a person do that justified such punishment?'

Komtsa explained that there were two categories of offences that led to warnings and perhaps ultimately to eviction. The first category was if an individual was negatively impacting environmental resources.

'For example,' he said, 'if a person went into the bush and decided on their own to start a grass fire.'

Lighting grass fires generated fresh shoots to attract antelopes and hence make hunting easier. But as Komtsa explained, this was a community decision based on seasonal conditions and individuals shouldn't make that decision alone. No mavericks, thank you. Another environmental example was if an individual messed with waterholes, which I couldn't imagine any-one doing, but if they did it could indeed have serious ramifications for the community's wellbeing.

The second category of offence that triggered warnings and potential eviction related to social harmony.

Komtsa used the elegant expression I mentioned earlier to describe this issue. 'The second reason for warnings is if the person was causing a pain in someone else's heart,' he said. So if someone was persistently offensive, rude, divisive or otherwise difficult to live with, warnings were given by the leader.

The next day, when I had my second conversation with !Gao, I asked him about his experience of camp discipline. I wanted to check whether his experience of the leader giving warnings and possibly evicting camp mem-bers was similar to Komtsa's, or perhaps what Komtsa had explained was unique to Bo's leadership. !Gao confirmed that occasionally a person was banished from the camp. He added to what Komtsa had told me. 'In being kicked out of camp, the person would go and live on their own or go find another group to join. After two or three months in the bush they might, if apologetic, be allowed back into our camp.'

There must be a compelling reason why the Bushmen's disciplinary practice mirrors what's regarded as good practice in workplaces. The reason is the balance between the interests of the individual and the interests of the group. On the one hand, for the individual, receiving warnings is fair so the person knows the potential consequences of their antisocial behaviour. They have a chance — a choice — to rectify their behaviour to permit them to remain a member of the group. On the other hand, a leader needs to protect the interests of the group. There needs to be a limit to what's tolerated. As an experienced HR executive, having worked in such diverse industries as mining, manufacturing, technology and professional services, it never ceased to amaze me the great relief that team members expressed when a socially disruptive person was dismissed from their team.

Komtsa's and !Gao's experience is consistent with the general practice of ancestral societies. According to anthropologist Christopher Boehm, there is a pattern that traditional communities use in disciplining an 'errant member'. The pattern involves steps of increasing severity of social isolation. First, the errant person is ignored and even shunned. At this stage, while still physically part of the group, the person is ostracised with no one speaking or cooperating with them. If that doesn't work to correct the offending behaviour, the next step is to expel the person from the group. The third and gravest form of social isolation is execution. Short of execution, the objective at each step of escalating discipline, Boehm points out, is for the disruptive person to be converted back to being a useful contributor to community life.[6]

With the challenges of social living, no wonder leadership is universal. No wonder someone takes a lead in influencing the social dynamics of a group. For the rest of this chapter, we'll track how the nature of leadership develops to match the level of social organisation — from village to division to nation. The experience of ancestral societies provides a template for structuring leadership roles in workplaces from small firms to large complex organisations.

Village Leaders Have Significant Authority

In hunter-gatherer societies such as Bushmen bands, leaders had limited authority to direct people. That changes as we go to the slightly more complex nature of village life compared to a hunter-gatherer band. Village life is socially more complex than life as a hunter-gatherer for three reasons. First, the village is generally larger than the band, numbering up to about 150 people rather than up to roughly 30 people in hunter-gatherer bands. Second, village membership goes beyond family members and friends, so group dynamics is more fraught. And third, there is slightly more effort required to leave a village and join another village than the flexibility in a hunter-gatherer community — which means people are less mobile which gives the leader more authority. With this greater social complexity of the village, the role of headman or headwoman emerges. The power of the village leadership role helps people live together peacefully and productively. The finesse of a village leader is to use their power well — not to be an autocrat.

Tjikoko is headman of one of the three Himba villages we visited in Namibia. We turned off the main road near Epupa Falls in the far north of the country and drove about 300 metres across a barren, grassless plain to Tjikoko's village. The dirt on the paddock approaching the village was as smooth as if it had been raked clean. Although we were expected, one of our guides went alone into the village according to custom to pay respects to Tjikoko and to check we were welcome. We were soon invited in through the outer corral of woven dead branches.

He greeted us warmly and showed us around the village. Given that we were visiting in the middle of the day, most people were out tending to the grazing goats and cattle. He led us back outside the corral to sit and talk. Tjikoko sat in the only chair. The rest of us — myself, our guide and our translator — sat in the dirt. Tjikoko's chair, like a throne, was symbolic of his power.

He was perhaps 40 years of age. Tjikoko founded the village that now numbered 33 men, women and children. He told us that he was ambitious to be a village headman, and his father gave him permission to leave his parents' village to start his own village. One of the subjects I was keen to understand was the nature of his power. Well into our conversation, I asked him, 'With 33 people living together, I imagine there are times when arguments occur between people.'

'There are always issues,' he said, smiling, sounding like a workplace leader lamenting the usual strains between people. 'Always problems. For example, one of my sons wanted to sell a goat to buy maize (corn) meal. I didn't agree with him so I called my two sons together and I fixed the problem. If for example the women have bad words with each other, I get them together and we talk.'

'What happens if people don't accept your decision?' I asked.

'I say to them, "I am the one who brought you here. If you don't follow my directions, then you need to leave my village."'

Tjikoko's power is the norm for village leaders in societies organised as villages. Another culture organised as independent villages, with no structure above the village, is the Yanomamo nation in Venezuela referred to in Chapter 1. In terms of the nature of leadership in the village, anthropologist Napoleon Chagnon witnessed headmen exercising significant power. One example provides insight into the power of a village leader. Chagnon wanted to film the harvesting of peach palm fruit. Picking the fruit involved using a set of climbing frames the Yanomamo had invented for this purpose. In one village, the headman Krihisiwa told a young man to assist Chagnon with his filming. The young man was told to make a pair of climbing frames and then climb the tree and pick the fruit. But after Krihisiwa left, the young man refused do what the headman had asked of him. Later that day, Krihisiwa asked Chagnon if the filming had gone well. Chagnon told the headman that the young man had refused to do what had been asked of him. Krihisiwa was furious and called the young man over and told him, 'Either you climb the tree as I ordered you to or I will banish you from this village.'[7] Given the likelihood of neighbouring villagers killing a lone stranger, banishment was a death sentence. The young man quickly complied. Obviously, the headman was to be taken seriously and there were consequences if he was disobeyed.

Traditional Māori society in New Zealand was also organised predominantly at the level of up to about 150 people. In my research, I was thrilled to find a 1967 book titled *The Changing Role of the Leader in Māori Society*. The author, Maharaia Winiata, had completed his PhD on the subject and the book was based on that research. He began his book by covering leadership in pre-European Māori society, which is my main focus. The three levels of Māori society that we covered in Chapter 1 provides a good example of the levels of leadership matching the levels of the social structure. The structure is the equivalent of a significant-sized organisation of teams, departments and divisions. One thing you'll notice is how 'clean' the Māori leadership structure is: there are leaders at each level of the organisation but, significantly, no unnecessary additional leaders squeezed between those levels, such as we often find in workplaces.

The basic unit in the Māori social structure was the biological family unit, the *whanau*. The 'first level' leader operated at this level of society. The leader of the extended family unit was the *kaumatua*. At this level of the organisational structure, the family leader considered any problems within the family and sought to resolve disputes. The leader was the link with family gods and the leader in work activities, such as cultivation and fishing. The kaumatua spoke at meetings and gatherings and represented the family at the next level of organisation.[8]

The next level of structure was the aggregation of family units into *hapū*. As mentioned in Chapter 1, hapū was the main organising unit of traditional Māori society and the basis for the ownership of the cultivating land and the fishing grounds. The 'second level' leader at this level of society was the *rangatira*. Importantly, given that the hapū was the key organising unit, the rangatira was the key leader in Māori society and could not be directed by the higher-level 'clan' chief. If a rangatira disagreed with any decision of the higher chief, they did not hesitate to state their position and disassociate themselves and their hapū from the clan decision. At the village ceremonial centre and meeting house, the hapū leader led the rituals, connected with hapū gods, welcomed visitors, supervised discussions of war and peace, listened to and settled internal disputes and decided marriage arrangements.[9]

For much of the period of Māori settlement in New Zealand, the hapū was the highest level of social organisation. With Māori society we see the transition of a population moving from the village level of social organisation to the clan or divisional level. The divisional level emerged in the late 1700s with an increasing need for people to defend against rival groups.[10] Members of hapū joined with other people with a common ancestry to form *iwi*. The leader of the iwi was the *ariki*, a position an individual held due to the seniority of their ancestry. The ariki's power was constrained by the absolute power of the rangatira — the hapū leader — over their people.[11]

Divisional Leaders Have Significant Power

Māori society shows the emergence of the organising level, and hence leadership roles, above the village. The pattern of levels of leadership matching the organising levels continues as we look at societies such as Maasai organised at the divisional level and Mohawk organised at the nation level.

Expanding on a point I made a little earlier, a clear theme of leadership that we will see is that there are clear hierarchical steps representing the different levels of leadership. You'll also note that there is no excess of leaders squeezed into Maasai and Mohawk societies that confuses the structure and impacts people's autonomy — a problem in many workplaces. Before we look at Maasai and Mohawk societies, here is an example of what I mean by an unnecessary layer of leadership in workplaces. A senior leader in the aged care sector once asked my advice about a manager who reported to her. We'll call the senior leader Alison and the manager reporting to her, Betty. Alison told me that Betty had two supervisors reporting to her, and the two supervisors had complained to Alison about Betty's leadership style; Betty was apparently micro-managing the supervisors and meddling in the work of the staff by bypassing the two supervisors and going directly to team members to allocate work and request information. Betty was apparently creating frustration and confusion for everyone. I asked Alison to draw her organisation structure on a nearby whiteboard. She drew Betty's organisation structure and stopped drawing after showing the two supervisory roles. I had expected her to draw more roles than just two supervisors. 'Oh,' I said, 'you've *designed* it to be dysfunctional.' The problem was that Betty's role was neither a team (family) leader nor a department (village) leader — Betty didn't have a team of four to eight direct reports and she wasn't leading a department of 25 or more people. Betty's role represented an unnecessary layer of management in the structure. With just two super-visors reporting to her, Betty's job was not demanding which meant Betty was duplicating the work of her two supervisors and getting too involved in the lower-level work of the staff. (The fix was to either: a) remove Betty's role and have the two supervisors report to Alison if Alison had capacity for more direct reports, b) remove the two supervisory roles if the number of people then reporting to Betty was going to be in the order of up to eight direct reports, or c) actually expand Betty's role by restructuring the wider organisation to have more supervisors reporting to her to give her a genuine and demanding leadership of a 'village'.) The problem of too many leaders and quasi team, department or division leaders doesn't happen in First Nation societies. Their leadership structure matches the organisation structure. There are leaders at each distinct level — family, village, divisions and nation — and no 'Betty roles' squeezed in between the layers that mess up the nature of leadership.

In Maasai society there are four levels of leadership: the head of the family, the village leader, the age set leader and the leaders of the older age sets in a district. The village is led by a 'village owner' (*olopeny enkang*). Because Maasai are organised at a level above the village, villages are not independent and the village owner has limited power. It's like in large workplaces where department heads report to a more powerful divisional head. People in a Maasai village can seek adjudication on issues from the higher leader — arguments they might have with their village owner or between two or more villages. One Maasai told me of a heated argument between members of two villages. The argument was over access to water for a herd of cattle. One village was on the move and wanted to rest so their cattle could drink at a river on another village's land. The resident group vehemently opposed the transitory group using their water. Before the argument turned brutal, the local chief of the oldest age set was asked to intervene to resolve the issue. The person telling me the story was a member of the resident village. He told me, 'After hearing the arguments, the chief adjudicated that the cattle coming through our territory really did need to drink. He gave the visitors permission for their cattle to drink our water. We actually thought the decision was fair, even though it went against what we were arguing.'

In Maasai society the level of leader above the village leader is the leader of an age set of warriors. In Chapter 1 we saw that warriors (*moran*), at the time of their circumcision, are organised into an age set and that, later, their wives become part of the age set. Each age set has a chief (*olainguani*). A chief might lead between several hundred and a couple of thousand warriors. Our good friend and first Maasai contact, Ngila Loitamany Johnson, is a member of an age set of 350 warriors at the time of its formation. His age set graduated from warriorhood after 12.5 years, to junior elder for another 12.5 years and then to elder. The chief of the warrior group remains their chief for life.

Ngila and I met over two visits at Lewa Conservancy in northern Kenya where he works as a safari guide. I was keen to know his story. Like most Maasai children, his early years in a village revolved around the family's livestock. At age four he shepherded the family's kid goats. By age six, he herded the adult goats. At about eight, he was given the awesome responsibility of the family's cattle. I knew from my preparatory reading that when Ngila was a child, the law required at least one child of a family to attend school.

'How old were you when you went to school?' I asked.

'I was a good boy,' he answered, 'so I didn't go to school until I was eleven.'

Yes, reader, you have read that right. Because Ngila was a responsible child, he was kept home to tend the livestock.

'I was too busy for school,' he quipped.

An irresponsible, mischievous child was highly likely to be the first sibling sent to school. Ngila said that in fact his father considered education important and sent more than one child to school. For Ngila, attending school meant a four kilometre (two-and-a-half mile) or 45-minute run every morning, and a run home in the afternoon.

We returned to the subject of chiefs. Ngila explained that the chief is the primary decision-maker and primary peacekeeper within an age set, and for an older chief, across various age sets. I commented, 'Your chief's role sounds like a big job.'

'But Andrew,' he said, 'the chief doesn't rule alone.'

'Tell me more, Ngila.'

He explained that the chief has what are poetically called 'feathers'. That is, his cabinet. The 'feathers' are highly respected individuals in the community who act as the chief's eyes and ears and who form the chief's inner circle — the executive team.

'How many feathers does a chief have?' I asked. Given the principle of a workable-sized group, I was anticipating the answer of seven.

'Seven,' Ngila answered! Then he added, 'Oh, plus the deputy and with the chief himself makes nine.' Still within the band of seven plus or minus two; a sensible number for a leadership council. The size of the Maasai leadership team matches recommendation #3 at the end of Chapter 1: that a functional executive team should number about seven people.

A key aspect of leadership in Maasai society is that chiefs are developed as they progress into more senior roles. When a new age set is formed, the prior age set of warriors progress to become junior elders. Given that the age set chief remains their chief for life, the chiefs are maturing in preparation for their move into more senior roles every 12 or so years. Each chief and their executive team are gaining experience, ready for when their age set is the most mature group of elders. This theme, where leaders are prepared for the level of role they move into, is present in each society organised as a division or a nation. For example, as we will see in a later chapter, in Haida society in the northern Pacific, a chief-in-waiting usually sits at the side of the current chief.

In Maasai society, the chief's role carries significant responsibility. The chief, with their feathers, makes decisions that are critical for a well-functioning society. My friend William Kinanta Sadera, the junior elder who as a five-year-old spent the first week of school vacation searching for his family, explained the nature of the decisions made by his chief (often the chief of the oldest age set). The decisions fall into two categories. The first category covers decisions made on a regular cycle — like for a workplace executive, the operational decisions you know you will make each year. The chief and their cabinet:

- Authorise marriages within the age set.
- Control the formation of the next age set of boys to be circumcised and become warriors.

- Punish any wrong doers. The chief has power to cast out the wrong doers — and to bless those who follow and obey the norms of the community.
- Take a lead in special occasions and ceremonies in the community.

The second category of decisions relates to occasional issues that require special attention and resolution — like the subjects that a workplace executive unexpectedly has to make time for:

- The chief of an older age set resolves conflicts between villages, such as in the example earlier when the cattle of one village transgressed onto another village's territory to access water.
- Serious issues between members of the age group might reach an older chief for resolution. For example, Maasai don't have wills so in the case of a family argument about inheritance of property, mainly cattle, anyone who feels unjustly treated can request a chief of an older age set to consider the merits of their case. Minor cases would be expected to be heard by the chief of the age set above where the issue is occurring, and only major cases would escalate up to the oldest chief.
- Issues involving two districts go to the oldest chiefs of the affected districts who will sit in conference. For example, there are occasional cases of cattle rustling. To avoid issues turning into bloody conflict, the two chiefs hear and try to resolve the issue between the competing parties. Cattle will generally be returned, the guilty party punished and peace restored between the two districts. William told me, with a smile, 'All cattle in the world belong to the Maasai.' I answered, 'I'll let the owners of the big cattle stations (ranches) in Australia know about that!'
- If grievances between districts are not resolved, the chief of the oldest age set issues the order for the warriors to go to war against the enemy. The most recent fight in William's part of Kenya was in April 2020 when two groups fought over cattle rustling and territorial boundaries. At least ten people died.
- Arguments about marriage partnering between two age sets are resolved by the chief above the age set of the parties involved in the argument.

- The oldest chiefs of the divisions led the Maasai decision in 2008 to protect lions — a major change for Maasai society. Up until that time, young Maasai warriors proved their manhood — and impressed future wives — by killing a lion with their spear. Even the chief's attire for special occasions, prior to lion protection, included a hat made from the mane of a male lion the chief had killed.
- Upon an outbreak of disease, the chief of the oldest age set and their cabinet make determinations about any districts to be placed in quarantine. Their deliberation includes deciding the punishment for disobeying the order. (Given the nature of COVID-19, the national government of Kenya managed the pandemic, not the Maasai chiefs.)
- Nowadays, the oldest chief deals with the Kenyan government and external parties, such as safari operators, on matters affecting their community.
- The oldest chief also tries to manage the influence of the external world pressing in on Maasai society — balancing, on the one hand, the Western lifestyle attractive to the younger generation and, on the other hand, retaining Maasai customs. It's a delicate balance for the chief to maintain interest from the young people in traditional customs yet not cause them to rebel.

I emailed William to check that I'd documented accurately what he'd told me about chiefly decision making. 'There's only one thing to add,' he wrote back, 'Remember to tell people in Australia that we Maasai are coming for our cattle!'

Leadership of a Nation

Mohawk and the wider Haudenosaunee nations show the highest level of organisation of traditional societies. The six nations are organised as a confederacy. In a corporate sense, the Haudenosaunee confederacy is, especially back in traditional times, the equivalent of a large, diverse organisation. As we would expect in a well-organised society, there were a number of distinct layers of leadership, with always just enough leaders and no more than required. A key purpose of those layers, one Mohawk person told me, was that 'a citizen had a clan liaison to share his or her voice with, and who represented him or her at each level of leadership'. Replace *citizen* with *employee* and you have a good principle for designing leadership roles in workplaces.

One of the Mohawk community leaders I met with on my visit to Canada is Teyowisonte Tommy Deer, manager of the Kahnawà:ke Language and Cultural Center. He's a sub-chief of the Wolf clan and is a student of Mohawk history and culture. Tommy was generous with his time, and because of his clarity of thinking, energy and tightness of explanation, we covered a lot of ground in our time together. He also generously clarified several subjects as I wrote this book.

The Haudenosaunee confederacy was formed, along with its constitution, 1000 years ago at a meeting on the northern shore of Onondaga Lake in today's upstate New York. We mentioned in Chapter 1 that in about 1650, the population of the Haudenosaunee confederacy was estimated at around 25,000. Of that number, there were an estimated 5000 Mohawk citizens.[12] Before the impact of smallpox and colonial warfare in the early 1600s, the Mohawk population might have been 11,000 people.[13]

The most distinctive aspect of the leadership structure in Mohawk and Haudenosaunee society is the top level of leadership, so we will start at the top and work down. As we work through the nature of leadership in Haudenosaunee society you'll see, as in the other highly organised societies, there are *just enough* leaders. At the top level of the confederacy is a leadership council, the League Council, made up of 50 chiefs representing each of the five founding nations. The Council still meets regularly on Onondaga Nation territory near Syracuse, New York. Each nation is allotted a proportion of those 50 positions, referred to as sachems. In the Mohawk language, the sachems are called *Roiá:ner*, which means 'He's good/He's on a good path/He has a good mind'. This Mohawk word gives a strong clue as to the leadership attributes of these top chiefs which we will come back to in the next chapter. Of the 50 sachemships on the League Council, the Mohawk nation is allocated nine. That number of positions arose from the nine extended Mohawk clans (three Turtle Clan sub-clans, three Wolf Clan sub-clans and three

Bear Clan sub-clans), with each of the sub-clans or divisions represented by a chief on the Council.

The powers of the sachems are prescribed by the constitution of the confederacy — The Great Law of Peace of The Longhouse People. The council of sachems 'assumed the charge of all matters which concerned the League. It declared war and made peace, sent and received embassies, entered into treaties of alliance, regulated the affairs of subjugated nations, received new members into the League, extended its protection over feeble tribes; in a word, took all needful measures to promote their prosperity, and enlarge their dominion'.[14] In reading the Great Law of Peace, an impressive document, my attention was captured by an important separation of duties that applied to leadership roles in traditional times. Article 90 specifies that in times of war, the leadership role was the responsibility of war chiefs. If a sachem chose to join a war party, he laid aside his civil duties and became a common soldier — an example of good corporate governance with military and civil roles separated.

Another insightful element of the Haudenosaunee leadership system is that the 50 sachems were and are required to represent the interests of the whole confederacy, not just those of their own clan or nation.[15] The designers of the Haudenosaunee constitution obviously knew what every member on a workplace leadership team knows: it's tempting but not helpful for members of an executive team to selfishly represent just the interests of their division. The primary focus should be making decisions in the interests of the whole organisation.

The next level of leadership, going down from the confederacy level, is the leadership of the nation. The number of chiefs at the national level replicates the number of Mohawk sachemships at the confederacy level, and comprises the same nine individuals who sit on the League Council. The nine chiefs of the sub-clans lead the nation. While there is and was no overall Mohawk chief, nor overall chief of any clan, in a practical sense at the council meetings of the nine chiefs, one of the Turtle Clan chiefs chairs the proceedings. In the next chapter we will look at the consensus decision-making process of the Haudenosaunee nations and the implications for executive decision making.

A Mohawk chief at any level, I was told, has to be 'fully dressed'. Fully dressed is similar to the Maasai concept of the chief having the support of 'feathers' or a leadership cabinet — the leader does not lead alone. A Mohawk chief being fully dressed means that the key roles supporting the chief have all been appointed. And not surprisingly, reinforcing the natural pattern, the number of roles on the executive team is in the range of seven plus or minus two. Supporting the chief are the clan mother, a sub-clan mother, a sub-chief, a male ceremonial keeper and a female ceremonial keeper. Including the chief, that makes six.

In this explanation of leadership layers in Mohawk society, we are now down to the middle-management layer. In traditional times, Mohawk citizens generally lived in large towns, with perhaps 3000 inhabitants (and before smallpox began to take its horrid toll from the 1630s, probably much larger).[16] Each town had its own village council that was made up of community chiefs. These chiefs were called *Ratishennawá:nens* — the 'big names'. The chiefs, appointed by the clan mothers, handled the affairs between villages and some forms of conflict in the community.

As we saw in Chapter 1, these towns were made up of a number of longhouses, each consisting of multiple families totalling 50 to 80 people. A longhouse was organised matrilineally. Women and unmarried young men living in a longhouse were related to one another through their maternal line. The adult men of the longhouse had married into the family. The internal affairs of the longhouse were led by the matriarch.[17]

In summary, the Mohawk and the wider Haudenosaunee confederacy was a well organised society, with distinctive levels of leadership necessary for a well-functioning society. As for other First Nation societies, leaders existed only at the distinct levels at which the society was organised. There were no extra leaders squeezed into the layers that results in more leaders than required which in turn causes the society — the organisation — to be over-managed with a resultant reduction in personal autonomy.

Actions for Workplace Leaders

Ancestral societies have gifted us leadership as a remarkable social mechanism. The universal existence of leadership demonstrates its importance as an enabling mechanism for the peaceful and productive operation of a group. The experience of ancestral societies shows that the nature of leadership needs to match the structure of the society or organisation. There are a number of actions that can be taken by workplace leaders to apply this wisdom.

1. **Be reassured that groups require leaders:** In our ancestral setting, leadership existed in every group and at each level of society. Significantly, leadership provided the means for humans to expand beyond bands of close relatives into villages and then to divisions and nations. This finding reassures leaders of their critical role in serving their group — if any leader doubts the significance of their role, the experience of ancestral societies should transform that doubt into feelings of empowerment.

2. **Appoint leaders at the levels that match the organisation structure:** A clear principle of leadership in ancestral societies is the hierarchy of leadership layers. There are leaders at each level in which the society is organised. There is a leader at the level of the family and then the band or the village, and then, for those societies organised at higher levels, the division and perhaps the nation. This is a match for workplaces, depending on their size, having leaders at the level of the team, the department, the division and the organisation.

3. **Avoid unnecessary leadership layers:** Ancestral societies are disciplined in having no more leaders than are necessary to match their level of organisation structure. Applying that wisdom, workplaces should avoid squeezing in extra leaders that distort the layers. Just the right number of leaders gives direct reports freedom to operate — freedom to live their lives in ancestral societies or freedom to do their job in workplaces. The way to test that just the right number of leaders exist in the organisation — not too many, not too few — is to review the population size of each leader's job:

- If the leader is leading a team, do they have about seven people reporting to them? As a general principle, if a manager has fewer than four direct reports their role should either be expanded or removed (and if removed, their direct reports absorbed under another manager). This general principle says that if a first-level leader has just two or three people reporting to them, the 'leader's' role is more of a hands-on contributor rather than a leader of a 'family' unit.

- If the leader is leading a department, do they have about seven direct reports and in the department for which this leader is responsible, are total numbers of staff between about 30 (the band) up to about 150 (the village)? In a small department, some of the direct reports to the leader will be team leaders and some will be individuals with no direct reports. In a medium-size department of about 50–80 staff, all direct reports to the department leader should be team leaders. In a large department — a department approaching 150 staff — some of the direct reports to the department head will also have team leaders amongst their direct reports.

- If the leader is a divisional leader, do they have about seven village leaders reporting to them and a divisional population of close to 1000 people?

- If the leader is an executive leader, do they have about seven divisional leaders reporting to them?

Generally, if a role doesn't pass that test and has too few people reporting to it, then it means the role is probably redundant and should be changed — the role should be made more demanding or removed.

4. **Prepare leaders for their roles:** From my career experience, one of the biggest leadership failings of workplaces generally is appointing people to leadership roles without the training to prepare them for their role. That's a big ask — to be asked to do something without training. Good organisations know that moving from a peer to a team leader role, being promoted from a team leader to a

department manager, or to a divisional leader or senior executive, are challenging steps for people. Individuals should be given help to succeed in their new role. They shouldn't be left to work it out for themselves by trial and error. The help in the form of training, coaching and resources should be tailored for the level of role the person is being appointed to:

- The team leader role is the entry position and specific people-leadership skills need to be gained by the person. The new leader needs to learn both leadership concepts and allowed to practise in the safety of a training room. The skills at this level are the foundation package for leading a team of direct reports at any level. The individual leader will keep developing and applying their leadership skills at each promotional step in their career.

- Being promoted to a department (village) leader means the leader is now a leader of managers and they have a whole new set of responsibilities. In preparation for taking on a village leader role, the person needs to be assisted particularly with enhanced communication skills and of holding lower-level leaders accountable for staff engagement and performance.

- Going from a village-level leader to a divisional leader is a big step up. Leaders at this level need to be given the appropriate preparatory education, especially around organisation systems to facilitate the desired culture that enables high performance.

- Leaders at the executive level need to develop their skills in strategic thinking and the future competitive position of their organisation. They'll continue to apply their people leadership skills they carried with them from their lower-level roles.

5. **Ensure leaders operate at the level required of their role:** The Kalahari Bushmen's inability to peacefully congregate at a level above their normal organisation level — above their band — is a sobering lesson. Every leader is required to do the level of job required of them at their level. For example, a village-level leader in a workplace needs to unify their teams, give clarity of purpose and direction, distribute resources equitably and ensure the working

environment is peaceful and productive. If they are not able to or not inclined to provide the necessary leadership, then the village suffers. Engagement and performance drops. Ensuring leaders operate at the level required is the responsibility of the next level of leader with the support of HR.

6. **Resolve conflicts:** A universal responsibility of leaders in ancestral societies is the resolution of conflict. It's not the most glorious of leadership responsibilities, but it is critical. The tendency towards interpersonal tension goes with being human; individuals have their own interests and motivations. Tensions existed periodically even in small nomadic bands of relatives and close friends. A leader has the role of keeping the peace, adjudicating issues and insisting on acceptable standards of behaviour. It's important that leaders know that this is an unrelenting obligation of their role and are given help to develop the skills to resolve conflict in their group.

7. **Ensure leaders act as guardians of group membership:** From time immemorial, as we heard from the Bushmen experience, leaders have had the responsibility to decide group membership — who gets to join the group and who gets to stay. In terms of who joins, leaders need to take care in recruiting people to the group. Leaders should be given the tools and training to help them make good recruiting decisions. In terms of occasionally dismissing individuals from their group, most leaders find that an onerous responsibility; as a leader, I never welcomed such conversations with people. But I knew that I had an obligation to the team to address any individual performance or attitude problems. A breakthrough for me in being more comfortable in talking with poor performers was realising that I didn't need the person's agreement to what I was observing and asking of them. For example, if someone was disrupting the normally happy working environment — 'causing a pain in other people's hearts' — then I was entitled to let that person know my observations and what was required. The person might debate my assessment, but I was still entitled to let them know my view. In being clear about what was required, I was giving the person a

choice — to comply or not. Their choice would soon be revealed by their behaviour. If they continued, say, to be nasty and rude to their colleagues, then their choice meant they now left the team. Like the decision of Komtsa's grandfather in the Kalahari, the interests of the group should not be compromised by an errant individual.

Having identified the significance and the nature of leadership roles, the next principle from the timeless experience of First Nations covers the attributes required for leadership. Not everyone who wants to be a leader qualifies. There is a mandatory attribute of leadership common to all the societies I visited and expressed by almost everyone I met.

CHAPTER 3

Attributes of Leadership

'Our chief is respectful of everyone.'

'I AM A REAL child of the Maasai,' said Koyaki Ole Sopia in Swahili to begin our meeting. We were sitting in the shade of a great canopy of Yellow Bark Acacias at Lewa in northern Kenya. Over my right shoulder, about 300 paces away, an elephant family bathed in a waterhole, two calves trumpeting as they played hide-and-seek around the legs of their mothers and aunts. Koyaki proudly painted a picture of his childhood, tending the family's livestock, his village moving every two months following the rain to find fresh grass for the cattle. He showed me his ear piercings and the extensions of his ear lobes. He described the removal of his four front teeth, all marks of being Maasai.

He told me about the attributes that qualify a person to be a chief in his society. He described leaders as having a calm temperament, being friendly and acting as a servant to the people. Koyaki made his point by stating, 'Our chief is respectful of everyone.'

It's a phenomenon. In my travels, everyone I talked to about leadership had *respect* at the top of their list of required attributes; the leader *respects* people. With just one exception, *respect* featured as the requisite leadership attribute in every society. (The fact that respect wasn't mentioned in conversations with Waorani in the Amazonian jungle will make sense when we look at that violent society in Chapter 7.) In every other society, if *respect towards other people* is not part of their character, a person is disqualified from leadership. Respect by the leader is mentioned by Bushmen, which is echoed in how Himba describe a well-regarded village head. In hereditary Haida and Māori societies, a 'candidate' (from a high-ranking family) for the role of chief will be passed over if they do not have in their character respect for other people. In Blackfeet and Mohawk societies people emerge or are appointed as leaders based in large part on respect for others.

The power of this finding of the universal theme of respect is to make undeniable what we all know to be the case, even if some leaders choose to ignore or deny the fact. If a leader deviates from the behaviours that universally demonstrate respect, the leader is self-sabotaging their effectiveness. And at the organisational level, the universal nature of leadership in traditional societies provides a template to build leadership systems (leadership selection, development and promotion) that enables teams and workplaces to thrive — or to suffer if we ignore ancestral wisdom.

The Prerequisite Leadership Attribute is Respect

Respect is the product of behaviour. There are behaviours that demonstrate respect and there are behaviours that demonstrate disrespect. In ancestral societies, aspirants to leadership who are rude and dismissive of others are disqualified from the leadership role. And if disrespectful behaviour emerges after the person is appointed, they either lose their role or lose their influence.

During leadership workshops, when I ask people to recall experiences of working for a leader who demonstrated *disrespect*, people instantly list a sorry set of behaviours. Even though participants might have worked for the disrespectful leader years before, people's recollections are vivid and the emotion attached to those memories is still raw. At the top of the list of disrespectful behaviours are: anger, yelling, volatile, moody, rude, offensive language, talking over/cutting off/interrupting, condescending, undermining and humiliation, public shaming, aloof and egotistical, taking credit for other people's work and hyper-sensitivity to criticism. These disrespectful behaviours are abhorrent to First Peoples. Universally in First Nations, they disqualify the perpetrator from leadership.

When participants on my workshops recall the wonderful leaders they've worked for who demonstrated *respect*, people are energised. The room is abuzz with people sharing joyful memories. The behaviours identified on workshops match the elements of respect mentioned by members of ancestral societies. We will cover in this chapter the attributes told to me by members of the societies I visited — behaviours all fitting under the over-arching attribute of respect. It was really striking to experience conversations about leadership attributes that were so similar across these societies in different parts of the world. The behavioural elements of respect that were almost always mentioned are:

- A calm temperament
- Absence of bad language
- Peacemaker (to resolve tension)
- Generosity
- Caring for the long-term interests of the community
- Knowledge of and respect for individuals
- Treating people equally (no favouritism)
- Humility, and
- Facilitating respectful meetings.

We will look at each attribute.

A Calm Temperament and a 'Good Mind'

In Mohawk society, *respect* is the first element of a relationship, including the relationship between leaders and followers. In my meetings with 12 people at Kahnawà:ke near Montreal, including 10 senior members of the community, a clear message emerged as we talked about mandatory attributes of leadership. Even though Mohawk society is organised up to the level of confederacy covering thousands of people, they have found ways to maintain respectful leadership. Being a 'big' organisation is not an excuse for leaders being disrespectful of people. In ancestral societies, respectful leadership is expected, from the family and village level all the way up to the divisional level and higher.

In my meetings at Kahnawà:ke, *respect* by leaders was mentioned often, usually through the expression that a chief must have 'a good mind'. The meaning of a good mind is explained in The Great Law of Peace, the constitution of the Haudenosaunee confederacy. In defining the required attributes of leadership, Article 24 states, in part, 'Neither anger nor fury shall find lodgement in their minds and all their words and actions shall be marked by calm deliberation.'

I've mentioned previously that Teyowisonte Tommy Deer is the manager of the Kahnawà:ke Language and Cultural Center. On the subject of attributes required of leaders in his society, Tommy explained the meaning of 'a good mind'.

'A good mind means the chief is fair, soft-spoken and has a good heart. He should be a man of the people. A leader cannot act independently of the people. He should know the minds of the people.' (There is a male bias in leadership roles that we will cover in Chapter 9.)

On the flip-side of the coin, Tommy explained an attribute that would erode the standing of the chief and might bring reprimand from the clan mother. 'We do not expect nor accept a chief speaking angrily,' he said. 'We say such behaviour is "throwing sparks". A chief speaking in this way is asked to calm down.'

Fran Beauvais is a Mohawk clan mother, the most powerful person in the clan (or the division as I termed it in Chapter 1). Like the chair of a board, she is the person who ultimately selects the chief. We had dinner together, and she told me about the attributes required — the character — of a person to be a leader in her society.

'A chief must have a good mind,' she said. 'He has good intentions, he has a good frame of mind, and has done no one any harm. He has no ego, or at least keeps his ego in check. He carries himself well. He can speak publicly; he has good oratory skills.'

An element of a calm mind is that the leader listens. Joe McGregor is a Mohawk faith keeper and a medicine man. He followed his grandmother in the calling. 'She was a medicine man,' he told me. 'The power was handed down to her and from her to me. Only the Creator can heal. The power is given to us.'

Joe is also a seer; he can see things not normally visible to people. He told me about a time when two young men were working on a scaffold and the derrick — a crane — hit the scaffold. The boys fell into the water and drowned. The rescuers failed to recover one boy's body. The boy's uncle came to Joe, desperate to find his nephew's body. It took Joe five minutes of meditation to know where the body was hidden. Joe directed the uncle to that place and the uncle found his nephew's body.

Joe and I were meeting in the kitchen of the Riverview Hotel, Kahnawà:ke where I was staying. The hotel, like many of the buildings in the street, dates back to the mid-1700s. The physical environment and the history of the place added to my sense of awe and gratitude at the privilege of talking with Joe.

'What are the attributes of a good chief?' I asked.

'A chief listens to people; listens to all the people and not just those who chose him or he is close to. A good chief does not have a swelled head. He does not put himself up high; the people put you high. A long time ago, the chief was the poorest in the community; he put others first.'

There will be many readers of this book who will bemoan the experience of working for a leader who didn't listen. Being a good listener is an attribute expected of a leader in such diverse social settings as the Mohawk confederacy and in a band of Bushmen. Beginning in 1951, a young Elizabeth Marshall (Thomas), on what must have been a series of amazing family adventures into the Kalahari, visited G/ui Bushmen several times with her mother, father and brother. (The G/ui Bushmen are a separate people from the Ju/'hoansi that I visited, although both societies are very similar.) Marshall Thomas wrote a wonderful book, *The Harmless People*, which she later updated as *The Old Way*. She described a number of the band leaders she met, and her description fits with what I found across the cultures I visited. For example, she described Toma, a highly popular leader, who listened to people. 'Toma listened diplomatically and intently whenever he was spoken to.'[1] It's indeed hard to imagine *respect* being attached to a leader who interrupts people or whose attention wanders when they are being spoken to.

The attribute of a calm temperament features strongly in the Maasai culture. Back under the giant Yellow Bark Acacias talking with the 'real child of the Maasai', Koyaki Ole Sopia told me about the extraction of his four front teeth: two middle teeth in the top row and two in the bottom row. The extraction occurred twice in his life: first his milk or infant teeth and then his mature teeth. Teeth are extracted by a person skilled in the operation using a chiselled instrument to punch the teeth clear of the gum. No self-respecting Maasai male will flinch in response to the excruciating pain caused by the operation. To do so would attract ridicule and accusations of cowardice.

I asked Koyaki to tell me more about his chief. 'My chief is a very good leader,' he told me, his eyes instantly glistening in adoration for his leader. 'He never gets angry. He is respectful of everyone and their rights. He is a good spokesperson. He upholds the Maasai law and justice prevails. He settles disputes, and he does so fairly with the outcome agreed by everyone.'

The top attributes nominated by Maasai I met are consistent, and roughly in the same order (with verbatim comments in quotations). Again, in Chapter 9 we will cover the theme that leadership in ancestral societies is overwhelmingly a male occupation.

- **Temperament:** 'He never gets angry.'
- **Sociable:** 'He spends time with people, he's in touch, he listens and talks to people. He relates to everyone. He brings people together.'
- **Wise:** 'He is intelligent and sees a long way into the future — which allows him to make good decisions.'
- **Strict:** 'He makes decisions that he needs to make. He is tough if he needs to be, but not in a bloody-minded way.'
- **Servant:** 'He acts like a servant to the people. He does a lot for the community. It's as though we are always on his mind.'
- **Fair:** 'He is respectful of everyone and their rights. He is fair in his decision-making. He has no favourites.'

After hearing on so many occasions that 'the chief never gets angry', I decided I should test with my friend Ngila Loitamany Johnson my assumption about why that attribute featured so prominently. I assumed that people were telling me that they appreciated their leader being a pleasant individual who treats people decently. Ngila and I were driving from the safari camp to a nearby village for him to introduce me to another person to talk with. We were distracted momentarily by a tower of giraffes. He stopped the car so we could watch the giraffes graze.

Upon resuming the drive, I asked him, 'Why do people almost always mention as a key attribute that their chief never gets angry?' His answer surprised me.

'It's about decision making,' he said. 'Being angry is like being drunk. In that state you are likely to make a bad decision. When a decision is made, we want to know that the leader was in the best frame of mind to make the decision. We will accept if a decision turns out to be a bad one, but we won't tolerate the decision being made in a poor state of mind. Sometimes we will postpone a meeting if the chief is not in a good frame of mind.'

No Tolerance of Bad Language

Mindset is revealed by language. The language of a leader reveals their respect for people, or their disrespect of people. As for Mohawk and Maasai societies, Māori society does not accept anger and hot tempers. While the three societies were prepared to engage in warfare, aggression was only acceptable in battle, not in interpersonal relations and community meetings. As I write this, I smile wryly thinking about a few hot-headed workplace leaders I've known. Their behaviour would not have been tolerated in Māori society, neither in traditional times nor now.

Samuel Marsden established the first Christian mission in New Zealand in the early 1800s. His seven visits to New Zealand from 1814 occurred in the very early days of European presence, so he had the rare opportunity to observe Māori society before European influence. At one point Marsden had to discipline one of his missionaries for offensive language and aggressive behaviour towards his hosts.

Marsden had arrived in Australia from Britain in 1793 to take up his position as assistant chaplain for the Anglican church in Sydney. The

British settlement in Australia was only five years old at that point and no European settlement had yet been established in New Zealand. From his first days in the region, Marsden took an interest in New Zealand. At the time, Māori chiefs and their sons and nephews visited Sydney, keen to learn about European ways of farming and warfare and also keen for adventure. Marsden provided them a friendly home, often supporting the young men if they'd been poorly treated as crew on whaling ships, such as being denied their wages. Consequently, when Marsden first visited New Zealand, he was warmly welcomed by the senior relatives of the young men he'd supported. Marsden was often making first European contact with people and was the first European to explore the inland of the North Island. Given that timing, his observations are particularly interesting, and fortunately he kept detailed journals of his seven visits, the last in 1837.

On Marsden's fourth visit in 1823 he turned his mind to interpersonal relations. 'A rude and violent (person) is very offensive to New Zealanders (as Māori were known at that time). Amongst themselves they live in great peace and harmony ... There is nothing that they despise more than a passionate (hot-tempered) man. They are not accustomed to fight amongst themselves excepting in regular warfare, and they cannot bear an angry man.'[2]

The subject was on Marden's mind because of the behaviour of one of his missionaries, a Mr Butler. Butler had been rude to people, using swear words and being aggressive. 'Swearing is a capital offence in New Zealand, and Mr Butler was accused of this sin,' Marsden wrote in his journal. 'The greatest insult that can be offered to a chief is to make use of bad language to him ... Hence it rarely happens that (Māori) who are men of rank use bad language one to another as the Europeans do, but are cautious in what they say.' Marsden added that if bad language is used, friends of the offended person will punish the offender to defend their friend's honour and the offence often leads to war.

Marsden received complaints of Butler's bad language and aggressive behaviour from a leading chief, Hongi Hika. At about this time, Hongi Hika had been the first chief to obtain muskets and was getting revenge on every other *iwi* (at that time called a 'tribe' by Europeans). At the time of Marsden's interactions with him, Hongi was terrorising neighbouring iwi with frequent and lengthy war campaigns, sometimes involving forces of 1000 warriors in 100 war canoes resulting in the burning of 500 villages and the capture of 2000 slaves.[3] Even Hongi, aggressive as he was in conquest, could not tolerate anger and bad language in interpersonal dealings. After talking with Hongi and Hongi's wife and others, Marsden concluded that Butler was guilty of 'unguarded expressions' and 'too much fight' and sacked him. His hosts pleaded with Marsden that if Butler was to be replaced, to send them someone with a mild temperament. Even a young Māori participating in the conversations requested, 'When you send us (someone), do not send us an angry, fighting man.'[4]

Anger and bad language do not work in Māori communities and other ancestral societies; nor, I'm saying, in workplaces.

Peacemaker (to Resolve Tension)

Because of the complexity of human groups, tensions occasionally arise and there is a need for conflicts to be quickly resolved. That role falls predominantly to the leader. It's therefore not surprising that facilitating peaceful relationships across a community was often mentioned in my discussions with people. Umuna is the headman of a Himba village. When I met him, Umuna was thirty-four years of age and had been headman for about three-and-a-half years. He told me that it's the role of the headman 'to make sure that the village doesn't fall apart. I have to step in if people don't cooperate with each other.' He's identifying an unrelenting obligation of leadership of resolving conflict to restore group harmony. In your workplace career, if you accept a leadership role you are signing up for that responsibility. And if you appoint a person to a leadership role, satisfy yourself that they'll cope with resolving conflict within and beyond their group — otherwise it's going to be a distressing time for them and exasperating for their people.

'What are examples of subjects when you have to step in?' I asked Umuna. He listed three subjects.

'For example,' he said, 'if a person wants to slaughter a goat to eat and I disagree with the timing. Another example is if people gossip about another person in the village. A third example is if a man wants to sleep with another man's wife.'

I asked him to tell me more about the village gossip and if there were any recent examples.

'Yes,' he answered. 'Last year there was gossiping between the women that became a big issue. The gossiping was about the headman's wife.' I think he was referring to his own wife and himself in third person. 'Some women were saying "the headman is married to an ugly woman". The wife heard what was being said about her. I called all the people together and sorted it out.'

'Was that the end of the matter?' I asked.

'No, this year the same thing happened.' It was still unresolved.

Each level of leader needs to resolve the quarrels at the level directly below them. In ancestral societies, this means village leaders like Umuna settling quarrels of people in his village. For workplace leaders, it means the team leader settling quarrels between team members and, at the next level, the department manager resolving disputes between teams. A problem arises though, in a workplace, if the leader that ought to be the peacemaker doesn't get involved in resolving disagreements. The problem for ancestral societies was if there was no level of leadership above where the dispute is occurring. For traditional Aboriginal society around today's Melbourne and Port Phillip Bay in Victoria, that issue of a leadership vacuum arose at the level above the village (or the clan in local terminology). Clans numbered about 120 people and given that each clan had a chief, disputes could be resolved amongst clan members. But what about disputes between the clans, where there was no leader to hear and settle arguments? In the early 1800s, thirty years before a first European settlement in Victoria, an outsider joined one of the clans and apparently served the role of peacemaker between hostile clans. The experience shows the important function of workplace leaders maintaining harmony at their level of the organisation.

In 1803, the British ship *Calcutta* arrived in Port Phillip Bay with a consignment of convicts and soldiers for the purpose of establishing a second Australian colony after Sydney. The settlement, later Melbourne, didn't go ahead at that time, but while the group was encamped, six convicts escaped. As they made their dash for freedom, one convict was shot in the leg and made it no further than the perimeter of the camp. That was enough for a second escapee to give up the dream. Another of the remaining four surrendered after just one night in the bush. Two of the others gave up after craving food and water for two weeks — one of those two individuals made it back to the camp, but the other was never heard of again. That left one, a William Buckley, who would spend the next three decades living a remarkable life in Aboriginal society and who later had his story documented.[5] In the first two weeks before his two friends left him, Buckley had made his way from the south-eastern side of the Bay to the western side around today's Geelong and the Bellarine Peninsula.

Somehow Buckley survived on his own for a year or two, but was in a desperate state of near-starvation and dehydration when befriended by a woman and man of the Wadawurrung balug clan. Fortunately for Buckley, just before the couple found him, he'd come across a grave, and stabbed into the grave was the spear of the buried man. Buckley carried the spear to help in his search for food. Many Aboriginal societies, including Wadawurrung, believed that dead people might return to life as a white person (as a ghostly figure). The couple, finding Buckley carrying the spear of their recently departed relative, believed that their brother and brother-in-law had returned to them. The clan rejoiced at the return of their relative and friend. Buckley, who became known as Murrangurk (the dead man), lived with the clan for 32 years.

Wadawurrung balug clan is one of 25 clans of the Wadawurrung people of the Kulin nation. According to Buckley, his clan numbered about 100 people. When clans mingled, invariably fighting broke out. Fighting was most often over women: either women being taken by another clan or over a woman betrothed to one man eloping with another. Occasionally, disputes were over alleged acts of sorcery and payback killings.

In the social structure of Aboriginal society in that region, there were chiefs of clans but no chiefs above the clans within a nation.[6] In the absence of a unifying leadership role, Buckley says that he served the useful role as mediator: '... by my harmless and peaceable manner amongst them, (I) had acquired great influence in settling their disputes. Numbers of murderous fights I had prevented by my interference, which was received by them as well meant; so much so, that they would often allow me to go amongst them (prior to) a battle, and take away their spears, and waddies, and boomerangs.'[7] Some of the disputes would have been the ritualistic settling of long-held grudges, but some fights presumably would have been due to more immediate grievances.

Thirty-two years after Buckley's escape, European illegal graziers (or squatters), intent on dispossessing Aboriginal people of their land, established a Port Phillip settlement. When Buckley received reports of their arrival, he headed to nearby Indented Head on the Bellarine Peninsula where a small group of whites were camped. He'd lost his ability to speak English but soon reacquired the skill and convinced them of his identity. He soon received the governor's pardon for his escape years before and lived another 20 years.

An enduring, humorous legacy of William Buckley, who against all odds survived so long in the bush, is the Australian expression, *Buckley's chance* (or more often shortened to simply, *Buckley's*). When an Australian expresses amazement at another person's foolhardy plans that have no chance of success, we don't say, 'You've got zero chance' or, 'You've got a fat chance.' Instead, an Australian says to their friend, 'You've got *Buckley's*'.[8]

While Buckley lived with them, the Wadawurrung and their neighbours apparently took advantage of the presence of someone filling the mediator role. In workplaces, we can't afford to rely on an external agent to diffuse tensions. That's the unrelenting role of a leader, at every level, and usually above the level in which the argument takes place. For a first-level leader, tension occurs between individuals. At the next level leader, as well as occurring between individuals who report to them, tensions occur between teams. On it goes up each level of the hierarchy, to the CEO level where tensions can be between divisions (as well as between members of the top team). No wonder leadership is universal.

Generosity

Along with the ability to keep the peace, respect towards people is demonstrated by being generous. Generosity was almost always mentioned to me as a leadership attribute.

Utjindisa Hembinda, also known as James from his school days, is a member of the Himba village led by Umuna who I mentioned above. James was twenty-seven years of age when I met him and speaks English. We sat near the banks of the Kunene River bordering Namibia and Angola. Before talking leadership, we chatted over a cool drink. I asked him about the main food Himba people eat. He smiled, as favourite food tends to make people do. 'We eat mainly sour milk, made from goat or cow's milk. To make sour milk you take a melon. The melon has been drilled out. You pour the milk in and you add the skin of a mopane leaf. We eat meat, mainly goat, about once every three weeks. We also eat a lot of maize (corn). We boil water and add maize meal and milk.'

I asked his opinion about the attributes of a good leader. 'A good leader looks after people. They treat people equally. They aren't rude and don't shout or insult people. They help people, such as those without a goat. A good leader shares and they settle tensions and quarrels.' James has neatly captured many of the leadership attributes universally mentioned.

'Who is a good leader in your district?' I asked.

'Umuna is good,' he said, nominating his own headman. 'Umuna recently went to Opuwo (the nearest town) and bought 50 kgs (110 lbs) of food which he shared equally with the whole village. A good leader avoids people going hungry.'

Generosity is not *just* about relieving hunger. It's a means of achieving group solidarity and social harmony. In ancestral societies, leaders were usually the most generous person in a band, a village or a clan. And because of this generosity, the chief was the unifying force of the community.

In Blackfeet society, for example, people changed bands if they believed another chief was more generous. Members of a band led by a stingy chief would have felt the same resentment as we do in workplaces working for a mean-spirited, penny-pinching boss. And in traditional Blackfeet society, a band usually dissolved after the death of a prominent chief if there was no one to take their place in the hearts of the people.[9]

I experienced the generosity of a headman in action. In Chapter 2, I mentioned my meeting with the Himba headman, Tjikoko, he sitting in his chair and the rest of us — my guide, translator and myself — sitting in the dirt. I wanted to pay or provide something as a 'thank you' for his time and for the knowledge he shared with me. Rather than taking a benefit for himself, he took us for a walk across the dry, grassless plain to a one-room shop. He requested that we buy bags of maize so all the people of his village could benefit. From the haul we lugged back, his people would have been happy that evening with plenty of gratitude towards Tjikoko.

Leaders being generous is not just an expected attribute of leaders of a village as in the case of a Himba leader. In the case of the highly organised Mohawk society, leaders in traditional times were expected to be generous. In 1644, still relatively early days of European presence in north-east America, a Protestant preacher wrote of his observation of Mohawk society. On leadership, he wrote, as medicine Joe McGregor had told me about the old days, 'The chiefs are generally the poorest among them, for instead of their receiving from the common people as among Christians, they are obliged to give to the mob ...'[10]

That attribute of leadership in Mohawk society continues today. Kimberly Kaniehténhawe Cross, the manager of the Kahnawà:ke Tourism Office, provided the perspective of a younger person in her culture. In our conversation over lunch in a café near the St. Lawrence River, I asked her about the attributes she admires in a chief. 'Honesty, clarity of thinking and communication,' she answered without hesitation. 'They are not there for themselves. They are a public figure. They have to be present; to be there in the community. A good leader knows the people. They know me. They are a good role model. They help others, especially older people.'

Caring for the Long-Term Interests of the Community

On the other side of North America, generosity is an expected attribute of Haida leaders. Elsie Gale runs Gwaii Naay guest house at Masset on the north coast of Haida Gwaii in the far northern Pacific Ocean of Canada. She is a cultural guardian. Like many first nations, Haida have had such a tough time keeping their culture alive that nowadays there are relatively few people with the knowledge. Their language and many of their practices were outlawed through the late 1800s and well into the 1900s. Like many traditional societies, the Haida population was devastated by European disease, including smallpox, in the early days of colonisation. By 1885 only 13% of their pre-colonial population survived.[11] Elsie is one of the people who acquired the old stories, mainly because when she was a girl, her grandmother saw in Elsie the qualities of a person who could carry the knowledge. Her grandmother deposited her oral stories with the young Elsie as the library.

During our several conversations, Elsie and I talked about the attributes of leadership in her culture.

'A good chief,' she said, 'takes care of their people; they make sure people have food, helps clothe them if required, gives them a good standard of living. A good chief adds happiness to people's lives. They respect everyone and in public gatherings they never talk over people. They have respect for the people and respect for the environment.'

I asked her to give me an example of a good chief.

'In my lifetime,' she said, 'Claude Davidson was a wonderful chief. He had a heart of gold. He was generous with less fortunate people, such as single-mothers and widows. He provided them with fish and seaweed. He was a loving person. And he followed cultural protocols.'

One day I returned to Elsie's guesthouse to find her drying seaweed. I'd been out to an isolated beach, where the only other living thing was a Bald Eagle standing in the shallow water of the bay feasting on a fish. Rain is a feature of Haida Gwaii weather, but this particular day was sunny. Elsie took the opportunity of fine weather to dry a bundle of seaweed. She'd erected a trestle and laid out the seaweed, turning it every few minutes so it dried rather than baked in the sun. The seaweed is a rich source of vitamins, a super food, which she will grind and use in salads and stews.

'A good chief,' she continued, 'respects the view of the community and our environment.'

Elsie explained that with big decisions, her people base their decision on the long-term protection and respect of the environment. 'In our decisions we take into account the effect of that decision on the land, the animals and the sea *for all time*.' (Her emphasis.)

'If a chief fails to demonstrate respect for the environment and the community's view, the chief will be counselled by the aunties,' Elsie said. The aunties are the matriarchs of the clan.

Elsie told me about one case when a chief refused to listen to the community. The issue related to an oil company wanting to transport oil through Haida waters. The people have vivid memories of the damage caused by the Exxon Valdez oil spill in nearby Alaskan waters years before and they didn't want to risk the same thing happening to the waters around Haida Gwaii. Despite the reservations of the community and warning by the aunties, the chief supported the oil company. The community decided that he would no longer be their chief. (In Chapter 6 we will look at the options available to the community if a leader is not fulfilling their role in the way the people expect.)

Respect for the long-term interests of the community often arose in my meetings with different societies. Mohawk clan mother Fran Beauvais told me, 'In our decision-making, we decide what's best for the entire collective, for the children seven generations from now.'

Chief Kahsennenhawe (Gus) Sky-Deer made a similar point earlier the same day. Gus is an elected councillor, a member of the municipal council. Hers is a leadership role but not one of the traditional positions. She made time during her annual leave to meet me. In her office I noticed a photo of her in football gear. She had attended college in Florida where she had played American football.

'A good chief,' she told me, 'has the utmost regard for the community — for the collective. They put the community before everything else. They don't put themselves above anyone. They are a representative on behalf of the people. They are humble; they don't let the title go to their head. Everything centres around peace and a good mind.'

The abundant environment of the Mohawk Valley supported large concentrations of people. In the arid Western Desert of Central Australia, small widely-dispersed bands eked out a living. Yet in both regions, leadership attributes are similar. I've mention previously that Pintupi is one of the last Aboriginal nations to interact with Europeans. Apart from being distant from the first British colony, the first European explorers who ventured into their country in 1873 assessed that the land was unsuitable for raising cattle. Consequently, while pastoralists moved into lands to the west and to the east of Pintupi country, they gave the Western Desert a wide berth. That meant Pintupi and neighbouring nations were spared the dispossession and dispersal that rode on the back of cattle. Lucky Pintupi. I mentioned earlier that in October 2019 I visited the town of Walungurru near the Northern Territory and Western Australian border. As for other First Peoples in most developed nations, Pintupi leadership today is a mix of traditional leadership and municipal leadership. In both leadership roles, ensuring community wellbeing is expected in the leader. The most senior woman in Walungurru is Irene Wilpinta. I asked two other female elders why Irene is the senior woman of their community. The two elders, Monica (Ampi) Robinson and Maureen (Mimala) Wheeler, are both highly respected, recently retired, assistant school teachers. They answered my question about Irene's leadership attributes by telling a story.

'We all lived in Papunya (the nearest town 450 kms or 280 miles away). That was not our country. In 1981 we decided to move back to our country — to Pintupi country. We called our town, Settled Down Country. When we first moved here, we had a meeting every morning. The main item we discussed was about how to look after our children. Initially we had no houses and no school. In 1982 we began a school under a large tree. Irene was the key person who created the school and although she was not trained as a school teacher, she was the first teacher. The next school was a shelter, with corrugated iron providing protection from the desert wind. We called it the Windbreak School. Irene got other people involved. With any community issues Irene is always involved. She is the speaker and people listen to her.'

I asked about attributes that are common to leaders in their culture.

'Leaders are involved in the community. They listen and they speak up. A leader listens to all the people and tries to help them. They listen to the elders — the old people — and they build up knowledge. Without knowledge the community goes downhill. Leaders identify young leaders — people aged 17 to 18 — who are emerging as role models. They involve the young people in meetings and in the issues of the community. Leaders are always walking towards the future.'

Knowledge of and Respect for Individuals

In taking into account the interests of the whole community, societies also expect the leader to have an interest in the individuals who make up their community. The leader values the identity of each person.

When my Maasai friend Ngila and I had stopped to watch the tower of giraffes, we were on our way to meet Nasha Kitonga just outside her village. Nasha is the mother of six children and about 40 years of age. Ngila provided the Swahili-to-English translation for Nasha and my conversation. I began by asking her about the most important part of her life.

'I want the best for my children,' she answered enthusiastically. 'I want them to be disciplined in the way they live. That they are well-behaved and god-fearing. I want them to be well-dressed.'

Upon being married, Nasha's husband's chief became her chief. I ask her whether her chief is a good chief.

'Yes!' she answered vigorously, accompanied by the customary welling of tears of admiration when Maasai think about their leader. 'He is a very respected person and we fear him. And we reciprocate that respect.' My interpretation of the word 'fear' which Ngila used in the translation was meant in the same sense she had used god-fearing.

Her chief is the leader of about 400 people. 'Does your chief know you?' I asked.

'Yes, of course!' she answered with the emphasis on *of course*, as though it was a foreign concept that her chief wouldn't know her as an individual within the group.

'What subjects does he know about you?' I asked, wanting to get a sense of whether the chief's interest in her was sincere or face-only recognition.

'He knows the family I come from. He knows the family I married. He knows my husband and my husband's nickname. He knows the name of my first child. The chief addresses me by the name of my first-born child. I became known as Mama Unero.' I gained the impression that Nasha felt well-satisfied that the chief knows and respects her as an individual.

Many workplace leaders at the 'village' or divisional level don't realise their impact when they demonstrate an acknowledgement of the individuals who work in their part of the organisation. Good leaders do. On her first day with a new employer some years ago, my wife, Jude, had the impactful experience of a CEO who made a point of acknowledging her as an individual being. Up until this point she'd worked in a large teaching hospital for over a decade, and then joined the pharmaceutical company, Merck Sharp & Dohme. Towards the end of her first day at Merck, the Chief Executive was walking through her department. At this stage, Jude was a staff member, not a manager, so was three levels below the CEO. When the CEO saw Jude at her desk, he introduced himself and sat down for a chat. He knew that a person named Jude Tasker was starting work that day. And he knew the role that she was engaged to do — a new role in the industry. Jude came home that night and as part of her report of newsworthy events from her first day, she enthusiastically told me about the chief executive introducing himself and having a brief chat. Leaders like this have a genuine regard for people, and, like Nasha's chief, they know the identity of the several hundred people in their division or organisation. The feeling of being acknowledged as an individual makes quite an impression, as it did on Jude, and that impression stays with you.

Treating People Equally — No Favouritism

Another element of respect that features prominently, linked to recognising the identity and worth of individuals, is that good leaders treat people equally. Across cultures, people frequently told me that a good leader has no favourites.

Not surprisingly, by the age of 18 a young Himba woman has worked out the desired attributes of a village leader. She knows how good or bad leadership makes her feel. She described the attributes of a good leader elegantly with telling simplicity.

Urprua (pronounced Waprua) lives in her grandmother's village. At the time I met her she had not long before moved from another village. We were sitting in the shade just outside the corral of her village. Urprua nursed her infant. A remarkable feature of Himba culture is the mixture of ochre and cow's butterfat Himba women apply to their skin as a make-up and for sun protection. We began our conversation, translated from Herero, with my asking how she begins her day.

'I spend time every morning on my make-up before coming out of my hut,' she said.

She had bright eyes and a ready smile. She was open and confident. She seemed to enjoy the stimulation of talking with a stranger interested in her culture. When I asked about the desired attributes of a leader, she readily named four things:

1. 'They say hello every morning with a smile on their face.'

2. 'They make sure there is enough food.'

3. 'They beat no one.' (I was sorry to hear this item. The equivalent in workplace leadership is that a leader does no one any harm, physically or psychologically.)

4. 'They have no favourites. A leader with favourites is like a grandmother who has favourites amongst the grandchildren.'

Poetically put! And she'd had no time to prepare her answer; they are the factors that were front of mind.

Her point about 'no favourites' is a critical one for workplace leaders. Given our social nature, humans are quick to detect if a leader has favourites amongst team members, or, in the case of a senior leader, favourite teams or sections of the organisation. The single fastest way to divide a team is for a leader to demonstrate favouritism for certain team members. People quickly intuit whether they are part of the in-group, and if not part of the in-group, they are pushed into an out-group. The top favouritism signals include a leader spending disproportionate time with some team members, speaking nicely to some team members and less so to others, sharing jokes with some people and not others, having coffee or lunch with only selected team members, demonstrating interest in the work of some team members versus others, allocating preferred tasks to some, and engaging in outside-work activities with only some team members. Realistically, a leader might have better chemistry with some team members than others, but the point is you can't show it — you can't show preference by your behaviours.

Four thousand kilometres (2,500 miles) from Urprua's village, roughly on the other side of Africa in northern Kenya, Jude and I visited the Samburu nation. I mentioned previously that the Samburu nation split with the Maasai only a few centuries ago. Given such a relatively recent split, Samburu culture is similar to the Maasai. The absence of favouritism featured as a desired leadership attribute.

When we visited Samburu society in August 2017, I spent most time with Lmusari (Mark) Lenanyankerra. Mark is about 50 years old, and had been elevated the month before to the respected position of senior elder of his clan. He lives in a village of 45 people, about two hours' drive from the Sarara camp where he works as a guide. He told me that a large village might have 100 people.

When I asked him about attributes of a good chief, one of the first attributes he mentioned is an absence of favouritism. 'They are free of bias. They have no favourites. A good chief can't be biased favouring their sub-clan over others. They treat everyone the same.' If the chief has favourites, the community would fracture around in-groups and out-groups. Social cohesion would be compromised.

A thirty-five-year-old Samburu woman, Nashangai, expressed the same point. 'A good chief does not have favourites,' she said. 'They treat everyone equally. This means there is no tribalism. Anybody can go to the chief and be heard.'

Humility

It's hard to imagine a leader demonstrating respect if they think they are the smartest person in the room. As we've already seen, a number of people referred to humility as a required leadership attribute. Mohawk people I spoke to mentioned that the leader 'has no ego, or at least keeps (it) in check', and 'the chief is not a peacock strutting self-importance'. The young Himba woman, Urprua, says that a good village leader 'says hello every morning with a smile on their face', a concrete picture of humility and of being in touch with followers. Richard Lee, the leading Bushman anthropologist, found that character was a major reason why someone became leader of a band. In describing the necessary characteristics, he stated that, 'None is arrogant, overbearing, boastful or aloof.' Behaviours such as arrogance and boastfulness would 'absolutely disqualify a person as a leader and may engender even stronger forms of ostracism.'[12]

During my visit to New Zealand, Keri Opai, my Māori host, stressed the importance of humility as a mandatory leadership attribute in his community. Keri and I spent three days together in his home region of Taranaki on the west coast of the North Island. As we drove around the district looking at important sites, or sitting in a café for a meal or a coffee, Keri added layer upon layer of Māori wisdom. On leadership attributes, he told me about the importance of humility — of being modest with a focus on enabling others. In his culture, to be respected and effective, leaders have an absence of arrogance and show no sense of superiority. They do not put themselves above others.

'In our culture,' he said, 'there are many proverbs for humility but none for arrogance. For example, "A kūmara doesn't tell you how sweet it is."' Kūmara is a sweet potato and was the primary food source of the population from the early days of Māori settlement — 97% of the population in traditional times lived in areas suitable for growing kūmara.[13]

'Another proverb,' he said, 'is "Be humble and your true chieftainship is obvious."'

Facilitating Respectful Meetings

Another indicator of respect for people is in the way leaders facilitate meetings. Across traditional societies, there is consistency in the way meetings are run. From what I was told, there are three themes about the nature of meetings in First Nation societies: first, everyone is heard; second, no one is interrupted; and third, consensus is developed through discussion. A lot of readers will smile, thinking how different that description is to their experience of workplace meetings, which are often impatient affairs dominated by the leader.

My Haida host, Elsie Gale, painted a picture of meeting protocols in her culture. 'When we conduct meetings, we gather in a circle,' she said.

'No one is sitting or standing at the back of someone's head. Everyone sees everyone else. There is no talking over people. Everyone who wants to speak is heard.' Likewise, Māori decision-making is a matter of discussion, compromise and consensus. Almost always acceptance of the outcome is and was through voluntary assent rather than obedience to any authority.[14]

Emma Kahente Ouimet helped organise my visit to Kahnawà:ke. She is about 20 years of age and passionate about her Mohawk culture. Emma shared with me her observations about the good leaders in her community. 'Good leaders listen to people. Everyone needs to speak. A good chief wants to hear from everyone.'

Mohawk and the wider Haudenosaunee society has a sophisticated decision-making process that has endured through the years. In our meeting at the Kahnawà:ke Language and Cultural Center, Teyowisonte Tommy Deer explained the process when meetings are held of the confederacy nations. 'Ours is a consensus-based system,' he said. 'When the League (of nations) meets, any issues are put into "the well". The Onondaga sachems (chiefs) go to the well to choose the issues to be discussed. The well-keepers — the Mohawk and Seneca — then decide the priority of the issues and stand up and identify the issue. The well-keepers send the issue to the other side of the house — the Oneida and Cayuga chiefs. The Oneida and Cayuga discuss the issue and develop solutions. These proposed solutions are sent back to the other side. The Mohawk and Seneca, in considering the proposed solutions, may endorse, amend or counter-propose. They can't reject the solution. When there is consensus between both sides, the solution is sent to the Onondaga.'

Tommy explained that this consensus system also applies at the nation level. Mohawk decisions are made in the same way with issues identified and then prioritised, sent to one side to develop possible solutions and sent back for consideration and only when there is a consensus is the decision made. It may take longer to make decisions, but I can imagine that implementation and compliance are more successful than decisions made in an autocracy. No doubt there were times in traditional Mohawk society when decisions needed to be made faster or with fewer people involved, such as in times of war. Likewise there are times when workplace decisions need to be made quickly. But the main point is to consider the advantages of calm decision making with more people involved in discussions which allow for better decisions, greater support and faster implementation.

'To achieve this consensus approach,' Tommy said, 'you need the right people in leadership positions. Leaders need to be good thinkers. They need to have ideas. They need exceptional problem-solving skills. At times there is conflict and differences of opinion, and a chief needs to find a solution. A chief must be able to communicate their ideas. They need good oratory skills.'

The basic meeting courtesies of Mohawk and wider Haudenosaunee society made quite an impression on Benjamin Franklin, one of the founders of the United States. In the mid-1700s, Franklin described the basic decency in the way speakers at the Haudenosaunee Grand Council are heard and never interrupted: 'He that would speak, rises. The rest observe in profound silence ... To interrupt another, even in common conversation, is reckoned highly indecent.'[15]

Actions for Workplace Leaders

For workplace leaders, there are two levels of implications from the ancestral experience that *respect*, and the behaviours that comprise respect, is the universal attribute of leadership. On one level there are implications for organisations and on the other there are implications for individual leaders.

For organisations, the call to action includes the following:

1. **Define leadership attributes:** Organisations should remove any mystery about how leaders are expected to behave by declaring the attributes expected of leaders in the organisation. The list removes the variability that arises when leaders determine for themselves how they choose to lead. That's too random. The attributes on the list should be the behaviours expected in every leader at every level — from first-level supervisors to the CEO. They apply to every leader in workplaces just as they apply to every level of ancestral societies — from leaders of small nomadic bands and villages up to leaders of divisions and nations; in my meetings the First Peoples'

respect for people didn't drop off the list at a certain level of the hierarchy. In defining the attributes of leadership, the wisdom of ancestral societies shared in this chapter provides a valuable list of attributes for leaders in your organisation.

2. **Hire and develop on the behaviours that demonstrate *respect for people*:** I was struck by the absolute consistency of people describing leadership in their society. The conversations were like a recording on repeat. From the Kalahari to the South Pacific Ocean and up via the northern Pacific to the eastern side of America, everyone spoke about respect for people. And they explained the behaviours that demonstrate respect. By defining the behaviours that demonstrate respect (Action 1 above), an organisation has a framework for hiring to that standard, for developing leaders with those skills and holding leaders accountable to lead according to those attributes. Organisations that appoint, or tolerate, managers who are disrespectful of their people are violating the universal leadership code and setting in train unintended negative consequences for staff engagement, retention and work performance.

3. **Hold to account disrespectful leaders:** Organisations, specifically their senior executives, need to counsel or remove leaders who operate without respect — who are angry, abusive or arrogant. These behaviours are self-sabotaging for the leader because they are repugnant and demoralising to staff. From my experience, leaders who are inclined to throw sparks of hot-headedness will moderate their dysfunctional behaviour on one condition: that their own boss, or a senior person in their line, calls them out on their behaviour. Being called out by an indirect person, such as Human Resources, usually doesn't motivate the aggressive leader to change their behaviour. We'll return to this point in Chapter 6 when we look at checks on leadership power.

4. **Provide tools to help leaders be generous:** Organisational policies can assist leaders to be generous towards their people. One of my brothers, Paul, told me about a time early in his career when his manager generously acknowledged a significant project Paul had

accomplished. As a 'thank you', his manager authorised Paul to engage a babysitter one night for Paul and his wife to enjoy a dinner out — the manager suggested his own favourite restaurant which made the experience extra special. The manager told Paul, in accordance with the company's policy, to submit his expense claim for reimbursement for the cost of the dinner and the babysitter. Paul vividly recalls that happy experience — because of the emotion attached to it — even though it was 25 years ago. As well as recognition programs (quite common in good organisations), other systems that support leaders being generous include:

- Communicating the expectation that managers will fully allocate their annual pay review budget (not being mean-spirited at pay review time),
- Programs that support the personal and professional development of staff, and
- Establishing the culture of generosity, such as an expectation that managers will, say, give people bonus time off work for sustained high delivery.

5. **Train leaders in people leadership:** Provided leaders have the right material in their make-up, leadership skills can be developed. Good leadership programs increase a leader's awareness of ideas and concepts, and help a leader apply those ideas in the training environment before they apply them for real in their roles. As most good workplaces do, organisations should invest in leadership training. The programs should include elements of respect for people: peacemaker and conflict resolution skills, the negative consequences of favouritism, practical ways to demonstrate respect for individual identity and the other subjects we have covered in this chapter.

6. **Conduct regular staff surveys that report down to the team level:** Good organisations close the loop on their expectations of leadership standards by conducting regular staff surveys. The loop is closed if the organisation (such as the HR leader) gets to see the survey results for each leader — so the HR team has data on leaders who are leading well and the leaders who need help. In selecting the

appropriate survey tool, a design criterion should be that the results can be reported down to the level of the individual leader (provided leaders receive, say, a minimum of four or perhaps five responses from direct reports to ensure the anonymity of people's answers). Only in this way can the organisation ponder the question: who are our leaders demonstrating respect and leading well, and who are our leaders who need to alter the way they are leading?

For individual leaders, the call to action from the universal code of respect includes the following:

7. **Beware random acts of anger and bad language:** The problem with occasional outbursts of anger by a leader is that those outbursts dominate the emotion people attached to that leader. How many times would a direct report need to be the recipient of, or even just an observer of, abuse before that behaviour dominates the leader's character in the eyes of the direct report? Once? No more than twice. The natural response by direct reports to angry outbursts is to keep a safe distance from such a leader — not a good place whence to lead. The societies I visited refuse to tolerate angry and abusive leaders.

8. **Be generous:** Leaders have an advantage if they are in an organisation that provides policy support for leaders to express appreciation for people. But even in organisations that aren't providing that support, a leader can still be generous by:

   a. Giving generously of their time, including welcoming 'interruptions',

   b. Responding quickly when people need work reviewed so that progress is not slowed,

   c. Providing resources so people can succeed without undue stress,

   d. Treating people out of the manager's own pocket to the odd coffee or equivalent,

   e. Accommodating people's personal circumstances, and

   f. Having a generous spirit and not being too quick to judge people.

9. **Demonstrate respect for individuals:** Workplace leaders should know what makes each person the individual they are. What's their story? What's their identity? When working for a manager who doesn't know them as an individual, staff will tend to say, disparagingly, 'My manager treats me just like a number.' The call to action is for each team leader (senior executives are also team leaders) to know, say, five things that makes each team member an individual. At the next level, leaders of 'villages' (of units up to about 150 people) should know all the individuals in their village. Remember, given the size of our brain, knowing 150 people is doable — if you have an interest in doing so. Above the village, the most inspiring executives know an incredible number of people in their organisation — people's faces, names, their role and something personal about them. I talked with one senior executive who I knew from insiders was very well regarded — he was loved. Years after he'd left the organisation, I asked him, 'Of the 3000 people in your organisation, how many did you know by name?' He said, in a humble tone, 'Maybe about 1200 people.' No wonder he was loved.

10. **Schedule regular time with your people:** A key leadership practice that combines the previous two actions (generosity and respect for individuals) is to hold regular reviews with team members. These are 'catch-ups' with people individually, perhaps once every two weeks or more frequently if a person is new to their role or they are working on a project that has pressing deadlines. The catch-ups achieve two key objectives. First, by allocating precious time, the manager is signifying to individuals that they and their job are important. Second, through regular catch-ups the manager is staying close to the tasks the person is completing so can offer help with ideas, remove barriers and detect if a project is heading towards trouble or about to miss deadlines. Part of the generosity mindset of the manager is to view the catch-ups as being the person's meeting as much as the manager's. This mindset leads to the manager accepting that each person will use the time according to their individual needs. In my time as a manager, one of my direct reports used the time to discuss high-level concepts for her projects which gave her greater clarity of

thinking. At the other end of that spectrum, another person used the time to go through his detailed action plans so that he and I knew his project was on track and he had the support he needed. I made sure that the catch-ups were informal. For example, I never asked people to prepare notes before the reviews. I considered preparatory notes unnecessarily formal as well as adding to workload. My approach was to keep a manilla folder for each person's catchup, and in the folder I'd have rough hand-written notes as memory joggers from one meeting to the next.

11. **Treat people equally — no favourites:** Showing favouritism towards a person or a sub-group is the fastest way for a leader to divide a team. A leader who shows favouritism drives people into one of two camps — the in-group or the out-group. Team leaders can self-assess on this point. Write down the names of your direct reports, then reflect on the amount of time you spend with people and the nature of those interactions. Is the amount of time and quality of the time roughly equal for each person? As a senior executive, as well as your own team, reflect on the way you treat the various units in your organisation. Does the time you spend demonstrate respect for all units, or are you creating elitism of some groups at the expense of others which will probably split your organisation?

12. **Communicate openly when delegating work:** One of the ways arrogant and aloof leaders burn people's energy is the way they delegate work — they withhold important information and opinions. The staff member is left to try to work out what's on the leader's mind. The staff member then spins their wheels trying to work out if they are coming up with the 'right answer'. It's a wasteful guessing game. In this guessing game, when the staff member reviews their output with the manager, the manager invariably points out the shortcomings of the staff member's analysis. 'Why didn't you tell me all that earlier?' the staff member bemoans to themselves. When delegating tasks, the best leaders have an open discussion about the issue at hand, why a solution matters and possible options for the staff member to consider as they complete their analysis or undertake the task.

13. **Follow protocols for respectful meetings:** Meetings don't just provide a rational vehicle for information sharing and decision making. Meetings have subtexts. One of the key subtexts is that meetings are a forum for a leader to demonstrate their style. How you run meetings reveals your mindset. Is your mindset one of respect for people: Do you have a view that everyone is a worthy team member? Do you want to hear everyone's view? Do you want to hear a range of views, including those that differ from your own? Do you believe that people deserve to be heard politely without interruption? Do you believe that meetings belong to the team and are not yours to dominate?

Having identified the attributes that qualify a person for a leadership role, we now turn to how First Nation societies choose *the one*: selecting *the right person* to fill a leadership vacancy. Traditional societies are incredibly diligent in their selection decisions. Samburu elder Lmusari (Mark) Lenanyankerra told me a key reason why in his society great care is taken in choosing the leader. His point sits strongly with me still. 'The chief,' he said, 'is given all powers, so you want those powers in the hands of a decent person. The powers include casting people out or cursing someone to die and the chief can punish anyone. You don't want those powers in the wrong hands.'

CHAPTER 4

Selecting Leaders

'The leader is chosen by the followers.'

OUT OF ELEVEN MAASAI and Samburu citizens I met, an astonish-ing ten people — 91% — were moved to tears just thinking about their chief. You'll recall in the Introduction to this book I mentioned that when I asked individual Maasai, 'What about *your* chief. Are they a good leader?' people instantly welled-up in adoration of their leader. All the Maasai and Samburu I met had a different chief — they lived in different districts or belonged to different age sets. Wouldn't we be ecstatic in our workplace if 91% of staff responded teary-eyed to the question, 'Is your leader a good leader?' And I don't mean tears of misery. How do Maasai, and their close cousins Samburu, get leadership selection so right? And is the Maasai approach similar to other ancestral societies to reveal a pattern of success-ful leadership selection? In short, yes, there is a pattern. And, excitingly, applying the elements of the pattern can improve leadership selection in workplaces. Having learned what I have about the First Nations approach to leadership selection, I regret that I didn't have this wisdom when I was in workplace roles that carried responsibility for leadership selection deci-sions; I would have done things differently.

In sharing the pattern of how ancestral societies select *the one* to lead, I'll focus mainly on the societies organised at the higher-levels of the division or the nation, rather than the band-level and village-level societies. This is because the selection decision processes used by Haida, Maasai, Māori and Mohawk societies are the most relevant to medium-to-large organisations; their big leadership jobs are most similar to the big leadership roles in large workplaces. Towards the end of this chapter I'll comment on the pathway to leadership in the hunter-gatherer and village societies, in which leadership roles are more similar to those found in small family-based firms.

Across the higher-level societies I visited, there are four elements that form the pattern for selecting leaders. First, extreme care is taken in selection decisions. Second, there is long tenure of the appointment. Third, followers are involved in the selection decision. And fourth, leaders come from within the culture. All four elements have implications for improving leadership selection in workplaces.

About two years after our first Maasai visit, Jude and I returned to Lewa in northern Kenya. We looked forward to spending more time with our friend Ngila Loitamany Johnson. I was keen to go deeper into many subjects with him, and the first was leader selection.

Jude and I flew by light aircraft to Lewa. On approach, the pilot swept low over the dirt airstrip to check that no animals, such as zebra, were grazing on the runway. All was clear and we touched down. Ngila met us. We were overjoyed to see him, and he us. In describing our friendship, Ngila pays me the compliment of saying that he and I are brothers from different mothers. After hugs and handshakes, we bundled our luggage and ourselves into Ngila's vehicle. The drive from the airstrip to the Sirikoi camp where Ngila works as a safari guide excites the senses. In every direction, animals dot the rolling grassland and emerge from groves of acacias. Soon after leaving the airstrip, we paused to watch giraffe loping across the plain. We hadn't progressed far before Ngila cut the car's engine for us to watch a white rhinoceros mother and calf grazing. Next, off to the right, a male ostrich fanned his white tail feathers at a small flock of females. His mating display only seemed to scare the females. They raced away. We lost sight of them over a distant hill with the male still in hot pursuit.

Having arrived at our lodge, Ngila and I soon settled into conference. I was keen to cover the Maasai process for selecting chiefs. There has to be an explanation for a 91% success rate in choosing leaders who followers revere.

Care and Time Taken in Selecting the Leader

I reminded Ngila of our conversations the previous visit when he educated me on the organisation of warriors into age sets, and that every age set has a chief who remains their chief for life as the generation ages.

'Tell me more,' I said, 'about the time it takes to select the chief of a new group of young warriors when a new age set is formed.'

'It takes between three and five years of observation to decide the chief,' he said. 'The candidates for the chief role come from high-ranking families. In my age set there were 350 boys, and in my clan of Laikipia Maasai there are four or five families from which we choose leaders. But birth is not enough. Character is the element that drives the choice of leader. After the age set is formed, a long period of observation of the potential chief begins. It will be a number of years before one is chosen.'

He continued: 'These few young people from the high-ranking families spend significant time with the elders. This investment of time allows the elders to observe them and to teach them the Maasai way. We have no documented history, so oral history is the only way that our laws and customs are maintained. During this time, as well as teaching them, the elders are observing their temperament, character and ability. The elders are assessing who amongst the candidates is the worthiest.'

In workplace terminology, this observation period is when the short-listed candidates are narrowed down. The main point is that the decision period to select the leader is years, not days or weeks or, in the case of external candidates for workplace leadership roles, a couple of interviews, reference checks and perhaps a battery of psychological tests and simulation exercises.

Ngila referred to high-ranking families. In some societies, heredity is a factor in leadership selection, sometimes a significant one. But as we will see, even in those societies where birthright plays a role, merit trumps lineage. While the hereditary system, where it applies, identifies a short-list of candidates or even a preferred successor, the community will not appoint to the leadership role a person who does not have the required character. (While Laikipia Maasai in the north of Kenya select chiefs from royal families, heredity is not a factor for Maasai in the south of Kenya.)

Haida society in the northern Pacific Ocean is one of the societies where birthright plays an important role in leadership selection. But again, merit and character override descent. In the Haida clan system, the matriarch has the responsibility, on the current chief's death, to 'invite the next chief'. The normal pathway of succession is to invite the eldest son of the eldest sister of the chief who passed away. (Again, we'll cover male dominance in Chapter 9.) That person can decline and if he does, the matriarch goes to the next eldest sister's oldest son. Yet the matriarch is not obliged to follow the protocol of inviting the eldest son. The matriarch still has to decide if the next-in-line is a good choice to fill the leadership role.

The Davidson family is one of the high-ranking families on Haida Gwaii. Before my visit, I'd read the life story of a late matriarch of the family, Florence Davidson.[1] Clearly, Florence was an amazing, active member of her community. On the occasion of 'raising a chief' in 1976, Florence donated bread rolls, baking a thousand buns in her kitchen oven. Apparently, that was not an unusual event. Her kitchen must have been a food factory, and I imagine a very happy one at that.

I was fortunate to meet three of Florence's descendants. One of them, Leona Davidson, is Florence's eldest granddaughter. She is now the matriarch of her clan in the Eagle moiety. She has the responsibility, upon the chief's death, of filling the role by selecting the next chief.

'What are the characteristics of a good chief?' I asked Leona.

'Respectful,' she nominated as the first attribute. 'A good chief binds the clan.'

Leona told me a story from her childhood which reveals a key stage of the process of inviting a chief. About 60 years ago, young Leona was in her grandmother's lounge room when grandmother Florence and the aunties met with the person being considered as the successor chief. From the side of the lounge room, wide-eyed little Leona observed the meeting. (I imagine grandmother Florence let young Leona observe the occasion as part of Leona's preparation as the clan's future matriarch.)

'In effect it was an interview,' Leona told me. 'The aunties were assessing the successor. After he left the house, the aunties talked and decided that he would be acceptable as chief.' And this final assessment was in the context that the aunties already knew the candidate extremely well, having observed him for years.

'What might have disqualified him?' I asked.

'If he was rude, arrogant or disrespectful.'

Given that a young man next-in-line knows from an early age that he is likely to be the next chief, he has plenty of time to prepare for the role. At the Haida museum at Skidegate, I was told by a guide that the successor has a long training period. He 'stands with the chief' and learns the role. But it's not a done deal that the next in line will be chosen. The museum official told me that the individual next in line could be blocked, or 'passed over'. The most likely reason for being passed over is if the matriarch has reservations about his character.

Like in Haida society, in Māori society the default for selecting the next leader is also hereditary. But also as in Haida society, the first-born could be passed over if that individual did not have the character, mental capacity and bravery to be the leader. Leading Māori academic Te Rangi Hīroa, discussing this topic in 1949, wrote that if the first-born did not have leadership potential, the people would turn to the next-in-line to provide the 'energy and administrative ability required for leadership'. Poor leadership would lower the prestige and security of the community. If they were passed over, the first-born still retained their honorary position for ritual and ceremonial functions.[2]

Finally on this point of the care and time taken to select a chief, in the Mohawk community of Kahnawà:ke leadership candidates are observed for years to ensure a quality appointment. When clan mother Fran Beauvais and I had dinner, she told me that she has her eyes on one lad of about 12 years of age who appears to have the character to one day be chief. As an example of the boy's character that impressed her, she said he recently excelled at a sports event. The boy's grandmother posted his accomplishment on social media. The young lad commented on the post, saying, 'Stay humble grandma'. Humility, along with other characteristics of the boy, appeals to Fran. She'll watch him for many years yet.

Lifetime Appointments to Leadership Roles

Maasai elder Koyaki Ole Sopia, the 'real child of the Maasai' who we met in the last chapter, was the first person who told me the second principle of leadership selection that's consistent across the ancestral societies I visited (including the band- and village-level societies). Leaders are in their role for life. I didn't expect that finding. It's a challenging concept, and one I have reflected on since I saw this pattern emerge in my research. Why? Why would ancestral societies consistently adopt that approach?

'We have to choose our chief carefully,' Koyaki said, leading to his telling point, 'because once in they can't be removed.'

Hear me out. I'm not advocating lifetime leadership appointments in workplaces, but it does justify exploring the reasons that lifetime appointments emerged, consistently, as the approach in ancestral societies. And consideration should be given to the possible lessons of this timeless wisdom for workplaces.

Being appointed to the leadership role for life — a Haida, Maasai, Māori or Mohawk chief and, as we will see, a Bushmen camp leader and a Himba village head — sounds counterintuitive. Wouldn't it be healthier to keep pressure on the individual to perform in their role? Wouldn't it be healthier not to risk being stuck with a bad appointment for the rest of that person's life? Not so. Ancestral societies have worked out over the long timeframe of their experience that the benefits of lifetime appointments far outweigh the potential downsides. From my reflections, there are eight reasons why ancestral cultures have landed on lifetime appointments. Several of them have implications for workplace leadership selection.

The first and the major benefit of lifetime appointments, revealed by Koyaki, is that permanent tenure means there is extreme pressure to make a superb choice when selecting the leader. If you're stuck with your decision, you do your very best, and take the necessary time, to make the right choice.

The second benefit of lifetime appointments is that being secure in their role allows leaders to lead without fear or favour. The role becomes less political and more focused on serving the community. If a leader is fearful of being deposed, they need to pander to small but powerful factions.

Associated with that second reason of the role being less political, third, it means that the leader is not subject to one of the main occupational hazards of senior executives of workplaces — being removed from their role based on a falling out with someone above them such as the CEO or Chair of the Board.

Fourth, associated with being secure in their role, the leader doesn't need to engage in dysfunctional behaviour to protect their position. If a leader is insecure in their role, defensive self-protective behaviours are often adopted by that leader. One common defensive behaviour of an insecure leader is to reduce the influence of other capable people, which means the group is denied the services of talented individuals.

Fifth, secure tenure removes the degree of political intrigue and undermining of the incumbent by ambitious rivals. Any attempt to usurp the leader is futile. Any attempt by an ambitious rival to become the leader is at least limited to the occasion of the current leader's death. When the current leader dies, although the line of succession might be known, in many societies there is a window for political manoeuvring as rivals take their chance. I've seen the same succession games played amongst senior executives when the current chief is wounded and weakened.

Sixth, extensive tenure of leadership appointments means that the political fallout that invariably follows a change in leader is minimised. We see in politics and in workplaces the predictable disruption that follows a change in leader. The new leader promotes their allies, or if they join from outside the organisation, they bring their closest confidants with them. People associated with the prior leader are pushed out as punishment for being part of the old guard. In the fallout, the organisation loses good people and plenty of knowledge. With lifetime appointments, the periods of political instability are spread out and the number of those events significantly reduced.

Seventh, the approach drives long-term perspective-taking by the leader, serving the greater good of the community rather than short-term political and personal interests.

The eighth and final benefit of lifetime tenure is the heightened legacy obligation of the leader. The leader is the custodian of the culture for their generation. They have a clear obligation to maintain the culture and to pass it on in a healthy state to the next generation. Being appointed for life means the leadership role is life's calling for the chosen individual. One Maasai told me, 'Mothers do not like their son being chosen to be chief.'

'Why not?' I asked, surprised. 'I thought a mother would be proud.'

'No,' he said. 'The mother knows that her son is lost to the family. He now belongs to the community.'

For workplaces, there are three main implications from this challenging perspective of lifetime appointments in ancestral societies. The first is about the care taken in leadership selection. The proxy for care in selecting a leader to fill a senior workplace role is to *imagine* the appointment is for life. *Imagine* the care you would take *if* the appointment is for life. The second implication is about leadership stability. Stability of leadership positions, and hence of membership of leadership teams, is generally undervalued. Stability is better than churn. Stability means members of a leadership team have a greater motivation to work with each other's style, personality, strengths and weaknesses and also to collaborate to achieve performance outcomes. Stability is a mindset; a chief executive who values stability will harmonise a team, acknowledge any tensions and see individual differences as strengths. With a stability mindset, a leader will fundamentally see things in the longer term rather than overreacting and spending excessive energy micromanaging short term issues. The third implication is the importance of a leadership legacy. The best workplace leaders have a strong sense of obligation to ensure the enduring success of their organisation. From this sense of legacy comes a willingness to prepare the next generation. In comparison to the focus of Maasai elders and Mohawk chiefs and clan mothers, senior leaders of workplaces generally don't spend enough time observing and mentoring the next generation. Limiting your observation of the next generation to glimpses of the young people presenting at meetings or attending planning conferences doesn't go anywhere near far enough. Such interactions are shallow exchanges no deeper than impressions of the young staff. Leaders with a drive to leave a legacy spend quality time with the next generation to mentor their development.

Although leaders are appointed for life, I just need to flag for completeness that there is in most societies an escape option that acts as a check on leadership incompetence or abuse of power. We'll look at checks on power in Chapter 6. In summary, these escape options, exercised only in the exceptional case, match the nature of the society. They range from people in Bushmen society voting with their feet and leaving camp up to, in the case of Mohawk society, a structured process involving three warnings.

Choosing a Chief the Followers Want as Their Leader

So far we've looked at the first two elements of leadership selection: extreme care taken in the selection decision and lifetime appointments. The next element goes a long way to explaining the phenomenal success of leadership selection in ancestral societies, including in Maasai society where 91% of followers adore their leader. In Maasai society, a person would only be chosen as chief if they have the enthusiastic support of their followers. In First Nation societies, followership is more significant than the role we allow it to play in workplaces.

Eric Ole Kasana is a Maasai elder who has travelled to the United Kingdom to speak to business audiences about Maasai leadership and culture. My friend Ngila drove me to the town of Nanyuki so Eric and I could talk over a cup of coffee. Eric spoke strongly about the role of followers in leadership selection. 'The leader is chosen by the age set — by the followers,' he said. 'The role of the elders is mainly to advise the warriors in their selection of leader.'

Ngila also introduced me to a young warrior, Legei Leiro. Because he was a current warrior, I was keen to hear of his recent experience of the leadership selection process. His striking clothing, featuring the red, blue and yellow-checked cloth of a Laikipia Maasai warrior, added to the privilege and pleasure of talking with him. Legei's broad smile and quick pace of talking revealed his enthusiasm for explaining his culture. He told me about the critical role the followers played in the selection of the chief of his age set. 'There is a cabinet of respected young men from within the age set. The cabinet plays a key role in choosing the chief. The cabinet and the elders identify the likely chiefs. The cabinet confers with the warriors to see who the warriors want as their chief. This process of the elders observing and conferring with the warriors goes on for three or more years.'

Legei continued: 'And right up until the end of the process, when the preferred chief has been selected but not yet announced, the elders will check with the warriors. "Are you still happy for this person to be your chief?" they ask one last time.'

Legei's cousin had been chosen as the chief of his age set. "Is he a good leader?" I asked.

Legei, even as a warrior, responded in the customary Maasai manner to that question — his eyes brimmed with tears of affection for his cousin. 'Oh yes! He never gets upset. He is always calm. He is never bad tempered. He is respectable and is liked by everyone.'

The key role of followers in the leadership selection decision applies in the other highly organised societies I visited. I mentioned earlier that in Haida society, the aunties select the leader. In this capacity, the senior women represent the followers and are choosing a leader that the community desires — the leader is not imposed on the followers. Upon appointment, the chief knows they are accountable to the aunties and to the community, not the other way around.

In Mohawk society, the Haudenosaunee constitution makes explicit that the chieftainship title is 'vested' in the women. The clan mother and the senior women are in touch with and represent the community. Teyowisonte Tommy Deer at the Language and Cultural Center added to what clan mother, Fran Beauvais, had told me. Tommy said that the final step in selecting a chief is a meeting of the candidate with the senior women of the clan. Men can also be present at this meeting, but only as observers. If the women agree with the clan mother's choice, they 'raise him'. The chief is responsible to the women and by extension, to the community. The followers decide their chief. (As a slight aside, the question arises as to how the clan mother is appointed. 'The community selects from amongst the women,' Tommy told me. 'Some communities look at blood before merit. But in our community we look at merit as the main attribute.')

In workplaces, why not ask the opinion of the followers when choosing their leader? I know it works. At one point in my career I worked as head of HR for a global professional services firm. For senior and mid-level management appointments, the chief executive sought the opinion of the direct reports of the vacant position. Most appointments were made from within the firm. Prior to deciding a leadership appointment the CEO talked with the direct reports, asking their opinion about the person he was thinking of appointing. The CEO knew that he did not have complete nor exclusive information on the candidates. The direct reports had both a valuable perspective and also a great deal invested in the person being appointed. The CEO also knew that the leader was more likely to be successful in their role if the team supported their appointment, rather than the opposite. On the rare occasion when an external candidate was considered, the direct reports were involved in the interview process. The CEO would not appoint someone who did not have the support of their team.

Leaders Come From Within

The fourth piece of the puzzle to the success of ancestral societies in selecting their leaders is that leaders come from within the culture — they don't hire from the 'outside'. While this is self-evident for traditional societies, it is significant and worth pondering for possible implications for workplaces.

In one of my conversations with Ngila about Maasai leadership, I commented that in Western workplaces we mostly advertise leadership roles and hire people from outside the organisation. 'How does that work?' he responded incredulously, frowning. 'How does it work hiring someone from outside your culture?' It was a foreign concept to him.

Catherine Rey is a school principal and has lived the sometimes painful experience of appointing leaders from outside a culture. Catherine is the founding Principal of St John Paul II College, a high school in the Catholic Archdiocese of Canberra & Goulburn, Australia. The school has around 950 students and 85 staff. As a new school with its first intake of students in 2013, the school was designed with a culture significantly different from conventional schools. For example, rather than having classrooms dedicated to a single class with a single teacher, classes are grouped so two teachers are pooling their skills for the benefit of two classes. Consequently, the physical space is extremely open compared to traditional schools. To facilitate a better connection between students and teachers, the physical design extends to staff rooms with glass walls positioned in the middle of the big open spaces. For some teachers from conventional backgrounds, the physical space feels like a fishbowl. Another difference is that the learning culture, based on a philosophy of individual and independent learning, involves teachers holding individual mentoring sessions with students each week. These practices can be confronting to traditional teachers.

The leadership systems of the school can be challenging to new leaders who are unfamiliar with the unique learning culture. In the first few years, middle managers were appointed both from within the school and also from other schools in the Catholic system. Too often, Catherine found, leaders appointed from outside the school — from outside the culture — found the environment too challenging. Significantly, this was despite the external leaders being good people with strong track records, and generally well known in the Catholic school system. 'In the early years,' Catherine told me, 'too often we found that new middle managers were overwhelmed and very unhappy. The challenge was that although we talked about our culture during the interview process, we could not actually prepare them for what they would face. Nowadays we appoint middle managers from within the school — we know they fit and they know they thrive in the culture. As well as fit, appointing from within has meant the accelerated development for early-career teachers within the college.'

Workplaces that as a matter of course fill leadership roles from the outside are understating the importance of culture. To habitually hire externally is a strong signal that an organisation is weak on culture — which is then, in fact, part of the culture. Organisations that value a strong, enduring culture prefer internal appointments. These organisations want to know that the person chosen is aligned to the culture; that the person has the same mental model driving their behaviour and decisions. Sure, there's sometimes a requirement to go outside. The question is one of preference and frequency. And if an external person is to be hired, especially into a senior position, that decision to go outside should only be made after balancing the risks, and not just as the default.

A big part of the attraction of external candidates for workplaces is that they tend to look better than internal candidates. There's a simple reason for this bias: the external candidate looks like the perfect person because during the recruitment process we don't get to know the whole person. The external candidate looks good on paper, they interviewed well and the referees (usually nominated by the candidate) speak glowingly about the person. It's really hard to look behind the mask to see the whole package, including their downsides (which we all have). By comparison, we know any internal candidate well. We know them as a total package — their strengths and any interference factors. Any weaknesses of the internal candidate feature prominently in the minds of the selectors. But in the case of the external candidate, we just don't yet know their potential interference factors. This drives us to invariably err in favour of the external person. Often, we are then surprised to find soon after appointing the external person that they aren't the perfect person we imagined them to be. They turn out to be human after all. In the meantime, we've overlooked and demoralised the good internal person who we might even lose from the organisation. Perhaps conveniently for some organisations, hiring from the outside also relieves pressure on the organisation to identify people early, to grow them and to give them opportunities in preparation for leadership roles.

The Pathway to Leadership in Bands and Villages

So far in this chapter we've looked at leadership selection in societies organised at the high level of divisions and nations. We will now look at societies organised as bands and villages as their highest organising unit. We will see that the same elements apply, although more informally than the approach in the higher-level societies. My proposition is that the elements served human groups well when, initially, all human populations were organised as bands and villages. And then as groups became more organised into divisions and nations, the elements were adopted more formally.

In band and village societies: a) leaders invariably hold their position for life; b) leaders come from within the culture (from within the band or the village); and c) followers have a say in who they want as their leader by choosing to stay or leave upon the transition to a new leader and in this way, merit still plays a role.

In Bushmen society organised around small bands of up to about 25 people, the element of lifetime leadership applied. The leader of a

Bushman camp was the founder of the camp and that person filled the role until their death or the camp disbanded. One of the reasons for disbandment was if, in the opinion of the followers, there was no suitable replacement leader to take up the leadership role. Upon the leader's death, if the group stayed together, the role generally passed to his or her eldest child. As 70-year-old Komtsa told me, when his grandfather, Bo, died, the leadership role 'would only be passed to his family'.

Even with lifetime appointments in Bushmen society, merit could still play a role. Elizabeth Marshall Thomas described one leader, Toma, mentioned earlier, who was leader of a band Marshall Thomas visited in the early 1950s. Toma had an unusual path to leadership. In Toma's case, the leader role was passed to him by his father-in-law. Toma had earned respect based on his character and hunting prowess. While in his late teens, Toma's 'powers in hunting attracted the attention of the headman of Gautscha Pan, who offered Toma the hand of his daughter, Tu, in marriage. Toma accepted, went to live with his wife's people, according to custom, and, when the old headman died, took over the leadership of the people in the area.' Thomas stated that Toma was not a true headman in that one of his children would not inherit the role when he, Toma, passed away. Two other family members who by birth could have been leader 'never contested Toma's position as leader, for it was not a position which Toma held by force or pressure but simply by his wisdom and ability, and people prospered under him'.[3] The followers were clearly happy with their leader.

The pathway to leadership in societies organised as independent villages is similar to the pathway to leadership in Bushmen society. For example, a Himba headman becomes the leader because either he or she established the village or it was passed to them by their partner or parent upon the current leader's death. The leader of a Himba village comes from within the village — from within the culture.

The leader of one of the three Himba villages we visited in Namibia told me her leadership succession story. We sat with Hyknodombu in her day shelter in the middle of her small village. Half-a-dozen toddlers, mainly Hyknodombu's grandkids, helped themselves to the remnants of a bucket of maize food. Several chickens held their own against the children in a fight for the scraps. Kid goats bleated in the village's inner corral, pleading for their mothers that were out grazing. Through the translator, I asked Hyknodombu about the Himba process for appointing the head of a village. 'The leader, before they pass,' she said, 'nominates their son or daughter who will become the headman when they pass away. The current headman lets people know his decision before he passes. It only passes to family. It is not possible to pass to a stranger. Leadership could be passed to a non-family member provided that person was born in the village.'

Earlier I mentioned that with lifetime appointments, any political manoeuvring by ambitious rivals is at least limited to the time when the current leader dies. When her husband died, Hyknodombu suffered a political coup. Her husband had named Hyknodombu as his successor. But apparently her husband's younger brother was ambitious to be the headman and, immediately upon the headman's passing, staged a leadership coup and forced Hyknodombu out. She moved out and started her own village about 300 paces away.

Earlier in this chapter, we saw in the First Nations societies organised as divisions and nations that, even if heredity plays a role in the shortlist of leadership candidates, merit trumped lineage. An interesting village-level example of merit trumping lineage is south-east Australia. In Chapter 1 we covered that in the abundant environment of the Western District of Victoria, people lived in communities of about 120 people and that chiefs had significant power. In traditional times, the pathway to leadership was primarily heredity — but still the heir had to be judged as competent and of desirable character. The Dawson family, the early settlers who took an interest in traditional Aboriginal society, were told by elders the process when a chief died. Upon a chief's death, the chiefs of the neighbouring communities appointed the best male friend of the deceased to take charge of the group until the first great meeting of the communities a year after the death of the chief. At this gathering, succession was determined by the vote of the assembled chiefs. The eldest son of the deceased chief was appointed unless there was good reason for setting him aside. If the heir was considered unfit to occupy the position, perhaps because of poor character or physical weakness, then he was passed over in favour of the second son. If the younger brother was considered more eligible by the other chiefs, he was invited to be chief. If that happened, the elder brother had to either fight for the role or yield to his younger brother.[4]

What about followers influencing the choice of leader in a Bushmen band or a Himba village, where the dying leader nominates their successor? The informal nature of the system had, and still has, a way of fixing the problem if a poor leader was nominated — the followers abandoned the band or the village. If too few followers remained, the band or village collapsed. People didn't need to put up with a nasty or incompetent leader. The informality at this level of society for followers to move away couldn't apply in the highly organised societies, where people couldn't quit their division or nation. So for the populations organised at the higher level, there needed to be a way to formalise the ability of followers to influence the choice of leader. Hence in Maasai society the warriors advise the elders of the person they want as their leader and in Haida and Mohawk societies, the senior women choose the leader on behalf of the community.

Curiously, in terms of mobility, workplaces are more similar to Maasai and Mohawk societies than Bushmen bands and Himba villages — which adds weight to the proposition of involving the followers when selecting leaders. At first glance, we might think that people in workplaces have great freedom to change employers. But it's not as free as might appear. For an employee disgruntled with their current leader(s), there are a number of things that need to fall into place for the person to change employers. There needs to be a decent alternative job. The person's application needs to generate an invitation to be interviewed. They need to impress the interviewers. They need to be comfortable with what they learn about the alternative job, including the quality of leadership in the new organisation. If they receive a job offer, the pay and benefits of the new job need to be attractive. As a person weighs up their options to escape a suppressive leader, there's pressure to continue to pay the mortgage or rent and keep food on the table. For many employees, then, resignation is not an easy or practical option. People will put up with a lot, and sometimes too much, from oppressive leaders. This inability to change employers calls for organisations to ensure quality leadership; the sort of leaders who people are delighted to follow.

Actions for Workplace Leaders

The approach of ancestral societies to leadership selection raises important implications for workplaces. Maasai and their close cousins, Samburu, set the benchmark that it's possible to get to 91% of followers being 'highly satisfied' — ecstatic, actually — with their leader.

1. **Take care and time in selecting leaders:** The single biggest reason that leads to the phenomenal success of highly organised ancestral societies in leadership selection is the care taken in the selection decision. They take the time necessary to ensure a sound choice — even in societies where heredity plays a part. The Mohawk clan mother has her eyes on teenagers and watches them mature. The Maasai elders, who know the young people already, observe the shortlisted candidates for three or more years before choosing *the one*. The implication for workplaces is to be diligent in the care we take, and the time we take, in leadership selection. For internal candidates, we can indeed observe high potential people over many years. We can give internal people extensive and varied challenges. We can observe their character and how they interact with people across the organisation, including how they behave under pressure. With external candidates the ability to observe is a greater challenge. But even with external candidates, we can choose not to rush a selection decision. We can organise multiple and varied interactions with candidates. We should vet them thoroughly. We should invest the time to get it as right as we possibly can.

2. **Select leaders *as if* the appointment is for life:** I didn't expect to find that leadership appointments in ancestral societies are for life. That's a challenging finding. It says that, on balance, ancestral societies found this approach works best. Workplaces can use this principle in a proxy form. Approach leadership selection *as though* the appointment will be for the duration of the leader's career. *Imagine* the pressure placed on the selection decision *if* the appointment is for life. We would indeed take great care in choosing the leader. In using this principle in leadership appointments, as you get close to a selection decision, ask yourself three questions:

- If this appointment is for life, how confident am I in the selection I am about to make?
- Do I have enough information to be confident (to appoint or not appoint)?
- What more do I need to know that will increase my level of confidence?

3. **Involve direct reports in leadership selection:** In the highly organised societies I investigated, leaders will only be appointed who the followers are happy to have as their leader (and in the band and village societies, people vote with their feet and leave if they get saddled with a poor leader). In workplaces, why not listen to the voice of the followers who will be reporting to the leader? The ability and wisdom to select a leader doesn't reside exclusively with the boss of the new leader. Direct reports are heavily invested in making a good appointment. Involving direct reports has three benefits. First, the direct reports have a valuable perspective that helps the person above the role make an informed selection decision (and with internal candidates, the direct reports will have a perspective likely to be more realistic than that of higher-level executives). Second, involving direct reports gives a strong signal to the candidate that maintaining the support of their followers is an important expectation of a leader. And third, it gives the new leader a confident start knowing that their team endorsed their selection.

4. **Give preference to internal candidates:** Where there is a sound internal candidate, I recommend erring in favour of the internal person. This counterbalances the usual bias favouring external candidates. As mentioned above, the bias favouring external candidates arises because we can't possibly learn the whole package of the external person. Their potential interference factors remain undetected and therefore ignored. Because we know the internal person as a total package, any of their interference factors are magnified from this unfair comparison.

5. **Value a proven cultural fit:** Internal leadership candidates have a proven fit with the organisation. The individual has absorbed the

often subtle dimensions that come into play when making decisions. Appointing leaders from within the culture leads to more consistent leadership quality. In turn, this consistency of leadership results in consistency of the employment experience enjoyed by staff. In contrast, organisations that tend to appoint leaders from the outside means that managers behave differently from each other — almost as free agents — resulting in a varied employment experience amongst staff. I've worked in both types of organisations, and I can vouch for the type that had higher morale and performance outcomes. In the prime example organisation of which I am thinking, one of the impressive outcomes of consistent leadership quality was the speed in which executive directions were implemented. Executives could decide a course of action, communicate it to managers and, wow, managers actioned the strategy consistently and quickly across the organisation. It was impressive to watch and was an intangible advantage to the organisation. This high quality of leadership through internal appointments mirrors the approach of First Nation societies, where the positive experience of followers is in part because leaders are totally immersed in the culture. Leaders know what is expected of them, how they are to behave, how they should treat others and the basis of their decision making.

6. **Favour stability of the executive team:** The approach of ancestral societies to leadership selection and long tenure results in stable leadership. In workplaces, stability of leadership teams is generally undervalued. Churn creates political alliances and self-interest. Churn reduces performance during the period people are distracted with changes at the senior level. Stability engenders a sense of obligation to each other — a view that 'we are going to be together for a long time' so we had better work together cooperatively and accommodate each other's style.

7. **Identify a personal leadership legacy:** A major driver for ancestral societies driving lifetime leadership appointments, I think, is that it establishes leadership as a calling. Leaders serve their community. An individual's period of leadership is a miniscule period of the society's existence. Leaders are motivated to protect the culture's

integrity for the period they hold the cultural baton. For workplace leaders, the implication is to contemplate the nature of your legacy: what will future generations associate with your period of leadership?

8. **Prepare the next generation:** A critical part of leaving a legacy is the development of the next generation of leaders. In workplaces, we don't develop leaders by sitting in talent review meetings. We don't develop leaders through shallow interactions and observing emerging leaders when they make presentations at executive meetings. Those interactions are fine, but not substantial. Current leaders equip the next generation by spending quality time with individuals and by giving them challenging experiences while all-the-while mentoring them.

Having decided the leader, the next step is to signal, to the community and to the chosen leader, the significance of the leadership appointment.

CHAPTER 5

Appointments and Status of Leaders

'Ko tō iwi te hiki o tō wae — Our people are the bounce in every leader's step.'

HAVING CAREFULLY CHOSEN THE next leader, societies organised at the division or nation level mark the appointment with appropriate ceremony. The ritual marks the significance of leadership appointments for both the leader and the community. In Western societies we happily incorporate this tradition for the swearing-in of heads of state. But, by contrast, in workplaces we are terribly understated. Generally, we distribute an email announcing a leader's appointment. How uninspiring. We miss the opportunity to send a signal of the significance of the appointment and of the obligations of the role.

I'm recommending that in workplaces we should follow the lead of ancestral societies and mark the significance of a person being given the responsibility — the privilege — of leading people. Part of the ritual should include a conversation with the new leader about their responsibilities in serving their people. The nature of the announcement ritual should reflect the level of the leadership appointment: the first-level manager, the village-level leader, the divisional leader or the executive leader.

Signals of Leadership Responsibilities

For the Mohawk nation and the wider Haudenosaunee confederacy, the Great Law of Peace specifies the ritual commemorating the appointment of a chief. Article 29 of the constitution specifies, 'When a chieftainship title is to be conferred, the candidate chief shall furnish the cooked venison, the corn bread and the corn soup, together with other necessary things and the labor for the Conferring of Titles Festival.' At the festival, the new chief will be crowned with deer's antlers, the sacred emblem of chieftainship. When the antlers are placed on a person making them a Confederacy chief, the person is said to acquire the deer's antenna-like sensitivity.[1]

The Great Law provides a script for the installation of the incoming chief. The script is beautifully worded, a succinct yet comprehensive statement of leadership. It contains many sentiments relevant to workplace leadership:

We now do crown you with the sacred emblem of the deer's antlers, the emblem of your chieftainship. You shall now become a mentor of the people of the Five Nations. The thickness of your skin shall be seven spans, which is to say that you shall be proof against anger, offensive actions and criticism. Your heart shall be filled with peace and goodwill. Your mind shall be filled with a yearning for the welfare of the people of the League. With endless patience you shall carry out your duty and your firmness shall be tempered with tenderness for your people. Neither anger nor fury shall find lodging in your mind. All your words and actions shall be marked with calm deliberation. In all your deliberations in the Council of the League, in your efforts at law-making, in all your official acts, self-interest shall be cast away. Do not cast over your shoulder behind you the warnings of your nephews and nieces should they chide you for any error or wrong you may do, but return to the way of the Great Law which is right and just. Look and listen to the welfare of the whole people, and have always in view not only the present, but also the coming generations, even those whose faces are yet beneath the surface of the ground — the unborn of the future Nation.

In Article 28, the constitution specifies that the incoming chief provides four strings of shells or wampum bound together, with the string symbolising 'the evidence of his pledge to the chiefs of the League that he shall live according to the Constitution and exercise justice in all affairs'.

The significance that Mohawk attach to leadership appointments is shared by other societies. In the northern Pacific, the Haida nation has an elaborate ceremony for 'raising a chief'. A clan chief is raised at a community event called a potlatch.

Potlatching is a practice widespread among First Nations peoples along the coast of northwest America and Canada. It involves the host, usually a high-ranking individual, providing a feast and presenting gifts to guests. Elsie Gale, who I stayed with on Haida Gwaii, told me that the potlatch is an essential part of the legal, social, economic and political life of Haida society. In terms of the legal aspects, a potlatch is the forum where laws are made and events are witnessed. As well as the host's clan, members of other clans are invited. All attendees are given gifts. 'By attending the event and by receiving gifts,' Elsie told me, 'the visitors become paid witnesses to the transaction and witnesses to any decisions made at the potlatch.'

In addition to the raising of a chief, in traditional times potlatches were held for weddings and funerals, the raising of a family story pole, conferring status on the child of a high-ranking family, claiming or conceding property (such as a riverbed for fishing), claiming a new family crest that tells a person's lineage and for conflict resolution or dispensing justice. Potlatches continue to be hosted for some of these reasons.

Moving to the southern Pacific Ocean, in Māori society the elevation to a chief's role is often marked by a new name being conferred on the chief. The name is an honourable one, chosen by the elders on behalf of the people. My host, Keri Opai, told me, 'Being named *by the people* is significant. It's a symbolic gesture meaning that the chief is responsible to and for the people. It's the people who put him or her in the role.'

Māori naming ceremonies are usually held at a sacred place, chosen because of its significance to the person being named. The location often has ancestral significance. The ceremony frequently includes a sacred water ritual, representing the sanctity of water being necessary for life and that water is life.

'What this means for leadership authority,' Keri said, 'is that a person elevated to a place of authority over others has that moment marked. It is not business-as-usual. For Māori people, like many indigenous societies, the significance is about defining the roles and responsibilities. You are our chief, and this means that you need to look out for your people.'

Keri is a practitioner of traditional ceremonial chants. 'There is a phrase in a *karakia*, a ritual incantation,' he said, 'Ko tō iwi te hiki o tō wae — Your people are the bounce in your step.'

It's a profoundly moving phrase, and I wasn't even the one to whom it was directed. Could a new leader, or a leader elevated to the next level, *not* be affected by being told that your people are the source of your energy?

'The incantation and that phrase,' Keri continued, 'tells the chief that you cannot move without the people and the people are part of you. The incantation may be used in the ceremony elevating a new chief.'

Maasai also appoint a chief with a stirring ritual. Over coffee and cake at a café in Nanyuki, northern Kenya, elder Eric Ole Kasana told me about the ceremony where the individual chosen to be chief learns of their appointment. 'It's taken three or more years to get to the point where the chief is chosen,' Eric said. 'At this time there will be a gathering of the warriors of the age set. The chief's appointment occurs at the conclusion of a week's ceremony. On the final night, the leader to be chosen spends the night in his mother's hut. Early the next morning, the warriors gather outside the hut. They are singing and carrying honey, blankets and new clothes for their new chief. Five of the warriors enter the hut and tightly hold the young man. The five warriors announce to their friend that he has been chosen as their chief. Outside there are perhaps 300 to 500 warriors, all singing.'

What an evocative mark of your appointment to a leadership role. If you were the chief, could you not be moved by this elevation to leadership?

'Once you are chosen,' Eric said, 'you can't say no. Once you are chosen, you no longer belong to yourself. You now belong to the age set.'

Mohawk, Haida, Māori and Maasai societies clearly decided that leadership appointments are worth celebrating — and signalling. Before we look at the implications for workplace practices, we need to cover a potential objection that people might have about recognising leadership appointments in workplaces.

Status Signals of Leadership

The reason that might cause people in organisations to hold back from celebrating leadership appointments is a reluctance to call out a leader's higher status relative to staff members. Yet I have found that status signals are a pattern in all ancestral societies, including in hunter-gatherer societies. My reflection on the question of status differentials has led me to two conclusions. First, status signals — provided they are culturally appropriate — are appropriate and even beneficial. Second, there is no First Nations society where leaders separate themselves — no society that I investigated where leaders decide that their rank warrants alienation from their followers. For example, in Maasai society the chief lives in the village, even it, in the case of the Laikipia Maasai clan, it is clear to any visitor the identity of the high-ranking individual because of their elaborate six-legged stool on which they sit. Chiefs don't build barriers between themselves and their followers, as we can often do in workplaces where senior people might, for example, base themselves in a separate building to their staff or pay themselves extravagant salary packages that alienate their followers.

A pattern across traditional societies is that people in high-status positions display their position. When I began my research, I wondered if even in hunter-gatherer societies there would be status symbols. There are. In the Bushmen culture, where the lifestyle involved frequent movement, the symbols were not elaborate dress, decorative regalia nor material possessions, but symbols nevertheless existed.

I've mentioned that I had the good fortune of having two conversations with Bushman !Gao who as a teenager lived the old way. Overnight between the two interviews, the idea struck me that maybe the placement of the grass shelters (*tshu*) in Bushmen camps might not be random. Maybe there was an order to the position of shelters, and if there was an order, what did that order reveal? So at the start of our second meeting I asked him, 'In your camp back in the old days, were people's huts positioned in a certain order?'

'Yes,' he answered enthusiastically with a twinkle in his eyes, 'there was an order and it was always the same.' !Gao was squatting and I sat in the dirt next to him. Using his two index fingers, rather long fingers relative to the size of his slight body, he marked in the sand the positions of the shelters.

'The grandfathers had the primary positions: east- and west-facing,' he said, marking dots in the sand. 'The grandfathers faced each other from one side of the camp to the other. This allowed the big leaders to talk to each other and to hear each other. The next most important people were the grandmothers and they had north/south-facing huts.'

Fancy that, I thought, suppressing a smile. Like the positioning of desks in open-plan offices, even in the absence of big individual offices there are positions of high status. With the way our conversation flowed, I didn't ask !Gao the reason for the grandfathers' shelters facing the rising and the setting sun. In continuing my reading after I returned home, I learned the location of the two Ju/'hoan Bushmen's gods; one lives where the sun rises and one lives where the sun sets.[2] That line of sight might be the reason for the high-ranking hut positions. Whatever the reason, the outcome is that in a Bushmen camp, there are two high-status positions for the placement of shelters. With the positioning of shelters, because it was culturally appropriate and the established order of things, there would have been no offence. There would, in fact, be functional benefits for this orderly positioning of shelters. First, it would have made establishing camp easy where everyone knew their place and second, strangers approaching a camp knew the people they first had to acknowledge.

There was a second status signal in Bushmen society. When a group of Bushmen, perhaps five or six people, undertook a gathering trek, they walked in a set order. They walked in the order of land 'ownership' or stewardship. Leading the group was the person with the longest connection to the land, usually the oldest female.

We tend to think of hunter-gatherer societies as highly egalitarian. Yet we can easily misinterpret the meaning of 'egalitarian'. Through our Western lens, we think egalitarian means equality in possessions and access to resources. But that's not the most accurate definition. If we apply the Western materialistic meaning to equality, of course in hunter-gatherer societies all people are equal. In those societies there was no difference in worldly possessions and no one controlled or rationed resources. But if we apply a different notion of equality, we find differences existed. Respected anthropologist Napoleon Chagnon stated unequivocally, 'If my teachers (and anthropology textbooks) got anything wrong, it was their misunderstanding of the notion of egalitarianism.'[3] He said that most anthropologists, looking at material equality, concluded that early societies were also equal in terms of status and power. He disagreed. Chagnon wrote, 'There are enormous differences in status among tribal communities (particularly arising from the strength of kin relationships).'[4] In other words, in his view, egalitarianism is a myth. Status differentials, and symbols associated with status, have existed and do exist in all societies.

Waorani in the rainforest of the Amazon rivalled Bushmen for being ultra-egalitarian in terms of material possessions and access to resources. At the Babeno community in the Yasuni National Park, Ecuador I met the elder of the community, Penti Baihua. His son translated from the Wao language to Spanish and my translator relayed the information in English. Penti explained that as a youngster he lived in a house established by his grandfather. The abundant water supply in the forest and food from their gardens allowed the Waorani to establish reasonably permanent settlements. They lived in substantial A-framed houses with thatched roofs of palm fronds. Houses usually accommodated about 40 people. Penti's childhood house was unusually large, accommodating about 60 people. Each married or adult woman had her own fire, so the interior of the house was a series of fires and hammocks down both sides. To test status signals with the hut layout, similar to the positioning of Bushmen shelters, I asked Penti if there was an order in which hammocks were positioned.

'There was a ranking,' he answered. 'My grandfather as the owner of the house had the premier position inside-right from the front door. The next highest position was opposite him, inside-left from the front door. That was the position for my grandfather's brother. His brother-in-law had the third position, next to my grandfather.'

On it went down both sides of the longhouse in descending status. Why was inside the front door the privileged position? Because that was the most dangerous location. Aggressive neighbours on a murderous rampage attacked through the only door. The leaders were putting themselves in harm's way to protect their community.

'Who had the position at the far back left?' I asked, smiling, thinking about desk positions in workplaces and who gets allocated the subordinate position nearest the print room.

The answer was lost as another topic was excitedly introduced, but I imagined, similar to the recently hired graduate getting the desk closest to the utility room, it was the most recently married young couple!

In traditional Aboriginal society the nature of status symbols appeared to follow the level of the society's organisation structure. Previously we covered the substantial settlements of people around today's Western District of Victoria. Every settlement had a chief. The old people who remembered the days before colonisation told the Dawsons, an early European farming family in the 1860s, that while the chief consulted with others, his authority was supreme and when he announced a decision, no one dared contradict or disobey him. Great respect was paid to the chief — as many as six young bachelors waited on the chief, and eight young unmarried women on the chief's wife. Even the children of the chief had servants.[5] The nearby Wadawurrung people who William Buckley lived with for 32 years also had status symbols. In 1802 before Buckley escaped from the camp on the eastern side of Port Phillip Bay, a scouting party landed on the western shore. Upon landing, First Lieutenant James Tuckey was approached by a group of Wadawurrung men. 'I could distinctly observe gradations of rank,' Tuckey wrote. The chief's cloak was superior in size to the cloaks worn by others. The chief wore 'a coronet of the wing feathers of the swan.' Some of the men had a reed stuck through the septum of their nose, with the chief's 'by far the longest and measured at least 60 centimetres (two feet).'[6]

When we shift from band and village societies to those organised at a division or nation level, the nature of status symbols becomes more elaborate — but still appropriate to the culture. We've seen that for the Haida society the hosting of potlatches confers significant status to the host. Clothing and accessories also demonstrated status in Haida society. The first missionary to Haida Gwaii, William Collison, arrived in 1876 and was greatly surprised to find that one of the status accessories in Haida society was a perfect match to that worn by the nobility back home in Britain: ermine pelts. 'The higher the rank of a chief, the greater the number of ermine skins he was entitled to wear,' Collison wrote. For Haida, the number ranged from three skins to six skins depending on the chief's rank.[7]

Another Haida status dimension observed by Collison at his first community gathering in a longhouse, which we can readily appreciate from our workplace experience, was that visitors were seated according to rank.[8] Not many years after Collison's arrival, in 1905, anthropologist John R Swanton visited Haida Gwaii as part of a major anthropological study. He also observed the hierarchical symbolism of seating arrangements at potlatches. 'The principal guests,' he wrote, 'sat in a circle or circles around the fire; the town chief in the most important place in front of the inside house-pole; and the others, to the right and left, at distances according to their social positions, while the commons assembled around the door or sat outside.'[9]

My research has caused me to reassess the role of status symbols in workplaces. Through most of my career in human resources, I've harboured concerns about displays of rank and have generally agitated for the removal of status symbols. I'm still right, I think, that when I worked at a manufacturing factory early in my career, I thought it was wrong to have separate dining rooms in the factory's cafeteria. There was one dining room for the workers and one for management. But I now think we can go too far in removing symbols. I'm persuaded from what I have learned from traditional societies. When First Nations people tell me about signs of rank in their society, there is not a trace of resentment in their description. Rather, it's the opposite. They speak with reverence about the symbols of the chiefly position. The symbols are a sign of respect. As I said earlier in this chapter, the most important two elements are first, that the symbols are culturally appropriate and second, that they do not involve leaders separating themselves from their people. If we swing too far with our concerns about status differentials, we get to the point of avoiding acknowledgement of a person's elevation to leadership roles (or promotion to the next higher level). We then resort to announcing the appointment by way of an email and we miss the opportunity to signal the significance of the responsibilities that arise from leadership — signalling the significance to both the leader and the followers.

Actions for Workplace Leaders

In ancestral societies, elevation to leadership is celebrated. And appropriate symbols of leadership add to the prestige of the position. What should we do in workplaces?

1. **Mark the appointment of a leader:** The appointment of a leader should be marked, with the nature of ceremony reflecting the level of the leadership position. A vital element of the ritual — for first, middle and top leaders — is that the leader 'faces' their people. For example, for a first-level manager, convening a morning tea with the team is appropriate. For a department-level leader, a gathering of the 'village' is appropriate. This village gathering should be a stand-up meeting at the work location(s), not a 'town hall' meeting which would be inconvenient to staff and in most countries would transgress status expectations. For the appointment of the chief executive (or top leader in a division or region), the personal interactions should involve a tour of key locations supported by 'virtual town halls' to connect with smaller locations. For senior executives, these gatherings are the vehicle for them to begin to tell their story, to share their vision for the organisation and as an opportunity to show they are human and worth following.

2. **Have a conversation with a new leader:** To signal to a new leader the weighty responsibility they now carry, senior people should *talk* with the new leader. Have a conversation. The chief executive (or other senior executive in a large organisation) plus the appropriate HR person should meet with the new leader. The conversation marks the moment and allows senior people to be explicit about their expectations of the leader. Even better, if the meeting involves the new manager travelling to the meeting, that gives the new manager the opportunity for reflection before and after the meeting. On their way to the meeting, the new manager can't help but ponder, 'The most senior person must think my appointment is important.' And on the return trip, the new manager will reflect on the discussion, where at least five topics should have been discussed:

a. Why leadership matters in this organisation.

b. Why they specifically were chosen as the new manager.

c. The various HR or people practices in the leader's toolkit in this organisation aimed at helping the manager (such as processes to give role clarity to staff, performance discussions, staff development, pay reviews, recognition plans, engagement surveys and leadership training for managers).

d. Sharing by the senior leaders their experiences that shaped their leadership. These experiences will include examples of good and poor leaders they have worked for and what they learned from those leaders about what to do and what not to do.

e. An invitation to the new manager to reach out for help if and when they need support in their new role.

For the elevation of higher-level leaders, given they are being promoted from a role already involving people leadership, a key topic of conversation is their role as a manager of managers. In their new role they are supporting and holding to account managers in their unit. In their senior role, they are setting the culture and direction for their village or division.

3. **Present a symbol of leadership to new leaders:** Symbols remind people of their place and responsibilities. In Mohawk and the wider Haudenosaunee confederacy, a person elevated to a chief's role is crowned with deer antlers. Apart from the metaphorical meaning of sensitivity we mentioned earlier, antlers were chosen because, back in the old days, deer were commonly seen by people.[10] So the symbol was a constant reminder. Workplaces should choose a symbol that represents the nature of leadership in their organisation. The symbol should be presented to the new manager at a suitable gathering, such as morning tea with staff. I'm suggesting that workplaces shouldn't be shy about reminding people, both staff and the leader, of the special responsibilities of a leader.

4. **Remember that culturally sensitive status symbols are acceptable:** We shouldn't be preoccupied with attempting to remove all signs

of rank. If we do try to quash them, they pop back up in another form. Signs of social rank exist in all societies. As societies became more organised, signs of rank became more obvious. The important learning from ancestral societies is that status signals are culturally sensitive. In Waorani society deep in the Amazon, the high-ranking position of a hammock is not offensive. Yet in relation to head-dresses of birds' feathers worn at festivals, the headdress of the community elder is no more elaborate than anyone else's. One is appropriate, one is not. Displays of status that are out of kilter with the culture risk offending followers and distancing leaders from their followers. The hands-down winner of the comic-display-of-self-importance-if-it-wasn't-so-serious award goes to the CEO of a major global corporation. He travelled the world in a corporate aeroplane for his exclusive use. That's not the winning part. The winning part that separates him from other nominees is that when he travelled, he was reportedly shadowed by a second jet — a spare in case the first jet broke down. Could you passionately follow this leader, or shed tears at the very mention of his name?

5. **Convene development programs for new leaders:** Another initiative that has functional benefits as well as appropriate value as a status symbol is training programs for new or potential leaders. We have covered elsewhere the obvious importance of leadership training (see Chapter 2, Recommendation 5 and Chapter 3, Recommendation 5). In terms of status, being selected for new leader training sends a signal of the importance of the leadership role and the high regard for the person chosen. Along with the prestige of being chosen is an obligation that the new leader will apply themselves diligently to the training and to the role if and when appointed.

6. **Provide offices to leaders to enable conversations:** A status symbol that has generally been removed from workplaces is the dedicated office for people leaders. In knocking down the walls we have compromised an important function of offices. Without offices, we inhibited conversations between leaders and their people. Given our incredible language capability, inhibiting conversations

compromises the single most important relationship mechanism available to humans (more on this in Chapter 11). I vote for the return of offices for managers. I know this view is 'old school' which only means it's out of fashion. But I'm writing this book for leaders over the next seven generations. In another generation or two the pendulum will, hopefully, swing back to the middle.

7. **Don't separate leaders from their people:** A Maasai chief lives in a village. A Waorani elder shares the common hut. There's no traditional society where leaders separate themselves. Waorani elders and Maasai chiefs would be bemused by the separation from their people that some senior workplace leaders fabricate. A friend of mine experienced an extreme example of a senior executive team separating themselves from their people. My friend works for a major Australian organisation, and he has been around long enough to experience the leadership style of several chief executives. During the reign of one CEO, my friend experienced the powerful negative symbolism of the top team cutting themselves off from their people. In the garage under the head office building, the CEO and his inner circle parked their cars in an exclusive caged area. A private lift conveyed the executives to their dedicated top floor, meaning that they were shielded from mingling with staff. The top team generally spent the day bunkered on their floor. Access to the executive floor was tightly controlled. On the rare occasions that my friend had to visit the top floor, even just to attend a meeting in one of the meeting rooms, he had to go through a strict process to break through the barricade. He had to first contact the concierge on the top floor. The concierge come down the lift to the ground floor to meet my friend and chaperoned him to the top floor. He was then left in a waiting area, with one more door blocking access to the meeting rooms. While waiting, people were generally silent and if they talked, they whispered. Just prior to the scheduled time of his meeting, he was admitted to the floor. What was the impact of this symbolism? My friend says he felt nervous and intimidated at the mere thought of venturing to the top floor. He felt like an unwelcomed outsider. It reminded him of his school days being

summoned to the principal's office. Ironically, my friend recalls feeling special in being escorted to the top floor, and in awe if he caught a glimpse of the CEO — even if the CEO didn't acknowledge him. Strangely enough, my friend says, these segregation symbols were accepted by staff as just the way things were done. It was only after a new CEO arrived, who quickly removed the extreme symbols, that people realised how insidious and disempowering the symbols had been.

Leadership was a fundamental mechanism to the peaceful and productive functioning of human groups. Leaders were carefully selected and appointed with culturally-appropriate ritual. But society also needed to contemplate the rare occurrence of a leader not being up to the job or being brutish. While leadership appointments were invariably for life, most societies had a way of checking leadership power, especially where a leader abused their power.

CHAPTER 6

Checks on Leadership Power

'If at any time it shall be apparent that a chief ...
has not in mind the welfare of the people ...'

BACK IN KAHNAWÀ:KE, MOHAWK medicine man Joe McGregor and I continued our meeting in the kitchen of the historic Riverview Hotel. We were interrupted momentarily by an odd sight. The Lawrence River Seaway cuts through the Mohawk territory and runs along the hotel's back fence. An oceangoing ship rumbled past on its way to The Great Lakes. For a visitor like me, the sight of a massive merchant ship sneaking past a kitchen window is a huge distraction. Joe had been telling me about leadership appointments. When the ship had passed, I asked him about what happens if a chief performs badly in their role.

'There is a process,' he answered, 'although it's highly unlikely to be activated because of the care taken in selecting a chief. But it can and sometimes does happen that a chief becomes errant in their behaviour. At which time, steps are taken.'

'What are the steps?'

'The process involves three warnings. The three warnings are issued by the clan mother. In traditional times the chief knew the consequences of being visited on the third occasion. Back in the old days, it was not the clan mother coming to the chief after the two prior warnings. The chief knew that *he* would visit,' he said, ominously.

'Who was "he"?' I asked.

'The war chief,' he answered. 'And the errant chief knew that the war chief would take the chief's horns even if he had to draw blood.'

That's serious performance management.

A thousand years ago, the founders of the Haudenosaunee constitution obviously had experience of the need to apply checks on leadership power. Either the founding nations were already using three warnings and considered it useful, or regretted not having the practice and fixed the omission while they had the chance. The three warnings must have been considered a fair, yet necessary, approach. The practice was included in their constitution.

Article 19 of the Great Law of Peace outlines the action if a chief is not serving the community. The phrasing of the Article places the welfare of the people front and centre: 'If at any time it shall be apparent that a chief of the League has not in mind the welfare of the people, or disobeys the rules of the Great Law, the men or women of the League, or both jointly, shall come to the Council and scold the erring chief ...' If the complaint is not heeded by the chief, then, after the third chance, 'If the chief is still disobedient, the matter shall go to the Council of War Chiefs. The War Chiefs shall then take away the title of the erring chief by order of the women in whom the title is vested.'

The Article even provides the script for the war chief when, as Joe McGregor told me, he confronts the errant chief who has disregarded the warnings and is about to lose his chieftainship and the deer antlers, the symbol of leadership:

> So you, (Name), disregard and set at naught the warnings of your women relatives. You fling the warnings over your shoulder to cast them behind. Behold the brightness of the Sun, and in the brightness of the Sun's light, I depose you of your title and remove the sacred emblem of your chieftainship title. I remove from your brow the deer's antlers which was the emblem of your position and token of your nobility. I now depose you, and return the antlers to the women whose heritage they are.

Senior Mohawk women have significant power. The clan mothers are part of the check on the chief's power, acting like a Board of Directors above the CEO. Ultimately, the clan mother is the most powerful individual. She appoints ('stands-up') the chief and can remove ('de-horn') the chief. I was told that, 'The clan mother holds the title; the chief works for her.'

Teyowisonte Tommy Deer told me that the clan mother monitors the chief. If the chief does something wrong, she admonishes him. The reasons for admonishing the chief might be bad behaviour in council or being disruptive during discussions. The chief must listen to her counsel and heed her warnings. I imagined, too, that the clan mother is good support to the chief in what must be, at times, a lonely role. I certainly found being a member of a top leadership team sometimes lonely. I also greatly appreciated the wise and fearless counsel of a senior colleague. Was it a coincidence, I wonder, that the person I mostly relied upon for counsel was a woman — an aunty?

Although the option exists to remove a chief, several Mohawk people told me that dehorning a chief is a last resort. They told of the bitterness that results from forcibly removing a chief. 'The lingering grudges divide the community for 60 years,' said one senior person. This, of course, highlights a key element of the ancestral approach to leadership: great care is taken in selecting a chief.

As I visited each society, I explored the options available to their community if a chief is performing poorly. I knew from my workplace experience that poor leadership takes two forms. First, the chief might misuse power, such as by verbally abusing people or burdening people with unreasonable demands, or using their position for personal gain. Second, the chief might lack capacity for the job. A First Nations chief must have been considered capable when they were appointed to the leadership role, but perhaps through life's events or increasing demands of the job they no longer function at the level required.

I found that First Nation societies have ways of dealing with errant leaders, and these don't always involve replacing them.

The Source and Nature of Power

A discussion about leadership power must include consideration of the nature of power. Power in ancestral societies differs from power in workplaces in two ways.

First, in ancestral societies, power comes from a different *source* than it does in workplaces. In ancestral societies, power comes from the community. In workplaces, leaders are appointed from above, so power ultimately comes from patronage. The nature of patronage in workplaces allows some people to progress to positions of power that they would otherwise not attain. This drives some managers to 'manage up' in order to retain the support of their patron. 'Managing up' is a greater motivator for many managers than 'managing down', or serving the people. I've worked with a few 'managing up' champions. There was one who we'll call Wayne. Wayne was head of a business unit, reporting to the chief executive. People reporting to Wayne found him beyond frustrating to work for — he was so preoccupied with pleasing the CEO that he rarely made a decision. As a consequence, his direct reports spun their wheels reacting to his whims. That was probably better than the alternative — when he did make a decision, he usually flip-flopped soon afterwards. One time at an executive team meeting I observed an act by Wayne that was emblematic of his sycophantic relationship with the CEO. As a matter of course, Wayne sat next to the CEO. On this day I happened to be on Wayne's other side. At one point during the meeting, Wayne went to a cabinet at the side of the room to pour himself a glass of water. He returned with two glasses, one for himself and one for the CEO — who hadn't indicated any desire for water. Wayne was so eager to please. However, he did manage up well, and progressed through the organisation under the patronage of the CEO.

The second major difference in power between ancestral societies and workplaces is the *nature* of power. In ancestral societies, leadership power relates to character. But in workplaces, power relates to the control of resources. In ancestral societies, a leadership position does not confer resource control. For example, in seafaring Haida society, fish stocks were abundant and no individual, or group of leaders, controlled the resource. In the 1870s, the missionary Collison observed a Haida couple fill their canoe with halibut in less than two hours.[1] No one controlled their right to do so. For Blackfeet and other plains nations, buffalo was the main resource. Before buffalo numbers were decimated from fur trading by the 1870s, the abundance of this key resource is hard to comprehend. In a visit to Blackfeet prairies in the mid-1800s, the government Chief Surveyor said, in awe, that one buffalo herd was so massive he was unable to see the end of the herd in either direction.[2] While chiefs controlled community buffalo hunts, no one controlled selective hunting, let alone hunting of the rest of the extensive fauna available to Blackfeet including elk, antelope, black- and white-tailed deer, mule deer, bighorn sheep, mountain goats, beaver and otter.

But in workplaces, control of resources gives leaders significant power. We've invented a warehouse of power tools. Workplace leaders have the power to hire and fire, to allocate budget, to delegate and reassign tasks, to set and review pay, to award bonuses, to approve training, to assess performance and allocate ratings and to complete 9-box assessments. In the wrong hands, these tools can be weapons. Power through resource control is less self-correcting than power through character. In ancestral societies, leadership is conferred by followers and can be withdrawn by followers. Followership has a much greater role in ancestral societies than in workplaces. A workplace leader who loses the respect of their followers can maintain their position through the control of resources — through the power systems we've invented — and through patronage from above.

Options to Address Poor Leadership

Of the societies I visited, the Mohawk nation is the most developed in its process to check inappropriate use of power or leadership incompetence. That relates, I think, to Mohawk society being the most politically organised. Being organised as a confederation calls for a different solution to being organised in hunter-gatherer bands or independent villages.

As we saw in earlier chapters, in hunter-gatherer bands the option available to followers was to opt out. Opting out of a camp was a very effective way to constrain a leader's power. In a Bushmen camp of up to about 25 people, if the camp was an unhappy one or if the leader was overbearing, people could easily vote with their feet. Membership of Bushmen camps was dynamic and turnover reasonably high. Each year around 13% of individuals changed camps and 35% of individuals divided their time between two or three camps.[3] A camp couldn't bear too much attrition. There had to be enough adults to spread the tasks — enough people gathering food, one or two people hunting, and a few people remaining in camp to look after the older people and children and to gather firewood and water. If too many people opted out, the camp collapsed. That's a powerful check on a toxic environment or poor leadership.

I asked the old Bushman, Komtsa, the options available to people if they disliked their leader. 'The only thing you could do was leave the camp. You would hear about a good camp and you would go and live there.'

'I imagine some camps were unhappy camps,' I suggested.

'We kept away from them. If we approached a camp and children were crying, we knew something was wrong with this camp and we kept going.'

Likewise, on the other side of Namibia in the Himba system of independent villages, people can fairly easily move villages. I asked the female village head, Hyknodombu, about the consequences of a bad leader running a village. 'People leave the village,' she answered. A despot runs a shrinking village.

On the continuum between the highly-organised Mohawk nation and the societies organised as bands or villages are the division-based societies. Curiously, in these societies there is generally no ability to remove a leader — tenure is paramount. Nevertheless, and I find this fascinating, ways do exist for the community to address inappropriate use of power or incompetent leadership.

For the Haida nation in the North Pacific, the main check on leadership power is through the matriarchs — the aunties. The female elders are the voice of the community and the chief has to listen to them. On Haida Gwaii I met Leo Gagnon who was about to be elevated to a chieftain role. As he contemplated his appointment and fulfilling his obligations in the role, he told me, 'Don't ignore the aunties.'

I asked matriarch Leona Davidson about her role as a counsellor to the chief. 'A chief is always asking the matriarch if they are doing right or wrong,' she said.

One person told me, 'One time a chief made an important decision alone. The aunties baulked. At the next community meeting, the chief publicly altered his position to that of the aunties.'

'In traditional times,' Leona said, 'you could not take away the chieftainship. It happens now, but people become bitter and divided and don't talk to each other.'

Ben Davidson owns an art gallery near Skidegate in the centre of Haida Gwaii. Along with his father, Ben is a key figure in the resurgence of traditional art. He told me of the consequences if a chief is an autocrat. He compared traditional chiefs (chiefs of clans) to municipal chiefs (councillors in Canadian local government). 'A chief is not respected if they become an autocrat. Today, as well as traditional chiefs, there are municipal leaders. These people tend to operate as autocrats. Traditional chiefs who act like that are not respected and they lose their influence.' Losing influence is a check imposed by the community.

Previously, I described the occasion when a Haida chief ignored community warnings and supported an oil industry proposal. Several people told me that the elders encouraged the chief to desist in his support for transporting oil through Haida waters. They warned him of the consequences if he didn't listen to the community. He ignored their warnings. A guide at the Haida cultural museum told me what happened next: 'The community organised a potlatch (a gathering) and declared, "He is not our chief anymore. That person no longer talks on our behalf."' The practical effect of this community declaration was that the chief continued notionally as the chief, but with no authority.

Similar to the Haida system of not removing a chief, Maasai society traditionally had no way of dismissing an errant chief. But my Maasai friend, Ngila, told me about a time when he and his age set friends heard about the novel idea of dethroning a chief.

'In 2004,' he began, 'our age set voted out our chief and his deputy. The chief had become a dictator, acting as though he was special. He was no longer a servant of the people. For example, when meat is consumed in the presence of the chief, the best part of the goat or cow is served to the chief. But when the chief is served the choice cut, it's polite for him to feign surprise and express his appreciation. But this chief demanded the best cut.

He didn't wait to be served. This is an insult to his hosts and to the community. Adding to that, he went with the wife of one of his own age set. That's tabooed.'

In traditional times, the age set would have been stuck with the chief. They might have treated him with contempt, he would have lost his influence, but he would have kept his job.

'But some of our clan saw on television that a political party in Britain voted to remove its leader. We thought that was a good approach for how we should deal with our chief. We talked to the "feathers" (the chief's council) and they took our concerns, and our planned action, to the other age sets and the elders. We gained support to remove our chief, which we did.'

As an aside, this story reveals the respondent who dragged down the result of my do-you-love-your-leader survey. Ngila is the only Maasai or Samburu I spoke with who did not shed a loving tear at the thought of their chief — he is the missing 9% in the 91% favourable result. Still, I could have reported 100% because he loves his current chief.

In the hierarchy of Maasai society, below the chief of the age set is the village leader (the 'village owner' or *olopeny enkang*). The age set chief provides the check on the power of the village owner by being a point of escalation. 'What are the options available to people,' I asked Ngila, 'if they live in a village with a poor leader?'

'The people go above the village owner to the age set chief. For example, if a village owner is treating his wife badly, the wife might go and report her husband to the chief, probably without her husband's knowledge. The chief will then say to the husband, "Why is your wife unhappy?" The chief might also say, "She is someone's daughter, so honour her and treat her nicely." If the husband is in the wrong, he needs to first apologise to the elders. And he then pays a fine to his wife. The fine might be one goat.'

'What's another example?' I asked.

'If a child is missing school because the father is not paying school fees, the child might go to the chief and ask him, "Can you please ask my daddy why he is not paying my school fees?"'

'Can people leave the village of a poor leader?'

'They can,' Ngila answered, 'although they tend not to. To leave a village you need the village owner's blessing to do so. But, yes, people can move and it's a sign of a bad owner if people move out of the village — and no one moves in.'

'What behaviour by the village owner would cause people to leave?'

'If he is too aggressive. If he is hot-tempered. If he is too strict,' Ngila answered. 'For the village owner to be admired and effective, they must respect people. Qualities that show respect are being a kind person, including to animals. Being fair. They are a big listener. They are a calm person. They are a uniting figure for the village, and are able to resolve conflicts. They're truthful. They're smart and want to keep learning. They teach others through advice and good practice. They are outgoing but not easygoing. When they must rule on an issue, they are firm and fair, and not blind or pig-headed.'

Actions for Workplace Leaders

The key implication from ancestral wisdom regarding leadership power is that power needs to be constrained — there need to be checks and balances. A good way for workplaces to approach power is to manage leadership power as a program. We should treat power in the same way we treat 'performance'. Most organisations have comprehensive practices helping leaders manage staff performance: setting job goals at the beginning of the year, conducting regular reviews through the year and closing out with end-of-year appraisals and, in many cases, performance ratings (I don't like this last power step, but that's another topic). The results usually feed into salary reviews and bonuses. High performance might lead to being included on a 'high potential' list. Low performance might lead to a performance improvement plan. 'Performance' is a system. We should implement a similarly comprehensive system to monitor power in workplaces — 'regulating power program'. Of course, performance of staff is easier to implement as it involves people with power assessing people with less power. Implementing checks on leaders is less comfortable — leaders holding leaders to account is like the police policing the police. Nevertheless, power is such a vital element of social dynamics that we should ensure it's a healthy part of our workplace. The 'regulating power program' should comprise the following elements.

1. **Develop a mindset that there should be checks on leadership power:** As for any initiative, regulating power first requires senior leaders to articulate their view on the subject. What's your mindset about the use of power? Do you have a view that there should be checks on leadership power? If so, you'll likely proceed with these recommendations. If not, then it's best not to embark on changes as the initiative is doomed. Here are a few questions to test your mindset and inclination to act: Does it concern you that there might be leaders in your organisation who bully their staff? Does it concern you that there might be leaders who abuse their power? Does it concern you that it's likely there are managers in your organisation who excel at 'managing up' but are incompetent at 'managing down'? You might be blind to some managers showing a rosy side to people above them while at the same time being foul to their staff. If you want to know the answers to these questions, then you have the mindset to proceed with checks on power.

2. **Explain power expectations:** The organisation — which really means the senior policy makers — should articulate expectations about power in their workplace. Power is not a dirty word. Throughout this book, we've seen the importance of leadership roles and the use of constructive power for group harmony. Leaders who use power well have the happy knack of being authoritative without being autocratic, appropriately dominating without being domineering, friendly without being a best friend, and involved in people's work without being a micro-manager.

3. **Educate leaders about the checks on their power:** When views about power have been crystallised, they should be incorporated into leadership training. Tell leaders about the way power can be used or abused. Tell them your stories about power usage — leaders you have observed, good and bad, and things you have tried. Use stories from within your organisation, where power has been used

appropriately, and stories of when the inappropriate use of power has been identified and addressed. Share with them research and concepts about power. And give them practice at using power well in a range of leadership scenarios.

4. **Ensure senior leaders model the good use of power:** It's obviously critical that the top leader and their direct reports model the appropriate use of power. The expectation on other managers collapses from hypocrisy if senior leaders act other than as role models. Modelling the good use of power involves both an absence of poor behaviours and the presence of constructive behaviours. There is obviously an absence of rudeness and aggression. Demonstrating the constructive use of power lifts people's energy. I observed this positive impact in the way one senior leader ran monthly sales review meetings. As is usual in sales organisations, analysts presented 'the numbers' every month to the top team. The leader, John, knew the numbers before people came into the room. Mostly, because we were in a growing market, the numbers were good. Invariably John cheerfully welcomed the lower-level analysts as they walked into the room, saying, for example, 'Welcome, Sam. Please share with us your lovely set of numbers!' Sam beamed. John's behaviour made Sam feel safe and confident. I imagined the positive chat amongst the analysts about how they enjoyed presenting to John's team. The point is that John used the power of his position to create a positive environment — he wasn't silent and snobbish.

5. **Senior leaders coach other leaders:** Senior leaders should incorporate the subject of power into their conversations with managers who report to them. And include power in the conversations with new leaders that we covered in Chapter 5 (Action 2) on Appointments. Hearing stories about power helps leaders determine their actions when they need to check other managers who are using power poorly. I was once coaching a senior leader who was struggling to decide what to do about a manager who reported to him. The senior leader was struggling to decide if the manager's poor treatment of staff justified the manager's dismissal after several

warnings had been flouted. In helping the senior leader make a decision, I asked a variation of the Maasai statement that 'this is someone's daughter — treat her well.' I asked the senior leader, 'Would you want your son working for this manager?' (The leader is a father of two boys.) The leader was stirred into action.

6. **Develop mechanisms to identify use of power:** A key part of the 'regulating power program' is having tools to monitor the actual use of power — to assess the current reality. Who are the leaders using power well? Who are the leaders who are passive or aggressive in their use of power? Mechanisms for monitoring power include:

   a. **Surveys:** Many organisations already use engagement and leadership 360° surveys to hear the voice of staff. A key design requirement is for results to be reported for each leader: how is *this* team feeling about *their* leader. (As I have commented before, a minimum number of responses to a survey are required to protect staff's anonymity.) For example, a good survey design incorporates a single 'index' which reports the average results of several key questions. The single score allows the HR sponsor or senior executive to compare the effectiveness of leaders in their organisation. The results allow senior leaders to know: a) the leaders who are using power well (so their behaviour can be affirmed); and b) the leaders who need help to improve their use of power or who, if they don't improve, ultimately might need to be removed from leadership. If an engagement survey only shows aggregated results at a department level, and doesn't allow the reporting of individual leaders' team results, they are not fit for this purpose; they are not an aid to check power.

   b. **Skip interviews:** There's other ways for senior leaders to get a good picture of power. One is the so-called Skip Interview. This practice gives each staff member the opportunity, say once a year, to meet individually with a leader at least one level above their own manager. The senior leader hears the perspective of staff on a range of topics. Themes regarding power tend to emerge. Apart from any issues emerging in the individual interviews, the program itself is a good check on leadership power — managers know that any poor use of power is likely to be exposed by this system. If a senior manager conducting a staff interview hears about bullying or other misuses of power, the matter needs to be investigated. This might need to be done in a way that respects the anonymity of the person raising the concern.

c. **Listen to the aunties and uncles:** Elders in our workplaces can play a key role in maintaining leadership standards. For every unit of 150 employees, there'll be one or two 'elders' who are protective of the desired culture. Tap into their voice. Who are the people in your organisation who are the custodians of the culture? Do they know they have a role to play? Are you in touch with these elders? Do you ask them what you need to know? Do you treat in confidence what they tell you? Of course, asking staff about their leaders is politically delicate. Initially, the aunties and uncles might be hesitant to share anything negative. But in time, when the senior leader demonstrates they handle information delicately and where it becomes 'part of what we do around here', it will be a healthy part of the system. As well as engaging the aunties and uncles as a feedback mechanism in your unit, engage one or two of them to check your own leadership and your use of power. Right now, who is your aunty or uncle?

d. **Listen to HR:** Listen to people who are in touch with staff. I know from my HR career inside organisations, HR professionals hear a lot of information about leaders — the good leaders and the poor ones. HR is a channel for senior leaders to easily tap into how power is being used in the organisation.

Through these mechanisms, managers know that there's a high likelihood of being exposed if they treat staff disrespectfully — they have 'Buckley's chance' of slipping through the net.

7. **Develop a culture of addressing poor leadership:** Managers quickly calculate the standards of leadership behaviour expected — and tolerated — in an organisation. In your organisation, are there

consequences for the misuse of power? The question to test whether your workplace has a healthy check on power is this: Can any manager who has been around for a while point to an instance of a manager being moved out of leadership because of poor behaviour? The desirable answer is along the lines of: 'Yes, there was Kim a few years ago. No one ever made an announcement, but I'm sure Kim was transferred out of management because of the way they treated people.' The undesirable answer is: 'No, you get away with anything around here. In the five years I've been a manager in this organisation, I can't recall any such occasion.' Given it's highly unlikely you've got a 100% success rate of leadership appointments, the undesirable answer is an indicator of unchecked leadership power.

8. **Reinforce the practice of three warnings:** The experience of ancestral societies gives us confidence, I think, that three warnings to errant leaders is a reasonable approach — balancing the interests of the individual leader with those of the community. The Mohawk nation leads the way with this approach. It's revealing, too, that at least one Maasai age set that lacked the approach adopted the practice in recent times. For Ngila's Maasai age set, the idea of replacing an insulting and antisocial chief struck them as a good approach after it came to their attention on television.

Through the long journey of human history, leaders have played a key role in social harmony. Ancestral societies had a comprehensive approach to leadership selection, leadership appointments and checks on leadership power. They also had other practices to help ensure a balance of individual autonomy with the interests of the community. We now turn to these practices.

CHAPTER 7

Clarity of Culture

'We'll keep it light today and only do a 500-year-old chant.'

WHEN WORKPLACE LEADERS REFER to the *culture* of their organisation, they are unconsciously referring to the extent to which individual autonomy is expected to be conceded in favour of group interests. 'What does it mean to be part of our culture?' really means, 'To what extent do we expect you to constrain your own interests in order to belong to our organisation?' There's a balance required, of course. If skewed too far towards individual autonomy, anarchy results. Skewed too far the other way — denying individual identity — results in a cult.

Balancing individual autonomy with group interests is a dimension that ancestral societies had to resolve. Of the societies I visited, I could have chosen any, except one, to show the impressive way that traditional societies balance group belonging with individual autonomy. I've chosen two societies — Pintupi in Australia and New Zealand Māori — to show how, by different means, the cultural objective of balancing group belonging with individual autonomy is achieved. We'll look at Pintupi and Māori in a moment, but let's first look at that one exception.

Waorani and Individual Autonomy

In Waorani society in the Amazonian jungle of Ecuador, to my thinking, the balance is out of kilter. Because it is such an extreme example, Waorani society provides a dramatic study of the violence and apparent anarchy that can happen when individual autonomy dominates group conformity. The approach must have worked for Waorani, but it doesn't recommend itself as a model for harmonious workplaces; it shows the end point of a culture where every person is for themselves. And even though the approach must have worked for Waorani, they themselves were quick to change this fundamental part of their culture when introduced to a new concept in the late 1950s. Their shift from a violent society to a relatively peaceful one was a cultural shift that makes any workplace culture-change program look pale by comparison.

Of all the societies studied by anthropologists, Waorani was the most violent. Up until the beginning of peaceful outside contact in 1958, a stunning sixty per cent of adult deaths were due to homicide, mainly from raids and vendettas between Waorani communities, and even spearings within their own household. In Waorani mythology there are no stories of old men; men were expected to die in skirmishes before reaching old age.[1] The violence was largely driven by a cultural mindset that the response to the frustration of individual autonomy was rage resulting in homicide.

Waorani (or Huaorani) live in the rainforest of the Amazon Basin of north-eastern Ecuador. I visited a Waorani community in May 2019. With a guide, the guide's son as camp helper, a translator and a local boat driver, we left the frontier city of Puerto Francisco de Orellana, known as Coca, and drove to the entrance to the Yasuni National Park. We then travelled in a 20-metre powered canoe, through squalls of rain, eight hours down the Shiripuno and Cononaco Rivers — two of the 1100 major rivers that drain into the Amazon. Our destination, deep in the jungle, was the Babeno community of 120 people. While some Waorani still live the traditional life, the community I visited is partly influenced by a Western lifestyle yet are very much in touch with their traditions and the jungle is still a great feature of their lives.

Waorani traditionally lived in semi-permanent large A-frame houses. The society was structured around independent family units living in a longhouse, or *nanicabo*. I mentioned in Chapter 1 that two or three allied longhouses made up a 'nexus' or settlement of around 90 to 120 people. Each allied longhouse was separated by a large tract of neutral territory several days' walk from the next settlement. Individuals were members of one and only one longhouse. If people stayed away from their longhouse for too long, they were considered outsiders and could not safely return to their old settlement. 'Outsiders' were either Waorani from other settlements (*warani*) or non-Waorani (*kowadi*, all of whom were considered cannibals). Outsiders of both types were considered enemies.

In the Babeno community I visited, the Elder is Penti Baihua. We met in his longhouse. With Penti was his peer, Ginto Tega and Penti's son, Omene. Omene is a school teacher and fluent in Spanish, so he translated what Penti and Ginto said in Wao into Spanish, and then my translator, Jorge Espinosa, provided the translation to English. Penti told us the history of the community. His grandfather, along with the grandfather's brother and brother-in-law, founded the longhouse of Penti's childhood. Because the grandfather was the oldest of the three founders, he was the elder of the longhouse.

A key subject I wanted to explore was the cultural question of balancing individual autonomy with the group's interest. I knew from my preparatory reading that in Waorani culture, individual autonomy is extreme. If a person's desires are violated, according to two anthropologists who studied Waorani society, the 'appropriate emotional response to such violations is homicidal rage'.[2] One story Penti and his friends told me reveals the Waorani response when an individual's interests are frustrated. The event happened only a decade before. There was an elder couple who became incensed at a noisy oil exploration helicopter hovering above their house. The couple relocated to another part of the jungle. Then an oil spill contaminated the land around their new house. Enraged at the infringement of their interests, they killed a second couple who had nothing at all to do with the oil — the homicidal response to the violation of their autonomy was culturally appropriate.

I wasn't surprised to hear this story. It fitted with stories I'd read before visiting the community. We can hardly begin to imagine the degree of individual autonomy in Waorani culture, and the rage expressed when individual autonomy is frustrated. For example, one anthropologist observed 'an occasion where a man returned from a raid in which (his brother) had been killed by *kowadi* (foreigners). The man sees his elderly grandmother lying in her hammock. "Why should a worthless old woman like you be alive when my brother is dead?" and drives a spear through her where she lies.'[3] He killed his own grandmother to express his anger at the violation of his interests.

Fancy being a manager, or even a colleague, in a workplace where the accepted behavioural response by an individual frustrated at failing to attain their personal objective is to lash out in uncontrolled rage. Imagine the response by a staff member whose performance rating disappoints them. Or a miserly pay review. Not to mention when a manager initiates a performance improvement plan. That would be one ugly workplace with blood constantly being mopped off the floor.

According to anthropologists Carole and Clayton Robarchek, in Waorani society there are few community rituals that link people together, which results in every household and every individual being independent and autonomous.[4] There are also 'no institutional structures of any sort that confer on any person more authority than another, or authority over another ... The authority of elders is limited to their ability to cajole and coerce. Even parents have little control over the actions of their children and cannot coerce them to do what they do not want to do.'[5]

Significantly, even the Waorani themselves made a dramatic cultural shift when an alternative concept was revealed to them: the concept of living in peace. The idea took off.

Up until 1958, Waorani society was a closed system. Waorani were isolated in the hinterland away from rivers. Their language has no connection to any other language. They had no trade and no peaceful relationships with any other society. The closed system itself didn't mean that violence must develop as the cultural mindset, but it meant that given it did develop, there was no alternative to the mindset of rage and murder.

And then in 1958 a new idea was injected into the belief system: outsiders are not all enemies and are not all cannibals. The new information was introduced by missionaries. In 1956 the first attempt by four American missionaries ended in the spearing deaths of the missionaries. Two years later, the wife of one of the dead missionaries and a sister of another bravely made peaceful contact with Waorani and brought the message of living in peace with your neighbours. Almost overnight the Waorani experienced a remarkable cultural change from being the most violent society on Earth to being relatively peaceful.

In studying this cultural transformation, Carole and Clayton Robarchek concluded that the transformation was due to new information that altered the Waorani world view and introduced them to the possibility of a different, peaceful, life. The Robarcheks said that the impact of the new information about the possibility of peace spread faster than what the missionaries could have achieved through direct contact with people — it spread by the people themselves sharing a new and compelling idea. The new information challenged a long-held belief and opened people to the possibilities of a different life. Almost overnight vendettas ceased and within months there was a 90% reduction in the number of homicides.[6] It was a remarkable cultural shift.

I met one man, Aboke Tega, aged about 85, who remembers the old days. We stayed one night in his hut, his roof of thatched palm fronds providing shelter from the rain. As my guide, José Aguinda, peeled and sliced potatoes for our evening soup, Aboke rested in his hammock close to his perpetual fire. He told us tales of his early days. Aboke was born well before Contact. He told us that as a youngster he was frightened by aeroplanes flying overhead as oil exploration staff mapped the forest. He told us that as a young man he was a member of a party of warriors that killed oil workers trespassing on Waorani land. He and his friends killed two oil workers and one, though injured, escaped to tell the tale. Through the English-Spanish-Wao translation chain, I asked Aboke whether he preferred the relatively peaceful years of his later life or the violent years of his youth.

'I preferred the old life,' he answered from his hammock, 'when we could walk, walk and walk in the jungle.'

Our boat driver, David Yasa, sat near Aboke's fire. Some years ago, David had moved to the Babeno community as a school teacher, met and married a local woman and they have two young children. I asked David, 'Is your wife happy that she was born in this generation with much less violence or would she prefer to have been born in the old days?'

Without hesitation he answered, 'Oh, she is very happy to be living now.'

Of the societies I have researched, Waorani is unique in that individual autonomy was supreme (and still is for some Waorani who choose to live their traditional life). For our purposes, the Waorani experience is an extreme example highlighting the importance of leaders articulating what it means to belong to the organisation and setting the boundaries of individual behaviour.

Pintupi Society and Obligations to Others

In contrast to Waorani, Pintupi society in Central Australia, like other Australian indigenous societies, has a sophisticated way of balancing individual autonomy with group identity. A person's autonomy grows through the development of relationships and obligations to the group. Obligations are developed through the privileged acquisition of knowledge of the Dreaming, of events during creation before the beginning of time. The slow acquisition of knowledge of 'the law' and the rituals of the society provide the means for individual growth, for a network of social relationships and for status within the community.

I was fortunate to be able to visit the remote Pintupi town of Walungurru with the charity, Red Dust. Red Dust supports remote indigenous communities with health and wellbeing outcomes. I mentioned in Chapter 1 that Pintupi is one of the last Aboriginal peoples to leave their traditional way of life. Some Pintupi remember living the life of their ancestors. Marlene Nampitjinpa Ross is one of them and she told me of the occasion, aged 11, when she first saw a 'whitefella'. Suddenly, she and her family were terrified by a strange beast appearing over the sandhills. 'I later learned,' she said with a broad smile and a laugh, 'that the strange beast was called a truck.' At the sight of the strange beast, her small family group scattered in fright. Marlene and her mother became separated from the others and hid in a cave. When all was quiet, she and her mother tentatively ventured from the cave. Her family — about four others — had disappeared. Strangely, all their footprints had disappeared at the same point, replaced by tracks she'd never seen before. They followed those strange tracks, the wheel tracks of the truck, through the sandhills and spinifex grass. She later learned that a government official had come to offer Pintupi people a lift into the nearest, yet distant, town for food and shelter. The rest of her family had accepted the offer and had clambered into the truck. Marlene and her mother had no idea what had happened, and decided their only option was to follow the tracks in search of their family. They followed the tracks for weeks, finally arriving at the town of Papunya where, with great relief and joy, they reconnected with their family. It was their first taste of a life different to what their ancestors had known for millennia.

Many visitors might find Pintupi country barren and uninviting. Not me. I grew up in the Australian outback town of Broken Hill, so the red soil and sparse vegetation is like going home. The country of my upbringing also gives me a deep respect for people who lived — who could survive — in the Australian desert. As a youngster, going 'out bush' with my family or on scout camps meant carrying all our water and plenty of it. It meant packing all our food. It meant taking our first-aid kit, our tents for shelter, sleeping bags for the cold desert nights and matches for lighting a fire. I can't imagine, but can certainly appreciate, the knowledge and skill necessary to find water, make tools and obtain and cook food in the Australian interior.

Earlier I mentioned that the tough environmental conditions, driven largely by low rainfall, drove the Pintupi social system. In traditional times, the population density was probably one person to 200 square kilometres (80 square miles).[7] Consequently, Pintupi groups were small and widely dispersed. Bands were based around family units of 6 to 10 people and sometimes aggregating into groups of 20 to 30 people.

In such a widely dispersed society, how did Pintupi achieve the social objective of balancing individual autonomy with group obligations? There are four elements which contribute to achieving the objective. In writing this summary, I am grateful to the anthropologist Fred Myers who, from his field work beginning in 1973, documented the sophisticated Pintupi approach.[8] Some of the people I met fondly remember Fred, and some remain in contact with him.

Own Country

The first element in Pintupi society of balancing group obligations and individual identity is the concept of 'country'. Each person has one's own country. Country is not exclusive to an individual, yet there are a small number of people with the same strong connection to an area or a landmark. One's own country is claimed based on a range of factors, including where a person's conception took place, their place of birth, where initiation occurred (for a male), where their mother or father was conceived or where a close relative died. The nature of country is that the person's identity is fundamentally connected with that place. And the person has a special bond with the few others who have the same strength of connection.

Arising from own country is the obligation of individuals to protect country. They have primary custodial rights to the area and to rituals that occur in the location or the sacred objects stored in that place. They have an obligation to protect and to 'pass it on'.

When visitors seek to visit a location, they must ask permission from the custodians. By being asked, 'one gains prestige, respect and personal autonomy'.[9]

The Dreaming

The second element of balancing individual identity with group obligations stems from the Dreaming, the creation period. The Dreaming explains every feature of the Australian indigenous universe.[10] A large hill, a rock outcrop, a waterhole is explained by the journey of travelling ancestors and spirit figures before the beginning of time. All features of the land, and all customs, originate in the Dreaming.

As a cultural system, the impact of the Dreaming is that actions and obligations for individuals arise from that law, not by being told by others what someone can do or cannot do.[11] It is a fundamental part of the balance between autonomy and compliance.

An individual is identified with their Dreaming and through it a place.[12] This becomes their own identity with their own autonomy, separate to any other person and not owed to any other person. No one possesses authority to force any other person to do one's will. The Dreaming does, however, provide group consensus to a shared code — which is the fundamental purpose of culture containing individual autonomy.

Status and prestige achieved through knowledge

The third dimension of the complex Pintupi cultural system, a system that manages to achieve individual autonomy and social obligations, is the acquisition of knowledge — a requirement to acquire all the Dreaming stories and knowledge and to appropriately pass them on.

In taking on this obligation, an individual is containing their own will. The person is driven to build and maintain relatedness with others — to maintain their social obligations and their social contribution. Indeed, status is achieved by the sharing of knowledge. The individual grows by 'looking after' a place and of teaching the Dreaming of that place and the myths, songs, designs and objects of that place.

The impressive cultural balance is that on the one hand, an individual gains respect and prestige by looking after country, by being the one from whom permission is sought and by being the one with the knowledge to pass on. And along with the prestige comes personal autonomy to that individual. Both individual autonomy and social obligation is achieved, in harmony.

Initiation for men and development for women

The fourth interwoven element of Pintupi society is initiation, particularly of males. A critical part of the initiation process is that initiation cannot occur with just one's own group. People far and wide are invited. This extends the social connections and the relatedness of people. The related-ness connects the adults who play a key role in the initiation, amongst the 'fathers' and 'mothers' of the young men being initiated and between the young man and his circumciser, and between the group of young men being initiated. The relationships continue for the rest of people's lives.

As a model for workplace cultures, Pintupi achieve the desired balance. Autonomy is connected to knowledge and responsibility which is inseparable from relatedness with others. That makes for a strong culture, where individual autonomy and the group's interest are in balance.

Not many workplaces achieve that balance. It's a rare but inspirational leader who has in their make-up a balance that allows individual identity within the group. For example, the balance of respecting individual expression free from expecting people to conform to the leader's image of desired behaviour, yet at the same time holding the boundaries on the rare occasion when an individual crosses the line and violates group norms. Leaders at every level can aspire to find that balance.

Māori's Elaborate Community Focus

Māori also achieve individual identity within community interests. The objective is assisted through the physical identity of a community centre, a marae, and through community ceremonies at the marae, called hui. Hui provide the avenue for community interactions, group identity and inter-group networking. People gather for weddings, birthdays, funerals, unveilings (a year after a death) and other significant events. Formal rules and protocols govern the planning and conduct of a hui.

A marae, the ceremonial centre with a meeting house and plaza, is generally owned by a hapū. (As covered in previous chapters, a hapū is the equivalent of a village-sized organisation unit as I am describing in this book.)

When I visited the Taranaki region in New Zealand in January 2020, I was given the honour of a ceremonial welcome, a powhiri, by my host Keri Opai and a female elder, Peeti Wātene. A powhiri is one aspect of the rich traditions at a marae. I knew from my preparatory reading, particularly Anne Salmond's book, *Hui*, that if the visitors include a person of high status, a chant of welcome, the powhiri, is delivered. When Keri Opai told me a few weeks before my visit that a powhiri would be provided to me, I felt incredibly privileged — and I found it to be an emotional experience.

Keri and Peeti's marae is called Taiporohēnui (pronounced Tie-poro-hair-nui). In the Taranaki region there are about 20 marae. Taiporohēnui is the marae of the Hamuna hapū. While many marae are named after ancestors, Taiporohēnui is named for an historical event. The name means 'the land floated off to the sea', referring to the time when the land was stolen by colonisers. The terminology is more positive than saying that the land was stolen, because saying that it has floated off leaves open the possibility that the land will one day return to the traditional owners.

Prior to arriving at Taiporohēnui for the powhiri, Keri coached me on what would happen, where I should stand and what I was to do. Knowing there are strict protocols, I welcomed his coaching. As instructed, I waited at the visitors' gate. Peeti and Keri stood on the porch of the meeting house. Peeti began chanting. I walked slowly along the 50 metre (yard) path to the house. As Keri had coached me, I walked slowly so I could think about people who have departed, including my ancestors and his. I felt the presence of my dearly departed mother and father, their smiling faces either side of me.

Keri had told me about the chant Peeti was delivering. The chant acknowledges the concept of conflict, dating back to a time when people believed they might be subject to black magic or physical attack from visitors — or the hosts attacking visitors. Inside the meeting house is a place of peace. Peeti's message was that she and Keri hoped I come into the house in the spirit of peaceful resolution.

I reached the house and removed my shoes. Keri invited me inside. As hosts, Peeti and Keri went to the left side of the house. I was sent to the right, the *tapu* or sacred side reserved for visitors. They greeted me with a *hongi*. Hongi is a greeting full of *aroha* (love), involving two people pressing their foreheads and noses together.

Keri signalled me to sit. He remained standing and incanted the next chant. As he recited the chant, he looked to the photos of his ancestors on the walls, he looked at me, he turned to the entrance door and then back to his ancestors. His chant acknowledged the marae and the protection it provided the people. In te reo (the Māori language) he was saying, 'Welcome, Andrew. Thank you for making our marae warm with your presence. We are honoured to have you visit.' Keri was acknowledging my status, or *mana*. He called on his ancestors to give us their blessings and to look after us. Keri was speaking on behalf of the people who have gone before. He told me later that in chanting, he had visions of the old people for whom he was speaking. He acknowledged the departed and their lineage that leads to us. During his chant, as well as feeling the presence of my mother and father, I felt the presence — the spirit perhaps — of Keri's ancestors. When he finished, I wiped a tear from my eye.

One of Keri's ancestors is Kupu, a navigator and the discoverer of Aotearoa (New Zealand). Kupu and his wife migrated to Aotearoa from Hawaiki (perhaps today's Cook Islands) in 900AD. Kupu's wife brought kūmara (sweet potato) and kūmara seeds with her. They landed at the Auckland isthmus, travelled south through today's Hamilton and on to Taranaki. They were in search of soil with a beautiful smell, as Kupu had been directed. The strength of Māori ancestry is a powerful way that people are bound together in a community.

Peeti and Keri had made me a local for that moment. 'You are as a bird lighted upon our marae. And then we leave together,' he told me.

A major aspect of the physical marae and ceremonial gatherings, the hui, is the balance of community identity and individual autonomy of community members. The two dimensions are in balance; one can't happen without the other.

Keri is a good example. Through his unique contribution to the community, his identity is enhanced. His special contribution is his language and chanting capability. He knows thousands of chants, some dating back 1000 years. 'But it's okay,' he said over breakfast before we drove to the marae, 'we'll keep it light today and only do a 500-year-old chant!' The longest chant he knows is twenty minutes. Chants have to be word perfect. Keri is too humble to acknowledge that he has a gift for chants. He merely says that he is lucky to have a photographic memory. He is frequently called upon to provide chanting services to his community, and represents his community across New Zealand. Keri adds that while he can be of service to his community with chants, there's a lot of other marae duties that are beyond him. One of them is cooking.

Food preparation for a hui is a well-orchestrated project. Marae prestige rests on the quality and quantity of the food. Elder Te Rangi Hiroa (Sir Peter Buck) in *The Coming of the Māori* describes the process in his own village he witnessed as a youngster in about the year 1900. He says there was a man called Mana who had become accepted as the public announcer in the village. When the time approached to commence the cooking, Mana toured the village to check that fires were set for lighting and the food was prepared. Mana then stood in the middle of the village and yelled, 'Ka tahu' ('Light up'). The cry was repeated from the nearest fireplaces to the outer edges of the village. The commander of each fire, usually a woman, applied a match and soon smoke was wafting from fires throughout the village. When the correct time had expired for the wood to burn down and the stones and charcoal were hot, Mana yelled out the next instruction, 'Ka tao' ('Cook'). The time allowed for cooking was an hour or more, and it was better to be on the safe side, for undercooked food brought shame to the family. When Mana was satisfied that the food would be cooked, he yelled out, 'Ka hura' ('Uncover'). The assistants at each fire scraped off the earth and stones from the oven and removed the kūmara and other vegetables and the fish or the meat. Mana's final instruction was, 'Ka hari' ('Carry'), issued when the women and girls carrying the food on trays were assembled. The women in two lines then marched slowly towards the marae, the leading women singing songs, joined by the chorus behind them.[13] Mana gained his identity through his contribution to the community.

At night in my motel room while visiting the Taranaki region I watched Māori Television. One of the programs featured the restoration of marae — marae that had deteriorated and in need of repair. It was striking, the focus the marae provides the community and the worth of each person through their individual contribution to the restoration project. Some people were good on the tools, some at cleaning, some at restoring faded photos of ancestors, some at cooking for the troops.

It's a delicate balance — community and individual identity — at which Māori excel. Individual identity is interwoven with community interests. Cultural identity is achieved in harmony with individuals containing their own motivations and interests in order to be part of the community, and in return individuals receive great respect and status through their community contribution. It's a wonderful model for workplaces. And it's a two-way street: to expect compliance by individuals to organisational standards, leaders need to know and respect each staff member as an individual.

Actions for Workplace Leaders

Ancestral societies are crystal clear about what it means to be part of their society — people know the values of their society and the extent to which they are expected to contain their individual interests in order to be a member of the community. Yet people are given personal autonomy and gain respect through their personal worth and the contribution they make. There are a number of actions that workplace leaders should take to achieve the balance of individual autonomy with membership of the group.

1. **Acknowledge the importance of culture:** The first action is to accept the importance of culture for a well-functioning group; bring culture on to your leadership radar and to the leadership practices of your organisation. Part of this acknowledgement of culture is that there is a balance of individual freedoms being constrained by group norms. The Waorani example of unconstrained individual autonomy does not recommend itself to workplaces. And cultish practices that result in an absence of individual autonomy are equally unattractive. The task for leaders is to have a sense of the boundaries. And this applies to leaders at each level — for top leaders thinking about the organisation down to team leaders thinking about their team.

2. **Ensure there are benefits to individuals in belonging:** For individuals to cede their personal interests in favour of the group, there need to be benefits arising from belonging to the group. In Pintupi and Māori societies, the benefits include the prestige associated with an individual's contribution to the group grounded in respect for an individual's identity. In workplaces, an individual's benefit from belonging isn't about pay and benefits — material rewards are purely transactional. The return needs to be the emotional benefit that arises from group belonging. The emotional return includes:

   - respect from colleagues and leaders,
   - being appreciated as a whole person and not being seen as merely an input in the production of goods and services,

- flexibility by the immediate manager to work to a person's strengths and accommodate their weaknesses,

- pride in being associated with the organisation and its purpose, and

- personal growth and professional development.

We'll return to the theme of individual development in the next chapter.

3. **Decide the extent of individual freedoms:** Waorani society represents the extreme option of almost complete individual freedom, unconstrained by group norms. Pintupi and Maori societies represent the more attractive option for workplaces — strong rules for belonging with scope for individual autonomy and expression. An organisation that attends to Action 1 above — that's prepared to talk about its culture and the expectations on staff to behave within certain parameters — will have laid a foundation for each department and team to be able to discuss the extent to which individual freedoms are constrained by group rules. It's useful to articulate this dimension of group versus individual freedoms because some of the conflict between colleagues within a department and across departments is when people operate on different assumptions about rules and priorities, often because those rules and priorities haven't been clearly codified. Tensions between functions within an organisation are often associated with compliance to rules relating to the common good. Some individuals might find this frustrating. In the pharmaceutical industry where my wife worked, debates between the marketing and medical departments invariably arose due to marketing staff, seeking to maximise sales, testing the boundaries of what could be said about the benefits of a medicine. The medical department played the important role of seeking to ensure medical accuracy according to the company's stated benefits of a medicine. One group can easily be considered bureaucratic and the other mavericks, depending on your perspective. Articulating the cultural priorities of an organisation helps individuals and teams make better sense of the rules of belonging.

4. **State your values:** In addition to rules of belonging and individual freedoms, 'values' should also be explicit. Values represent the basis on which members of the group are expected to behave and the basis on which decisions are made. People can work out the rules over time, but leaders can save people time, energy and frustration by articulating the values. There are two ways to develop the values of an organisation. One is to develop them bottom-up through staff focus groups, identifying the values that people strongly associate with. Through this process the list is compiled, narrowed and filtered up through the organisation for sign-off by the top team. The other way is to have the top team, mainly the top leader, state their values. I favour the latter. I do so because in reality the values of an organisation are those of the top leader. That's why the cultures of companies such as IBM, Google, Tesla and Amazon.com differ. They don't differ because of the country in which they are head-quartered. They don't differ because of the nature or occupation of the staff they employ. They differ because of the character of the top leader. Some years ago I consulted to a company that had a special culture. Not surprisingly, it was led by a respectful and capable chief executive. People loved working for this leader and were greatly saddened when he announced he would be leaving the organisation. In the window of time between the dearly loved, long-term CEO leaving and his replacement arriving, most of the top team were of the view that, 'Our culture is so strong it will endure no matter the style of the new CEO.' They were seriously disappointed. The new CEO, people quickly found, was narcissistic and demeaning — which created defensiveness and disunity across the organisation. Almost like flicking a switch as the new CEO walked through the door, the culture changed dramatically, for the worse. That's the impact of the top leader on culture.

5. **Express values as behaviours:** If there are any conflicts between the proclaimed culture and what's experienced in practice, the practical wins. That's because what the top leader *does* trumps what they *say*. The best approach, then, is for the top leader to articulate their values through the set of behaviours people should live

by. Stating the demonstrable behaviour brings a value to life and is more understandable. Values mean different things to different people; behaviours are clearer. What does a value of 'customer service' or 'continuous improvement' or 'respect for each other' really mean — how would someone know they are living the value? The clarity comes from *observable* behaviours. When I assist leaders and teams to express values as behaviours, I prompt them to list what a fly on the wall would *observe* in the team living the value. 'Or expressed differently,' I say as a facilitator, 'if we record a video of you living that value, what would we see on the video? Or if a visitor, such as me, joined your team for a day or a week, what would the visitor observe to conclude that you are living that value?' With these prompts, team members easily express values as observable behaviours. For example, the value of 'respect for each other' might be expressed as: *We demonstrate respect for colleagues by listening politely to the views of others without interruption.* Or, *We demonstrate respect by asking a colleague to explain their ideas so we avoid jumping to our own conclusion.* Yes, you could shoot a video that shows a group of colleagues listening attentively to another person speaking and people asking questions to allow a person to explain their point.

6. **Address deviations from the standards of behaviour:** Clarity on the behaviours that demonstrate the key values of the team or the organisation provides clarity to individuals about what's acceptable and what's not. It draws the line on the extent to which individuals need to conform to group norms — to the group's culture. For the culture to live, transgressions of behaviour need to be addressed. As I developed as a leader and contemplated the occasional challenge of a poor performer or disruptive member of my team, there were three realisations that helped me to be more confident to fulfil this leadership task. First, as mentioned previously, I realised that as the leader I didn't need the wayward team member's *agreement* to what I was observing and requesting; I realised that as the leader I unconsciously *wanted* the person to agree to what I was saying about my perspective of their shortcomings. But I realised that it's okay if

the person was not about to agree with me, which would perhaps involve them changing their view about self. Yet as the leader I am entitled to my standards, entitled to my observations, and entitled to require adherence to my standards of behaviour. The second realisation was that if I followed the process of three warnings, starting gently, I was giving the person a chance to listen to my request and to correct their behaviour. If they didn't change, then they were making an alternative choice. If they didn't amend their behaviour, then I felt more comfortable in hardening my position and escalating my warnings. The third realisation was, as covered earlier, that I felt the overarching obligation as the leader to protect the welfare, harmony and outputs of the group.

7. **Demonstrate confidence in existing staff to be part of a culture change:** One of the lessons from the Waorani experience is that even well-entrenched cultures can change if there is a convincing reason to do so; convincing to the members of the group. Some senior leaders might think that to shift a culture, there needs to be a 'clean-out' of managers and staff. But Waorani, within the one generation, shifted from being the most violent society on Earth to being a relatively peaceful one. It was based not on 'clearing out the dead wood' or 'deciding who's on the bus' or 'sacking people and starting again' (all cop-outs saving top leaders from being convincing and inspiring).

8. **Implement initiatives for social cohesion:** Another lesson from the Waorani experience is that the society had little in the way of communal rituals that connected and united people. In Chapter 11 we'll look in detail at the initiatives that generally apply in traditional societies to create a sense of community obligation and cohesion. The implication for workplaces is that social rituals are critical to develop a collaborative culture.

Before we depart from culture and autonomy, there is one other way, universally, that traditional societies achieve the balance of individual identity *and* group membership. That method is through intensive individual learning.

CHAPTER 8

Individual Identity Through Learning

'See that tree? In the old days we made spears from that tree.
Would you like to have a go?'

TRADITIONAL SOCIETIES ARE LEARNING organisations, superb at developing the next generation. Part of the genius of the traditional learning approach is to validate the identity of the individual. From what I have observed, it's impossible in traditional societies for an individual to be anonymous. Unfortunately, in workplaces, many staff feel unsupported, with a sad number harbouring the horrible feeling of being anonymous. They are lost in the crowd. As well as preparing the next generation for their roles ahead, learning is the remedy for any sense of loneliness or anonymity amongst staff.

In my visits to traditional societies, I was amazed that *every time* I asked someone how they learned their cultural knowledge, *everyone* instantly nominated a single person. While the person I was meeting with might have subsequently nominated a second or third person, there was always a single teacher who stood out above all other adults in their life.

For Alan Palmer, growing up in Alice Springs in Central Australia, his tutor was a great uncle. Alan works with the charity Red Dust and was one of the leaders of the volunteering group I was fortunate to join in October

2019 to visit the Pintupi community of Walungurru. I was one of seven volunteers in the expert hands of Alan and three other Red Dust leaders. We drove the 640 kilometres (400 miles) west from Alice Springs to Pintupi country in a convoy of five vehicles. Knowing my interest in culture, our head leader allocated me to travel with Alan. It's hard to believe that a six-hour drive can go by so quickly. Alan gave me a mobile seminar. Given that I'm an uninitiated person, I know Alan was careful with what he was permitted to share with me. What he was culturally permitted to share, he did so generously.

Almost the whole drive from Alice Springs to Walungurru is on gravel road, the loose stones smacking the inside of the wheel hubs and the undercarriage of the car. The dust created by the car ahead meant the convoy was well spread out. Alan and I talked and talked. The only interruptions were a brief stop at the single town, Papunya, at about the halfway point and another stop an hour or so later to check that all vehicles were accounted for. It was the best road trip, ever.

One of the subjects I asked Alan was, 'Who taught you about your culture?'

'My grandmother's younger brother,' he said. 'As an uncle two generations above me, he had the responsibility — the obligation — to teach me. But only if I wanted to learn, which I did.'

'When I was a boy,' he continued, 'we would be sitting around home — my siblings, my cousins and me — and Uncle might say, "Do you want to go out bush?"'

'"Sure, Uncle, let's go." I always jumped at the offer. Hardly any of the others wanted to go. There were plenty of distractions for young kids.'

'Then out bush, my uncle might say, "See that tree? In the old days we made spears from that tree."'

'There would generally be a pause in our conversation,' Alan told me. 'Then Uncle said, "Do you want to have a go at making a spear?"'

'We sat and made a spear, talking as we worked,' Alan smiled at the memory of being at the side of his devoted uncle. And clearly Alan was an eager pupil.

'The style of teaching was subtle. My uncle didn't say, "Son, I want to teach you our culture and the old ways." If he'd said that it would've put pressure on me — putting me in the role of a student with the burden to acquire and retain knowledge. He never made me feel that way.'

As we approached Walungurru and the start of the Western Desert, the number and variety of trees surprised me. There were stands of Desert Oaks and thickets of mulga, which we would later investigate for crafting boomerangs. Alan pointed out Corkwood trees and Bloodwood gums, which in season carry bush coconut (a worm).

'My uncle's approach to teaching,' Alan said, 'also allowed him to assess when I was ready for the next stage of learning.'

'How did he do that?'

'He assessed if I was curious. Was I well-motivated — was I learning the customs and the knowledge for good reasons and not for boasting rights? Was I respecting the knowledge? Was I smart,' Alan tapped his head, 'meaning that I was enquiring, thinking things through and starting to give back?'

What a generous approach to learning. How could Alan not feel validated, to have someone devoted to his education and development? How could you not be deeply affected by that attention, and at the same time associate strongly with your community?

Can this method of teaching and learning be adopted in workplaces? Yes, I think so — I know so. I know because I had the good fortune twice in the early stage of my career to work for managers who invested in me — in my learning — as one of their priorities. I started my career as an industrial (labour) relations advocate, and I was fortunate to have as my first boss Norm Amos. Norm coached and guided me. He made time for me, he shared his experience, he provided me opportunity to develop and gave me feedback on my progress as I began to represent our member companies before industrial tribunals. I welcomed his feedback because first, I wanted to learn and second, I knew he was sharing observations entirely for my benefit. What's not to like about a manager devoted to your development? Under Norm's tuition, I did things I had no idea I was capable of doing, and certainly faster than I could have imagined was possible. As I talked with Alan in the car heading to Walungurru, I could see that Norm's style of teaching all those years before was similar to Alan's great uncle. Alan's uncle asking him, 'Would you like to have a go?' was the same as Norm asking me, 'Would you like to present the next case in the industrial tribunal?'

Norm and I worked in a small organisation. But the size of the organisation wasn't significant. The critical factor was that Norm was motivated to teach me — he would have been like that even in a large global corporation.

My next role was with a large manufacturing firm. Again, I was fortunate to work for a generous manager, Jim Neville, who was also dedicated to my learning and development. Jim and I chatted frequently about projects and challenges. We shared ideas and tested solutions. He offered observations to help me grow. He gave his time and shared his knowledge. Working with managers like Norm and Jim, I felt strongly validated and grew as a professional. And consequently, I had a strong sense of identity with both organisations. There's no way that I could feel lost, alienated or anonymous.

In fact the individual-oriented approach to learning I've described so far in this chapter *is* replicated quite closely in some workplace roles. In the apprenticeship model, used particularly in the trades, a young person gains the bulk of their knowledge alongside an 'elder' in the field. It was probably natural that this form of learning was adopted by the trades, those being the first occupations that emerged in the Industrial Revolution when Western society was still in touch with our human traditions. With the much later emergence of knowledge work and other office occupations, we have become distant from our ancestral past. The fundamental concept that underpins apprenticeships remains a good one to apply more broadly.

Lifelong Learning and Individual Mentoring

In traditional societies, there are two broad components in a person's lifetime of learning. The first component, beginning in infancy, covers the skills and knowledge to survive. The second component is cultural and spiritual knowledge.

The curriculum for surviving in the bush or the rainforest is extensive — the equivalent of a double degree in botany and zoology, and more. Waorani in the Amazon know the fruits of 152 species of trees and palms.

Bushmen in the Kalahari know 200 plant species, with 105 of those plants edible for their fruits, nuts, berries, gum, roots or bulbs. Add to that, Bushmen know 58 mammals, about 90 bird species, 25 species of reptiles and amphibians and around 85 species of invertebrates.[1]

In their first stage of learning, toddlers are generally guided by their parents. Then when the person progresses into their teenage years, the teaching responsibility usually shifts to a close relative other than a parent. As this pattern emerged from my meetings with people, I wondered why this was so — why not their mother or father in a person's teenage years and beyond? Elsie Gale on Haida Gwaii told me, 'Sometimes tough lessons are required for a young person. Having an older relative as the teacher means the young person always has a safe place with their parents.'

Māori Keri Opai's learning experience is almost a match to Alan Palmer's experience. Growing up in the 1980s, Keri told me, he was bashed and ridiculed for being Māori. At school he suffered the butt of 'jokes', not just from the other children but also from most teachers.

'As a teenager, I was at a crossroad,' he said as we explored his ances-tral district around Mount Taranaki on New Zealand's north island. 'One path would lead me to join a gang. I'd hate to think where I'd be now if I had chosen that path. The other path led me to be respectful of the Māori world and my heritage. A switch went on in my head and I chose the Māori path.'

He told me that, tellingly, a community elder took an interest in him at that critical time. 'My elder showed me a glimpse of the Māori world. It was nuanced, it was marvellous. I resolved that I would live and sleep Māori.'

I commented, 'The elder must have seen something special in you. What do you think he saw?'

'He saw a confused boy, but a curious one who had capacity for learn-ing. He saw that I was dedicated and interested to learn.'

'What was the elder's style of teaching?' I asked.

'He fed me small bites of knowledge, and then bigger bites. We never went backwards. He taught by osmosis. I acquired knowledge at a pace set by him and no-doubt matching my ability. "Come to the mountain with me," he might say. "Let's go for a walk," he would suggest.'

'Learning was experiential. He posed questions for me to reflect on and come back, sometimes weeks, months, or even years, later. We would have a lengthy conversation about my answer. The important thing to my elder wasn't whether my answer was right or wrong — he was interested in my thought processes and the depth of my reflections.'

Keri left school to dedicate himself entirely to learning his Māori language and customs. He studied Māori language, te reo, during the day and learned chants and recitations at night.

'In the Māori language,' Keri said, 'the word for "teaching" and the word for "learning" is the same: *ako*. So teacher and learner are the same word: *kaiako*. That gives insight into the nature of the relationship and the equality of the learning and teaching experience in our culture.'

In traditional societies, learning is not exclusively individualistic. Learning in Māori society included schools of learning, or *whare wananga*. The school may or may not have been a physical structure. Keri told me that in the old days, schooling was generally conducted in winter when there was less work in the fields and during periods of peace.

There were various subjects taught at school, including genealogy, chants and invocations, esoteric or mysterious law, agriculture and conservation, wood carving, weaving, tattooing, storytelling, entertainment and warfare and weaponry. Graduating from a school carried great prestige. At graduation, a student was gifted a new name in honour of their progression.[2]

Each section of the school was led by a master, a *tohunga*. Tohunga are highly regarded and are people of great influence. Keri told me of one tohunga who lived in the Taranaki region perhaps around the year 1700. He was a master of conservation. Periodically, he travelled from the north, visiting all areas along the coast of Taranaki. His purpose was to check how each hapū, each community, was treating their fishing grounds, their horticultural land and the purity of the water in their streams and rivers. If the tohunga deemed that a hapū was not caring for their precious resources, he would pass the land or the water to a different hapū that was expected to treat the resource better.

A Role of Elders was to Teach

In ancestral societies, elders are revered. In large part, their prestige is due to their knowledge. The admiration is in sharp contrast, I think, to the general lack of respect for older workers in Western workplaces.

Bias against older workers is, in my experience, a relatively recent phenomenon. I detected a shift during the 1990–91 recession. Before that downcycle, older staff were valued and there was no stigma attached to grey hair and wrinkles. But in 1991 the language, indicative of mindset, shifted. With jobs being slashed, pressure was applied to older staff to sacrifice their employment in favour of younger colleagues. And then as the economic cycle improved, young people continued to be favoured for job vacancies. The stigma attached to older age remained. To further make the point that language reveals mindset, another shift happened in the 1991 recession. Before that time, in answer to the casual question from a colleague, 'How are you going?' no one answered, 'Really busy!' That response became fashionable out of the need to demonstrate usefulness from fear of layoffs. The language stuck.

A consequence of bias against older workers is that we undermine the value of knowledge in workplaces — knowledge gained from worldly experience. Getting back in touch with the experience of ancestral cultures that older people are revered for their wisdom and knowledge would add substantially to the quality of our workplaces.

In traditional societies, older people are honoured for their knowledge. My guide in the Amazon, José Aguinda, told me about his traditional Kichwa upbringing in the 1970s and the role of his grandparents. 'I was born in the jungle. My mother never went to a hospital, not even for a pregnancy check-up. My grandmother was the doctor and knew all the jungle medicine. My grandmother assisted in my birth and I was born healthy! I grew up in the jungle with my parents and grandparents. My grandparents told me many stories about their own hard life, and also what their own parents had experienced — the hardships and the triumphs. My grandparents taught me to respect and love Mother Earth, how to use her medicine and where to find food in the jungle. They taught me which plant or animal to take care of in order to avoid encountering a harmful spirit. I remember many Kichwa stories, legends and myths — some were exciting, others terrifying, but none was boring or that you let pass without asking a question. All that remains of my grandparents is their knowledge. I treasure that knowledge. My spiritual knowledge is mostly thanks to my grandfather and my father. From a very young age I participated in *ayahuasca* ceremonies where my father and my grandfather transmitted their power to me through blows on my head, my hands, my feet, my nose, my tongue, and I took tobacco and ayahuasca. This experience marks you for life. I always have in mind where I come from, moments that mark the history of this land and my deep cultural roots.'

Elizabeth Marshall Thomas, in recalling her time among Bushmen, wrote that while old people reach a point when they can't contribute to production — to gathering and hunting — they are valued for something even more valuable: they are valued for what they know. The old people hold the largest amount of important information. The most important information critical for survival often related to events that might occur only every fifty years or so, and this information is known only to people in their 60s or older. For example, when a major drought occurred, it was probably only the older people who knew where to find water. Perhaps that was because their own grandparents showed them where to get water during the previous major drought years before. Marshall Thomas wrote, 'Few attributes could be as useful as a long memory, or contribute as much to survival.'[3]

The workplace equivalent of a once-in-a-generation drought in the Kalahari is a national recession. For example, as a consequence of the COVID-19 pandemic in 2020 national economies nosedived. For workplace leaders, as well as local, state and country leaders, COVID required quality decision making in tight timeframes. Decision making in those demanding conditions is helped if a leader has lived the experience. And here's the point about age (which is really a proxy for experience). In Australia, the prior recession to the 2020 COVID recession was way back in 1990–91 (we avoided the recession most countries suffered during the Global Financial Crisis in 2008). That's 30 years between recessions for Australian leaders. A leader in the COVID pandemic would need to be at least 50 years of age to even have been in the workforce in 1990. To have been in leadership roles or even close to decision-making roles last time, they would need to be at least 60 years of age in 2020. If a leader in the early hectic days of the COVID recession couldn't rely on their own experience, it was invaluable if they had experienced heads around them to give advice and counsel about 'last time'.

The Use of Story

The elders pass on much of their knowledge through stories. Before humans had written language, we had stories. Our language capability allows us to communicate about places, events, people and concepts. Humans are instantly engaged by a story. In a relevant and well-told anecdote, we easily imagine the characters and put ourselves in the narrative. Our imagination allows us to interpret the events and the story's relevance. When we hear information by way of a story, the information is easily stored in our memory for later recall.

In workplace communication, from my observation, the use of story is underrated and many leaders have overlooked this skill.

In contrast, the use of story is emphasised in every society I visited. For example, in Central Australia, my conversations with Pintupi people invariably commenced with an invitation from my host, 'Andrew, sit here and I'll tell you a story'. People always shared information by seamlessly incorporating story.

Keri Opai taught me that there are three main types of stories used by First Peoples. One day Keri and I took a break from our drive around Taranaki to have lunch. While we waited for our food, I commented that he'd shared with me many stories over the last couple of days. He explained the three types of stories.

'The first is *pūrākau*. These are foundation or creation stories that describe the world and our traditions. Taranaki *maunga* (Mount Taranaki, the dominant physical feature of the region) is an example of a pūrākau. The story tells how the maunga came to this place. Taranaki maunga once lived in the centre of the north island. Taranaki fell in love with a female mountain Pihanga, but she was desired by other maunga, including Tongariro. Tongariro was the eventual victor and Taranaki left his home travelling west. He was led in his travels by a stone, Te Toka a Rauhoto (which Keri had just shown me). The mountain and the stone travelled west, where the journey ended when Taranaki settled next to two other maunga named Pouākai and Kaitake where he has stood ever since.'

Consistent with this explanation, Keri told me, modern science says that Taranaki is the most recent of the three mountains where it stands, and the lava flows in that part of the North Island in the direction that the old people say Taranaki travelled.

Keri explained that pūrākau stories show that indigenous people are part of the cycle of life. 'We have a place and our connection is the land and the water. I am the mountain and the mountain is me.'

Keri's explanation that origin, or creation, stories connect people to a place reminded me of an informative moment of my youth when I learned my first Aboriginal creation story. I was about 13 years of age. In writing this book, I refreshed my memory of that story. I was not surprised that, prior to rereading the story, I had retained its fundamentals. This was despite not having read or heard the story all my adult life. That's the power of story. The story tells the origins of my favourite flower, the Sturt Desert Pea, known to many Aboriginal people as Flowers of Blood. The flower is a ground cover, and in bloom has a black centre within two spectacular deep red petals.

The Sturt Desert Pea is my favourite flower because witnessing a massive bloom of the flower as a teenager was my first experience of being in awe of Nature. My dad had reason to visit a sheep station (a farm) about two hours' drive from our hometown, Broken Hill. The city is remote. Leaving town in any direction means being in the bush, hours from any other town. We drove south, not seeing another soul, and then turned off the sealed road onto a rutted bush track towards the homestead we were visiting. Not far from the sealed road, the treeless patchy plain miraculously transformed into a blanket of red and black flowers. The flowers were so abundant they encroached onto the bush track and we couldn't avoid driving over them — wincing with each patch of flowers crushed. We travelled through the enchanting display for perhaps 15 minutes and we never reached the end of the bloom. Dad had never seen anything like it. He told me that conditions have to be 'just right' for Desert Peas to flower, perhaps flowering once a decade, and never in his experience as abundant as this. He or someone else, perhaps the station owner, must have mentioned that an Aboriginal legend explains the origin of the flower, because at the first chance after we got home, I visited the local library to research the story.

Two young lovers had to separate for the male to go hunting. He gave the young women a red cloak, which she promised to wear until he returned. The young man had not returned by the time the community had to move on. The young woman refused to leave. She sat on a rocky outcrop waiting for her lover, the red cloak wrapped around her. When the community returned to the site a year later, there was no sign of the young woman. But in her place was a spectacular flower, with a black centre covered by red petals very much like a black head encased by a red cloak. Having read that story as a teenager, I never looked at Sturt Desert Peas the same again. From that moment, the flower has a deeper, emotional meaning for me, and gives greater significance to the environment. (Different Aboriginal nations have different versions of the story. This version is the story of the Wilyakali people of my hometown.)

Keri told me that, 'the second type of story is *pakiwaitara* — ancestors' stories. These stories include people's adventures from about 1000 years ago to the present. Pakiwaitara are usually stories of daring exploits, often with a moral lesson.'

We had just visited the Parihaka community, the site of non-violent resistance by Keri's forebears on 7 November 1881 against land stealing by *pākehā* (white people). The events at Parihaka reveal to Keri and his community the character of their ancestors. Tensions over the control of land had been escalating, and on that day the village was plundered by white people intent on stealing the land. Keri's ancestors did not run in the face of cannons aimed at their village, and the women fed the constabulary when they stormed the village to drag the men off to gaol. The peaceful resistance ultimately caused a shift in colonial attitudes. The success of Parihaka's non-violent resistance influenced Mahatma Gandhi years later to adopt a similar approach in India. 'These stories carry wisdom and give you instruction on how you should think and act,' Keri said. 'The stories demonstrate what the old people thought about things.'

'The third type of story is *kōrero paki*,' Keri said. 'These are jovial stories or ditties about contemporary people or events.'

Our food arrived.

I smiled as I recalled a contemporary story told to me by an emerging leader when I was in Central Australia a few months before. The story reveals information about an uncle character, the old ways and how stories are memorable. I'll share at the expense of the poor bird involved. At Walungurru, Farren Major and I leant on the bonnet (hood) of his car watching a group of kids play basketball. I asked Farren how he acquired knowledge about traditional times. Farren nominated his grandfather as the key person. 'When I was about 13, he began to teach me country.' We talked briefly about his grandfather for whom he clearly retains great affection. Farren then nominated his mother and an uncle as key people in his development. He then ever so naturally transitioned into a story to reveal a lesson from his uncle.

'Every time I see an emu, I think of my uncle,' he began. For readers not familiar with emu, it's a large flightless bird similar to an ostrich. 'One time when I was a boy, my uncle and I were driving to Alice Springs. We came across two emus a little way off the road. My uncle said he would teach me how men in the old days hunted emus. But as the car slowed, the emus ran away. I said to my uncle that the birds have run away so it's no use stopping. Uncle still stopped the car and said, "'I'll show you how the old men killed emus. I'm going to use a rifle, but in the old days they used a spear." By the time my uncle got out of the car the emus were a long way off, far in the distance. I said, "But Uncle, the emus are now so far away." "Don't worry, son," my uncle said, "you just watch."

'My uncle lay on his back cradling his rifle across his chest. He began to move back and forth in the red dirt, creating a cloud of dust. After a little while, the emus stopped. They looked back. They must have been curious, maybe wondering if another emu was in distress or enjoying a dust bath. The emus started walking back. My uncle kept up the dust cloud, jerking backwards and forwards, squirming in the dirt. The emus kept coming. Finally, the emus had come all the way back and peered down on my uncle from directly above him. My uncle fired his rifle and shot an emu.

'My uncle stood up. I got out of the car and he said to me, "That's how in the old days men hunted emus — they lured the emus in so close they could use their spear." I never forgot that experience,' Farren said, 'and every time I see an emu on the Alice Springs road I think of my uncle.'

As in any field, in workplace leadership the use of story enriches communication. A well-chosen story reveals meaning. In one particular organisation where I facilitated leadership workshops, the managing director often spent a session with the participants. The business operates in the heavy industrial sector. People across the organisation knew that their managing director was obsessed with safety protocols, but might not have known the reason for Mike's obsession. By his use of story, Mike revealed why he was obsessed with safety. Early in his career he worked in underground mining. As a young engineer he was put in charge of commissioning a heavy vehicle to be used underground. His job involved shipping the component parts of the vehicle deep underground via a cage (a lift) and then having the vehicle reassembled. The day came when the vehicle was given a test run. Proper safety steps appeared to have been taken, but inexplicably soon after moving down the decline the vehicle careened out of control. As the vehicle gathered pace, the driver jumped from the cabin and the vehicle hurtled down the passage, smashing into the rock face at a far point where the tunnel took a turn to the right. Mike described the horrible feeling of wondering if anyone was run over or crushed against the rock face. By incredibly good fortune, no one was in the way of the runaway vehicle and no one was hurt. But in describing the haunting experience, Mike told the leaders how he vowed never again to be in a position of risking life or limb.

Actions for Workplace Leaders

The nature of learning — and teaching — in traditional societies has profound implications for workplaces. Selected initiatives modelled on traditional societies make all the difference to both individual identity and knowledge acquisition in workplaces.

1. **Create an individual learning focus:** The genius of the approach of traditional societies is that the nature of learning achieves individual

identity within group membership. That has exciting possibilities for workplaces — to avoid the cursed anonymity that happens in many workplaces. Traditional societies achieve this outcome through a smart, straightforward approach: one person takes responsibility for a young person's education, generally passing from a parent to an older relative as the content of education expands. The learning approach of traditional societies is a great blueprint for workplaces. For a manager, the blueprint has two elements. First, the manager is the first teacher (in the parent role). Second, when the junior person is ready and shows the right level of curiosity for learning, the manager encourages the connection of the individual with an older person who will guide their further learning. Most older people — the elders in a workplace — have a naturally generous propensity to pass on knowledge. And please, don't contemplate bonuses or appraisal points to reward older workers for passing on their knowledge. That's insulting and demotivating, and undermines the legitimacy of the initiative. All the elder needs as motivation to share knowledge is for the junior person to appreciate the elder's knowledge and to demonstrate, like Alan Palmer and Keri Opai, an eagerness to learn. For workplaces wanting to know that managers have facilitated the connection between a junior and an elder, there are only two questions that need to be asked of a junior person: Q1: Do you have a teacher in the organisation (Yes/No)? Q2: How satisfied are you with what you are learning? The young person's manager 'owns' the results of the questions.

2. **Encourage managers to have a genuine interest in individuals:** Everything depends, of course, on a manager having a genuine interest in each person as an individual. Without this interest, staff will consider their manager unqualified to be their teacher and mentor. The manager's mindset is revealed to staff through the manager's behaviours and conversations. I first met Mark LeBusque when he was in a sales leadership role in a large corporation. I was impressed that Mark's team had an extremely high level of engagement coupled with exceptional sales results. Mark had a genuine interest in the people he worked with. One of his initiatives was

incorporating into the annual goal setting and performance reviews at least one non-work goal nominated by each person. Mark told me, 'They could choose anything, as long as it was meaningful to them as an individual and would be a factor in them bringing their best self to work. I wanted to know what inspired them and what drove them as humans.' The range of lifestyle goals people shared with Mark was as rich as the diversity of his team. One person's goal was to have twice-weekly walks on the beach with their partner. Another's was to spend more time playing with their young nieces and nephews. Yet another person's was to run a marathon within the next 12 months while another colleague declared they wished to write a book. A manager prepared to actually have these conversations should not be as rare as it is. A big part of the power in Mark's initiative was that it was his creation; it was not a corporate initiative. There's a danger with a good idea like Mark's being adopted as a corporate requirement. The problem is that managers who have not yet developed the appropriate mindset tend to mess up these conversations; or, more accurately, their mindset is revealed in the way they conduct the conversation. The result of a corporate initiative in the wrong hands is that the requirement for a lifestyle goal comes to be regarded by staff as a tick-the-box exercise. And if it's required of all managers, then the good managers doing something like this don't get the credit from staff. The finesse in organisations implementing such ideas is to encourage managers to develop the desired mindset, and then allowing the managers to decide the right initiative for them and their team. A variation on ensuring that it is not viewed as a corporate requirement is for a senior leader to model an initiative like Mark's. Managers who report to this senior leader will value the experience of working for a manager who engages in these conversations. There's a good chance that those managers will adopt the initiative themselves — or something like it — without it being mandated on a form.[4]

3. **Task immediate managers as developers of staff:** The manager of a team has the responsibility to encourage development of their staff — no one else can fill that role. A young friend of mine, who

we'll call Peter, has been fortunate with his first career experience — his first manager encouraged his development. The manager invested time with Peter, and helped Peter in three ways. First, his manager encouraged Peter to think about where he wanted to go in his career. Second, his manager discussed with Peter the development courses and experiences that would help him along his career track. And third, his manager helped Peter establish an internal network by often advising Peter as to who he should talk with to get his work done (which meant Peter was using his own time and other people's time effectively). In expressing his appreciation in working for a manager who took a genuine interest in him and his development, Peter told me, 'I'm really appreciative of both my manager and the organisation. I know I'm lucky.'

4. **Develop a mentoring culture:** Over the years as a HR Director, I was disappointed with mentoring programs — they didn't endure. But I can see now from my current research the essence of a valuable concept was suffocated in its implementation. In traditional societies, there is no need for an orchestrated mentoring program; an older relative knows they have an obligation to mentor, at least of a curious young relative. But mentoring programs in workplaces tend to falter under the complexity of matching mentor and mentee, the weight of expectations and the pressure of forced compliance and reporting. The challenge for workplaces is to find the balance between establishing a culture of mentoring without killing the idea with bureaucracy. The solution, I suggest, is for senior executives to take three actions. First, the top leaders should mentor one or two individuals at any point in time. This obviously sets the example and sends the message of the importance of mentoring. Second, senior leaders should talk to staff and managers about mentoring being an important principle in the organisation. And third, senior leaders should chat with other elders to ask about their experience in mentoring young people. The elders, generally, will be keen to pass on their knowledge. And on the young person's part, they need to demonstrate an eagerness to learn. When the mentoring relationship is established in this more organic way

than through an orchestrated program, the relationship is likely to be deeper and longer lasting.

5. **Choose a term for describing individual learning focus:** Words have meaning because of the emotion attached to the word — so terminology is important. If you adopt the recommended learning initiatives, or extend your already good practice, what might you call the initiative? Keri's Māori term has great pathos, I think. *Ako*. The word covers both learning and teaching. I recommend researching the term for learning and/or teaching of the First Peoples in your neighbourhood and adopting that term (provided of course the people you contact give consent and that you are true to the word's intent). Using the term becomes an important aspect of explaining the nature of the initiative, the reason for adopting these practices in your organisation and the roles of the main people in the learning relationship.

6. **Use low-budget teaching methods:** In encouraging and developing their staff, leaders shouldn't feel constrained by their department's budget. There are many development options other than paying to attend seminars, conferences and workshops. At one point as a manager I had two young HR professionals reporting to me. I initiated a book club. For each cycle of book club meetings, we agreed the next book to read, and about month or so later we convened the book club. We strolled to our favourite café, and over coffee and cake the three of us discussed the learnings from the book. Generally, the books covered skills for effective interactions with other people and later the books were more specific to our profession. The young pair named our club the AOK Book Club after my initials. My point is, the cost of the initiative was miniscule, yet the development of the two young people was accelerated and we had fun. The test question for whether a leader is effective at providing an environment for staff development is if team members answer a resounding 'yes' to the statement: I have grown as a consequence of working with my manager. The spirit of this statement is that a staff member should be able to look back, after six months or more

working for a leader, and think, 'Yes, for sure, now that I think about it, I've grown significantly during my time working for this manager.' Like I felt about my two early managers, Norm and Jim, the person working for a teacher-manager will think, 'I'm able to do things I never thought possible.'

7. **Tailor the pace of teaching to the individual:** An integral aspect of learning in traditional societies is that teaching is tailored to the individual. Alan Palmer's and Keri Opai's shared experience of the style and pace of teaching by their elder is an inspiring model. The elder assesses the pace that suits the student. Bite-sized pieces of knowledge are given as the student absorbs the last dose. Learning progresses. The student is stretched but not discouraged. The student's confidence steadily builds. It's a great model for workplace learning, and can really only be achieved through a manager and an elder attending to each person.

8. **Give elders a role in teaching:** Traditional societies provide a startling comparison to the role of elders in their community compared to workplaces. In traditional societies, elders are venerated. In Western workplaces we don't regard elders, and their wisdom, highly enough. Valuing the role of elders in workplaces starts with a leader demonstrating their respect for the wisdom of older workers. A senior leader seeking advice and counsel from elders elevates the role of elders. Involvement of elders in educating younger colleagues helps. And an untapped resource is the elders who have retired — invite them to be mentors of young staff.

9. **Use stories:** Mid-way through my career I sensed that using story in communication was important. I read a number of books on the subject to improve my own leadership communication. But it took a while for me to see clearly what 'using story' meant in practice. The lightbulb moment came when I realised that the use of story is, most often, through *the use of example*. For workplace leaders, the categories of stories to inform and inspire are on a continuum. At one end of the continuum are stories in the form of examples being used to make a point. By incorporating an example when explaining

a point, a leader's communication comes to life — the listener readily associates with the story. The number of topics where example can be used is extensive: why service is important, why quality is crucial, why sharing information is important, why collaboration with other departments is important, why we avoid surprises, why our team culture matters, why following safety protocols is vital. The clue to whether you are using story is that story mostly starts with a date and time stamp, 'There was a time when ...' or 'About three years ago ...' or 'Early in my career ...'. At the other end of the story continuum are the larger or more developed stories explaining complex issues such as the creation of the organisation, its purpose and strategy. These stories provide a compelling reason for people to connect with the organisation, its mission, current direction and perhaps its transformation journey.[5]

Most of the Principles of First Leadership are positive principles from the wisdom of ancestral societies and their enlightened leadership approach. In the next two chapters we cover two negative aspects of ancestral life. Being forewarned about the negatives helps workplace leaders avoid the predictable obstacles to success.

CHAPTER 9

Gender Equity — To Avoid a Feature of Ancestral Life

'Growing up in the jungle, the roles of men and women were clearly defined.'

TRADITIONAL SOCIETIES, AS I have shown in this book so far, have a lot to teach us about effective leadership. But ancestral societies are not perfect. If we expose the imperfections, leaders will be alert to the negatives that interfere with building successful workplaces. Armed with this insight, leaders can take proactive steps to avoid engagement and performance being sabotaged.

There are two key challenges for leaders that emerge from this study of ancestral societies or, more accurately expressed, two challenges that arise from human nature that come to light from this study of traditional human social systems. In exploring the two challenges, I don't want to be seen as being overly critical of First Nation societies. I am being critical of human nature. My study of traditional societies provides a lens on the positives and negatives of human nature and of our social systems. The first challenge is gender inequity in favour of males which we'll look at in this chapter. The second challenge is inter-group hostility which we'll cover in the next chapter.

Gender inequity has been a fixture of human societies, probably forever, and in Western society we have only made significant progress towards equity over the last generation or two. I'll show in this chapter universal gender inequity against women and women's roles in First Nations societies. Just one outcome of this discrimination was that leadership was almost exclusively a male occupation. My discomfort about this finding is offset by the fact that at least if we know the deep-seated source of gender inequity, we can choose to take tangible actions necessary to fix the problem.

I'm sensitive about gender equity because, fortunately, I grew up in a family where males and females were equal and there was no gender stereotyping. My mother and father were equals in terms of strength of character and education attainment, and they treated each other as equals. My mum, for example, after completing high school went on to university which was unusual for a woman in the 1940s. She travelled 1000 kilometres (700 miles) from Broken Hill to attend The University of Sydney — the first woman from the town to go to university. Growing up in a family where genders were equal meant my siblings and I were assigned household tasks free of gender stereotyping. Us boys had to help in the kitchen as well as doing the labouring jobs such as clipping hedges and weeding the garden, while my sister had to work in the garden and sweep paths as well as doing her preferred tasks in the kitchen. I carry that healthy conditioning with me, so my wife Jude and I share the load — I do the cooking, food shopping and washing dishes, we do our own ironing, and Jude does the cleaning, clothes washing and is head barista. My dad was a leader in gender equity in his work. He worked at one of the major mines in Broken Hill, promoted through the trades and engineering department to ultimately become Chief Engineer. As head of engineering, he introduced in the early 1970s female apprenticeships into the mining industry in Broken Hill, which also influenced apprenticeship equity in the industry beyond Broken Hill. That initiative opened up the option for young women to follow a career in the male-dominated trades and become boilermakers, fitters and electricians. Dad talked about these subjects at dinner times and in our late teenage years often asked our perspective. With that personal and professional modelling in my upbringing, I hope to think that as a leader I provided an environment of equal opportunity. And I hope to think as a senior executive, I positively influenced the practices of organisations where I worked.

Gender Division of Labour

In ancestral societies, life was lived according to a strict division of men's work and women's work — men hunted and women gathered. That rule applied across all societies. At a symposium in Chicago in April 1966, 75 leading anthropologists who specialised in studying hunter-gatherer societies shared their knowledge. At the time, there were 27 surviving groups of hunter-gatherers. One of the universals observed at the symposium was the 'strikingly uniform division of labour — women gather and men hunt'.[1] The outcome is that the strict gender division resulted in men's work being more valued than women's work, leading to deep-seated gender inequity.

My Kichwa guide and friend, José Aguinda, described the role of men and women in his early days growing up in the Ecuadorian Amazon. His and his mother's experience is characteristic of life in our ancestral setting. José and I had this conversation by email with the help of Google Translate converting José's Spanish to my English. 'Growing up in the jungle,' José wrote, 'the roles of men and women were clearly defined. Women worked the garden, took care of the children, cleaned the house and prepared food and drinks. Men made the tools and weapons, hunted, built the houses and protected the community. When houses were being built, the women kept up the supply of chicha drinks made from yucca (a root vegetable). In the garden, men did the heavy work of cutting trees and clearing the ground for planting yucca, plantain, corn and beans. In our traditional society, all the community leaders were men. That part has changed a lot. Today, women have leadership roles in many communities and indigenous women have important positions in state government.'

I was keen to hear José's mother's experience of gender differences when she lived the old life in the jungle. I emailed my questions to José and he travelled to his childhood home to talk with his mother, María Grefa. She and his shaman father live on the edge of the jungle in a small community of 90 adults and children. They work their garden plot each day, growing green bananas, cocoa, corn and yucca. José emailed me his mother's answers to my questions.

'Did you enjoy your life in the old days in the jungle?' I had asked.

'Yes, I enjoyed it a lot! Our community was together. Life was healthier and we all shared whatever little thing we had. We had no limits — we had no borders. Everything about the jungle was enchanting.'

'José explained to me the different roles of women and men,' I had written. 'What are your feelings about the roles of women and men?'

'In my time, we women were not very important. Rather, we were only in charge of doing the housework, taking care of the children, working the garden and looking after the husband! While the men — they were taken more seriously and did many things, such as dealing with enemies, taking care of the whole extended family, they could become a shaman and even be the leader of a community.'

'Were you happy doing the jobs that women did?'

"Yes! We were happy because we were always together as a whole family — sisters, brothers, cousins, uncles and aunts. We shared any little thing we had at the time. When working, we all worked together and completed jobs in quick time. We were more united as a family and a community.'

'Were there things women were expected to do that you didn't enjoy?'

'Oh, yes! For example, men could do anything they liked, but women were not taken into account. A man could abuse his wife. He could even cause her to suicide by ingesting a toxic root.'

'José told me that in the old days, community leadership roles were filled by men. Why was that?'

'The reason was because men were always taken as being stronger. He was also a shaman, so he could face a fight either physically or spiritually with any rival. Back in those days, women had no rights. Their parents and then their husband made all decisions that affected them. Marriages were arranged, sometimes before a girl was born. Even as adults, women were unable to do what you wanted or say what they thought. We had no choices. We were practically slaves — parents gave you a husband and you had to be with your husband and do what he wanted until one of you died. If a woman outlived her husband, only then did the tie get broken and she gained freedom. In that context, women could not be leaders of the community.'

'Did women resent that men were in the leadership roles?'

'Not at that time. Rather, we felt protected and safe. That's how things were. Today, times have changed and many women excel. I hear that women even become presidents of a country and that makes me very happy! Many women have had the opportunity to enter colleges and universities. Education has given us this opportunity to lead — to lead communities and countries. This includes Amazonian indigenous women who up until only recently were not taken seriously.'

The division of labour and value of work that José and María described matches the other societies I investigated; there was women's work and men's work, and men's work was valued more than women's work. (It's like in our society that women tended not to go to university in the 1940s.) In Bushmen society, men hunted antelopes and women gathered nuts and dug tubers. Significantly, women's work contributed the majority, around 70%, of calorific intake but hunting was valued more.[2] In traditional times in Aotearoa (New Zealand), fishing was men's work.[3] In Waorani society in the Amazon, only men hunted while the women tended the garden. In traditional Mohawk society, while very different in so many aspects from Waorani society, the same gender division of labour applied. According to a visitor in 1634, 'the village and adjacent (corn) fields were the domain of the women and the forest the domain of the men'.[4] In Blackfeet society on the Great Plains of America, men hunted while women performed almost all other tasks: they tanned the animal skins, dried the meat, made the tipi, cooked the food and carried the wood and the water.[5]

The strict division of labour in ancestral societies even extended to the way women and men procured protein — if women were involved at all in obtaining meat or fish. As a kid, José accompanied María and his grandmother when they fished in small rivers with poison from the roots of toxic plants and nets made from the fibre of palm leaves. Fishing in the small rivers, José told me, meant women only caught small fish. Along the big rivers, the fishing was done by men using either large nets set overnight or lines and hooks to catch fish up to three metres (yards) long. If toxins were used in the big rivers, fishing was a communal activity because of the number of fish killed. The women also dug traps and set snares to catch small mammals and birds, such as agouti (a rodent), rabbits, squirrels and partridges. Meanwhile, men risked the dangers of the jungle by travelling further afield hunting larger animals using spears and blowpipes with poison darts.

Pintupi women and men in the Australian desert both collected various reptiles, including lizards and goannas. But otherwise in Pintupi society, men hunted kangaroos and emus and women gathered 'bush tucker'. In my own neighbourhood, back in traditional times, the First Nations people of Sydney Harbour had a strict gender division for the critical task of fishing. While men and women both fished, there was a male technique and a female technique. Women pushed off from shore in a canoe and fished using lines from bark and hooks made from shells. Meanwhile, men fished from the rocks using a multi-pronged spear. While the men might spear fish from a canoe, according to a member of British First Fleet, men are 'never seen fishing with a line, and would indeed consider it was a degradation of their pre-eminence'.[6]

There are two sides of the universal division of labour. On the positive side, the division acknowledged the critical role of both genders. The family and band couldn't survive without the contribution of both genders. The partnership was critical. In 1980 a member of the Blood division of Blackfoot society in Canada wrote a book based on the memories of older females. The author observed that with women working hard around the home and the men travelling far afield on hunting expeditions and defending their families from prowling enemies, there was respect for the roles of both genders.[7]

On the negative side, the gender division resulted in men's work being more valued than women's work. This was despite, in many hunter-gatherer societies, men as the hunters contributed only about 30% of the diet. Not only did women contribute the bulk of calories, the food they gathered was more dependable than the risky task of hunting.[8] And in their gathering work, women in most societies used the most critical tool available to early humans — the humble digging stick. Except in environments like the frozen tundra, in most societies each woman had her personal digging stick. The tool gave humans a unique food source — root vegetables. No other bird or animal that would otherwise consume root vegetables could dig, so with the aid of a digging stick, our ancestors could get to food sometimes a metre (three feet) under the ground that no other animal could access. Yet despite this critical role of women supplying most food with more security of supply, as anthropologist Marjorie Shostak observed in relation to Bushmen, 'Being the hunters of meat gave men more influence than women'.[9]

My point is that from our ancestral heritage we carry a deep-seated cultural mindset that there's women's work and there's men's work and that more value was attached to men's work. Unless we realise how deep-seated this bias is, we'll continue in modern workplaces stereotyping work on gender grounds resulting in inequality for women. Shortly I'll come to the possible reasons for this historic gender inequity.

Leadership was a Male Occupation

The strict division of labour and lower value attached to women's work led to leadership roles being exclusively filled by males in every society I investigated, except for Himba and Māori societies where there are rare exceptions to the rule. Perhaps the societies I investigated are atypical? No, unfortunately. In the 1970s a group of female anthropologists mainly connected with Harvard and Stanford examined this topic. They concluded that there is no First Nations society in which women have power and authority passing that of men. 'Everywhere we find that women are excluded from certain crucial economic or political activities, that their roles as wives and mothers are associated with fewer powers and prerogatives than are the roles of men.'[10]

In the ancestral societies I visited, males occupying the leadership roles was particularly pronounced in the highly organised nations such as Haida, Maasai and Mohawk. But even in the hunter-gatherer and village societies, while I was sometimes told that the leader could be male or female, the evidence of women in leadership roles was scarce. Hyknodombu, the Himba headwomen who started her own village after losing out to her husband's brother, told me that a village head can be a man or a woman. But when I asked her how many of the dozens of villages in her Epupa Falls region of northern Namibia are led by a woman, her village was the only one. In the anthropological literature on Bushmen, all the leaders referred to in the 1950s and 1960s were men. This is despite land 'ownership' being mainly held by the most senior woman with the longest association with the land.

And in their respective childhood camps, the three older Bushmen I spoke with about the old days described their *grandfather* as the leader.

Even in matrilineal societies (where individuals gain their clan identity from their mother) where women have significant power, men dominate leadership roles. In Haida society, the senior women appoint the chief. Despite this, in traditional times, 'Haida society was still a male dominated one. Men were the final authorities of the household and the holders of positions of political authority. They alone were the hosts of the most important types of potlatches (gatherings), the owners of the most important property (houses and story poles), and performers of the most prestigious rituals ...'[11]

In Mohawk society, women have significant power and influence. The clan mother appoints the chief, yet the chief is a man. Why are chiefs always male? I was told that in the Mohawk tradition, men were responsible for any activity that took them away from the village, such as hunting and warfare. Women were responsible for any activity associated with the village. Diplomacy was an activity outside the village and hence men's business.

Arguably the involvement of the senior women in leadership appointments in Haida and Mohawk societies placed the role of women in leadership at a higher position than existed historically in the West. In Haida and Mohawk societies, women may not have been able to fill the formal leadership roles, but at least their wisdom in choosing a leader was recognised.

Of the societies I visited, traditional Māori society came closest to equality and to women occupying leadership roles. While succession to chieftain roles was in the male line, there were exceptions and women did become chiefs. Keri Opai knows the oral history of his ancestry in an unbroken line from 950AD. He knows of several women who became chiefs. In teaching me about gender in traditional Māori society, Keri's main point is that the roles of women and men were different, but complementary. This reflects a key Māori spiritual belief of Earth Mother and Sky Father — both are necessary and equivalent. In ceremonies at a community's centre, the marae, both genders play a key role — complementary but different. Women dominate the chant of welcome, and inside, in most regions, men make the speeches. Even though the key speechmaking role is limited to men, women still have influence. If a man breeches marae protocol, it is the women who correct him. If a man speaks too long or becomes boring, the women will make their opinion known. And if a man becomes insulting, the older women might apply the ultimate sanction of a *whakapohane*. They stand with their backs to him, bend over and raise their skirts in derision.[12]

Possible Explanations of Gender Inequity

The rest of this book has been a joy to write. I'm flat as I write this chapter. Reading and writing about the dominance of males makes me downhearted about the challenges to overcome gender inequity in workplaces. Gender equity is about individual rights. I think especially about my nieces and great nieces — fortunately they live in a time and place where they have a fair chance of living according to their choices. If we keep up the progress in workplaces, then by the time my great nieces join the workforce they will enjoy gender equity.

One of my nieces, 26-year-old Heather O'Keeffe, lifted my pessimistic mood a little. When I told her about my findings and described the life of women in our ancestral environment, she said, 'We've come a long way!' That's true. It's only one hundred years ago, almost to the day, that in 1920 USA women won the right to vote nationally. That followed New Zealand's lead in 1893 and South Australia in 1895. Britain was slower and only implemented full suffrage in 1928. In terms of employment, we have also come a long way. Australian media celebrity Lisa Wilkinson was interviewed recently while the interviewer, Anh Do, painted her portrait. Lisa described how she got her start in the media industry. In the late 1970s she applied for her first job. The stunning part of her story was that to search for a vacant position, she looked in the *Women and Girls Employment* section of Sydney's main newspaper. She and Anh laughed incredulously at that antiquated practice of a bygone era. 'I know!' Lisa said, enjoying a full belly laugh. 'How hilarious is that! And I love the fact that that is now funny — that we could ever think that was okay.'[13]

Yes, we've come a long way, but we still have a way to go. For a decade from 1986 I was employed with IBM when good companies such as IBM started to focus on gender equity. Thirty-plus years later we are still on the task, with gender equity showing great resistance. In the largest organisations in America and Europe only 20% of top executive roles are filled by women. And take out human resources and corporate affairs roles and the percentage would be significantly lower. In Australia the number is 25%. In Asia, the number is only 4%.[14] We need to keep pushing along the path of gender equity so that the work of women is valued the same as men, and that women have the same opportunity of progression as men.

Why might it be that throughout history, human societies had unequal gender roles and that overwhelmingly men filled the leadership roles? It's important to explore the question as part of the call to action. There are at least three possible reasons for the origins of gender inequity.

1. Biological Differences

The first possible answer relates to biological differences between women and men, and that this led to different roles for women and men and a different value attached to those roles. Women lactate and bear children. Pregnancy and nursing infants impose significant demands on women and on their time. The biological contribution of men in pregnancy, while vital, is minuscule. And men's involvement in rearing children is discretionary. While a woman is carrying or nursing a child, her husband can be out hunting and fighting. Without obligatory childcare responsibilities, men had more time for ceremony and for long initiation periods. This time discretion also translated into leadership activities.

Biological differences can transfer into the role definition, and role definition can become ingrained in society. In turn, ingrained mindsets show in people's behaviour. Heather, my niece, works for a large management consulting firm. She shared with me an academic paper that demonstrated the link between gender, role definition and behaviour: women are more inclined than men to volunteer for mundane projects. Not only that, if it fell to a manager to choose one member of their group to volunteer for a low-value task, women received 44% more requests to 'volunteer' than men. Significantly, the gender of the manager made no difference: female managers were just as likely as male managers to ask a woman to volunteer. The paper supports the proposition that the less valued work is assigned to women.[15]

A year after she shared that research with me, I asked Heather what she'd done since the subject had been on her radar. I'm proud to say she had not been powerless. She'd done four things to ensure her work is valued and that she resists undertaking less meaningful tasks merely because she is a woman. First, she assesses whether a task is a valued versus a routine one, and she is selective in volunteering for routine work rather than doing so from a sense of duty. Second, she doesn't volunteer for a routine task if she's not the most junior person in the room — she'll hold back. For example, she attended a meeting recently that ran into lunch time. Would someone volunteer to take lunch orders? Heather was the only woman in the meeting but not the most junior person. She held back from volunteering to run lunch orders. No one else volunteered and the leader didn't ask the junior male to take on the task — so everyone went hungry! Third, Heather tells people — women and men — about the research. She tells them about her response to the article and the difference between routine tasks and valued tasks. The research gives her male colleagues a fresh perspective on something they have been blind to, and her female colleagues become aware of maintaining personal power and not being presumed upon. And fourth, Heather still does routine tasks, such as data clean-up after a major project, which isn't a fun task and one not many people do. But in doing data clean-up, she'll communicate to her manager her observations of process improvements for future projects. In this sense, she makes perceived mundane work valued. In reviewing this chapter, Heather told me, 'If someone has to pick berries, then make sure everyone knows how important those berries are to their diet!'

2. Control of Economic Value

The second possible explanation of gender differences in ancestral societies relates to the control of economic value in society. In the study by female anthropologists in the 1970s, one anthropologist observed that women's status in ancestral societies was greatest where women's contribution to subsistence was relatively equal to that of men.[16] Status and influence follow the control of production.

In the relatively egalitarian societies such as Bushmen and Pintupi, the economic contribution of women and men was roughly equal. But in Maasai society, for example, where men control the cows as the measure of wealth, genders are unequal in favour of men. In Maasai society, differences between men and women are part of the property system. Property rights in Maasai society include rights to livestock and rights over people. Girls, boys and women are 'owned' by their father and husband. Only men of a mature age are free of being owned. The owner, being the father and husband, has complete rights to dispose of his property as he wishes.

Not only are wives and daughters owned by the husband and father, women are excluded from full ownership of livestock. When a woman marries, she's allocated a number of animals from her father's household herd. But she has limited rights to those animals. She has the rights to the milk from the animals and she has rights to use or sell the hides of animals that die or are slaughtered for celebrations. But she never has absolute rights to the animals, such as choosing to sell them. Those rights pass through to her husband and settle on her sons when they come of age.[17] A husband may slaughter or give away any of his wife's animals, including any that may have come to her from her own family.

My email communication with William Kinanta Sadera led into the role of women in his society (you'll remember William's story from when he was five years of age and at the start of school vacation he had to first search for his family across the Maasai Mara savannah). William emailed me to tell me of his personal awakening to gender inequity in his society. He realised the unfair treatment of women when he became the father of girls. 'There are so many injustices for women in my society,' he wrote. 'That's the tradition that I grew up with and that's just how things are. For example, women are held responsible for mistakes that happen in their home, even if the mistake is not their fault. If a family loses cattle, even though the wife was not looking after the cattle, she is often beaten for the mistake and forced to try to find the cattle. If she can't find the missing cattle, her punishment is to go to her parents' home and get replacement cattle to cover the loss to her husband's herd. In most families, a wife is never consulted in decision making, and the husband's decision is final even when he is wrong. Consequently, the self-esteem of women is generally low and they are voiceless. After I got married and had daughters, I realised that their rights and freedom are important and they deserve everything in life. I have five daughters in my house, ranging from 13 to three years of age. Three of the girls are my biological children, and two are my brother's, which in our society is the equivalent of biological children. For my daughters, I am doing a number of things that help them grow as valued individuals:

- Give them a quality education as a priority
- Love and respect them, and value their work
- Help raise their aspirations about what's possible in life
- Listen to them and ensure that their point of view counts
- Prohibit early marriage and sexual harassment.

For me to achieve all this I have to take the initiative to teach them and talk to them about these topics, and to be an example in the way I treat and support their mother.'

The link between wealth and power is critical. Through the 20th Century, as the rate of employment of women in Western society increased, women became more equal contributors of household wealth. Women's social status and power increased. This is why in workplaces pay equity and promotion equity are vital — equity is connected to economic value which is connected to equal status. We'll come back to this point when we talk about actions.

3. Our Primate Natures

The third possible explanation of the universal pattern of gender inequity relates to our primate natures. From my collaboration with the Jane Goodall Institute in the last 15 years, I've been in and out of zoos with workplace leaders teaching them about our social instincts. In listening to primatologists talk about apes and monkeys, one key element on gender equity stands out: in every primate species one of the genders is dominant. In some species, such as the chimpanzees and gorillas, males are dominant. In some species, such as ring-tailed lemurs and bonobos (once known as pygmy chimpanzees), females are dominant. It stands to reason that in early human history one of the genders was dominant. For humans it looks like we are more inclined towards the chimp model than the bonobo model. This factor would explain the finding of one of the contributing authors to the study by female anthropologists in the 1970s: 'The secondary status of women in society is one of the true universals.'[18] It would also explain why the unrelenting march towards gender equity shows great resistance.

Fortunately, even if there is something in our natures that adds to the explanation of gender inequity, we humans have the capacity to act differently to our natures; we can choose to create a society and workplaces where gendered roles are left behind. In Western society, the history and progress of women's equality over the last 100 years demonstrates that we are not bound by our cultural or natural heritage. Today's women, and their mothers and grandmothers, are exceptional. They are winning the rights to equality like no women before them in the long journey of human history. That's to be admired, celebrated and supported.

Actions for Workplace Leaders

Mindsets come from our conditioning — from our collective family, community and culture. In turn, conditioning, largely unconscious, drives our beliefs and behaviours. Conditioning about gender comes from a long way back. By being aware of the source of a mindset we have the choice of changing both our beliefs and our behaviour. For workplaces to continue to make the shift towards gender equity, we need tangible actions where people are valued irrespective of gender and where men and women have equal access to leadership roles.

Being a male, I'm conscious that if I recommended the actions for gender equity I'd perpetuate the male presumption of speaking for women. So in identifying actions for this chapter I sought the counsel of 15 women, including my wife and two of my nieces. I sought their ideas for concrete solutions — we need to go beyond statements of good intentions and admirable aspirations. The actions below relate to gender inequity, but also apply to other forms of workplace discrimination such as race, religion, age and physical capability.

1. **Ensure awareness of gender inequity:** Awareness of a problem isn't enough, but being aware is a necessary first step. Awareness helps open-minded people see gender inequity in a fresh light. In turn, that insight motivates many people to take action, like my Maasai friend William mentioned above who gained insight upon becoming the father of daughters. Training in gender equity is an early helpful action to increase awareness. By participating in equity training, many people experience a light bulb moment when they realise how blind they are to gender bias and behaviours that signal bias. One of the women I spoke to about this chapter told me that a behaviour she frequently encounters in meetings is where men avoid eye contact with her and other women. Men often make eye contact with the other men in the room, but do not look at the women. That behaviour undermines the confidence and sense of worth of female colleagues.

2. **Lead from the top:** Not surprisingly, given our hierarchical natures and the influence of leadership, establishing a culture of equity starts from the top. If meaningful change is to happen, the CEO and the leadership team must lead the way. They signal their leadership by being the first to participate in the awareness training. They signal their leadership by being willing to air opinions and to challenge conventional beliefs. They signal their leadership by having zero tolerance of sexual discrimination and harassment. And they signal their leadership by sponsoring reviews of practices that impede equity and inclusion.

3. **Fix discriminatory pay practices:** The next action step is to review pay in the organisation to ensure there is no pay inequity based on gender: are women on the same job level paid the same as men in a similar role? To ensure the review is robust, it should be sponsored

by the CEO (or in a mega-organisation, by the divisional head). Pay equity is vital because, as we saw in Maasai society as an example, power and status follow the control of wealth.

4. **Implement gender-friendly policies:** After the review of pay and job levels, employment policies should be reviewed to ensure women are not disadvantaged. Most employment practices date from when workplaces, 50 to 100 years ago, were primarily populated by men. The new suite of policies suitable for today recognises modern approaches to family responsibilities — for both women and men. Policies should include keeping in contact with women on maternity leave so that they stay connected with their team and possibly keep their development ticking, if they wish to, so they minimise the professional impact of their parental leave. Gender-friendly policies should include genuine flexibility and sensibly designed part-time roles for women returning from maternity leave, making it *okay* to have taken a career break. Gender-friendly policies should also mean that excessive working hours does not elevate a person's chances of promotion. For example, in law firms and other professional service firms, people's chances of promotion to partnership are increased if they work excessive hours — which means that a person raising a family has little chance of competing in the promotion stakes.

5. **Ensure progression is independent of gender:** Another practice with a negative impact similar to pay inequity is promotion to higher-level roles. In your organisation, do women and men advance equally? The elements of good practice in this area are:

   a. **Determine talent pools:** A cadre of high potential leaders should be identified across every business unit. Lists of high-potential people are developed by the immediate manager and reviewed by the next level of leader. These reviews go on all the way to the top team, so there is an organisational pool of high-potential leaders. The pool will probably number about 5% of total staff numbers. There are sound methods that help unbiased identification of talent, such as scenario assessments and role plays. To avoid bias in identifying the talent pool, people making assessments need to be attuned to mindsets, and in turn that mindsets are revealed by language. One senior woman I spoke to has participated in many talent review meetings. She says that gender bias often slips in. She's observed that when discussing a female candidate, 80% of the time the senior executives in the room say about a female, 'She's just not ready yet'. This phrase, she says, is never used in reference to a male. Women are judged on past performance whereas men are judged on future potential. At a recent meeting, after letting the discussion run for a little while, she called her colleagues' attention to the discriminatory language. The senior people in the meeting were surprised but agreed with her observation, and went back over the female candidates who had been passed over and made a fresh assessment much more attuned to gender bias.

b. **Develop and prepare candidates for progression:** Individuals in the high-potential pool should have an individual development plan prepared with and by them. The plan includes their progression objectives and the actions necessary to get them 'ready' for the next step. A pathway is built for each person.

c. **Establish promotion criteria:** Develop the criteria against which promotion decisions will be made. Ensure that the criteria are legitimate and not the means of perpetuating bias. One senior woman with a track record of successful implementation of equity programs told me that she has found senior male leaders too often use 'business acumen' or 'budget responsibility' or 'client impact' as criteria that is irrelevant to many roles and also discriminates against most women in the organisation.

d. **Promote from the talent pool:** High-potential programs sometimes break down at the point of filling vacancies. If the system of appointments is not actively sponsored and controlled by the HR executive and CEO, a creeping practice develops where divisional leaders promote people who aren't necessarily on the high-potential list. The whole program fails at that point. Those ad hoc appointments are often based on stereotyping, favouritism and personal networks. If the person was such a strong candidate, why didn't they make the high-potential list?

Two of the recommendations in Chapter 4 Selecting Leaders will help with gender equity. Recommendation #3 is to involve direct reports in choosing their leader. Especially if a candidate is within the organisation, the direct reports to the vacant position are usually in the ideal position to know the capability of candidates and be less affected by gender bias. Recommendation #4 is to give preference to internal candidates. Gender stereotyping is less likely to occur with internal candidates because the organisation knows their track record and has the complete picture of the person.

6. **Decide whether to have separate leadership programs:** A subject that polarised the women I spoke with for this chapter relates to Women in Leadership programs. Many business schools, for example, offer short programs aimed at women-only participants. There were strong views in favour of and against programs exclusive to women. The women I spoke with who were in favour of separate leadership programs argued that the programs provide a safe place to learn, without domineering men talking over the women. The women I spoke with who oppose the women-only programs expressed their opinion more forcibly than those in support of the programs. Those against women-only programs stated as their primary objection that the programs 'perpetuate the belief held by some men that women can't cope with the real world'. The important dimension here is that in deciding initiatives that support gender equity, think about the purpose and implications from initiatives such as separate development programs. And if you support them, do so because they fit your purpose, not because they are fashionable.

7. **Involve men as mentors:** Involving men in the mentoring of women gives men the opportunity to see the female perspective. Senior men will be challenged to question their own assumptions, and be better equipped to contribute to overcoming gender inequality.

One woman I spoke with suggested that several organisations, perhaps from different sectors, could form a cooperative network for matching high-potential women from one organisation with senior male mentors in another organisation. Mentoring from outside the organisation creates a safe place free of concerns about internal judgements. These mentoring interactions between women and men achieve several objectives. First, the high potential women benefit from being mentored by a senior person (man or woman). Second, the senior male gains insight into the frustrating behaviour that women uniquely face. Third, the conversation the man has with the woman they are coaching helps them then have similar conversations with women in their own organisation. For example, 'I've been mentoring a senior woman in another organisation. I now better appreciate the obstacles women face. She's shared with me behaviours she experiences in her organisation. Do you or other women face similar behaviours in our organisation?' The CEO can then sponsor a discussion amongst their own executive team regarding behaviours in their organisation and the actions necessary to achieve gender equity. From the anthropological evidence there's an important reason for involving men in the mentoring of women and not just leaving mentoring of women up to women. In ancestral societies, girls stay in the company of their mothers and aunts. But boys, through initiation rites, leave the company of their mothers for their development to then be in the hands of a wider group of males. In workplaces, we follow the same biased path if, beyond their junior career years, women are coached by women and men are coached by men. In workplaces, men are over-represented in top leadership. We need the men coaching women, and not perpetuate the cycle of a male coalition bringing forward the young male leaders.

8. **Set targets:** Given the deep roots of gender inequity, we need to push for progress. The women I spoke with told me that targets set by the organisation, which many good organisations already do, is an important step. The targets should include women filling leadership roles in at least the same percentage as women in the organisation's

workforce. I asked the women whether our society should go the next step beyond targets: should government policy makers impose quotas on organisations to achieve a certain percentage of women filling senior leadership roles? Quotas were generally opposed, and often passionately. As one woman said, 'I'm a staunch opponent of quotas. I earned my senior role in my own right. I'd be embarrassed and my credibility would be undermined if I got the role because of my gender.'

9. **Increase the pipeline of female candidates:** Proactive organisations expand the pool of quality female candidates. Men seem to be more comfortable with self-advocating than women. To overcome this potential reticence of women, organisations could offer to coach women for the purpose of lifting their confidence as a candidate for senior roles. The coaching equips them to present their best self at interview. In adopting this action, organisations don't need to limit this service to existing female staff. Organisations should offer the service to external female applicants who are considering applying for one of their senior roles (including senior women identified by a search firm). It will be a powerful message to a female candidate: 'If you are interested in our role, we will coach you to make your strongest application so we are seeing the best you.'

Good organisations have worked hard at overcoming our deep-seated biases that inhibit gender equity. We need to help other organisations to keep progressing on the unrelenting path away from our ancestral heritage. By keeping up the pressure, we'll achieve a working environment that when my great nieces enter the workforce, they'll enjoy equal opportunity. Like Lisa Wilkinson and Anh Do sharing a laugh about the antiquated *Women and Girls* jobs vacant section of the 1970s newspapers, my young relatives will be able to laugh with their friends about what used to apply back in 2022.

CHAPTER 10

Inter-Group Harmony — To Avoid a Feature of Ancestral Life

'We are the true people of the jungle.'

THE SECOND BIG NEGATIVE of the human experience that we bring into life at work is the frequent antagonistic relationships between groups. Combative out-group relationships are the downside of the human tendency to form strong in-group affiliations. As we will see in this chapter, ancestral communities often engaged in hostilities with their neighbours. This in turn meant that, generally, the fiercest rivalries were between members of the same language group. A modern version of this human trait commonly plays out in workplaces where people often tribalise into rival groups and engage in petty contests and territorial fights. These antagonistic relationships sabotage organisational performance. By being aware of this unrelenting tendency of human nature, leaders can avoid being blindsided by the behaviour and can take proactive steps to avoid it — and quick remedial action if and when it appears.

The greatest threat to early humans wasn't lions and tigers, leopards and jaguars. The greatest threat was other humans. For most ancestral peoples, the threat of attack was a constant, niggling fear. I've experienced the strains and sub-performance associated with inter-group hostility in workplaces. But I never dreamed, up until my trip into the Amazon, that I would experience the constant dread of an attack that most ancestral humans lived with.

My Fearful Experience in the Amazon

In planning my visit to a Waorani community in the Yasuni National Park in the Ecuadorian Amazon, my guide, José Aguinda, knew that I wanted to meet Waorani who live close to their traditional life. He gave me a more genuine experience than I bargained on. While I knew beforehand that the Waorani had been a violent people, I didn't know that attacks still occur. If I had known of the danger I would not have gone.

As explained in Chapter 7, the great feature of Waorani traditional life was intra-ethnic killings. In the ranking of violence in traditional societies, Waorani topped the chart. They were the most violent society on Earth. In traditional times, a staggering 60 percent of adult deaths were due to killings, mostly by members of opposing bands of their own ethnic group.[1] What I wondered, and what I found out, is that killings still periodically occur.

The era of 'Pacification' for Waorani is rather recent, only beginning in 1958. The Babeno community I visited live a peaceful life. There's a problem though, in living a peaceful life, if your neighbours don't share your peaceful intentions. And that's the problem for the Babeno citizens.

From the early days of outside contact, one group of Waorani, the Tagaeri, turned their backs on the peaceful life offered by missionaries and the government and chose to continue their life in the jungle. And living the traditional life means engaging in killing raids on 'others', meaning anyone not part of your immediate neighbourhood of about 120 people. The Babeno community I visited is located in the dreaded Tagaeri Zone and they fear an attack at any time. And for the week I was in the jungle, I shared their horrible, niggling fear.

It took me a while to put the picture together, and by the time I'd connected the pieces it was too late to pull out. The first piece of the puzzle came on the first day at the entry point to the Yasuni National Park. We drove from the frontier city of Puerto Francisco de Orellana, known as Coca, to the entrance of the park to travel by canoe eight hours downstream on the Shiripuno River that feeds into the Cononaco River and ultimately into the Amazon. Being first-time visitors to the National Park, my translator and I were given an orientation by park staff. The main point of the orientation was a warning that if we came across the Tagaeri on the banks of the river, we were to stay calm, be quiet and not make any hand signals. 'You don't know what your hand signal means to them,' warned the park officer (a wave can look like throwing an imaginary spear). This was the first time I'd heard of Tagaeri, and I didn't know enough at that time to worry.

My curiosity about Tagaeri shifted to anxiety the first night on the river. We travelled two hours downstream in our 20-metre powered canoe until dusk caused us to camp for the night. We would have another six hours' travel the next day. I was travelling with my guide José, his teenage son Anderson, my translator Jorge Espinosa, and the canoe driver David Yasa, a local who knows every bend of the river and where every submerged log lurks.

José and David chose a sandy bank with just enough room to pitch three tents and build a fire. My mind turned to staying safe in this strange environment. I'd never spent a night in the jungle, but having grown up in the Australian outback I knew enough about the bush to know that dangers that are common sense to the locals need to be explained to visitors. After a simple meal of barbequed meat, I requested a safety briefing. José didn't provide any specifics, so I offered some examples.

'Do I need to be careful of caiman (alligators) at the river bank?'

'No,' he answered, 'because the river here is narrow the caiman are small and not a threat.'

'Okay. If I get up in the night, do I need to be careful of jaguars at the edge of the clearing?'

'No, the fire will scare them away.'

I was about to learn that in the jungle, the greatest danger is not from cats, alligators, snakes, scorpions and fire ants. The main danger, at least in this forest, is human.

At the end of his elementary safety briefing, José went to the edge of the clearing to collect firewood. David, the local boat driver, continued the safety instruction. In a grave tone, he said that he needed to explain something. He spoke in Spanish and Jorge translated. 'Tomorrow morning after about two hours travel, we will enter the Tagaeri Zone. If we come across Tagaeri, stay calm, be quiet and don't make any hand gestures.'

David spoke with such gravity, I wondered if he chose to share the information at the moment our leader moved away to collect firewood. David then went further than the park officials and told us of a section of the river where the Tagaeri had attacked an innocent Waorani couple.

The unfortunate Waorani husband and wife were travelling down the river in their powered canoe. Their progress was blocked by a tree that had fallen into the river, and at that point the river was so narrow that the tree blocked the river from one bank to the other. The tree might have been deliberately felled by the Tagaeri, or a band of Tagaeri had chanced upon the fallen tree and decided it presented an ideal ambush site. The Tagaeri waited, easily hidden behind the curtain of jungle vines. The unsuspecting Waorani couple came around the bend of the river. Halted by the fallen tree, the husband began chopping branches with his machete to clear a passage through the thinnest part of the tree. His wife controlled the outboard motor. The Tagaeri attacked, first spearing the wife to disable the canoe. And then, as it was told to me, 'A storm of spears rained down on the husband'. Both were killed.

When exactly the attack had occurred, I didn't learn until back in Quito after the trip. I had to wonder if the murder occurred last week or last year. But David was clearly telling us that the trip involved serious risk and our lives could be in danger.

I immediately thought of my darling wife, Jude. Imagine if, from my indulgence of wanting to visit traditional communities, my life prematurely ended and she was left to live the rest of her life without me? Jorge, thinking of his wife and three-year-old daughter at home near Quito, told me later that he would not have volunteered as translator for the expedition if he had known of the danger. He'd innocently responded to a call that José had posted on Facebook. No mention was made in the post of the Tagaeri danger! I was ready to abandon the adventure and have us turn around the next morning.

When José came back to the fire, arms loaded with firewood, I told him what David had said. José responded sharply, 'Yes, I heard him.'

I said, 'We need to reassess going on. I didn't come here to put myself in harm's way of Tagaeri killings.'

'We're not going that far!' José stated firmly, referring to the site of the killing of the Waorani couple. I concluded that I must have misunderstood David's warning, perhaps his meaning being lost in translation.

We continued the next morning. Soon after we'd left the camp site, a pair of Scarlet Macaws flew high overhead. The Waorani believe macaws are a model of a happy marriage — they fly together, care for each other, feed each other and never separate.[2] I thought of Jude and considered it a good omen.

Two hours after setting off, suddenly around a bend of the river, we came to the killing tree. So much for 'not going that far'. We were in the Tagaeri Zone.

At every bend of the river David eased off on the throttle. I assumed he did so to avoid submerged logs. But surely not every one of 400 to 500 bends had underwater danger.

When I first heard the sketchy information of the attack, I understood it was a revenge killing. Optimistically, I thought that I would not be a victim of a revenge killing. But sitting for hours on a hard bench of a canoe gives you time to think, and I recalled the real nature of revenge killings by Waorani: killing is their way of expressing anger and frustration. It's their response to rage. A killing didn't need to be directed at the party causing the offence — killing anyone will do. And so it turned out to be the case with the killing on the river when I added another piece of the puzzle. Later I was told, 'A son of the killer's family had at that time died. The killers were looking to kill someone to avenge the death of their son.' The unlucky couple in the canoe were random casualties. It could have been anyone. It could have been me.

The narrow Shiripuno River finally fed into the Cononaco River and with the increased volume of water the river widened and we made better speed. We finally reached the Babeno community. But my Tagaeri anxiety escalated further when I learned that the local people live in constant, niggling fear of an attack by their terrorising neighbours. When people make light of a fear, you know the fear is serious. At one lunch time, David dropped us and one of the locals at our camp. As David turned his canoe around to go to his home for lunch, the local staying with us yelled out to David in a joking farewell, 'Watch out for the Tagaeri!'

Because of the amount of time travelling to and from, we only had 48 hours with the community. I confess I was happy when soon enough we said farewell. Our return journey was longer because we were going upstream against a strong current. Whereas the downstream journey had taken about eight hours, the return journey was 13 hours. Even against the current, approaching every bend, David slowed the canoe. On one bend well into the journey we hit what felt and sounded like a submerged log.

'Did we hit a log?' José asked David.

'There are no logs here!' David answered in a tone of wounded professional pride.

Like a London cab driver who knows every corner of the city, David knows every bend of the river and where every log lies. We probably hit one of the turtles, he said, that had scurried into the water at our approach. Only then did I realise that he was probably easing off on the throttle on every bend to check if any Tagaeri were lurking along the banks of the river. A slow pace allowed for a quick engagement of reverse gear if suddenly we confronted or surprised a group of Tagaeri. I didn't clarify my suspicion; sometimes leaving a shadow of a doubt is comforting. Yet if he had been easing off to help spot human danger, the chances of seeing people hiding in ambush was near impossible, so thick and close was the jungle screen. Along most of the Shiripuno, the river is only 15 to 20 metres wide and at times narrower with vines and branches overhanging the river.

We had to break the return journey with an overnight camp, and then after five hours travel the next morning it was announced we were outside the Tagaeri Zone. I could now relax. And I could reflect. I'd inadvertently experienced, if just for the total of five days including travel, what most ancestral humans experienced: the constant, niggling threat of attack by 'others'. I have empathy for their state of fear.

As we moved further away from the Tagaeri Zone, David no longer eased off on the throttle around every bend. We made it safely back to the city of Coca and the next day, with great relief, I flew back to Quito.

By the time I'd reached Quito, Jude had arrived in Ecuador to join me for a holiday. She was settled into our hotel room. With great relief I hugged her, even more tightly than normal. Fortunately, she'd had no knowledge of the risk I'd run until I told her this tale over coffee at a nearby cafe. Only back in Quito, with a further conversation with José, was I able to put the final piece of the jigsaw together. The ambush of the Waorani couple by the Tagaeri had occurred two-and-a-half years before — so it wasn't yesterday, yet recent enough to be fresh in people's minds.

And maybe the Tagaeri's motivation for murdering the Waorani couple was indeed payback. José told me that some of the Babeno community I'd met had, ten years before, attacked and killed a Tagaeri couple.

Feuding Between Neighbouring Groups

Around 95% of ancestral societies engaged in war.[3] In one sample of 50 early societies, 66% were almost continuously at war — defined by at least one battle per year. And around 90% went to war at least every five years.[4] Almost all ancestral societies had weapons of war, such as special spears, clubs and shields. Of the societies I visited, only the Bushmen and Himba didn't have weapons of war. All other societies had hunting tools plus *fighting* tools, and the men always carried both sets just in case.

Fighting was for a range of reasons. Often, wars were for the purpose of claiming or defending territory. Almost always, hostilities were to avenge previous raids. Often, fights were over women and, in some societies, to capture slaves. In Australia, Aboriginal people didn't engage in fights about land because territory was decided in the time of creation. But fighting and raids were commonplace. The raids were either to avenge previous killings, as payback for alleged acts of sorcery or to abduct women. One of the first Aboriginal persons with whom British colonists communicated was Bennelong of the Wangal clan on the southern shore of Sydney Harbour (the point of land where Sydney's famous Opera House stands is named in Bennelong's honour). Englishman Watkin Tench was a marine captain of the first British settlement. Tench was struck by Bennelong's antagonism towards his neighbours on the northern side of the harbour.

Tench recorded that Bennelong's 'most violent exclamations of rage and vengeance' were against his sworn enemies, the Gai-mariagal. 'He never failed to solicit the governor to accompany him, with a body of soldiers, in order that he might exterminate this hated name.'[5]

As part of my research, an Aboriginal elder suggested I read the book, *The Red Chief*. This superb book describes life of the Gunn-e-darr clan in pre-colonial times in northern New South Wales. The remarkable element of *The Red Chief* is that the narration is by the last of the clan's traditional holder of stories and tells of events around the year 1700, ninety years before European colonisation irreversibly changed Aboriginal society. A stunning aspect of traditional life in Gunn-e-darr society was that *every day*, men who weren't out hunting or raiding were assigned to one of two squads — one squad was assigned to lookout duty to watch for menacing neighbours sneaking on to their land, and another squad acted as guards of the women and children foraging for food. The guards were to protect the women and girls from being kidnapped as wives and to ensure the young boys weren't stolen to be raised as warriors of the abductors. Most of the hostile neighbours were of the same Kamilaroi nation as Red Chief's Gunn-e-darr clan.[6]

In almost every society I investigated, life involved frequent skirmishes with neighbours, often people of the same language group. Keri Opai told me that in the early days of Māori migration to Aotearoa (New Zealand), peace generally prevailed. But from about the year 1500 the increasing population from waves of migration added pressure on inter-community relationships. At about this time, pā (fortified hilltop short-stay villages) became common. Almost all Māori communities had access to a pā which provided refuge at times of attack — to protect both themselves plus their kūmara crops and seeds. Pā were usually positioned in naturally near-inaccessible terrain. One early European observer, a military officer, observed in 1820 that 'pā are situated in high, steep and generally conical hills, ascended by a narrow pathway so rugged' that one climbs the path at their personal danger.[7] Half a century earlier, explorer James Cook was struck by the signs of frequent warfare: 'At whatever place we set in at, or whatever people we spoke to upon the coast, they generally told us that those who are a little distant from them were their enemies.'[8]

In the highly organised societies, like Mohawk and the wider Haudenosaunee confederation, large armies could be amassed to inflict carnage on hostile neighbours. The Seneca nation is one of the Haudenosaunee nations. In 1755, a 12-year-old daughter of Scots-Irish settlers, Mary Jemison, was taken captive and adopted by two Seneca sisters. Mary's forced adoption was to replace, for the Seneca sisters, their recently deceased brother. After her initial trauma, Mary had a comfortable life with her new family and voluntarily lived the rest of her life with her Seneca family. In her memoir she told of the exploits of her second husband, Hiokatoo. Hiokatoo lived a long life, dying at age 103 (as best Mary could estimate his age). War campaigns were a major feature of Hiokatoo's life. He participated in 17 campaigns against enemy nations, four of them against Cherokee. 'He was so great an enemy to the Cherokees, and so fully determined upon their subjugation, that on his marches to their country, he raised his own army for those four campaigns, and commanded it ... He brought home a great number of scalps, which he had taken from the enemy, and ever seemed to possess an unconquerable will that the Cherokees might be utterly destroyed.' In 1731, one of Hiokatoo's campaigns was against the Cherokees and a nation called Cotawpes. After that campaign, the Cotawpes were so thoroughly routed with 1200 dead that, so Mary believed and a Google search appears to support, the Cotawpes no longer existed as a nation. Hiokatoo's people suffered immense losses as well, but in being victorious they gained the hunting ground that Mary said 'was their grand objective'.[9]

Almost everywhere I looked and in almost every book I read, evidence of inter-group hostility featured. On the other side of the American continent, in the northern Pacific, hostility towards neighbours was similarly a feature of traditional life. During my visit to Haida Gwaii one local joked about the old days: 'Haida were the Vikings of the Pacific, or maybe the Vikings were the Haida of the Atlantic.' In 1874 the first missionary William Collison and his wife began forty years of missionary work on Haida Gwaii (at that time called the Queen Charlotte Islands by Europeans). Soon after arriving, Collison realised the brutal purpose of the design of Haida houses. Houses were impressive buildings, about 13–16 metres (40–50 feet) in length and the height of the roof ridge was about five metres

(16 feet). The entrance to the five-tier lodge was through a small oval doorway, cut in such a way that compelled those entering to bend in order to enter. The design of the door helped in case of an attack.[10] 'On one occasion a large number of Haidas of another tribe had been slaughtered on the threshold of the great lodge in which I was. (Upon being invited to make peace at a feast) they determined to avail themselves of this opportunity to revenge themselves and came to the feast with their weapons concealed under their garments. (But) a report of their intention had been secretly conveyed to the chief who had invited them … Within the narrow doorway were posted two powerful warriors, one on either side, each armed with a war club. The guests arrived in a long line, led by their chief, each prepared for deeds of blood (with the concealed weapons). But as each entered with head bowed low through the low and narrow portal, one powerful blow from the concealed guard was sufficient, and as the body was dragged aside quickly by them in waiting, they raised a shout of welcome in chorus to disarm suspicion in those following. In this way the entire number was disposed of, and only two great heaps of corpses to right and left of the entrance remained to tell the tale.'[11]

To encourage bravery in war, and perhaps as a forerunner to workplace recognition awards and incentive plans, Blackfeet society had a program of graded war honours (*namachkani*). In their region on the north-western plains near the Rocky Mountains, Blackfeet were reputedly the major military force.[12] Life involved a near-constant war footing against their neighbours — Crows, Sioux, Crees and Assiniboine. The Blackfeet incentive program was based on the degree of courage involved in a heroic deed. The highest honour was to capture an enemy's gun. Next ranked the capture of a bow, shield, war bonnet, war shirt or ceremonial pipe. The taking of a scalp ranked below these deeds, but ahead of the capture of a horse — the capture of a horse was too common to rank highly. Any peace agreed between the leaders of warring groups was generally short lived, frustrated by ambitious young men keen to gain war honours to help advance their economic and social standing. Blackfeet had a saying, 'It is better for a man to die in battle than to die of old age or sickness.'[13]

For workplace leaders, the undercurrent of in-group identity and consequential alienation towards out-groups is an unrelenting challenge.

It can appear as rivalry between teams with different priorities — 'close neighbours' — such as between Finance and Human Resources, Sales and Service/Installation, or Engineering and Production. Thankfully the use of physical violence associated with such rivalries is absent — not to mention illegal — but antagonism can manifest in many other behaviours. It can show as bad-mouthing other leaders and teams. It can show in competition for resources, especially when setting budgets. And I've seen it show as undermining to weaken a leader of another division.

A time when in- and out-group identity is particularly likely to surface in workplaces is when groups are being realigned — mergers, acquisitions, restructures and relocations. If leaders are attuned to sensitivities associated with group membership, they can take early action to smooth the tensions around realignments, and also to take quick remedial action when inter-group hostilities appear. A few years ago, I was involved in a change project involving relocation of staff. Part of the relocation plan involved a group moving to an office where staff of the same organisation were already located. As soon as the existing staff heard that other colleagues would be moving into their building, they labelled these new staff as *invaders*. That expression is straight out of the handbook of hostile treatment of 'others'. The project team took immediate action to remove the suspicion attached to new people. Wendy Stamp, the project manager, scheduled the new people in small groups to visit the site. One of the resident staff was allocated to host the visitors, including hosting a morning tea. A different individual hosted each group of visitors, so that most of the resident staff hosted at least one visit. After meeting and mingling with their new colleagues, the existing staff no longer categorised the new people as 'strangers' and the 'invader' label quickly disappeared. Because she was aware of in-group and out-group tendencies, Wendy could respond quickly at the first sign of internal hostility.

We are People — Others are Not

What allows people to brutalise members of other groups, whether in ancestral societies or in contemporary societies, or even just to treat others as second-class citizens? I was surprised to discover how often one group of indigenous peoples considered themselves 'true humans', and by extension seeing members of other nations or groups as non-human. Considering 'others' as non-human allows members of one group to do seriously nasty things to members of other groups — including killing, torturing and enslaving.

The Wadawurrung people around Melbourne, who William Buckley joined for 32 years, had a distinct 'us and them' view of the world. 'Us' were the Kulin nation, the common language group that Wadawurrung are part of. In the Kulin language, Kulin means 'man' or 'person'. 'Others' were all other people on the outer edge of their cosmos. Those others were described as *mainmait*, *warragull* or *gulum gulum*, meaning 'wild black-fellas'. Those *others* were undesirable foreigners, the source of evil, to be treated with suspicion and animosity.[14]

Pintupi people who I visited in Northern Australia considered distant travel from their own country dangerous. Distant strangers — *munuwati* or 'non-human' or 'different people' — were suspected of evil intentions and unpredictable behaviour.[15] The Walbiri nation, Pintupi's neighbours to the north-east, had a similar outlook. In traditional times, Walbiri had a view that there was 'either we who are Walbiri and those unfortunate people who are not'.[16] Their view about outsiders varied considerably. Some were regarded as friends, with whom they engaged in marriage exchange. Others were regarded as enemies to whom they attributed various disgusting non-human practices including eating their own children.

From the desert of Australia to the desert of southern Africa, the same distinction of 'us and them' in language occurred. Ju/'hoansi Bushmen called themselves *Zhu/twasi* meaning 'real people'.[17] They saw themselves as the only people, and other tribal groups as non-people. Yet their neighbours the Hottentots called themselves 'men of men'.[18] Both can't be right!

One of the terms Mohawk use in referring to themselves is *Onk-wehón:we*, which nowadays is used to distinguish indigenous and non-indigenous people. But when Joseph Bloomfield, the fourth governor of New Jersey, visited Mohawk Valley in 1776, he noted that the word meant 'man surpassing all others'. 'They think of themselves by Nature superior to the rest of Mankind, and assume the Name of Ongue-honwe, this is, Man surpassing all others.'[19] The Blackfeet people don't call themselves Blackfeet. That name was given by others because of their black leggings and moccasins.[20] They call themselves *Nit-si-tuppi* meaning 'One' or 'Only People'.[21] In the Haida language, Haida means 'people'.[22]

My guide in Ecuador, José Aguinda, is Kichwa. 'In our culture,' he told me, 'we say that we are *kikin rune*, "true people" of the jungle!' Likewise, the word 'Waorani' in their language means 'true human beings'. I've mentioned previously that in Waorani society, the division into in-groups and out-groups was at two levels (and, as I described earlier, for some Waorani still is). The first distinction is between Waorani and non-Waorani or *cohuori*. The non-Waorani cohuori are seen as cannibal predators who steal people to butcher their bodies. The second distinction was within the Waorani people. Every individual is categorised as either *waomoni* 'us' or *warani* 'enemy others'.[23] The 'us', as covered in Chapter 1, comprises small groups of about 120 people living in intermarrying longhouses separated by vast stretches of unoccupied forest.

Maasai speak the Maa language. I asked my friend William Kinanta Sadera about this subject of categorisation revealed in the language. This pattern of 'we are the true people' only emerged in my research after William and I had met in Kenya, so I emailed him. In asking him about the meaning of the word 'Maasai' in his Maa language, I didn't at first give him the background to my question — I didn't want to suggest any answer to him. William emailed back, that the two components of 'Maa-sai' mean we are the speakers of the Maa language and 'sai', doing God's work.

I then shared with him my findings about 'true people' and asked him if in 'doing God's work' there is any sense of 'we are the chosen people'. He answered that the word Maasai itself does not have that meaning, but the sense is strongly portrayed in other ways.

'For example,' he wrote, 'the Maa language is common to all Maasai people. As long you speak the language you are one of us — if you don't speak the language you can't be one of us. In the old days, Maasai used language to protect our territory and to identify our own people versus others. Anyone unable to speak Maa was a stranger. In times of peace, that wasn't a problem — strangers were welcomed and treated well. But in times of war, on the battlefield, anyone who couldn't speak the language was an enemy and would not be spared. Also, we consider our culture to be unique and exclusively ours, and no other tribe is permitted to own our culture.'

'Owning cattle, sheep and goats,' William continued, 'is part of the true definition of the Maasai people. We believe livestock drop from heaven and owning them, especially cows, makes you a true Maasai. No one else in the world is permitted to own the cattle. They are ours! Finally, most places in Kenya have Maasai names. For example, Nairobi, the capital city, means "cold place". Many large towns and many mountains have Maasai names. We Maasai believe we own Kenya because we are the true people.'

In workplaces, the in-group 'superiority complex' that has endured through human history doesn't show up as conspicuously as 'we are people — others are not'. But it's only more subtle by a matter of degree. It shows in the guise of 'we're smart — others aren't', Or 'we get it — others don't'. Or 'we're the ones who drive the business'. A proactive way to overcome in-group superiority is to tap into and challenge what a group says about 'other' groups. One group I assisted with this process was part of an aged care organisation. The team ran an aged care facility, and relied on a centralised kitchen team for food served at their facility — the makings of a potential 'us and them' clash. In this case, the relationship between the facility and the kitchen team was indeed poor. The leaders of the facility complained about the lazy kitchen staff and the late delivery of the food — food that when it did arrive was cold and crummy anyway.

In a workshop with the facility staff, we went through the following process to help them realise that their own mindset was not helping and for them to decide the few actions they should take to help fix the problem. The staff were split into small breakout groups, and each group considered four questions. The four questions were given one at a time so the groups focussed on each question, rather than jumping too quickly to the last question. *Question 1*: What do *you* currently say about *them*? The breakout groups were encouraged to capture on their flipchart paper the actual words they use: the kitchen staff are lazy, they're slow, they don't care. *Question 2*: What do we imagine *they* currently say about *us*? The confronting nature of the answers to this question provides the breakthrough: we're ungrateful, we're demanding, we're the worst facility the kitchen has to deal with. 'No wonder we get food delivered last,' one of the managers said in a moment of insight. *Question 3*: What do we *want* them to say about us? The mood shifted to the positive: that we are pleasant to deal with, we're appreciative, we're respectful of them, we respond to requests quickly. The final question is based on the premise that 'we' are entirely responsible for the quality of the relationship with the 'other' because our attitude is reciprocated. *Question 4*: What actions will we take to create the desired future state within 30 days? The leaders identified a few concrete actions. One action was to invite the kitchen staff to conduct a menu review. Apparently, the kitchen staff had been wanting to complete a menu review with the facility, but the managers had never taken up the offer. They did so immediately after the workshop. The facility manager contacted me about 10 days later to let me know that the relationship with the kitchen had been transformed. And that the facility was now getting tasty hot food delivered on-time for their residents.

Actions for Workplace Leaders

Inter-group rivalry shows in workplaces as silo behaviours, rivalries, turf protection and bad-mouthing 'others'. The attitude sabotages collective effort. If we know our natural tendencies, we are better placed to establish the conditions that reduce the likelihood of destructive behaviour, and when it does occur we are able to spot it quickly for what it is and take immediate remedial action. The pull towards creating rival divisions is so strong that workplace leaders can't afford to be passive on this subject — being passive allows the natural antagonism between sections of an organisation to develop. Leaders have to be proactive to ensure unity and collaborative effort.

1. **Foster a collaborative top team:** The fastest way to create rival groups within an organisation is for the top team to be divided. If rivalry and turf protection exists within the top team, then disunity infects the entire organisation or division. Deep down in the organisation, staff become acutely aware of any tensions within the top team and are compelled to take sides — to be part of their in-group and not suffer the risk of ostracism from their group. The top team, of the organisation or of a large division, needs to show

genuine collaboration and camaraderie. Part of a collaborative culture means leaders — at every level — need to be careful of how they talk about other teams. A frustrated leader who says in a team meeting, 'I can't believe that Finance is getting in the way *again*' is sending a divisive signal. And that language tends to be mimicked by team members.

2. **Demonstrate that every group is valued:** Once the top team has its relationships in order, the next step is for senior leaders to show that they value every group in the organisation. They signal that just like the human body, every part of the system is critical to the healthy operation of the body — the lower intestine might not have the most glorious function, but it's as critical as the head and the heart. Checking their calendar allows a senior leader to quickly self-assess how they perform on this dimension. Look at your diary over the last 30 days to see where you have spent your time. Have you distributed your time roughly equally across departments that report to you? Or does the way you spend your time send the signal of elitism favouring one or two groups? If you favour one or two groups, you are likely creating the conditions where in- and out-group rivalry will emerge, if it hasn't already.

3. **Establish the common purpose that connects people:** As we have covered in the beginning of this book, the default for human groups beyond about 150 people is to splinter into sub-groups. For larger groups — divisions in large organisations for example — leaders need to actively overcome our natural tendencies towards 'us and them'. One critical action is to develop and communicate the mission of the division or of the organisation. The mission emotionally connects people and unites people around a common and compelling purpose. From the mission, the strategic goals can cascade through the organisation with each group seeing the role they play and how it connects them to other groups.

4. **Encourage actions not aspirations from top leaders:** People are attuned to the signals from top leaders. People detect what's expected of them, and what's not acceptable. In processing and prioritising

signals, people are particularly persuaded by a leader's actions — their behaviours. An organisation might state as a value that 'We Are a One-Firm Firm' or 'We Are One Team'. But the aspiration has to be backed-up by the behaviour of the top leader and the executive team. *Behaviour* is about what the top leader does and equally what the top leader refuses to accept. In Chapter 7 on Culture, in Action #4, I mentioned a company I once consulted to that had strong values driven by the CEO, who we'll call Alex. I heard one story several times from the managers in the organisation:

> 'Alex is serious about our collaborative culture. He once hired an outsider to head up one of the state offices. In the first week of his employment, the new state manager held a meeting of his team. He said to the team, "My measure of success of our state is not how well we do in pure sales numbers, but how we compare to the other states. We just have to beat the rest." That attitude is totally against our culture. Within days Alex got to hear about what the state manager had said. Alex flew to the state office to meet the manager. Alex said to him, "I've been told what you apparently said to your team." Alex repeated what he'd been told and the manager confirmed it was true. Alex didn't mess around. He said to the manager, "I am very sorry. I've made a terrible hiring mistake. Your competitive approach against other sections of the firm is the opposite of our culture and you can't be part of this business. All that you and I have to decide now is the arrangements for your leaving us."'

The storytellers invariably concluded the story by saying, 'Alex is serious about our collaborative culture.' Actions are not always as dramatic as that, of course. But those are the type of choices leaders make, and the signals they send.

5. **Individual leaders work at building friendly relations:** The importance of reducing inter-group hostility doesn't just fall to the top leaders. Every leader in the organisation plays their part. And again, being passive is not a good option for individual supervisors

and managers. Action is required. Workplace leaders should invest time and energy in maintaining friendly relationships with internal groups they interact with as either suppliers of services or as receivers of services. The suite of activities should include friendly chit-chat (we will cover this prerequisite action in the next chapter), visits to each other's locations, shared social or bonding events, participating in joint planning sessions and business review meetings. The default, from the long journey of human history, is that we treat people as strangers until they prove they are friendly. To ensure inter-department relationships are between 'friends', the managers leading the relevant departments need to take action to build positive relationships.

6. **Be ready for times when 'us and them' is most likely:** I've mentioned earlier in this chapter that of all the organisational changes that leaders implement, one form of change can particularly trigger anxious feelings around group identity and rivalry. If the change involves or even threatens the possibility of changes in a group's membership, then staff become particularly wary. The prospect of changes in group membership, with people possibly joining or leaving a group, arise with mergers and integrations, restructures and relocations. Leaders need to lead such changes with respect — to not disregard or denigrate people's concerns about belonging. Leading with respect allows the change to be implemented faster and smoother, with less distraction from productive work. Andria Wyman-Clarke was HR Director of North America for Thales, a systems and professional services company. One of Thales's divisions acquired another business that would be integrated into Thales. Andria was acutely aware of the human condition of people being suspicious of 'others' — the in-scope staff would be wary about Thales. She wanted to overcome that wariness, and knew the first step was for Thales leaders to engage in friendly conversations with in-scope staff. So, at the first briefing of staff, Andria organised the seating so that at each table, at least one Thales executive sat with the staff of the acquired business. By having easy conversations before the formal presentations, the Thales executives became

more human in the eyes of the in-scope staff. It was an important early step for a smooth integration. Subsequent actions built on that positive first impression.

This attribute of the human experience — of the potential conflict with 'other' groups that can flare at any moment — calls for constant effort by leaders. Being passive about or staying remote from the potential of hostility is not an effective leadership option. Ancestral leaders and their community certainly worked hard at attempting to minimise hostility with their neighbours. And they invested heavily in maintaining harmonious relationships within their own group. As we will see in the next chapter, a happy, harmonious and productive existence didn't just happen — it took time and resources.

CHAPTER 11

Initiatives for Social Cohesion

'That one there, she's your sister. This one is your little mother.'

PART AND PARCEL OF the dynamics of human groups is the constant contest between social tension and harmony. The dynamic can shift from harmony to conflict in a heartbeat. Within their group, leaders and group members need to constantly work at maintaining harmony — to at least minimise moments of interpersonal tension and hopefully avoid episodes of group dysfunction. And as we saw in the previous chapter, the struggle between tension and harmony extends to our relationship with 'other' groups — our neighbours on the savannah or the other divisions at work. For me, the standout feature of what I learned about this aspect of ancestral life was the considerable investment of time, effort and (food) resources First Nation communities devote to the fostering of social cohesion. Initiatives range from the informal to the sophisticated, and many provide ideas to help build cooperative relationships in workplaces.

Bonding Through Chit-Chat

The first and primary mechanism promoting social cohesion in ancestral communities, and in workplaces, costs nothing and is in ample supply — informal conversations. 'Chit-chat' is a prerequisite bonding practice for every human group. Indeed, every social species has a way of bonding.

With my leadership education work over the past 15 years, I've had the honour and good fortune of spending time with, and I'm proud to say becoming friends with, chimpanzee researcher and environmental crusader Dr Jane Goodall. On one occasion she and I discussed the social practice of grooming (using the primatological meaning of the word, not as it is latterly used in reference to illicit behaviour). Chimps groom to maintain harmonious bonds between group members.

'Andrew,' said Dr Goodall, punching a closed fist into her palm for emphasis, 'two chimps cannot *possibly* be bonded if they spend no time grooming.'

Dr Goodall was recalling her days from 1960 onwards observing chimps in the forest of Gombe, Tanzania. For her, it beggars belief that individuals could be bonded if they don't invest time in grooming. It isn't possible to be connected without it. Grooming is social glue.

Whereas chimps groom physically, humans, with our language capability, groom through chit-chat. In workplaces, chit-chat is about subjects other than technical and task work (subjects other than project updates, sales reviews, inventory levels, production targets, key performance measures and the like). Subjects that fit within the definition of chit-chat include interests and hobbies and also chatting about what's going on in the organisation that might help a colleague or that reveals social information. (Although chit-chat can be used maliciously, its social function is overwhelmingly positive.) The point is, to paraphrase Dr Goodall, we can't be bonded with other people or as a team unless we engage in chit-chat. If almost all your conversations with direct reports or your boss or your colleagues or your clients are task-related, while those topics are important, they do not constitute grooming and the quality of your relationships will suffer.

In our ancestral setting, chit-chat was the second most important activity after foraging for food — that's how important chit-chat is for group cohesion. The amount of grooming a group needs to engage in each day relates to population of the community which in turn, as we covered in Chapter 1, relates to the size of our brain. Robin Dunbar and his colleagues extended their work linking brain size and group size to calculate the proportion of a day a community of primates needs to spend grooming in order to keep their community unified. Chimps, with their brain size and living in groups of up to about 50 individuals, need to spend at least 10% of their day grooming. Humans, with our much bigger brain and living in ancestral groups of up to about 150 individuals, need to spend around 30% of daylight hours grooming. As I say to participants on our leadership workshops, don't try that back at work! The point at this stage isn't to scare you with that number; the point is that chit-chat is a critically important social mechanism.[1]

Although the amount of time required for chit-chat was large, in our ancestral setting that wasn't a big challenge. There are at least four reasons why extensive chit-chat was not a problem.

First, food was relatively plentiful. Even in the dry Kalahari, except in exceptional drought years, people didn't have to work hard to gather enough food (calories) to sustain themselves. Anthropologist Richard Lee found that Bushmen only needed to spend a modest 17 hours' effort per adult per week, or 2.1 days' work, to gather enough food.[2] Compared to the gatherers, hunters spent a little longer at their task — about 2.7 days per week — mainly because of the distances covered tracking prey. This low number of hours spent gathering food meant there was plenty of time for bonding — chatting while sitting around the camp occupied with other tasks such as making or repairing equipment or fetching water. The waterhole was indeed the office water-cooler of the savannah, with treks late in the afternoon to the waterhole an occasion for social interaction.[3]

Second, because we groom vocally, we can groom while our hands are occupied. This option isn't available to chimps. Chimps either have their hands occupied on a task — such as foraging for food or climbing trees — or grooming. They can't forage and groom at the same time. But humans have a great bonding advantage. While members of a Bushmen camp might be busy collecting mangetti nuts under a tree or digging tubers from the ground, they could chat — they could work *and* bond. Further, because we don't need our hands to engage in grooming, people didn't need to be stationary in order to bond; people could chat while moving from one gathering site, such as a grove of nut trees, to the next.

Third, whereas chimps can only groom one-on-one, with our vocal capability we can groom several people at once which gives a productive return on the time spent grooming. How many people can groom at the same time? Up to four. You'll be familiar, even unconsciously, with the dynamic involved. At a coffee-break during a conference, or standing around having a drink at a party, observe the size of the groups people gather in. The group will be between two and four individuals. And what happens if a fifth person joins a group of four? Within 30 seconds, one of two things happens. Either the group of five splits into two conversations, one with two people and the other group with three people. Or the other option is that one of the five people finding themselves no longer involved in the conversation excuses themselves and breaks off and joins another group. This universal phenomenon of up to four people in an informal group is because our grooming ability is one speaker to up to three listeners, making a group of four. Add one more listener and it's a stretch for everyone to be engaged and to have their say.[4]

Finally, on the challenge of enough time for grooming to keep a group bonded, ancestral humans came up with a creative solution. We weren't limited to squeezing enough grooming activity into daylight hours. With the domestication of fire, we could extend the hours available to us into the night, chatting around the campfire. And music and dance provided the means for high-leverage grooming with many people bonding at community festivals.

Bonding through chit-chat is fundamental to group unity. The clear implication for workplace leaders is that chit-chat is vital — irreplaceable as a means of bonding. Leaders at every level need to engage in chit-chat and need to facilitate chit-chat within and across teams. Participants on our leadership workshops often tell us that in the past, prior to this realisation of the science and logic of bonding, they considered informal catchups with people, team lunches, standing around talking and the like as a waste of time — a waste of their time and their team members' time. Those leaders can now see that their relationships and team cohesion suffered. With that realisation came a shift in mindset. For a leader to bond with their people and to ensure the team is unified, two things are required. First, leaders must spend time with individuals in relaxed conversations about topics other than task, and second, leaders need to facilitate team or departmental activities that constitute bonding rituals. In leadership workshops we ask groups to identify the activities that they use, or have heard other groups use, that they can now see serve as group bonding rituals. The list is always extensive and always falls out effortlessly with high energy and good humour. Here is an example list from one leadership workshop:

Coffee catchups	Charity events	Business success celebrations
Walk to coffee	Team challenges	
Team morning tea	Onboarding morning teas	Cultural lunches (food)
Milestone successes		Sharing important crises
Team building days	Provide food for all	Health initiatives (e.g. steps)
Offsite activities	Working lunches	
Corporate games	Home-hosted drinks	Team breakfasts and lunches
Carpooling to meetings	Paint a mural together	
Festive activities	Monday morning check-in	Celebrate birthdays
Football tipping		Site social club
Bowling	Lunch time exercises	Fundraising efforts
	Daily quiz	Barbeques

In many workplaces, the opportunities for grooming have been declining in recent years. Workforces have shrunk and become 'leaner'. And under pressure to keep up, many people are 'too busy' for team morning teas and lunches or easy chit-chat in the first few minutes of a team meeting. Remote and hybrid work adds further challenges. But ancestral leaders would never have considered bonding practices a luxury and would never have sacrificed time devoted to bonding.

Cooperative Relationships Through Skin Names

As we saw in the previous chapter, most ancestral societies had tense and hostile relations with their neighbours. In workplaces, similar tense intergroup relations, territorial rivalries and silo behaviour can easily occur unless we work at unifying people.

Aboriginal people have a sophisticated solution to reduce intergroup tension. The system of kin and family relationships in Aboriginal society goes far beyond blood relations or genetics in Western society. In the old days and still now, an Aboriginal stranger can travel through different regions of the continent and connect with locals, immediately shifting from being a stranger to becoming a relative through the concept of 'skin'.

When I visited Pintupi country, along with most of the other six Red Dust volunteers in our group, I was given a skin name when we were welcomed to country. A few nights later, six female elders took us out bush for a talk around the campfire. The sun was close to setting when we arrived at the chosen spot, and we all chipped in collecting firewood so the fire was alight by dark. When the flames died down, our hosts buried kangaroo tails in the coals to cook along with damper (a bread). Later, the billy (a tin of water) was boiled for tea. The senior host was Ampi Robinson. While we waited for the food to cook, Ampi looked at me across the fire.

'Andrew, what's your skin name?'

'Tjapangati,' I answered, giving the name that I had been honoured with the first night.

'That one there,' she said, pointing to a woman across the fire, 'she's your sister.'

My hosts love a laugh, so I exclaimed, 'My long-lost sister!' I jumped up and dashed around the fire, knelt in the dirt and hugged the woman roughly my age. Raucous laughter. That's how I met Lorraine.

'This one 'ere,' Ampi said, tapping the knee of a young woman sitting next to her, 'she's your little mother.' Being much younger than me, possibly in her 20s, I thought it appropriate that I stayed sitting and waved to Rachel.

I am now connected with Lorraine and Rachel. There are obligations in the skin relationship. As my little mother, if in my older age I become infirmed, Rachel will look after me as though I was her infant son.

Some obligations are easier to fulfill than others. At the start of our six-hour drive from Alice Springs to Walungurru, I asked Alan Palmer about his and my skin relationship. I was keen to meet my obligations to him. He obviously knew the translation of my Pintupi name to the equivalent Arrernte name in his society. 'You and I are cousins,' he said.

'And what obligations do I have to fulfill?' I asked in a serious tone.

Equally as serious he answered, 'As cousins, we can joke with each other.'

'Oh,' I laughed, 'I can deliver on that responsibility!'

As it was told to me, the skin system works like this. At border communities, a translation is made from the skin names of one nation to the equivalent skin name of the nation the person is entering. This translation is completed despite different languages and a different number of skin names. For example, Arrernte have eight skin names, whereas Pintupi have 16 names. So when an Arrernte person like Alan first visited Pintupi country or interacted with Pintupi, he made the match of his skin name to the Pintupi equivalent. Having made the match, the person immediately has relatives in the new country — a new sister, brother, great uncle and aunt and so on — with reciprocal responsibilities between the relatives. The visitor is no longer a stranger. In ancestral times, neighbours were potential enemies but skin names went a long way to support social harmony across Aboriginal nations.

The skin name conversation continued later in Sydney. When in Central Australia I'd met Marlene Ross, who you'll recall was 11 years of age before she saw a European. Towards the end of our conversation in Alice Springs she mentioned that she would soon be in Sydney for a conference — she's active in community health, social enterprises and is an accomplished artist. She said she would make contact and we could meet up and she would tell me more stories. I agreed enthusiastically and we exchanged phone numbers. I said that I'd love to introduce her to my wife, Jude, and we'd take her to dinner. Marlene called a few weeks later from her Sydney accommodation. The three us had dinner, and Marlene shared with us more about her early life.

While we were waiting for dessert, Marlene said to Jude, 'I'll give you a skin name'. This was an honour, as not every non-Aboriginal person receives a skin name. I had been told that elders such as Marlene assess spiritually whether a Western person is ready for a skin name.

'Your skin name,' she said smiling at Jude, 'is Nampitjinpa.'

'Thank you!' Jude beamed, checking the pronunciation. 'What's the significance of Nampitjinpa?'

'It means that you and Andrew are of the correct skin names to be married.' We thanked her for that!

'And second,' she continued, 'you and I are sisters.' Overjoyed, Jude grabbed Marlene's hand.

Dessert arrived. Marlene said that young Pintupi couples still respect skin name marriage partnering. If they are the 'wrong side' the elders talk to the young people. 'If they are the wrong side, we say to the girl, "that's not the way our grandmothers did things". And we say to the boy, "that's not the way our grandfathers did things."'

Marlene had brought a gift for me: *The Lizard Eaters* by Douglas Lockwood. The book describes a 1960s government expedition into Pintupi country, with the author making first contact with some of Marlene's people. At the time of the trip described in the book, Marlene was still living the old life and had not yet seen her first non-Aboriginal person. I read the book as Marlene's story. Marlene, living the life she has lived, having experienced the old way before European contact, is, surely, an Australian national treasure.

Building Trust With Neighbours

Another way Aboriginal communities maintained harmonious relationships with neighbours was lending sacred objects into the safe keeping of selected neighbours.

In 1899, FJ Gillen and Baldwin Spencer completed a major study of Arrernte people around Alice Springs. Given that the Overland Telegraph was only completed in 1872, this was in the early days of European contact and at a time when Aboriginal people overwhelmingly lived their traditional life. Gillen was the manager of the telegraph station and appears to have been trusted by the local people. With anthropologist Spencer, they observed and extensively documented Arrernte practices and rituals in *The Native Tribes of Central Australia*.

Arrernte (or Arunta) society comprised 'a large number of small local groups each of which occupies a given area of country'.[5] The small groups were comprised largely of individuals who were connected to a totem animal, plant or object, such as emu, sun or water. For example, the caterpillar people 'comprised 40 individuals; men, women and children'.[6] Each band had its headman, or *Alatunja*. Each band had a storehouse of sacred objects, and the Alatunja was the custodian of the storehouse. Bands occasionally lent sacred items, *churinga*, 'to a neighbouring and friendly group as a very special mark of goodwill'.[7]

Gillen and Spencer observed a group of elders of the emu totem lend sacred objects to another totem group. Through a messenger, permission to borrow had earlier been requested and granted. The elders of the group borrowing the objects arrived at the emu camp. After sunset, the visitors were taken to the corroboree (ceremonial) ground. Performances lasted several days. At the end of the ceremony, the local emu headman went to the sacred storehouse and chose the churinga to be lent. At daylight the next day, the objects 'were solemnly handed over to the visiting Alatunja, the lender saying in a grave tone, "Keep the churinga safely, they are of the *Alcheringa* (the Dreaming); we lend them to you freely, gladly; do not be in a hurry to return them."'[8]

In reply, also in a low tone, the receiving headman said, 'We will watch over them with care, and return them to you after some time; the emu churinga are good, and emu men are strong and good.'[9] Spencer and Gillen observed the borrowed churinga being returned after a little more than two years, again with appropriate ceremony.

Imagine a workplace where divisions of an organisation treat each other with the same level of respect demonstrated by the emu totem group and their neighbours; I've had that experience. When I worked at Cable & Wireless Optus, the number two telecommunications company in Australia, two of the main sales divisions were the Mobile Phone division and the Enterprise division. I was head of Human Resources for the Enterprise division. The top leaders of the two divisions regarded each other highly. My boss in the Enterprise division was Stephen Beynon. The head of

Mobiles was Paul O'Sullivan. In describing the close relationship between the two, Stephen said. 'If I was unable to attend an important meeting and Paul O'Sullivan was attending, I'd be happy for Paul to represent me and our division, and the same applies for Paul.' In my experience on top teams, that closeness is highly unusual — Stephen and Paul were prepared to entrust their sacred objects to each other. Developing and maintaining trust between groups is obviously critical, and groups that could be rivals need to find ways to build trust if they are to have a cooperative relationship. Arrernte bands established trust through sharing sacred objects. Workplace teams and divisions need to spend time together, engage in bonding through combined activities and where leaders make and meet commitments to each other. In the Optus example of Beynon and O'Sullivan, their trust of each other set the tone across the two divisions that we were in the one organisation and not in rival camps.

Cooperation Through Sharing

Sharing food within a community was a vital element of social cohesion — don't hoard resources is the leadership message in this section (or at least be aware of the social cost of hoarding). In describing her observations of Bushmen in the 1950s and 1960s, anthropologist Marshall Thomas wrote that 'sharing was perhaps the most important element of the social fabric ... Continuous sharing reassured the people of their membership in the social fabric, and failures of sharing, or perceived failures of sharing, suggested the fear that people felt of marginalisation and exclusion, the deathlike state of being alone'.[10]

For Bushmen, sharing meat and nuts, the two most important food items, provided an opportunity to unite people, yet it could also generate jealousy if distribution was not equitable. If sharing failed, the group fractured. Given the importance of meat and the sensitivity of equitable sharing, Bushmen had strict rules for distribution. The sharing of meat was initiated not by the successful hunter, but by the owner of the arrow used to kill the animal. Arrows were made by any adult and given to the hunters. Upon returning to camp from a successful hunt, the meat became the responsibility of the owner of the arrow to share equitably amongst the group.

The only other food item Bushmen were obliged to share was mangetti nuts. Mangetti nuts comprised about half the vegetable component of their diet, which in turn was about 70% of the diet, making nuts the single most important food item.[11] Nuts were shared in a similar way to meat, and the distribution started not by the person who brought a bag of nuts into camp, but by the person who made the bag. (Other fruits and vegetables belonged to the person who gathered them and did not need to be shared.)

Marshall Thomas observed one group of people returning from a gathering expedition. She was struck by the social cohesion of the group, demonstrated and reinforced by sharing. The group of nine approach the camp as a small procession, 'all together, no one far ahead of the others, no one lagging behind, all carrying enormous bundles bulging with mangetti nuts, balancing their bundles with their walking sticks ... All were tired, yet all seemed glad to be home after their successful journey and happy with the pleasure that was blossoming around them. Soon, the bundles had been opened, the bounty had been shared and shared again, and everyone was roasting and eating mangettis. These nine strong men and women had brought important food to sixteen other people, including the children, two elderly men and three elderly women, one very pregnant woman, and the other able-bodied adults who had stayed home to take care of the encampment ... Never has there been a better example of a well-functioning group'.[12]

Another unifying practice of Bushmen, a practice common to ancestral societies, is gift giving. Almost every person had a set of gift-partners, on average about 15 people spread out over 160 kilometres (100 miles), with whom he or she would exchange gifts. There were strict rules associated with gift giving: gifts must be given, must be received and must be reciprocated. Yet a return gift could not be given too soon as that would look like a trade.[13] The Marshall family unwittingly entered the gift-giving (*xaro*) system. On one visit, they had with them cowrie shells from the Pacific which they gave as gifts upon their departure. As they said their farewells, they gave 20 shells to each woman of the group. When the Marshalls returned a year later, not one of the women had a shell in her possession. The shells had entered the xaro system and had been distributed across the whole Nyae Nyae region of the Kalahari.[14]

The universal practices of sharing and gift giving in ancestral societies link to the leadership character of generosity we covered in Chapter 3 (see for example Action 4 in Chapter 3). A workplace leader who shares resources, time and knowledge with other leaders builds a foundation for cooperative relationships with that other leader. And a leader who has a generous character is more likely to have quality relationships with, and loyalty of, their people.

Harmony Through Trading

While trading as a commercial exchange is different to gift-giving, it was also an important way that most ancestral communities maintained harmonious relationships with neighbours. Aboriginal society had extensive trading networks criss-crossing the continent, radiating from major trading centres.

In the Western District of Victoria in south-east Australia in the mid-1800s, the settler family, the Dawsons, were told about the trading practices of the traditional owners prior to colonisation. A favourite trading place was a hill called Noorat near today's Terang. People from Geelong (Djillong), 150 kilometres away, brought the best stones for making axes and a wattle tree gum used as an adhesive for fixing the handles of stone axes and for attaching splinters of flint to spears. People closer to Terang traded sandstone that was useful for grinding greenstone. People from around today's Dunkeld brought obsidian, a volcanic glass, for scraping and polishing weapons. Mallee saplings for spears were brought from the Wimmera area to the north. Red clay for paint and marine shells were brought from the coast. Trading was accompanied by celebrations, and attendance was compulsory to the members of all invited clans.[15] With hundreds of people attending, trading took place at a time and place when food was in abundant supply. Providing food for this purpose, and for other celebrations, was a significant investment of time, effort and resources.

Likewise, in North America trading networks extended across the continent. For the Blackfeet nation, stone for making tools came from across the Rocky Mountains, shell ornaments came from the Pacific Ocean and cowrie shells came from the Gulf of Mexico. Horses were reintroduced in North America by the Spanish in the south and were soon obtained — by trading and raiding — by nations across the continent. Before trading took place between groups, peace treaties were made. By smoking the peace pipe, trading could take place in a spirit of friendship where everyone lived up to their obligation.[16]

Sharing labour was another form of trading that helped inter-community harmony. In Australia and New Zealand we use the term 'working bees' for people pitching in to help each other. A major element of the Māori economy and social life was the production of kūmara or sweet potato. The preparation of land for cultivation was often an opportunity for collaborative effort, both within a community and possibly with people from neighbouring communities who were potential enemies. In traditional times, land was owned by the *hapū* (the village equivalent we covered in Chapter 1). Plots of land were allocated to families, and the family was responsible for planting seeds, weeding the plot and harvesting the crop. Each family was responsible for storing their own crop in their own store pits.[17] But the preparation of the plot for planting was usually a community affair. Cooperation took the form of working bees (*ohu*). If a host village wished to use the task of clearing land as an opportunity for harmonious interactions with another community, the leader sent an invitation to the other group who would clear the land for them. The home group 'provided the food and entertainment and the visiting *ohu* put forth their best efforts to gain the approval of the hosts. Such exchanges gave pleasure to both sides and served to maintain friendship between the two tribes.'[18]

It can't be coincidental that sharing food was an integral part of trading camps and working bees. Enjoying a good meal tends to stimulate the release of the feel-good hormone dopamine in the human brain. And the region of the brain where dopamine is released is the area associated with reward and sensory perception. On top of eating a good meal, positive social interactions can release a second positive hormone, oxytocin. Oxytocin is associated with the warm feelings that come with feelings of empathy, trust and positive communication. Even without knowing the neurochemistry for bonding over food, workplace leaders who are effective at unifying their people instinctively know that an event that involves food is a sure way to make people feel good and want to repeat the experience.

Unity Through Marriage and Blending of Clans

Given the almost constant risk of hostility with neighbours that we covered in the previous chapter, overwhelmingly First Nation societies diligently facilitated harmonious relationships between groups. Marriage and the blending of clans are two methods generally utilised. Back again to the Western District of Victoria, Australia, marriage taboos within their group caused people to connect beyond their community, beyond their skin group and even beyond their immediate neighbours. The two chiefs of the respective communities agreed to the partnering of the two people. Then to help build relationships between the two communities, prior to marriage the man and the women lived with each other's community for 12 months prior to the wedding.[19]

Then the wedding ceremony was attended by members of both communities — perhaps 200 people. The bride was introduced by her bridesmaid, the nearest unmarried female relative of the groom — further cementing relationships of the bride with her new in-laws. The groom was attended by one or two bachelors. The ceremony was accompanied by amusements and feasting — the pantry included emus' and swans' eggs, possum, kangaroo and wild fowl, and even perhaps what early colonists called the native sloth bear (koala). The wedding celebrations continued for several days, with plenty of dancing, pantomime, laughter and more feasting until the wearied guests headed home — well bonded, I imagine.

Okay, in workplaces we aren't going to arrange marriage partnering across groups (although a lot of people meet their partners in workplaces), but the ancestral practice shows that fostering intergroup relationships is important — if we don't invest in unifying practices then we risk disharmony.

In Maasai society, marriage is one of three ways that communities are bonded to help reduce the risk of clans or divisions breaking into separate entities. The consequences of people having greater identity with their clan than with Maasai as a nation would, in time, drive the clans into different entities (such as what appears to have happened several centuries ago when Samburu split from Maasai and now have a distinct identity). The same risk arises in workplaces if people have such a strong in-group identity with their division that they have combative relationships with colleagues in other divisions.

Maasai are prohibited from marrying a member of their own clan. As a consequence of this taboo, villages are blended with members of all five clans. And of course, it's hard to treat a person you live with as anything other than a friend. My friend and key contact William Kinanta Sadera told me the story of his childhood village as an example of how clan membership is blended within a village.

'Thirty-five years ago, my father moved from his village in a different district to this district to meet a respected elder called Ole Kipira. Ole Kipira was the owner of that village. He is a good leader and his homestead was peaceful and a pleasant place to live. My father and Ole Kipira belong to different clans — Ole Kipira belongs to the Ilmolelian clan and my father belongs to Iltaarlosero clan. My father was keen to marry one of Kipira's daughters and to live in his village.

'When my father arrived at Kipira's village, he was welcomed and given the role of looking after Kipira's cattle for seven years. This earned him permission to marry Kipira's daughter. They remained in Kipira's village, building a house in the village and my father becoming a member of the village even though he belongs to a different clan. His wife, Kipira's daughter, was a member of her father's clan but upon marrying my father she became a member of his clan. Their children belong to my father's clan — so children grow up with friends of different clans. That's how clans become blended in a village and it helps ensure friendly relationships across the clans.'

The key point is that leaders need to find ways to keep a community together and avoid a silo mentality. While workplace leaders and ancestral leaders have different mechanisms at their disposal, both need to work at maintaining unity across sections that could break into rival divisions. For example, when I worked at IBM in the mid-1980s through to the mid-1990s the company was good at seconding people from one division to another.

A steady stream of transfers across divisions meant that people appreciated the contribution of each division and this helped to avoid an 'us and them' rivalry. And although a few lower-level leaders selfishly tried to hold on to their good people, higher-level leaders in IBM overrode leaders who tried to hoard their human resources to ensure that transfers happened (see Action 7 at the end of this chapter).

Group Belonging Through Initiation

In addition to marriage and the associated blending of clans, initiation, most often of young males, is a common practice in ancestral societies. In Maasai society, the male fraternity is formed when boys in a province are ready for circumcision and initiation as warriors (*moran*). Because all five clans are represented in the villages of the region, all five clans are also represented in each age set. The initiation ceremonies and the protocols of the fraternity firmly bond the young men. And the young women, as we will soon learn, value the emergence of quality men in the community. The age set of men remains together for life. Upon graduation from warriorhood after about 12 years, the now junior elders are permitted to marry.

A feature of the age set is that an individual becomes part of a unit above their village. It's similar in workplaces where above our team and department we might identify with a group or groups that run across the organisation. In professional organisations for example, communities of knowledge run across divisions. Similarly, in firms that hire significant numbers of college graduates, the young people hired in a year become an 'age set'.

I was keen to hear the perspective of a young Maasai who had recently commenced his warriorhood period. William Sadera introduced me to one of his young relatives, Wilson Nashula Kipira. Wilson is 17 years of age and last year began his long period as a warrior, or moran. He has another eleven years as a moran ahead of him. A key focus of this period is the bonding of the group of warriors and their education in Maasai customs. Wilson and I had our 'conversation' through a series of emails.

'About a year ago,' I asked, 'just before becoming a moran, what were your feelings about your upcoming warriorhood?'

'I was really excited to be a moran — to prove my manhood by defending my community, amongst other things. That is the desire of every Maasai boy. Early in the morning the day after my circumcision which begins the moran process, my father said to me, "Wake up, Wilson, you are now a man." Those words motivate me to do what has to be done for my community.'

'What were you most looking forward to in becoming a moran?' I asked.

'When I was growing up, during storytelling sessions, we were told about the great moran of past generations. One of the legendary moran I loved hearing about was Ole Surum. He was tall, well-built and brave. He was gifted with wonderful singing abilities and he could jump higher than anyone else. He was popular with the girls. He became very famous and was super respected. Above everything, Ole Surum was courageous. He showed great courage in facing lions and in defending his community from attacks by rival tribes. He also showed great bravery and cleverness at cattle rustling — groups led by Ole Surum rustled large numbers of cattle during their time. The stories of Ole Surum and other warriors motivated me and I was ambitious to be among the great moran of our generation.'

'Now a year later, is your age group becoming closely bonded?'

'Yes, we are bonding — but not as strong as previous generations. Our age set is influenced by the Western lifestyle which reduces the strength of our Maasai cultural education. For example, most of my age set is at Western school, so they have less time for moran business and less time in the villages. Cattle rustling is now a criminal offence and the government deals harshly with any offenders, so our age set will miss the adventure of stealing cows. Also, today we are not allowed to kill lions. In the old days, part of the proof of manhood was to kill a lion with your own spear. Killing lions is prohibited now under the Wildlife Protection Act, so our generation won't have that experience.'

There are roughly 800 boys in Wilson's age set. The qualifying age to join an age set is ten years — meaning that a boy of nine years of age who just misses out joining an age set will join the next group in 12 years' time. So members of an age set range from ten years to even 21 years of age at the start of their warrior period.

'How are bonds created between the members of your age set?' I asked Wilson.

'The name of our age set bonds us. We have the name, Ilmirisho, which means winners. It took us about a year, including with guidance from the senior elders, to decide our name. When I hear the name and know that person is one of my age set, a great sense of respect, love and belonging arises within me. Wherever we travel, and whatever village we visit, we first introduce ourselves by our age set name. That comes before my name and my family's name. If I am visiting a village where I don't know anyone, I will be directed to the house (hut) of a member of my age set. He will look after me and give me accommodation. Immediately I feel as though I belong, which I do.'

'What are the processes or ceremonies that bind an age set of warriors so closely together?'

'The process actually starts in childhood. In a village, children of the same age play together. On moonlit nights, we played games for many hours. On nights when there was no moonlight, we gathered at the fireplace to hear stories. The play and the stories unite children — to love and respect each other. You can now imagine that every Maasai boy has close friends within the circle of his age group.'

'The next stage is when we are circumcised,' Wilson continued. 'Circumcision happens just before warriorhood commences. You prepare for circumcision with your closest friends in your age group. Then we undergo circumcision together and surviving the pain of the knife without shaming the community means you are courageous enough to start the warrior period. Circumcision is done in public for all the people to witness. In being circumcised, there is no pain-relief medication and a boy must not produce any noise nor shake any part of his body — otherwise society declares you a coward and you are then not recognised by society. As I prepared for my circumcision, I remembered the stories of Ole Surum who had the courage to survive circumcision pain. After circumcision, during the healing period, we travel to all the villages, visiting each other as members of Ilmirisho.'

'What are the main ceremonies during your period of warriorhood?'

'Moran don't stay at home. Instead we travel around the community, eating meat and sleeping in the bush. We have a temporary meeting point, an *emanyatta*, which is also our home for short periods. This is where moran come together and perform our ceremonies. The first ceremony is laying the foundation of the emanyatta, which is called the *emanyisho* ceremony. Temporary houses are built mostly by the mothers of the moran. During emanyisho, the senior elders guide us on how to conduct ourselves during the moran period.

'After a further five months, another ceremony is held to close the emanyatta. After this ceremony, the mothers and the elders are released back to their homes and the moran start going around the community where the main role is displayed. We travel around to protect the community, to grow and mature, to harden up and to learn many things.

'We come together regularly throughout our 12 years. There are many ceremonies and some of the ceremonies take many months because of all the things involved in those ceremonies. The senior elders are actively involved with us during our warriorhood — teaching us all we need to know to live according to our Maasai culture. The elders remain our close consultants even after warriorhood. They are highly respected, they are the eyes of the community, and nothing is done against their will.'

Workplace leaders who believe in the value of culture as the glue for unifying people and giving people a sense of common purpose will identify with Wilson's remarks. It's hard to deny, I think, and hard to imagine a group of people being unified without mechanisms that create a sense of belonging. In terms of initiation, good organisations will already invest in formal orientation of new staff. There are three key objectives of quality orientation. One objective is to make explicit for new people the rules of belonging — the culture of the organisation and the operating rules. The second objective is to create a fraternity of new starters. The third objective is that orientation is a key vehicle for leaders to reach new staff. The best leaders use orientation as a vehicle to share their view about the culture, to gain support to the mission of the organisation and to gain emotional connection with their followers.

'At the end of our moran period,' Wilson concluded, 'another emanyatta is constructed to hold the final ceremony. Then we go back to our homes to be shaved and to start the next stage of life — marriage.'

Meanwhile, young Maasai women are observing their brothers and the boys they grew up with going through the warrior period. So I could hear the female perspective about male initiation, William Sadera introduced me to his niece Grace Nyamalo Sadera. Grace is 16 years of age and is in her final year of secondary school. She hopes to continue her education by going to university to study medicine and becoming a surgeon. We conversed via email.

'What are your views,' I asked, 'as you watch the boys of your age going through their moran period?'

'I have great admiration for the boys developing into brave, responsible and heroic moran to look after us. I expect to see through the moran period the transformation of boys into quality men.'

I asked Grace to talk with some of her girlfriends to see if they have a similar opinion. She emailed back a couple of days later. 'I took some time to visit my friends to enquire about the information you requested. I managed to speak with three of them. They all said that they admire watching the boys transition into quality men — because the girls wish to have quality men and husbands in our community.'

'What are the qualities of a good husband?' I emailed back.

'They are responsible, hardworking, respectful, brave and caring,' she answered. 'During the moran period we see the boys we grew up with transform into good men.'

'The warrior period is also great fun for us girls,' Grace wrote. 'When the moran come from the bush and gather in the emanyatta, we join them. I assume you know the layout of a village. The village is organised in a circular manner, with the houses around the edges of the village and in the middle of the village compound is a big space where the cattle are kept at night. When the moran come into the village, they gather in the vacant middle space. Moran line up and sing and jump (Maasai jumping to a rhythmic beat is a spectacular sight). When the moran are jumping, the women and girls join them. Each girl matches with a moran. We sing and dance with him, nodding our heads and shaking our shoulders. The moran you line up with is random. You give a gift, an *enkononkoi*, to the one you stand parallel with. The gift is a beaded necklace. We will then serve the moran milk to drink before they go back to the bush.'

My impression from what Grace told me is that the moran period is significant for the whole community — men and women and the emerging generation of young men and young women. It's not just about growing warriors to protect the community. It's a tradition that unifies through broad participation, the excited chit-chat created in anticipation of key events and the clear purpose and outcomes it delivers to the community.

Regular Ceremonies and Festivals Reinforce Identity

Like the Maasai, all ancestral societies used ceremonies to unite people — and to add joy to people's lives. Significant time and resources were and are invested in ceremonies as a vital way to generate social harmony.

For some societies, the cycle of festivals focused on giving thanks for Nature's gifts. For example, Mohawk celebrate six festivals each year. The first of the season is the Maple Festival, the liquid maple sap signalling the passing of winter. Next is the Planting Festival, to invocate the Great Spirit to bless the seed. Third is the Strawberry Festival to express thanks and to celebrate the first fruit of the season. The fourth is the Green Corn Festival to acknowledge the ripening of corn, beans and squash, the staples of Haudenosaunee life. The fifth is the Harvest Festival, celebrated after the gathering of the harvest. Last is the New Year's Festival. Some of the festivals are single day events while some were longer. In traditional times, the Green Corn Festival and the Harvest Festival both ran over four days, with a feast at the end of each day. The New Year's Festival ran for seven days.[20] The festivals serve the purpose for thanksgiving, religious expression, community celebrations, dance and games. The festivals unite the community.

In Aboriginal society, the major reason for ceremonies is to fulfill the spiritual obligations of each nation, though ceremonies also serve to facilitate harmonious relations between neighbours. In Alice Springs, Alan Palmer explained to me the key aspects of ceremony. 'The ceremonies follow the Dreaming lines. All nations have obligations in the Dreaming. It's like a baton, passed from one group to the next, extending into neighbouring nations. The host of a ceremony sends out invitations to the neighbouring nations — the nations that the law specifies will attend the ceremony.

Perhaps two or more nations gather in celebration. The next group knows when the 'baton' is passed to them, and they in turn hold their ceremony. In this way there is a path of ceremonies extending across the continent following the Dreaming lines. Ceremony is a major way that society keeps functioning. There are various reasons for ceremony. One reason is to share time and knowledge with people from different nations. Another is to settle squabbles before they escalate into blood feuds. When people gather to resolve differences, we are reminded that there are forces bigger than the individuals involved — ceremony is bigger and more important than our feelings. Disagreements are set aside, and everyone is a witness.'

The key connection from the ancestral experience to workplaces is an appreciation that gatherings of people are not just for functional reasons (such as to inform or to educate). When I was at IBM we had a regular cycle of events or festivities. The annual cycle started with a kick-off event where staff heard about the plans for the year. Through the year, each division convened regular information and celebratory events, and about halfway through the year a gathering of all staff in a location, such as across Sydney, was held. A Christmas function was also a good reason to get everyone together. Part of the cycle of events included an annual leadership conference for all managers. Formal education was only one purpose of these conferences. Equally important was the message that the role of managers was vital. The time, effort and expense invested in the development programs demonstrated this message, as did the involvement of the executive team.

Shaman Role Vital for Social Cohesion

Without exception, every ancestral community had a spiritual leader, variously called a shaman or medicine person or in Māori society, a *tohunga* or priest. That's phenomenal — that the role was universal. For a role to exist in every society, in every band and village, in every environment across every continent, the shaman role must have served (and in many cultures still does serve) a critical purpose for human communities.

I met with Kichwa shaman, Humberto Bartolo Aguinda Tapuy on the banks of the Napo River in north-east Ecuador. Bartolo is the father of José who guided me on our visit to the Waorani. Upon our safe return from the jungle, José introduced me to his father. We talked over breakfast, with the indefatigable Jorge Espinosa translating. I asked Bartolo about his role as a shaman.

'As a shaman, my key role in serving my community is to cure sickness and to protect the community from bad shaman who might curse people,' he said. 'In traditional times, shaman also had a spiritual role and the role unified the community. Nowadays most people are Christians so my role is less spiritual than in my grandfather's day — today the role is mainly to do with people's health and curing sickness.'

'In the old days,' I asked, 'how did a shaman unify a community?'

'A good shaman,' he said, 'kept a community together. They did this in four ways. First, they helped people stay calm when bad things happened. Second, a good shaman helped keep the peace between people when any issues arose or tensions occurred. Third, they protected people from attempts by bad shaman to do harm. And fourth, the presence of a good shaman meant people didn't feel a need to leave the community to join a community with an effective shaman.' Living in the Amazon Basin is very different to life in modern workplaces. But given the universal nature of the human condition and the dynamics of our groups, Bartolo's description is a match to the contribution of effective workplace leaders: helping people stay calm when bad things happen, keeping the peace between people, protecting the people from outside forces and avoiding the need for people to leave/resign to go elsewhere to work under a better leader.

Protecting the group from enemy raids and helping them in attack was a common responsibility of shaman across societies. From my wide reading of anthropology, any society that engaged in warfare and raiding, which covers almost all ancestral societies, had a shaman involved in the warfare or raiding. In the northern Pacific, every Haida war party was accompanied by a shaman.[21] On the Great Plains, Blackfeet always had a medicine man on a raid — information provided to them in their dreams was vital for the success and safety of the party. And when Māori war parties left home, a tohunga joined the expedition.

Many tasks in the job description of the shaman role are beyond the scope of workplace leaders! But one service provided by shaman is important for workplace leaders: explaining events. As Bartolo just said, shaman provided explanations of events that allowed people to move forwards. For workplace leaders, the implication is that people need to make sense of events. And making sense of events is easier if the explanation of the event is *plausible*.

An event in traditional Aboriginal society that required a plausible explanation was the death of a community member. That was one of the roles of healers, or medicine doctors, in Aboriginal society. In 1944, anthropologist A. P. Elkin published a study on medicine doctors of 80 Aboriginal nations. Elkin respectfully called the role, *persons of high degree*.[22] Whenever someone died, the band's person of high degree was required to explain the death. Aboriginal people generally held the view that death was not due to natural reasons but caused by human interference — from a curse inflicted by an enemy. When a person was dying, they often whispered in the ear of the medicine doctor the name of the person who was to blame for their death, but even if the dying person didn't name the culprit, the medicine doctor did so soon after the death occurred, including the direction in which the culprit lived and the group to which the culprit belonged. It might have been two or three years before the culprit was discovered and retribution was then organised.[23]

In the workplace, the plausibility principle guides leaders to communicate candidly to staff, especially when communicating negative news. If a leader's explanation of a decision is *implausible*, then people are likely to fret and gossip with others in an attempt to make sense of what's going on. People make up their own story with the fragments of apparently plausible information they have been able to access. Even if the news is bad, people are less anxious with a reliable explanation than if they can't make sense of what's happening.

For example, there was one managing director who had a large team reporting to him. The team was too large to function well and was restructured to reduce the number of direct reports to the managing director. One of the functions, the legal team, was moved 'down' so that its leader now reported to one of the direct reports of the managing director, rather than directly to the managing director himself. The problem was that neither the managing director nor the head of the legal department fronted up to the legal team and explained what was happening and why. It would have been a straightforward explanation, even if a disappointing outcome. The two leaders probably avoided meeting the lawyers because they didn't want to face the barrage of questions from lawyers feeling diminished in status by being dropped down the hierarchy. The problem is that when leaders don't face up to communicating disappointing news, it makes it worse because people have no plausible explanation. In this case, by not meeting with the legal team, the senior leaders left it to the lawyers to make up their own explanation, which became increasing sensationalised.

A good example of a leader who helped her team make sense of a major change was a department head in another organisation who called her team together immediately after the organisation announced a potential merger. She briefed members of her department on what she knew, what she didn't yet know, about the steps that would likely unfold and of her commitment to keep her team informed. One of her team told me how appreciative the team members were and the trust they had in their leader that she would 'look out for them'. What the leader told them made sense and they didn't need to engage in conjecture. This aspect of the shaman role — removing uncertainty and making events plausible — is an important role of workplace leaders.

Actions for Workplace Leaders

Ancestral societies regarded social cohesion as a top priority. They employed a significant number of initiatives and invested substantial time and resources to achieve that objective. The consequences of not investing in social cohesion would have been the likely disintegration of the community and increased conflict with neighbours. For very similar reasons, maintaining social cohesion is a vital element of effective workplace leadership.

1. **Devote time and resources to social cohesion:** Ancestral societies devoted significant time and resources to maintain social unity. Gatherings for various reasons — trading, marriage, initiation,

settling grievances, festivals — were a major part of the calendar. People took a break from anything else they might have otherwise been doing and, if they were hosting the gathering, put time and effort into stocking up on food. Why bother? Because without investing in social cohesion, communities were less harmonious places to live, bickering escalated into feuds and groups risked disintegration. What if ancestral leaders had to do an annual budget of resources as workplaces do? Imagine if, upon the ancestral budget committee convening, a young colleague floated the novel idea, 'We could save a lot of effort and food this year by cutting a festival, or perhaps we could skip hosting the trading camp this year?' Ha. Imagine the astonished reaction of the leadership group to such a hairbrained idea. The chief, recovering their wits first, would have spoken for the cabinet, 'No. We are not about to sacrifice social cohesion.'

2. **Engage in healthy chit-chat as leaders:** As we covered at the start of this chapter, quality relationships require a healthy level of chit-chat. Leaders at every level need to be part of the chit-chat — with individual team members and at group gatherings. Bonding happens when we talk about topics other than task and technical subjects. If a leader doesn't engage in chit-chat, bonding can't occur and relationships suffer. Leaders need to engage with people, for example, on a Monday morning to chat about weekend activities, engage in brief corridor conversations, at the beginning of team meetings (in-person or on-line) and at the beginning of regular reviews with staff. It also means that leaders have to be prepared to share a little of their own 'news' — being appropriately open with staff is reciprocated, and being closed and secretive is also reciprocated. Easy informal conversations are not time-wasting — they are mandatory for people to bond and to maintain harmony.

3. **Establish team bonding rituals:** As well as bonding individually with team members, a leader needs to ensure that their team gathers periodically for informal interactions. One leader, Daniel, shared his experience of fixing team tension by way of grooming. He was a participant on one of our leadership programs. His organisation operates in a heavy industry sector. On the leadership

program, Daniel and his colleagues returned for a day of training, four months after the prior day when we'd covered the subject of grooming and bonding. At the start of this return day's workshop, each participant shared just one way they'd applied the leadership ideas covered in the last training session. Daniel volunteered to share first. He told us about the tension that had existed between members of his team. He said that the chit-chat topic provided the breakthrough — he realised that up until now he and his team spent no time bonding, so no wonder relationships were poor, he said. He also realised that the fix should be easy — he just needed to provide an environment where chit-chat would naturally occur. 'So,' he said, 'the first Friday morning back at work after the last training session, I took the team out for coffee. What a difference! Almost all the topics of conversation were chit-chat — hobbies and the like. From that moment, team tension disappeared. Even a new team member who'd had trouble fitting in suddenly was more included. Friday morning coffee is now our ritual.'

4. **Establish village bonding rituals:** As with team bonding, bonding amongst members of the 'village' and the 'division' in a large organisation is vital for people to be unified. Rituals are necessary. Village leadership teams should decide the ritual(s) that best suit their group — for some groups, a regular informal barbeque is ideal. For others, gatherings in a hotel function room might be more suitable. An important element of a ritual is that it is a regular event and has the characteristic that 'this is what we do'. Celebratory events should be held through the year, with a mix of events at the village level and the divisional level (or in medium-sized organisations, the whole organisation). The Skills Group in New Zealand has experienced significant growth and has grown to about 300 staff. Staff are spread across the major cities of the country. To ensure unity of the group, the company invests in annual gatherings of all staff. The investment involves both lost productivity and the cost of travel and accommodation. Despite the significant cost, the leadership team invests in the activity as a critical mechanism to avoid the company splintering into divisional entities. This became

especially important after the Group grew significantly beyond the natural village size of 150 people. The executive team is of the view that the cost of the initiative is returned in the intangible benefit of staff commitment and through the enhanced productivity that comes from people being closely connected and knowing who to go to to get things done.

5. **Invest in bonding, even if working remotely:** The importance of chit-chat and bonding rituals of ancestral communities helps leaders who are leading dispersed teams or where team members spend a high proportion of their week working from home. Bonding is obviously easier when people are physically together. But at a distance, chit-chat can still happen — we have the technology. As well as formal reviews with distant people, leaders should have informal contact replicating as best we can the informal conversations that happen when people work in the same office. In one of my HR Director roles I had team members in different parts of the world. One of the team, Helen Connor, was in Manchester, UK and I was in Sydney. Our informal catch-up time was on Fridays, early evening my time and Friday morning Helen's time. We chatted about our week. I shared bits of news from Sydney head office and Helen shared her news from the UK office. The call was different to our regular review meetings — task topics were left for our regular reviews and not mixed in with this chit-chat call. After I'd left the organisation, Helen told me that she really missed those Friday conversations.

6. **Give gifts:** Gift giving and sharing resources is and was a practice of all ancestral societies (and in terms of trading, the only society I have come across that didn't engage in trading was Waorani who isolated themselves in the Amazon jungle). Think about the colleagues you are close to. They are probably the people with whom you have a sharing relationship — you share ideas and resources and help each other where you can.

7. **Organise transfers across departments:** Ancestral societies carefully orchestrated blending of their communities — their villages and divisions. In the ancestral setting, genetic diversity provides a

compelling reason to do so. But blending has an additional benefit that applies to any large group — it breaks down barriers between individuals and between sub-groups. Earlier in the chapter I mentioned that a steady stream of transfers across divisions of a workplace is important to facilitate an appreciation of the contribution of each division and to avoid an 'us and them' mentality that can so easily and naturally develop. Senior leaders should institute ways to override leaders who selfishly try to hold on to their people. One way is for the top team to orchestrate transfers of people and not allow a lower-level leader to block a move. Another way is for internal roles to be publicised, and to allow people to apply for a role without requiring their immediate manager's approval. Then to ensure a transfer happens, any internal person appointed to a role must be freed up for the transfer with 30 days' notice.

8. **Use orientation as initiation:** Good organisations will already invest in formal orientation of new staff. Workplace induction or orientation is a long-standing practice because it's so fundamental to creating a sense of belonging. As mentioned earlier, there are three key objectives of quality orientation. One objective is to make explicit for new people the rules of belonging — the culture of the organisation and the basic operational rules. The second objective is to create a fraternity of new starters. The third is for leaders to use orientation as a key vehicle for them to reach new staff — to share their view about the culture, to gain support to the mission of the organisation and to gain emotional connection with their followers.

9. **Give plausible explanations for decisions:** We covered earlier the importance of candid communication by leaders. People search for meaning by making sense of events. Candid communication makes the reasons for decisions *plausible*, which saves people making up their own story. Good leaders explain to people what's going on and why. When the news is bad, good leaders have the courage to face up to people to give them the truth. On the other hand, when the news is bad, poor leaders tend to make up part of the story in an attempt to soften the blow for people (or to ease the

emotional strain on themselves as the communicator). But thanks to the power of chit-chat, people check out what's going on and are particularly attentive to bits of information on the grapevine that fills any gap in the explanation provided by a leader.

Leadership of human groups is a challenging occupation. The timeless wisdom of ancestral leaders gifts to workplace leaders a set of practical principles. The nine 'positive' principles we've covered help workplace leaders know the actions that will make the biggest difference. And the two 'negative' principles help leaders know the traps to avoid. This wisdom of first leaders helps workplace leaders achieve the objective of group harmony and performance. After all, work should be enjoyable and productive.

Conclusion and Resources

WHEREAS WORKPLACES HAVE BEEN practising leadership for about 100 years, First Nation societies have been refining it for millennia. They have been at it long enough to work out what works and what doesn't. They've been at it long enough to work out the component pieces that make up the comprehensive social system. It's long enough, for example, to work out the solutions to how populations should be structured, the attributes that leaders have to have in their character to be successful, to give followers a say in the selection of their leader and the investment needed to keep a community together.

The ideal time to learn a subject is just when the student is ready. I regret that I didn't discover the significance of ancestral leadership earlier in my career. But then again, if the subject had presented itself too early, when I hadn't had the experiences I have had, maybe I wouldn't have been ready for the lessons and would have missed seeing their significance for workplace leadership. In my first discussions with Ngila Loitamany Johnson and William Kinanta Sadera seven years ago, it was as though a light was switched on that illuminated the possibilities. When I asked them about leadership in their society, I had no idea that I was about to launch on such an adventure. But their answers inspired and intrigued me. I was inspired by the misty-eyed reaction of people at the very mention of their leader's name. And I was intrigued to discover the answer to their leadership success and the component pieces that explained the whole picture. I was then excited to embark on a learning journey to identify the patterns across different societies and how that wisdom can assist workplace leaders.

The people I met inspired me, and I hope through the vehicle of this book, they have inspired you, too, to begin your journey in embracing the Principles of First Leadership. A summary list of the actions recommend for each principle is provided in an Appendix that follows the Acknowledgements section.

While the principles provide a comprehensive blueprint of workplace leadership, there is no requirement to implement the practices in the order in which I have distilled them. Start anywhere and build from there.

Your journey is likely to mean applying the principles to your own leadership and also to the leadership practices of your organisation. For individual leaders, in addition to ensuring that respect for others is your overarching style, you might start by making more time for easy chit-chat with your team or by playing a more active part in the professional development of individuals. Likewise, at the organisation level, the possibilities for transforming the leadership systems don't require you to adopt all the principles at once, nor in a set order. Some organisations might start by improving their selection of leaders to ensure that the number one attribute, respect, is given greater prominence. Some might start by giving followers more influence in the selection of the leader and by giving greater recognition to the appointment of leaders. Some organisations start by implementing the family/village structure, and even then, some have implemented the principle slowly rather than as a major restructuring initiative.

To help you with your journey, more information on First Leadership is available at www.firstleadersbook.com. The website includes resources for:

a. individual leaders

b. senior executives

c. facilitating group discussions for leadership development

d. facilitating group discussions for Reconciliation Action.

The facilitation resources help leadership teams or leaders on workshops discuss the implications of First Nations insight for their own leadership and the leadership practices in their organisation. Facilitating group discussions on the Principles of First Leadership also contribute significantly to an organisation's Reconciliation Action Plans to enhance the respect for First Nations wisdom and leadership practices.

In applying the wisdom we have covered in this book, start with any of the Principles that are most relevant to you and progress in whatever sequence makes sense. But above all, start.

.

Photo Gallery

HERE ARE PHOTOS OF some of the amazing people I met and two of the ceremonial centres I visited. Please note that the photos may include, and in time will include, images of people who have died.

Ju/'hoansi Bushman, Komtsa, enjoyed talking about his teenage years living the old way. He talked about the three warnings given to an errant camp member who was causing a pain in someone else's heart.

!Gao !Naioi, who spent his teenage years living the old ways of Kalahari Bushmen, demonstrates his hunting skills. To help towards social harmony, meat from a successful hunt was shared according to a strict protocol.

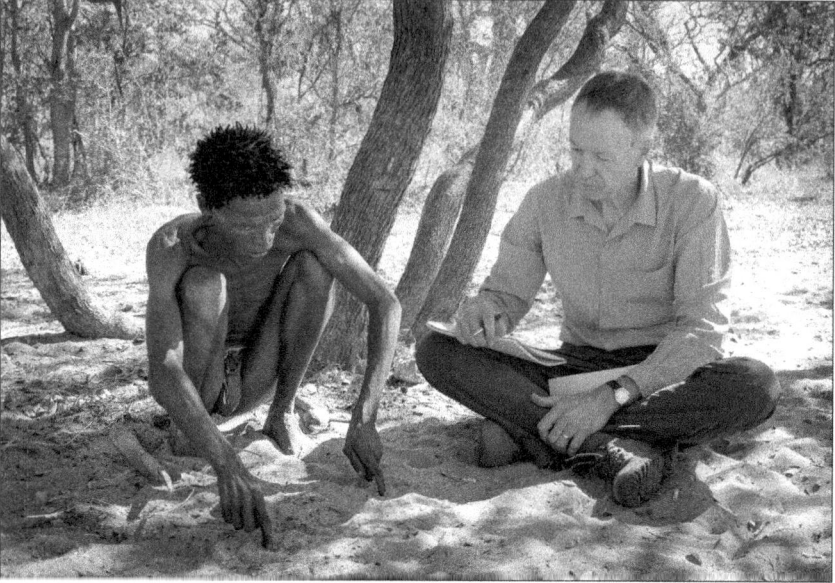

!Gao !Naioi draws in the sand showing the positioning of huts in a traditional Bushman camp. The key leaders took the high-status positions.

Himba headwoman, Hyknodombu, started her own village when her leadership succession plans were blocked by an ambitious rival.

One of the leadership attributes nominated by young Himba woman, Urprua, is that a village leader has no favourites: 'A leader with favourites is like a grandmother who has favourites amongst the grandchildren.'

Himba headman Umuna begins another day — possibly involving settling any squabbles between members of his village.

Tjikoko demonstrates the traditional way of starting a fire. We'd just trekked across the grass-less plain to a one-room shop to buy bags of maize so all the people of his village could benefit from our thank-you gift to Tjikoko.

As the first person I interviewed about First Nations leadership, Maasai Ngila Loitamany Johnson holds a special place in the story of this book.

As a five-year-old, William Kinanta Sadera (left) began school breaks by looking for his village in the Maasai Mara. Using his village as an example, William explained how clans are blended within a village which ensures harmony across clans. Here he is pictured with a village owner (or olopeny enkang).

Maasai Nasha Kitonga described how her chief knows her as an individual. It was a foreign concept to her that a leader would not know her amongst a group of 400 people.

Samburu senior elder Lmusari (Mark) Lenanyankerra told me that a chief is given all powers, including casting people out, so you want those powers in the hands of a decent person.

Pintupi Marlene Nampitjinpa Ross was 11 years of age before she saw a European. By skin name, Marlene and my wife Jude are sisters.

Respected Pintupi elders Ampi Robinson (L) and Mimala Wheeler showed me around Walungurru and told me stories about leaders helping their community.

As the sun sets, Pintupi women choose the site for the camp fire. While the kangaroo tails and damper cooked, they told us stories.

Respected Pintupi leader Irene Wilpinta, left, with Arrernte Alan Palmer. Alan told me how his great uncle encouraged Alan's curiosity and tailored his teaching to suit Alan's pace.

As a teenager, Māori Keri Opai was fortunate to have an elder who patiently taught him, encouraging Keri's curiosity. The elder 'fed me small bites of knowledge and then bigger bites, never going backwards'.

Taiporohēnui marae in the Taranaki region is the centre for gatherings, festivals and celebrations (hui) for Keri Opai's community.

Kichwa couple, María Grefa and shaman Bartolo Aguinda. María told me, 'I hear that women even become presidents of a country and that makes me very happy!'

My guide into the Amazon, José Aguinda, grew up in a traditional Kichwa community. A community consisted of 10 to 12 families numbering up to about 70 people.

At a bend in the Shiripuno River there was just enough room to camp. I was about to learn about the danger of an attack by Tagaeri.

In places, the Shiripuno River is so narrow with thick curtains of jungle that an attack by Tagaeri would have been impossible to avoid.

We slept a night in Waorani Aboke Tega's hut and he told us about his first interaction with Europeans. Pictured from left to right, Anderson Aguinda, translator Jorge Espinosa, Aboke, local boat driver David Yasa and guide José Aguinda.

Penti Baihua is the elder of the Waorani Babeno community in the Yasuni National Park in the Ecuadorian Amazon.

Only since 1958 has Waorani society shifted from the most violent society to a relatively peaceful one. I was told that women much prefer today's relatively peaceful relationships with 'others'.

Armed with blowpipe, Ginto Tega leads us into the Waorani jungle on a hunting exercise. No monkey suffered as a consequence of the demonstration.

My Haida Gwaii host, Elsie Gale, takes the opportunity of a fine day to dry seaweed. When she was young, her grandmother entrusted her with cultural knowledge.

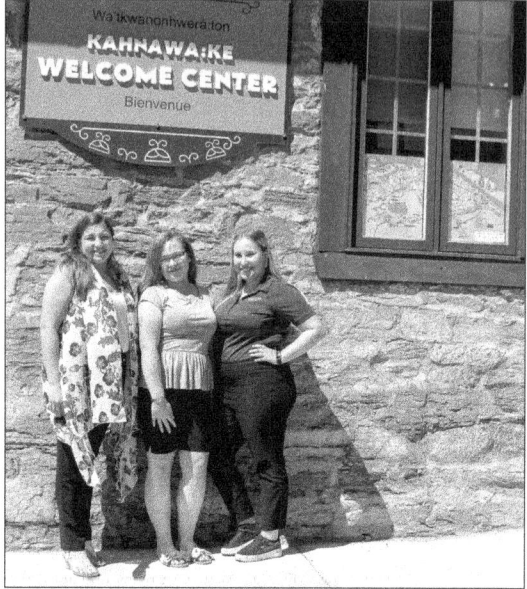

The team at the appropriately named Kahnawà:ke Welcome Center who organised my visit to Mohawk territory. From left, Kimberly Kaniehténhawe Cross, Ravyn Regis and Emma Kahente Ouimet.

As for all the Haudenosaunee (or Iroquois) confederacy nations, the longhouse is the centre of a Mohawk community's gatherings, ceremonies and decision making.

Mohawk medicine man, Joe McGregor at Kahnawà:ke, described the process on the rare occasion that a chief is 'dehorned' — which occurs mainly if the chief disregards the voice of the women who speak for the community.

As for the Kahnawà:ke community, First Nations societies have, since time immemorial, invested significant time, effort and resources in initiatives that support group cohesion.

Acknowledgements

WHILE WRITING THIS BOOK, Jude and I lived on the land of the Wangal people (we have only recently moved out of Sydney). Wangal country is on the southern edge of the Parramatta River leading into Sydney Harbour. To acknowledge the traditional owners of the land where I wrote this book, I was keen to meet with a local elder. I was fortunate to be introduced to Dennis Foley, a Gai-mariagal elder of the north side of the harbour. Dennis is the last of the story holders of his people and one of the last in the whole Sydney area. Dennis responded immediately to my email and that afternoon we sat on a bench in Hyde Park in the centre of Sydney and chatted. I was able to acknowledge him and his ancestors as the traditional owners and custodians of the land.

I most want to acknowledge and thank the First Nations people I've met and the people who assisted me in my adventure. When friends and clients become aware of my adventure, they invariably ask how I managed to arrange visits to such interesting places. As I express my thanks here, in the order of my visits, I'll explain the circumstances that led to my good fortune of meeting the wonderful people I did.

The first 'thank you' is to Maasai Ngila Loitamany Johnson who, being the first person I met to ask about ancestral leadership, launched me on my quest. We met when Jude and I holidayed in Africa and stayed at the safari camp, Sirikoi, in Kenya where Ngila works as a guide. *Ashe*, Ngila, for your enthusiasm, your generosity in sharing, and your encouragement. You lit my fire. Thank you for being Jude's and my friend. Special *ashe*, too, to William Kinanta Sadera who has also become Jude's and my close friend. William tirelessly checked what I had written about Maasai society and contributed vital information. William introduced me to his young relatives, Wilson Nashula Kipira and Grace Nyamalo Sadera, who provided their critical perspective as young Maasai. *Ashe* Wilson and Grace. And *ashe oleng'* to other Maasai who shared with me, in order: Koyaki Ole Sopia, James Lenkai Sadera, Eric Ole Kasana, Legei Leiro and Nasha Kitonga.

From the beginning, I had in mind visiting the Himba people in Namibia. Jude and I had visited a Himba community 20 years earlier and I was keen to learn more about their society. A big attraction was that Himba, like Maasai, overwhelmingly continue to live their traditional lifestyle. Shortly after resolving to investigate ancestral leadership wisdom, I was introduced to an Australian travel guide and professional photographer, Ben McRea (benmcraephotography.com), who conducts tours to Namibia and in particular to Himba villages. When Ben and I talked on the phone and I explained my purpose, he said that in addition to his close Himba contacts, he is also friendly with two Bushmen communities and he would be happy to take us there as well. My heart skipped. For me, the Bushmen of the Kalahari carry a special aura. With his local Namibian guide, Morne Griffiths, Ben guided Jude and me to the Bushmen and Himba. Thank you, Ben and Morne, for introducing us to your friends and because of their respect for you, they welcomed us and enjoyed sharing their knowledge. And as an added bonus, thanks for being good company to travel with.

Thank you to the Ju/'hoansi Bushmen I met, all three having lived the old life: *mi ui i!a* Komtsa, !Gao !Naioi, !Asa !Amace and translator Ghau (who was with me for my meetings with !Gao and !asa).

Okuhepa shenene to the Himba people in the Epupa Falls district who generously welcomed us: Hyknodombu, Tjikoko, Utjindisa (James) Hembinda, Urprua, Umuna and Timoteus.

After the Namibian leg we revisited Kenya to continue conversations with Maasai and to see Ngila again. Before reaching his Sirikoi camp, we went further north in Kenya to meet the Samburu nation. Here I was fortunate to meet Lmusari (Mark) Lenanyankerra, a guide at the Sarara camp. Mark is an elder of his community. While at Sarara I also met with two Samburu women, Agatha Nashangai and Nanemu. *Ashe oleng'* Mark, Agatha and Nanemu.

The next nation was Haida in Canada. From reading anthropology, I'd developed a keen interest in the coastal nations of north-western America and Canada. In traditional times, with their abundant environment, coastal people lived in permanent villages. That was an interesting comparison to the nomadic or semi-nomadic people I had met up to that point. At about this time, Jude decided to attend a conference on Vancouver Island. 'Great,' I said, 'While you're at the conference, I'll try to visit Canadian First Nations.' At that point I didn't know the two nations would be Haida and Mohawk. Things fell nicely into place, mainly because of welcoming and encouraging people. As luck would have it, at just the right time as I was thinking about the Pacific Northwest, I received a tourism brochure advertising trips — I wasn't interested in joining an organised group but a photo of an unidentified lodge caught my eye. The greenery of the northern Pacific is the greenest in the world; greener than Ireland. My hunch that this was the north Pacific was confirmed through a quick Internet search matching the photo to a lodge, Haida House, on Haida Gwaii. I contacted the lodge manager and we talked so I could explain my project. She generously suggested I contact Elsie Gale at Masset on the north of the island. I contacted Elsie, received an instantly warm response and we arranged the visit. Elsie was a wonderful host and introduced me to some of her friends. *Haw'aa*, Elsie and the wonderful people I met on Haida Gwaii: Merle Andersen, Leona Davidson, Ben Davidson, John Brent Bennett and Leo Gagnon.

At the same time as investigating the Pacific coast possibilities, I reached out to a Canadian contact. Liz Weaver is co-CEO of the Tamarack Institute, a community support organisation. Liz and I had met when we'd been keynote speakers at a conference a few years before. We'd stayed in touch. I reached out to Liz to see if she had contact with and could introduce me to any First Nations communities. She said she unfortunately did not, but she introduced me to her colleague, Mark Holmgren. Mark and I spoke and he told me about his work supporting the Kahnawà:ke Mohawk community. Even growing up in outback Australia, I knew the Mohawk nation. Again, I felt lucky — honoured — that I might meet representatives of such a significant nation. Through Mark, I was introduced to Kimberly Kaniehténhawe Cross at the Kahnawà:ke Welcome Center. I emailed Kimberly and then we spoke on the phone. She enthusiastically agreed to arrange my visit of May 2018. A special *niá:wen* to Kimberly for your immediate support and tireless work in organising such a busy agenda to meet with leaders of your community who generously made the time to meet me. In order of the people I met, I sincerely thank Kenneth Deer, Dwayne Stacey, Joe McGregor, Chief Kahsennenhawe (Gus) Sky-Deer, Teyowisonte Tommy Deer, Grand Chief Joe Norton, Steve Bonspiel, Emma Kahente Ouimet, Otsitsakenra Charlie Patton, Fran Beauvais and Kevin Kanahsohon Deer. *Niá:wen*. It was a great honour to meet you and to be entrusted to pass on the knowledge you shared with me. And thank you, Liz Weaver and Mark Holmgren for your support.

How did I get to travel down the Amazon of Ecuador? Jude and I have enjoyed many holidays with American friends Charles (Chuck) Bergman and Susan Mann. They took great interest in my project and encouraged me in my research — thank you both. Chuck mentioned he'd travelled several times on birding conservation trips into the Ecuadorian jungle with a guide and good friend, José Raul Aguinda Grefa (also known as Waira). Chuck said, prophetically, 'Waira will keep you safe in the jungle.' Chuck introduced me to José and, with the help of Google Translate converting my English into José's Spanish and vice versa, we organised our trip deep into the jungle. *Gracias*, José, for your leadership, happy disposition and jungle knowledge. Our relationship developed into a friendship during and after the trip and we are in regular contact. *Gracias* also to José's son Anderson for his camp and cooking contribution, Jorge Espinosa for his indefatigable translating of Spanish to English and David Yasa for his river navigation skills and local knowledge. *Waponi* to the Waorani Babeno community who gave us a warm welcome and passionately shared their knowledge with me: Penti Baihua, Omene Baihua, Ginto Tega and Aboke Tega.

After we returned from the jungle, José introduced me to his shaman father, Humberto Bartolo Aguinda Tapuy. Bartolo and I, again with Jorge translating, talked about his role of shaman in Kichwa society — *pagrachnu*, Bartolo. And *pagrachnu* to José's mother, María Grefa, for sharing your perspective on the role of women in traditional Kichwa society.

I experienced frequent moments of serendipity. One of the first books on Aboriginal societies I read as part of this research was Donald Thomson's book, *Bindibu Country*, describing his 1950s visits to Pintupi (Bindibu) country in the Western Desert of Central Australia. Visiting Pintupi went to the top of my wish list. First, the dry outback of Australia is the land of my youth so I have a strong affinity with the environment and second, the impact of European contact with Pintupi is relatively recent. Subsequently I was discussing my project with a friend, Scott Stirling. Scott is the CEO of the charity Red Dust which supports remote Aboriginal communities. Scott and I had become friends when I ran leadership workshops for his prior employer. Scott was supportive of my project and introduced me to several colleagues to check that they were also supportive. He then invited me to join one of their community visits to Northern Australia. Of the communities his organisation supports, he said the one that I would most likely visit was Walungurru in Pintupi country. 'Scott, Pintupi country is at the top of my list of dreams!' Red Dust is greatly appreciated in the local communities, so I was given a warm welcome in Walungurru. This appreciation of Red Dust reflects on the nature of their staff over the years and on Red Dust's focus of enhancing local capability. It reflects on the wonderful team that led my trip, Brett Wheeler, Paul Saverin and Tatiana Marinho. Thank you, Scott, Brett, Paul and Tatiana. *Palya lingku* to the Walungurru elders and emerging community leaders who I had the honour of meeting: Irene Wilpinta, Joe Young, Monica (Ampi) Robinson, Maureen (Mimala) Wheeler, Marlene Nampitjinpa Ross and Farren Major.

Another Red Dust staff member, Alan Palmer, had just started with the organisation. Alan is of the Arrernte nation at Alice Springs. Alan trusted me with the Arrernte knowledge that he was comfortable and permitted to share to a non-initiated person such as me. Through our skin names he and I are cousins and we maintain regular contact. One of the most stimulating experiences I have had was the travelling seminar Alan gave me on our drive from Alice Springs to Walungurru; the 640 kilometres (400 miles) slipped by to the sound of stones from the gravel road hitting the undercarriage of the car. *Kele mwerre*, Alan.

At the outset I was keen to learn about Māori society. New Zealand is our neighbour and I have a warm regard for New Zealanders. A client and close friend, Anna McNicholl was very supportive of my project and introduced me to one of the leaders in her organisation, Theresa Rongonui.

Theresa is one of the younger generation inspired by her departed ancestors to connect with her Māori culture. Theresa began my Māori education. Another New Zealand client and close friend, Simon Batters, was also interested in my research and the leadership patterns I would discover. At that time, Simon had on his team a cultural leader, Keri Opai. Simon introduced us. Keri and I talked so I could outline my project. He was keen to host me if an elder of his community approved my visit and permitted Keri to share his knowledge. Keri introduced me to Peeti Wātene. I called Peeti to introduce myself. 'I can't talk right now,' she whispered politely. 'I am with the children and while at school we don't speak English.' We talked a day or so later and Peeti approved my visit and for Keri to share his knowledge with me and obviously to share with readers of this book. Keri welcomed me to his country around Taranaki on the North Island and was an exceptionally knowledgeable, thoughtful and generous host. I greatly value our friendship. *Ngā mihi nui* Keri, Peeti, Anna, Theresa and Simon.

Early on I imagined that I would visit a Great Plains nation of North America. At the beginning of my project I had no fixed idea of the nation I would visit. Thanks to Amazon.com I became inspired by the Blackfeet nation. I downloaded a number of books on North American nations and Amazon.com quite rightly calculated that 'a top pick for me' was any book by James Willard Schultz. Schultz was a prolific writer of fiction and non-fiction from his time living with Piegan Blackfeet in the later part of the 19th Century. I quickly devoured Schultz's books for the quality of his writing and the anthropological information contained in his novels. That led me to the extensive non-fiction literature on Blackfeet — the literature is extensive because anthropology was emerging at the time that Blackfeet were still in touch with their traditional life. Blackfoot elder Darrell Norman was keen to host me and I planned to visit in May 2020. But unfortunately the COVID-19 pandemic hit and the trip had to be cancelled.

Charles Bergman, who introduced me to his Ecuadorian guiding friend, José, also gifted me the title of this book. We had brainstormed title ideas, at first in-person and then via email. After much toing-and-froing Chuck emailed what he called his final contribution: *First Leaders*. I loved the title instantly. The title succinctly captures the sentiment I was hoping to portray. Thank you, Chuck.

Sincere thanks to the women who enthusiastically shared their ideas to improve gender equity. I sought the input of my wife Jude (Tasker) and two of my nieces, Heather O'Keeffe and Nellie O'Keeffe. And I sought the opinions of a number of women whose life-path has fortunately connected with mine: Tracey Ayson, Vicki Baker, Sarah Bateup, Julie James, Liz Leverett, Darsha Masin, Anna McNicholl, Ruby Otero, Simone Robards, Nicole Sullivan, Sylvie Vanasse and Andria Wyman-Clarke. Thank you for your perspectives, insights and recommended actions.

A big thank you to my brother, Paul, who was chief reviewer of my manuscript. Paul has worked as a senior executive in the US and has extensive leadership experiences to draw upon as he reviewed each chapter. He tirelessly read every draft of every chapter and then the entire manuscript. As a reviewer, Paul has the ideal capability of conceptual insight coupled with attention to detail. Thank you, Paul.

To my editor, David Brewster (davidbrewsterwriter.com), thanks for polishing my manuscript. David has a background in business, so in addition to making valuable readability suggestions, he asked insightful questions about the implications of my research for workplace leaders. Thanks to my book designer, Sheila Parr (sheilaparr.com). I've had the pleasure of working with Sheila on my three books and I admire her creativity and project management. She demonstrates that book cover and interior design is a creative art form of its own.

I have the good fortune of being married to my best friend. Jude and I support each other in our separate interests that give us energy, and encourage the other in our personal and professional growth. I am incredibly grateful for Jude's support and encouragement in this project. She was entirely supportive of my desire to visit First Nations people so I could conduct primary research — and for me to enjoy the adventure and stimulation the visits provided. We shared some visits and some I did alone. She saw the enjoyment I was having and the personal growth I was experiencing. And from her experience as a senior executive, she shared with me the significance that ancestral wisdom provides to workplace leaders. Thank you, Jude.

Checklist

HERE IS A SUMMARY checklist of the Actions of the 11 Principles of First Leadership recommended in each chapter.

Principle 1: Organisation Structure

The objective of this principle is to organise your population in a way that helps people belong and that best enables them to perform. Ancestral wisdom identifies what works for people, and how to avoid dysfunctional organisation design. To achieve that objective:

1. Keep organisational structure on your radar

2. Design your organisation around 'family units' of about seven people

3. Organise leadership teams with about seven members

4. Design 'villages' of *up to about* 150 people

5. Structure village membership according to a compelling purpose

6. Organise villages into divisions

7. Monitor spans and layers

8. Avoid matrix reporting — ensure everyone is a member of a single family and village

9. Enable family and village members to work closely together.

Principle 2: Nature of Leadership

The objective of this principle is to create leadership roles that fit with the appropriate organisation structure. At higher leadership roles, leaders need to accept their roles as the equivalent of village leadership roles, as leaders of a division or leaders of a nation. To achieve that objective:

1. Be reassured that groups require leaders

2. Appoint leaders at the levels that match the organisation structure

3. Avoid unnecessary leadership layers

4. Prepare leaders for their roles

5. Ensure leaders operate at the level required of their role

6. Resolve conflicts

7. Ensure leaders act as guardians of group membership.

Principle 3: Attributes of Leadership

The objective of this principle is for organisations to specify the characteristics of leaders that First Nation societies know work. To achieve that objective, at **the organisation level:**

1. Define leadership attributes

2. Hire and develop on the behaviours that demonstrate *respect for people*

3. Hold to account disrespectful leaders

4. Provide tools to help leaders be generous

5. Train leaders in people leadership

6. Conduct regular staff surveys that report down to the team level.

For **individual leaders** to achieve the objective:

1. Beware random acts of anger and bad language
2. Be generous
3. Demonstrate respect for individuals
4. Schedule regular time with your people
5. Treat people equally — no favourites
6. Communicate openly when delegating work
7. Follow protocols for respectful meetings.

Principle 4: Selecting Leaders

The objective of this principle is for organisations to increase their success of selecting leaders by adopting the processes proven by ancestral societies. To achieve that objective:

1. Take care and time in selecting leaders
2. Select leaders *as if* the appointment is for life
3. Involve direct reports in leadership selection
4. Give preference to internal candidates
5. Value a proven cultural fit
6. Favour stability of the executive team
7. Identify a personal leadership legacy
8. Prepare the next generation.

Principle 5: Appointments and Status of Leaders

The objective of this principle is for organisations to decide how to signal the significance of the appointment of a leader — a signal to the leader and to the followers the significance of leadership responsibilities. To achieve that objective:

1. Mark the appointment of a leader
2. Have a conversation with a new leader
3. Present a symbol of leadership to new leaders
4. Remember that culturally sensitive status symbols are acceptable
5. Convene development programs for new leaders
6. Provide offices to leaders to enable conversations
7. Don't separate leaders from their people.

Principle 6: Checks on Leadership Power

The objective of this principle is for organisations to monitor the way in which leaders use their power, so that on the rare occasion a leader misuses their power, remedial action can be taken. Ancestral societies worked out that even with great care in leadership selection, the process is not infallible and corrective action is occasionally required in the interests of the community. To achieve that objective:

1. Develop a mindset that there should be checks on leadership power
2. Explain power expectations
3. Educate leaders about the checks on their power
4. Ensure senior leaders model the good use of power
5. Senior leaders coach other leaders
6. Develop mechanisms to identify use of power:
   a. Surveys
   b. Skip interviews
   c. Listen to the aunties and uncles
   d. Listen to HR
7. Develop a culture of addressing poor leadership
8. Reinforce the practice of three warnings.

Principle 7: Clarity of Culture

The objective of this principle is for organisations to decide the key dimensions of their culture and the extent to which individual autonomy is to be regulated in the interests of the group. To achieve that objective:

1. Acknowledge the importance of culture

2. Ensure there are benefits to individuals in belonging

3. Decide the extent of individual freedoms

4. State your values

5. Express values as behaviours

6. Address deviations from the standards of behaviour

7. Demonstrate confidence in existing staff to be part of a culture change

8. Implement initiatives for social cohesion.

Principle 8: Individual Identity Through Learning

The objective of this principle is to ensure individual identity within the collective and to help people grow. To achieve that objective:

1. Create an individual learning focus

2. Encourage managers to have a genuine interest in individuals

3. Task immediate managers as developers of staff

4. Develop a mentoring culture

5. Choose a term for describing individual learning focus

6. Use low-budget teaching methods

7. Tailor the pace of teaching to the individual

8. Give elders a role in teaching

9. Use stories.

Principle 9: Gender Equity — To Avoid a Feature of Ancestral Life

The objective of this principle is to ensure that the organisation is free of bias, especially gender bias and inequity. To achieve that objective:

1. Ensure awareness of gender inequity

2. Lead from the top

3. Fix discriminatory pay practices

4. Implement gender-friendly policies

5. Ensure progression is independent of gender:

    a. Determine talent pools

    b. Develop and prepare candidates for progression

    c. Establish promotion criteria

    d. Promote from the talent pool

6. Decide whether to have separate leadership programs

7. Involve men as mentors

8. Set targets

9. Increase the pipeline of female candidates.

Principle 10: Inter-Group Harmony — To Avoid a Feature of Ancestral Life

The objective of this principle is for organisations to be attuned to the signs of internal rivalry that sabotage overall performance and to be ready to take remedial action if and when required. To achieve that objective:

1. Foster a collaborative top team

2. Demonstrate that every group is valued

3. Establish the common purpose that connects people

4. Encourage actions not aspirations from top leaders

5. Individual leaders work at building friendly relations

6. Be ready for times when 'us and them' is most likely.

Principle 11: Initiatives for Social Cohesion

The objective of this principle is to invest in initiatives that support unity to overcome the tendency of groups a) to fracture and b) to engage in rivalry with other groups in the same organisation. To achieve that objective:

1. Devote time and resources to social cohesion

2. Engage in healthy chit-chat as leaders

3. Establish team bonding rituals

4. Establish village bonding rituals

5. Invest in bonding, even if working remotely

6. Give gifts

7. Organise transfers across departments

8. Use orientation as initiation

9. Give plausible explanations for decisions.

About the Author

ANDREW O'KEEFFE's interest in the human-side of workplaces goes back a long way. As a youngster growing up in the outback mining town of Broken Hill, Australia (Wilyakali country), Andrew was intrigued by the city's rich industrial relations history. He observed how the cooperative relationship between unions and management brought benefits to the whole community. This interest eventually led him to study industrial relations and economics at The University of Sydney. He started his career in the mining and manufacturing industries and later filled senior HR roles with large organisations including IBM and Cable & Wireless Optus. For the past 15 years, Andrew has run his own consulting and leadership education business, Hardwired Humans, with a focus on helping organisations and individual leaders align their leadership practices with human instincts. His two previous books are *Hardwired Humans* and *The Boss*. For most of his adult life, Andrew lived in Sydney (Wallumettagal and Wangal lands). He now lives near Urunga on the mid north coast of New South Wales, Australia (Gumbaynggirr country).

www.firstleadersbook.com

Notes

Introduction
1. Taylor 1911, e882, e858, e617

Chapter 1
1. see Barnard 2019. The term 'Bushmen' is controversial because of the derogatory translation from Afrikaans, but the people I met call themselves Bushmen so I am using the term.
2. Dunbar 1996
3. Chagnon 2014, e90
4. Chagnon 2014, e1805
5. Myers 1991, 27
6. Thomson 1975, 21
7. Spencer 1899, e189
8. Dawson 2009, 10
9. Dawson 2009, 10
10. Yost 1981, 99
11. Personal communication with Professor Laura Rival of The University of Oxford.
12. Ballara 1998, 161, 164
13. Ballara 1998, 124
14. Anderson 2015, e2530
15. Personal communication with William Kinanta Sadera.
16. Collison 1916, 127; Personal communication with a guide at Skidegate museum.
17. Murdock 1934, 356
18. Blackman 1982, 665
19. Gallagher 2007
20. Ewers 1958, e231, 671
21. Grinnell 1892, e44
22. Grinnell 1892, e2386
23. Personal communication with Teyowisonte Tommy Deer of the Kahnawà:ke Language and Cultural Center.

24. Morgan 1962, 26; Starna 1980, 377
25. Morgan 1962, 322
26. Van der Donck 2010 first published 1655, e1312
27. Starna 1980, 378
28. Gehring and Starna 1988, e294
29. Williams 2018, e1116
30. Gehring and Starna 1988, e505
31. Starna 1980, 375
32. Gehring and Starna 1988, e258
33. Gehring and Starna 1988, e300

Chapter 2

1. Lee 1979, 343
2. Shostak 1981, 220
3. Lee 1979, 351
4. Lee 1979, 397, 446
5. Lee 1979, 369
6. Boehm 2001
7. Chagnon 2014, e5883
8. Winiata 1967, 34
9. Winiata 1967, 33
10. Hiroa 1949, 333
11. Winiata 1967, 31
12. Morgan 1962, 26
13. Starna 1980, 377
14. Morgan 1962, 66–67
15. Morgan 1962, 62
16. Morgan 1962, 317
17. Personal communication with Teyowisonte Tommy Deer.

Chapter 3

1. Marshall Thomas 1989, e2358
2. Elder 1932, 388, 395
3. Elder 1932, 129, 173
4. Elder 1932, 403
5. Morgan 1852
6. Dawson 2009, 5
7. Morgan 1852, e1073
8. Part of the joy of language is that the origin of sayings can be debated. The main other contender of the possible source of the 'Buckley's' expression is the name of an old Melbourne department store. The store was named Buckley & Nunn, with the expression 'Buckley's' a play on the word 'Nunn' for 'none'.

9. Ewers 1958, e1502

10. Snow 1996, 46

11. Blackman 1982, 45

12. Lee 1979, 345

13. Anderson 2015, e1952

14. Ballara 1998, p145

15. Quoted in Williams 2018, e4859

Chapter 4

1. Blackman 1982

2. Hiroa 1949, 345

3. Marshall Thomas 1989, e2541, e2547

4. Dawson 2009, 5–6

Chapter 5

1. Williams 2018, e1835

2. Lorna Marshall 1976, 66

3. Chagnon 2014, e5739

4. Chagnon 2014, e5756

5. Dawson 2009, 5

6. Cahir 2019, 36–37; Courtenay 2020, e310

7. Collison 1916, 135–136

8. Collison 1916, 136

9. Swanton 1905, 155

10. Williams 2018, e5763

Chapter 6

1. Collison 1916, 209

2. Ewers 1958, e4141

3. Lee 1979, 54

Chapter 7

1. Robarchek 1998, 3

2. Robarchek 1998, 120

3. Robarchek 1998, 122

4. Robarchek 1998, 106, 143

5. Robarchek 1998, 102

6. Robarchek 1998, 159

7. Long 1971, 264

8. Myers 1991
9. Myers 1991, 99
10. Myers 1991, 48, 145
11. Myers 1991, 70
12. Myers 1991, 131
13. Hiroa 1949, 376–377

Chapter 8

1. Lee 1979, 98, 158, 438
2. Hiroa 1949, 361–2
3. Marshall Thomas 2006, 204, 206
4. Mark LeBusque is passionate about treating people as humans and this interest led him to start a consulting practice to spread his message: marklebusque.com
5. The best book I have read on the use of stories for workplace leaders is *Putting Stories to Work* by Shawn Callahan: Callahan 2016.

Chapter 9

1. Washburn and Lancaster 1968, e8861
2. Shostak 1981, 218
3. Salmond 2005, 106
4. Gehring and Starna 1988, e680
5. Wissler 1911, 27
6. Tench 2019, e2998
7. Hungry Wolf 1980, 110
8. Berndt 1977, 119
9. Shostak 1981, 218
10. Rosaldo and Lamphere 1974, 3
11. Blackman 1982, 51
12. Salmond 1975, 127
13. *Anh's Brush with Fame*, Series 5, 2020
14. 20-first consultancy, 2017 study. For Australia: CEW ASX Senior Executive Census 2020
15. Source: https://hbr.org/2018/07/why-women-volunteer-for-tasks-that-dont-lead-to-promotions
16. Sanday 1974, 189
17. Llewelyn-Davies 1981, 334
18. Ortner 1981, 67

Chapter 10

1. Robarchek 1998, 3

2. Rival 2002, 138
3. Keely 1996, e632
4. Keely 1996, e741
5. Tench 1793, e687–709
6. Idriess 2003, 45
7. Cruise 1824, e356
8. Ballara 1998, 56
9. Seaver 1824, e1145, e1267
10. Collison 1916, 101
11. Collison 1916, 104–105
12. Ewers 1958, e495
13. Ewers 1958, e1608, e2135, e2184. See also any of James Willard Schultz's novels based on his life with the Blackfeet, such as Schultz 1911.
14. Courtenay 2020, e1030
15. Myers 1991, 101
16. Meggitt 1965, 34
17. Lee 1979, 31
18. Davie 1929, e4636
19. Bloomfield 1776, 282
20. Catlin 1861, e539
21. Schultz 1914, e656
22. Blackman 1982, e665
23. Rival 2002, 51–52, 62

Chapter 11

1. Dunbar 2014
2. Lee 1979, 455
3. Lee 1979, 120
4. Robin Dunbar 1996
5. Spencer 1988, e173
6. Spencer 1899, e189
7. Spencer 1899, e2944
8. Spencer 1899, e2984
9. Spencer 1899, e2984
10. Marshall Thomas 2006, 216
11. Lee 1979, 182
12. Marshall Thomas 2006, 212–213
13. Marshall Thomas 2006, 222. See also the classic study on gift giving by Mauss 1950.
14. Marshall Thomas 2006, 223
15. Dawson 2009, 78
16. The Blackfoot Gallery Committee, 66

17. Hiroa 1949, 376
18. Hiroa 1949, 378
19. Dawson 2009, 30. For the male, this 12 month period was part of initiation into manhood.
20. Morgan 1962, 183
21. Swanton 1905, 40
22. Elkin 1977
23. Spencer 1899, e7609, e7619

Bibliography

Arrernte, Pintupi and Other Aboriginal Societies

Attenbrow, Val, *Sydney's Aboriginal Past, Investigating the archaeological and historical records*, UNSW Press, Australia 2010.

Cahir, Fred, *My Country All Gone The White Men Have Stolen It — The Invasion of Wadawurrung Country 1800-1870*, Australian History Matters, Australia, 2019.

Courtenay, Adam, *The Ghost and the Bounty Hunter: William Buckley, John Batman and the theft of Kulin country*, ABC Books, Australia 2020.

Berndt, Ronald M and Berndt, Catherine H, *The World of the First Australians*, Ure Smith, Australia, 1977 (first published 1964).

Blainey, Geoffrey, *The Story of Australia's People — The Rise and Fall of Ancient Australia*, Viking Australia 2015.

Davenport, Sue, Johnson, Peter and Yuwali, *Cleared Out, First Contact in the Western Desert*, Aboriginal Studies Press, Australia, 2005.

Dawson, James, *Australian Aborigines — The Languages and Customs of Several Tribes of Aborigines in the Western District of Victoria, Australia*, Cambridge University Press, USA 2009 (first published 1881).

Elkin, A P, *Aboriginal Men of High Degree: Initiation and Sorcery on the World's Oldest Tradition*, Inner Traditions, USA, 1977 (first published 1944).

Foley, Dennis and Read, Peter, *What the Colonists Never Knew — A History of Aboriginal Sydney*, National Museum of Australia Press, Australia 2020.

Howitt, Alfred W, *The Native Tribes of South-East Australia*, Cambridge University Press, USA, 2010 (first published 1904).

Idriess, Ion, *The Red Chief*, ETT Imprint, Australia, 2017 (first published 1953).

Lambert, J (ed), *Wise Women of the Dreamtime: Aboriginal Tales of the Ancestral Powers*, Inner Traditions International, USA, 1993.

Lockwood, Douglas, *I, The Aboriginal*, New Holland Publishers, Australia 2004.

Lockwood, Douglas, *The Lizard Eaters*, JB Books, Australia 2006.

Long, Jeremy P M, 'Arid Region Aborigines: The Pintupi' in Mulvaney, D and Golson, J (eds), *Aboriginal Man and Environment in Australia,* Australian National University Press, Australia 1971.

Maddock, Kenneth, *The Australian Aborigines: A Portrait of Their Society*, Allen Lane, UK 1972.

McKay, Helen F (ed), *Gadi Mirrabooka, Australian Aboriginal Tales from the Dreaming*, Libraries Unlimited, USA, 2001.

Meggitt, M J, *Desert People: A Study of The Walbiri Aborigines of Central Australia*, The University of Chicago Press, USA, 1965.

Morgan, John, *Life and Adventures of William Buckley* 1852, reprinted by The Perfect Library.

Myers, Fred R, *Pintupi Country, Pintupi Self: Sentiment, Place and Politics among Western Desert Aborigines*, University of California Press, USA, 1991.

Parker, K Langloh, *Wise Women of the Dreamtime — Aboriginal Tales of the Ancestral Powers*, Inner Traditions International, USA 1993.

Peasley, W J, *The Last of the Nomads*, Fremantle Press, Australia, 2009.

Reed, A W, *Aboriginal Stories*, Reed New Holland, Australia, 1994.

Rintoul, Simon, *Lowitja: the authorised biography of Lowitja O'Donoghue*, Allen & Unwin, Australia, 2020.

Spencer, Baldwin and Gillen, F J, *The Native Tribes of Central Australia*, first published Macmillan & Co, 1899.

Stanner, W E H, *The Dreaming & Other Essays*, Black Inc Agenda, Australia, 2009.

Tench, Watkin, *A Complete Account of the Settlement at Port Jackson: In New South Wales, Including an Accurate Description of the Situation of the Colony; of the Natives; Its Natural Productions: Taken on the Spot*, Hardpress, Australia 2019 (first published 1793).

Thomson, Donald, *Bindibu Country*, Thomas Nelson Limited, Australia, 1975.

Blackfeet

The Blackfoot Gallery Committee, *The Story of the Blackfoot People — Niitsitapiisinni*, Firefly Books, Canada 2013.

Catlin, George, *My Life Among the Indians* 1909 (First published 1861).

Ewers, John C, *The Blackfeet — Raiders of the Northwest Plains*, University of Oklahoma Press, 1958.

Gallagher, Marsha V (ed), *Travels in North America, 1832-1834 — A Concise Edition of the Journals of Prince Maximilian of Wied*, University of Oklahoma Press, USA 2017.

Grinnell, George B, *Blackfoot Lodge Tales — The Story of a Prairie People*, A Public Domain Book (first published 1892).

Grinnell, George B, *When Buffalo Ran*, Yale University Press USA 1920.

Hungry Wolf, Beverly, *The Ways of My Grandmothers*, Harper USA 1980.

McClintock, Walter, *The Old North Trail: Or, Life Legends and Religion of the Blackfeet Indians* by Macmillan and Company 1910.

Schultz, James W, *On the Warpath*, 1914.

Thompson, David, *David Thompson's Narrative of his Explorations in Western America, 1784-1812*.

Wissler, Clark, *The Social Life of the Blackfoot Indians*, American Museum of Natural History, New York 1911.

Bushmen

Barnard, Alan, *Bushmen — Kalahari Hunter-Gatherers and their Descendants*, Cambridge University Press, UK, 2019.

Lee, Richard B, *The !Kung San: Men, Women, and Work in a Foraging Society*, Cambridge University Press, UK 1979.

Marshall, Lorna J, *The !Kung of Nyae Nyae*, Harvard University Press, USA, 1976.

Marshall Thomas, Elizabeth, *The Harmless People*, Vintage Press, USA, 1989.

Marshall Thomas, Elizabeth, *The Old Way: A Story of the First People*, Picador, USA, 2006.

Shostak, Marjorie, *Nisa — The Life and Words of a !Kung Woman*, Harvard University Press, USA, 1981.

Haida

Blackman, Margaret and Davidson, Florence E, *During My Time: Florence Edenshaw Davidson, A Haida Woman*, University of Washington Press, USA, 1982.

Collison, William H, *In the Wake of the War Canoe*, The Musson Book Company, Canada, 1916.

Dawson, George M, *On the Haida Indians of the Queen Charlotte Islands*, Geological Survey of Canada, Franklin Classics, 2018 (first published 1880).

Murdock, George P, 'Kinship and Social Behaviour Among the Haida' (1932 visit) in *American Anthropologist* 36, 1934.

Swanton, John R, *Contributions to the Ethnology of the Haida*, Publications of the Jesup North Pacific Expedition; v. 5, pt. 1, 1905.

Himba

Crandall, David P, *The Place of Stunted Ironwood Trees — A Year in the Lives of the Cattle-Herding Himba of Namibia*, Continuum International Publishing Group, New York, USA, 2000.

Shields, Sandra, *Where Fire Speaks: A Visit With the Himba*, Arsenal Pulp Press, Canada, 2002.

Maasai

Lekuton, Joseph L, *Facing the Lion — Growing Up Maasai on the African Savanna*, National Geographic Society, USA, 2003.

Llewelyn-Davies, Melissa, 'Women, warriors and patriarchs' in Ortner, Sherry and Whitehead, Harriet (eds), *Sexual Meanings — The Cultural Construction of Gender and Sexuality*, Cambridge University Press, USA, 1981

Saitoti, Tepilit Ole, *The Worlds of a Maasai Warrior — An Autobiography*, University of California Press, USA, 1988.

Māori

Anderson, Atholl et al, *Tangara Whenua, A History*, BW Books, NZ, 2015.

Ballara, Angela, *Iwi — the Dynamics of Māori Tribal Organisation from C. 1789 to C. 1945*, Victoria University Press, NZ, 1998.

Buller, James W, *Forty Years in New Zealand — Including a Personal Narrative, an Account of Māoridom, and of the Christianisation and Colonisation of the Country*, Hodder and Stoughton, UK, 1878.

Cook, Captain James, *The Journals of Captain Cook*, Penguin Classics, UK, 2003.

Cruise, Richard A, *Journal of a Ten Month Residence in New Zealand*, Longman, UK, 1824.

Elder, John R (ed), *The Letters and Journals of Samuel Marsden 1765-1838*, Otago University Council, NZ, 1932.

Hiroa, Te Rangi (Buck, Sir Peter), *The Coming of the Māori*, Whitecombe and Tomes, NZ, 1949.

Salmond, Anne, *Eruera — The teachings of a Māori Elder*, Penguin, NZ, 2005.

Salmond Anne, *Hui — A Study of Māori Ceremonial Gatherings*, Penguin, NZ 1975.

Tregear, Edward, *The Māori Race*, A D Willis Ltd, NZ, 1928.

Winiata, Maharaia, *The Changing Role of the Leader in Māori Society*, Blackwood and Janet Paul, NZ, 1967.

Mohawk and Haudenosaunee Society

Bloomfield, Joseph, 'Journal of Joseph Bloomfield 1776' in Snow, D et al (ed), In *Mohawk Country: Early Narratives about a Native People*, Syracuse University Press, USA, 1996.

Brandao, Jose A, *Nation Iroquoise — A Seventeenth-Century Ethnography of the Iroquois*, University of Nebraska Press, USA, 2003.

Charles River Editors, *Native American Tribes: The History and Culture of the Mohawk*, USA, 2013.

The Great Law of Peace (Kayanerenkó:wa) of the Longhouse People, fifth printing, 1977.

Gehring, Charles T and Starna, William A (eds), *A Journey into Mohawk and Oneida Country, 1634-1635: The Journal of Harmen Meyndertsz van den Bogaert*, Syracuse University Press, USA, 1988.

Megapolensis, Johannes Jr, 'A Short Account of the Mohawk Indians' in Snow, Dean et al (ed), In *Mohawk Country — Early Narratives about a Native People*, Syracuse University Press, USA, 1996.

Morgan, Lewis H, *League of the Iroquois*, Corinth Books, USA, 1962.

Reid, Gerald F, *Kahnawake — Factionalism, Traditionalism, and Nationalism in a Mohawk Community*, University of Nebraska Press, USA, 2004.

Seaver, James E, *A Narrative of the Life of Mrs Mary Jemison*, USA, 2014 (first published 1824).

Snow, Dean et al (ed), In *Mohawk Country: Early Narratives about a Native People*, Syracuse University Press, USA, 1996.

Starna, William, 'Mohawk Haudenosaunee Populations: A Revision' in *Ethnohistory*, Autumn, 1980, Vol 27, No 4, pp 371–382.

Van der Donck, Adriaen, *A Description of New Netherland (The Iroquoians and Their World)*, University of Nebraska Press; Reprint edition, USA, 2010 (first published 1655).

Williams, Kayanesenh Paul, *Kayanerenkó:wa the Great Law of Peace*, University of Manitoba Press, Canada, 2018.

Waorani

Davis, Wade, *One River*, Simon & Schuster, USA, 1997.

Kane, Joe, *Savages*, First Vintage Books, USA, 1996.

Robarchek, Clayton and Robarchek, Carole, *Waorani: The Contexts of Violence and War*, Harcourt Brace & Company, USA, 1998.

Rival, Laura M, *Trekking Through History — The Huaorani of Amazonian Ecuador*, Columbia University Press, USA, 2002.

Yost, James A, 'People of the Forest: The Waorani', in Acosta-Solis et al, *Ecuador in the Shadow of the Volcanoes*, Ediciones Libri Mundi, Ecuador, 1981.

Ziegler-Otero, Lawrence, *Resistance in an Amazonian Community — Huaorani Organizing Against the Global Economy*, Berghahn Books, USA, 2004.

General

20-first consultancy, 2017 study. For Australia: CEW ASX Senior Executive Census 2020

Babcock, Linda, Recalde, Maria and Vesterlund, Lise, 'Why Women Volunteer for Tasks That Don't Lead to Promotions' in *Harvard Business Review*, July 16, 2018.

Boehm, Christopher, *Hierarchy in the Forest; The Evolution of Egalitarian Behaviour*, Harvard University Press, USA, 2001.

Bridges, E Lucas, *Uttermost Part of the Earth — A History of Tierra Del Fuego and the Fuegians,* Rookery Press, USA, 2007.

Callahan, Shawn, *Putting Stories to Work*, Pepperberg Press, Australia, 2016

Chagnon, Napoleon A, *Noble Savages: My Life Among Two Dangerous Tribes — the Yanomamo and the Anthropologists*, Simon & Schuster, USA, 2014.

Chagnon, Napoleon A, *Yanomamo: The Fierce People*, Holt, Rinehart and Winston, Inc, USA, 1983.

Charles River Editors, *The Roman Army: The History and Legacy of the Military that Revolutionized Ancient Warfare and Made Rome a Global Empire*, USA, 2017.

Davie, Maurice R, *The Evolution of War — A Study of Its Role in Early Societies*, Dover Publications, USA, 2003 (first published by Yale University Press in 1929).

Dunbar, Robin, *Grooming, Gossip, and the Evolution of Language*, Harvard University Press, USA, 1996.

Dunbar, Robin, Gamble, Clive and Cowlett John, *Thinking Big: How the Evolution of Social Life Shaped the Human Mind*, Thomas & Hudson, UK, 2014.

Johnson, Allen, *Families of the Forest: The Matsigenka Indians of the Peruvian Amazon*, University of California Press, USA, 2003.

Keeley, Lawrence H, *War Before Civilization: The Myth of the Peaceful Savage*, Oxford University Press, USA, 1996.

Lee, Richard and DeVore, Irven (ed), *Man the Hunter. The First Intensive Survey of a Single, Crucial Stage of Human Development — Man's Once Universal Hunting Way of Life*, first published Transaction Publishers, USA, 1968.

Mauss, Marcel, *The Gift — The Form and Reason for Exchange in Archaic Societies*, W. H. Norton, UK, 1990 (first published 1950).

Ortner, Sherry and Whitehead, Harriet (eds), *Sexual Meanings — The Cultural Construction of Gender and Sexuality*, Cambridge University Press, USA, 1981.

Rosaldo, Michelle Z and Lamphere, Louise (eds), *Women, Culture and Society*, Stamford University Press, USA, 1974.

Sanday, Peggy R, 'Female Status in the Public Domain' in Rosaldo, Michelle Z and Lamphere, Louise (eds), *Women, Culture and Society*, Stamford University Press, USA, 1974.

Taylor, Frederick W, *The Principles of Scientific Management*, Digireads.com Publishing 2011.

Turnbull, Colin, *The Forest People*, Simon & Schuster, USA, 1961.

Washburn, Sherwood L and Lancaster, G S, 'The Evolution of Hunting' in Lee, Richard and DeVore, Irven (eds), *Man the Hunter*, first published 1968 by Transaction Publishers, USA.

The Weekend Australian Oct 31–Nov 1 2020 (page 44)

Wrangham, Richard, *Catching Fire — How Cooking Made Us Human*, Profile Books, UK, 2009.

Index

Page numbers followed by *f*, *m*, or *p* refer to figures, maps or photographs, respectively.

CPSIA information can be obtained
at www.ICGtesting.com
Printed in the USA
LVHW100141310123
738243LV00008B/299/J

9 780645 627909